Praise for Authentic Selves

"*Authentic Selves* gives us a gift of truth so crucial in this time of fear and violence. Readers are *invited in* to stories of abundant possibility. The unapologetic truth is that trans and gender creative people live, love, become, and belong—and always have."

> —Dr. Kia Darling-Hammond,
> Director of Education Programs and Research
> for the National Black Justice Coalition

"Peggy Gillespie continues her pioneering work, this time by offering a safe space for trans and nonbinary people and their families to discuss the joys and challenges of openly living their authentic lives. These inspiring accounts offer indisputable proof that love conquers all. The words and photographs found here have the potential to save lives and make the world a safer place for everyone."

> —Lesléa Newman, author of *Heather Has Two Mommies*
> and *Sparkle Boy*

"As a Black, genderqueer woman, I had no role models or positive representation of what it meant to be someone who identified outside of the binary. The narrative presented to us is one shrouded in misinformation and shame. For me, the lack of visibility for those who were just like me led to a long and arduous road to self-acceptance. I did not discover or accept that I could live outside the prescribed lines until my late forties. I wish I had a book like *Authentic Selves* on my journey. The beautiful images in this book are more than pictures; they represent freedom. The stories in this book are not merely words but medicine for our wounds created by a society that's not yet ready to accept our truth. It's critical that we see and learn about the full spectrum of our identities; it is just as essential for the world to see."

> —Stacey Stevenson, CEO of Family Equality

"It feels wildly ambitious to create a single resource that is able to provide the reader with a window into the rich, varied lives of gender-diverse people. Yet *Authentic Selves* does just that by introducing us to everyday trans and nonbinary people and the family members who are brilliantly and lovingly on the journey with them."

—Aidan Key, founder of Trans Families and
author of *Trans Children in Today's Schools*

"*Authentic Selves* is exquisite proof that transgender and nonbinary people don't have to ask for permission to participate in the creativity of our own survival. Here are our families. Here is our love. There's no denying."

—Taylor Mac, theatre artist and author of *Joy and Pandemic*,
Gary: A Sequel to Titus Andronicus, and *A 24-Decade
History of Popular Music*, among others

"As the mom of two trans kids, *Authentic Selves* brought tears of recognition to my eyes. And as a professional in the national LGBTQ+ community and as an ordained pastor and director of a non-profit that supports LGBTQ+ individuals and those who love them, it brought me joy to know that this beautiful book will become a lifeline for the increasing number of faith leaders, educators, and families who will now have an expertly crafted volume to guide and inspire with real stories from real lives."

—Rev. Marian Edmonds-Allen, Executive Director of PARITY

"I've always believed in the power of stories to crack our hearts wide open with fierce love and empathy as we listen to the unique journeys of the people we encounter. Peggy Gillespie's interviews open windows into the powerful stories of these amazing trans and nonbinary people and their families. Their stories will bring tears to your eyes, widen your aperture of compassion, and make a knowing smile curl on your lips. Though each human is unique in their beauty, we are also so much alike in our yearnings to be seen, known, and loved. *Authentic Selves* will help create such spaces that begin in the mind and heart of each reader."

—Rev. Dr. Jacqui Lewis, public theologian, author of *Fierce Love*,
and Senior Minister of Middle Collegiate Church

AUTHENTIC SELVES

Celebrating Trans and Nonbinary People and Their Families

Interviews by Peggy Gillespie
Photographs by Robin Rayne, Jill Meyers, and others
Alex Kapitan, Consultant

In Collaboration with PFLAG National, The Transgender Legal Defense & Education Fund, and Family Diversity Projects

Based on an exhibit originally created by Jack Pierson with Peggy Gillespie and Gigi Kaeser for Family Diversity Projects

SKINNER HOUSE BOOKS • BOSTON

Copyright © 2023 by the Unitarian Universalist Association.
All rights reserved. Published by Skinner House Books,
24 Farnsworth St., Boston, MA 02210–1409.

skinnerhouse.org

Printed in the United States

Cover design by Larisa Hohenboken
Text design by Jeff Miller

print ISBN: 978-1-55896-896-7
eBook ISBN: 978-1-55896-897-4

5 4 3 2 1
27 26 25 24 23

CIP information on file with the Library of Congress.

All photographs copyrighted by credited photographers. Special thanks to
Clare Bertrand; Diane Bondareff (dianebondareff.com); Alyssa Botelho
(oakandorangephotography.com); Robert Brooks; Celeste Burns (celesteburns.com);
Joy Flanders; Priscilla Harmel; Brianna Harris; Patrick Jervis, Jr.;
Gigi Kaeser; Simran Malik (simimalik.com); Sarah McBride; Carla McDonald;
Jill Meyers; Adam Miller; Erik Mohn; Hannah Moushabeck; Robin Rayne
(creativerayne.com); Sansskruty Rayavarapu; Aurie Singletary (Thecliqueshotit.com);
Haia Sophia; David J. Spear (instagram.com/davidjspear); Josh Stringer (joshstringer.com);
Shana Sureck (shanasureck.com); Cherie Tolliver (ctolliverphotography.zenfolio.com);
Krysia Villón; Cody Young (cdyphotos.com)

To my beloved, generous, and wise adult offspring, Jay Gillespie. You have always been a teacher to me since early childhood, when you first began to challenge societal gender norms. For so many reasons, I feel so lucky to be your mom! You have been at the center of my life for thirty-five years and always will be. You have always added literal and figurative spice to my life. Dumplings rule forever!

To my fabulous, smart, witty, and loving life partner, Jill Meyers. You not only contributed your excellent photography skills to this book, but you gave me your full support during the long process of working on this book. Your enthusiasm always encourages me to do my best. I'm so grateful that we met six years ago on April's Fool Day and have had the joy of sharing love from that day forward. May the bluebirds of happiness always come to the sound of your whistle.

To all the remarkable people who generously shared their authentic selves with me and with the readers of this book, thank you for your dedication to making this world a safer place for the next generation of trans and nonbinary people and their families.

Contents

Foreword

In the early 2000s, when we began our journey as a very young trans child and her family, we felt so alone and isolated. There were no books about transgender or nonbinary kids, almost no resources, and barely any positive representation in the media. It was like we had no echo. Our first chance to be part of a community, a place where we might be able to be ourselves and connect with others who mirrored our experience, was a family picnic hosted by a local LGBTQ center. We were so excited to be a part of a community, a place where we felt that we could be ourselves and bond with others who mirrored our experience. Unfortunately, there were no other transgender kids at the event. All the kids were cisgender children of same-sex couples. We felt so out of place. So disappointed. We just wanted to belong somewhere . . . anywhere.

Jazz (*she/her*) and **Jeanette Jennings** (*she/her*)

Those early years were tough. Our family was on a long journey with no map, no compass, no captain, and other than our therapist, no one to guide us. Then the discrimination began. Bathrooms became inaccessible. The bullying surfaced, and the silence continued.

It's a very long story, but the producers of the popular ABC television news show *20/20* heard about our family and the fact that we had a five-year-old transgender daughter. They presented our family with the opportunity to share our story publicly. We resisted. We were asked again and again, but the idea of putting ourselves out there on national television to expose a reality that was unknown but frowned upon by so many was terrifying.

After about a year of contemplating, we finally decided to move forward with appearing on *20/20*, but only if the renowned journalist Barbara Walters would do the interview with our family. Our entire family participated because we wanted to show the importance of love and support for a transgender child. In our heart of hearts, we know we made the right choice so many years ago. The world needed to know that transgender children like me (Jazz) exist and are special and beautiful. Most importantly, we wanted other families like ours to know they were not alone.

From that moment forward, a tidal wave of families with young transgender children came forward. It reminded us of the scene from *The Wizard of Oz* when the Munchkins felt safe enough to abandon their hiding places and reveal themselves. We learned about the immense power of visibility. To us, visibility provides knowledge, and without both visibility and knowledge, we can't expect the world to change.

Authentic Selves is a perfect and fantastic ensemble book that truly embodies the importance of visibility and the power of love. Love glows from every page. The reader is invited into a world of families, biological, adoptive, and chosen, that may be very different from their own, and in doing so, provides a new perspective. Learning more about people of different gender identities, expressions, and experiences and different ways of being a family help those of us who are trans and nonbinary to see that we belong to a larger community and that there are so many unique ways to express our authentic selves and live authentic lives. For those of us who are cisgender, it gives us a chance to deepen our understanding of, connections with, and empathy for our trans and nonbinary family, friends, and acquaintances.

In this foreword, the word *alone* is mentioned quite a lot, because both our family and the contributors to *Authentic Selves* want others to know they are *not* alone. Helping to create a safer world for trans and nonbinary children and adults and their families is why we have continued to live our lives so publicly and why we want to add our voices of praise to this powerful book. We decided to write this foreword because, like everyone who chose to be part of *Authentic Selves*, we want to celebrate love. Being a part of a loving family of any kind means you are a branch in a beautiful tree that will embrace you for the rest of your life.

Sharing true stories is often the only way we can connect deeply and authentically as humans. Real stories of lived experience give readers a chance to learn from other peoples' experiences and in doing so can shape, strengthen, or challenge our opinions and values. *Authentic Selves* offers readers an opportunity to grow both spiritually and emotionally and to gain amazing insight into how to take action to protect trans and nonbinary rights.

Thank you, Peggy Gillespie for your heartfelt interviews and your vision to create *Authentic Selves*. And thank you to all the terrific photographers, and to everyone who was interviewed and photographed for this book, for creating a gorgeous visual gift, because sometimes words alone just aren't enough. Visibility matters!

JAZZ JENNINGS *(she/her) is the star of the award-winning TLC documentary series* I Am Jazz. *She is a twenty-one-year-old LGBTQ rights activist, author, and student at Harvard University. Jazz wasn't allowed to use the girls' restroom in her elementary school for five years and was prohibited from playing girls' soccer in her state for more than two years. After a long battle, the United States Soccer Federation (USSF) created a policy to include all transgender athletes who want to play soccer. In 2021, The Smithsonian National Museum of Natural History in Washington DC opened an exhibit called* Girlhood . . . It's Complicated, *which included Jazz's life story, making her the first transgender girl to be featured as an historical figure.*

JEANETTE JENNINGS *(she/her) is married to her soulmate Greg and a proud mom of four adult children. Jeanette spreads her message of unconditional love and acceptance through media and speaking engagements all over the United States and is the co-founder and president of the Transkids Purple Rainbow Foundation, which helps to support transgender youth.*

The entire Jennings family was featured in a documentary special for Oprah's OWN network called I Am Jazz: A Family in Transition *when Jazz was eleven. Currently, the Jennings family is filming season 8 of the popular TLC reality series* I Am Jazz.

Preface

When I was asked to write a foreword to this important and beautiful new book, I honestly wasn't sure that I was the right person for the job. I mean, I'm a cisgender gay man. What could I possibly have to contribute to a book on the lived experiences and stories of transgender people and their families?

I grew up in a very conservative and religious part of rural Missouri, knowing I was different in a way that brought me shame and fear. Like many of the people in this book, I loved my family dearly and I worried every day that they would

Brian K. Bond
(*he/him*)

Executive Director,
PFLAG National

find out who I really was, and that my truth would be a disappointment to them. As for my peers, I felt safer with Rufus, the 2,000-pound steer I showed at the local fair, than I did walking the halls of my school. Societal stigma and prejudice weighed heavily on me.

Then I came out—and how fortunate I was. My family supported me. My immediate supervisor at work kindly, firmly, lovingly moved me toward the direction of getting help, supporting me every step of the way. The more of us who came out, the more society moved forward. Slowly, people started to acknowledge the lived experiences of gay, lesbian, and bisexual people. Our work was honored, our marriages finally legal. This was a major step forward.

But with that step forward came a fast and furious backlash, not against cisgender lesbian, gay, and bisexual people, but against transgender and nonbinary people.

As I write this, there are hundreds of bills across dozens of states seeking to harm transgender and nonbinary kids and their families. Bills that, if passed, would prevent access to gender-affirming healthcare, prevent trans kids from joining their friends in playing on sports teams, and deny them access to bathrooms and locker rooms. Bills that would criminalize their parents for making informed, loving, and very private decisions. Still other bills are working to prevent even the mention of gender identity or sexual orientation in the classroom. Essentially, the full weight and impact of all of these harmful bills is an attempt to legislate trans and nonbinary people out of existence. In truth, no amount of legislation can erase the authentic identities and lives of our trans and nonbinary loved ones; it can only serve to make trans and nonbinary people more vulnerable to harm as they simply try to live their lives.

But I have hope, based on my own experience—and that hope is my contribution to this book.

I remember what made the difference when I came out to my family and to the people who knew me: they knew me. They knew my story, they knew my life, they knew my heart. And when they found out I was gay, it was a moment of reckoning for each of them: to take what they thought they knew about gay people—much of it learned from, frankly, terrible and uninformed sources—and align it with the Brian they knew, had grown up with, and loved. Their hearts softened, and in nearly every case, their minds changed.

PFLAG has been in the heart-softening, mind-changing business since 1973. I've seen firsthand the difference stories like the ones found in this book can make.

So here is my request of you: if you are someone who already knows and loves a person who is trans or nonbinary, please share this book with someone who might need to learn more. When you give it to them, gently suggest that they read with an open mind, because someone you know and love is trans. If you are someone who has never knowingly met or gotten to know a person who is trans or nonbinary, and none of what you know on the subject was from a trans person, do everything you can to take in the stories of the people on these pages. Any one of them could be your neighbor, your friend, your local official, a person you know from your faith community—or your own child.

Sharing our personal stories is critical. Pairing them with portraits only deepens the experience. Here is to more hearts softened and more minds changed.

BRIAN K. BOND *(he/him) is the Executive Director of PFLAG National. Founded in 1973, PFLAG is the first and largest organization dedicated to supporting, educating, and advocating for LGBTQ+ people and their families. PFLAG's network of hundreds of chapters and more than 250,000 members works to create a caring, just, and affirming world for LGBTQ+ people and those who love them.*

Introduction

I was privileged to interview the remarkably kind, fierce, brave, and delightful people featured in *Authentic Selves* and help get their words and images in front of you. I come to my role in putting together *Authentic Selves* as a 74-year-old bisexual and queer cisgender woman and as the mother of a nonbinary 35-year-old. Despite the many relationships I've had with trans, nonbinary, and genderqueer people throughout my life, I still feel like I am an aspiring ally, learning as I go. I picture you, dear readers, as a gorgeously varied community of people who are also lifelong learners about yourselves and the people you love.

Peggy Gillespie
(she/her)

I've dedicated much of my work life as a journalist to Family Diversity Projects, the national non-profit organization I co-founded thirty years ago with photographer Gigi Kaeser. Our mission has been to fight prejudice, bullying, and violence by helping to teach children, teens, and adults to respect all people without exception. To do this, we created eight traveling photo-text exhibits about marginalized groups, including trans and non-binary people, which have been shown in thousands of schools, colleges, libraries, museums, workplaces, and houses of worship nationwide. Our most well-known exhibit, Love Makes a Family: Portraits of LGBT People and Their Families (also published as a book), was the subject of a federal lawsuit in 1995 after some parents tried to prevent it from being shown at our local elementary schools. One sixth grader who finally got to see the exhibit wrote in the guest book, "We're all created equal!!! Remember????"

Clearly, a huge number of people still don't remember or live according to this core statement in our US Constitution. While I've been working on *Authentic Selves*, horribly transphobic and homophobic bills have been passed or on the path towards becoming law in many states in our divided nation. All over the country, books about LGBTQ+ people continue to be removed from school libraries and classroom shelves. Sadly, I can easily imagine that *Authentic Selves* may join the ranks of banned books.

I spent the past year interviewing the trans, nonbinary, and gender nonconforming people and many of their biological, adoptive, and chosen family members that you will meet and get to know in *Authentic Selves*. I don't think I made it through any of the interviews without crying at least once—often due to the descriptions of pain, discrimination, bullying, and violence many of them had faced, but more often due to stories of healing, transformation, joy, and triumph made possible by authenticity in the face of immense challenges.

This book is coming out at a time when the increased visibility of trans and nonbinary people has resulted in increased violence and incendiary political rhetoric. It is more important than ever for trans and nonbinary people to be recognized and celebrated in their full authenticity. I'm grateful to everyone who agreed to share their story to help counter these violent political narratives and to offer representations of families who fully embrace the authenticity of their trans and nonbinary members.

I continue to hold onto hope that this world will someday be a safe and welcoming place for all people. Although I suspect that *Authentic Selves* will not lose its relevancy for many years to come, my most fervent hope is that someday—in the not-too-distant future—this book will be valuable because beautiful depictions of beautiful families are always inspiring but won't be needed in the same ways that it is now. I try to envision a world where every person can come into their own understandings of their authentic selves without fear of what that revelation might do to their relationships and their ability to navigate the world with safety and joy.

For now, I urge you to look into the eyes of these magnificent human beings and read their words. Breathe in the love and wisdom they are offering you. Know in your heart the truth that all people are created equal and that all people are worthy of being celebrated. Period. No exceptions. Then go out and make that fact guide all your actions.

PEGGY GILLESPIE *(she/her), MA, CSW, is the cofounder and director of Family Diversity Projects, and editor of all of the organization's exhibits and books, including* Love Makes a Family: Portraits of LGBT People and Their Families.

A Note on Making Room for All of Who We Are

In the pages that follow, you'll be introduced to a beautiful diversity of people who are trans and/or nonbinary, as well as those they call family. This book features people of many different ages and generations, races and ethnicities, class and educational backgrounds, disabilities and abilities, sexualities and relationship structures, religious and spiritual paths, and other cultural identities.

Alex Kapitan
(ze/per, he, none)

Senator Sarah McBride, who is featured in this book along with her parents and brothers, puts it best: "There is no one way to be trans." And yet, for far too long, narrow narratives of what it means to be trans have limited not only how cisgender people think about trans people, but also trans people's authentic expression of who we are, from whether we feel "trans enough" in comparison with those narratives to whether we are able to access gender-affirming medical care based on how closely we hew to what medical providers expect.

This book offers one antidote to the narrow narratives and stereotypes about trans and nonbinary people that are so prevalent—but only if you, dear reader, regardless of your own gender identity, enter these pages with an open heart and mind, leaving behind any assumptions about who trans and nonbinary people are.

Some of the people in this book knew who they were from their first conscious moments; some came to understand the truth of their gender late in life; and others are still questioning and exploring who they are. Some have endured incredible suffering, violence, and/or rejection and others have experienced nothing but affirmation and celebration of who they are. Some suppressed or hid away their truths for decades; some never have.

Some of those you'll meet in this book understand "transition" as referring solely to the medical steps that can help their body reflect the internal truth of themselves, with a set beginning and end; others consider transition to have social, legal, and medical dimensions; and still others consider life to be one extended transition into ever-greater expressions of authenticity. Some have experienced intense dysphoria in bodies that feel wrong while others love their bodies and have never experienced dysphoria; some have a deep need to access medical intervention while others don't desire to change anything about their physiology.

Some want to blend in with the rest of the world and some want to clash in fabulous fashion with all that is seen as "normal." Some have an unwavering identity and expression and others understand and express themselves in fluid and ever-changing ways. Some view their trans- or nonbinary-ness in medical terms, some in spiritual terms, and some in terms of simple human diversity.

The language used by those in this book reflects this diversity. Identity terms (like *woman, man, genderqueer, agender, transsexual, Two-Spirit, māhū,* and so many more) are not only informed by people's understandings of their gender but also by all their other cultural identities and experiences. Different people have different understandings of different words, including "transgender." Some trans women think of their child selves as being boys and have no aversion to the names they were given at birth; others think of themselves as always having been girls and women and never want to see or hear their "deadname." Some nonbinary people experience dysphoria whenever they are referred to in gendered ways; others feel affirmed by a variety of pronouns and gendered words. Some trans men's children call them "Dad," some call them "Mom," and some call them by their first name or an invented term.

Just as trans communities stretch and alter the meanings of words to suit our realities, we also stretch and alter the definition of "family." Although there are many families in this book composed of two parents and one or more children, trans and nonbinary people create family in so many ways. You'll meet foster families and adoptive families, chosen families of close friends, drag families, polyamorous families, families of divorced spouses who continue to love each other and raise children together, families with one parent, two parents, three parents, or four. There's no one way to be trans, and there's no one way to be a family.

The people featured in these pages have opened their hearts and their homes to you. Some of them are eager to be seen and known as trans and/

or nonbinary, and others are taking a risk to disclose and share their gender histories. My hope is that you will receive their gift with an openness of spirit. This book is not a manual for how to understand or relate to the people in your life who are trans and/or nonbinary, nor is it a guide to understanding your own identity. Rather, it is a testimony to the power of being exactly who we are meant to be. May it inspire you to be your authentic self and celebrate authenticity in all those you love.

ALEX KAPITAN *(ze/per, he, none) is a trans and queer educator, editor, activist, and faith leader. Alex is the founder of Radical Copyeditor (radicalcopyeditor. com), an anti-oppressive language project, and the co-founder of the Transforming Hearts Collective, a faith-rooted LGBTQ healing justice collaborative. Alex lives in western Massachusetts with partner Teo Drake and a menagerie of furry and feathered friends.*

Jack Pierson

Jack. Photo by Hannah Moushabeck

(they/them)
preschool teacher,
creator, dog lover

In the summer of 2006, I had an internship with Family Diversity Projects, the creator of the Love Makes a Family traveling photo exhibit and book. It also turned out to be the summer I changed my name from the one I was given at birth and started exploring different pronouns—certainly no coincidence. I'd been thinking specifically about my gender a lot in the previous months and gender in general ever since arriving in western Massachusetts as a college student three years earlier. At Smith College, I was surrounded by trans folks and gender variance of all kinds. It was a haven! I felt safe to explore my identity not only with my friends but also amongst my larger college community. It felt like there was so much room to claim whatever identity felt best, and I eventually came to understand myself as genderqueer.

Although Smith was and still is known as a women's college, I wasn't overcome with fear about letting my peers and professors know that I was going to be using a new name, Jack, and that I wanted them to use both she and he pronouns interchangeably when referring to me. There was already such an established presence of transmasculine folks on campus using he/him pronouns that I wasn't an anomaly. That said, there were not too many folks using multiple pronouns or gender-neutral pronouns like they/them in the same way that we see people using them today. I was clear that I didn't identify as a man, so I wasn't drawn to using he/him pronouns exclusively, and while they/them resonated with me, I wasn't ready to go out on a limb when there were so few people using those pronouns around me. However, using both he and she pronouns felt like a way to try on greater visibility as a genderqueer person, and it meant that I immediately felt part of the larger trans community.

During my internship that summer, I approached the codirector of Family Diversity Projects, Peggy Gillespie, with the idea of creating a new traveling photo and text exhibit about transgender people, which would eventually come to be called Pioneering Voices: Portraits of Transgender People. What a gift it was to be invited into people's homes and to bear witness to their stories—both their pain and their joy. I photographed them and interviewed them and opened the exhibit at Smith College's newly opened Resource Center for Sexuality and Gender.

When I initially reached out to Peggy with the idea of helping to create a trans-based project, in no way did I foresee how vital it would be to my own personal journey. I'm so very grateful that things unfolded as they did. It was through working on this project and meeting so many incredible trans people of all ages and stages that I was finally able to see and begin my own gender journey. I gained the confidence to move forward with changing my name and pronouns, start binding my chest, and exploring my own gender identity—ultimately including myself in the exhibit and coming out to my family.

At the time of creating the exhibit, and for quite some time after, I was quite certain that I'd never start taking testosterone or have top surgery. Friends, peers, and professors so easily called me Jack and I felt good about using both he and she pronouns, so what was there to change? However, after graduating and spending a year out in the real world, I started rethinking some of these ideas. I had come to prefer he/him pronouns, but besides my close friends, no one was using them. I still didn't feel like a man, but being called "she," "ma'am," and so forth felt increasingly uncomfortable, whereas being called "he" and "sir" didn't make me feel like I was being misgendered.

> *Every step of my gender journey has been slow, dipping my toe into various changes to see what they felt like. From choosing a new name to pursuing medical transition to wearing lipstick and having a beard, I have always allowed myself to try things on, feeling pleasantly surprised with everything that has helped me to feel more myself.*

Despite some trepidation, I finally decided that I would try taking testosterone in mid-2010, about two and a half years after graduating college and four years after coming out as trans. I started on a very low dose, uncertain of what changes I might begin to see at first and if I'd like them or not. As my natural sideburns began to thicken and my voice slowly deepened, I eventually increased to a regular dose over the following year. It was very exciting when both coworkers and random people started to use he/him pronouns for me without fumbling or second-guessing themselves.

I was almost surprised by how relieved I felt when this shift began to happen. I felt just as genderqueer as ever, but I hadn't even realized the emotional weight I was carrying until I wasn't constantly being misgendered as a woman. Being seen as a man wasn't as painful or wrong-seeming in the same way that being seen as a woman was. I had felt constantly bombarded every day by a pronoun that felt so wrong, and not having to bump up against that made a huge difference. But beyond that, I began to really enjoy the effects of testosterone. The greater sense of ease I felt wasn't just from people calling me he/him; I also started to like how I looked and how I felt about myself.

A year later I entered my first summer at Smith School for Social Work to get my MSW degree. In my first week of school, I was talking to a classmate and learned that she was from Connecticut. Without thinking it through, I blurted out that I'd gone to Miss Porter's, a well-known all-girls boarding school in Connecticut. She gave me an odd look and immediately asked, "How is that possible?" I was still so used to being perceived as a woman that it was easy to forget that certain parts of my history were no longer so simple to share without putting myself in the vulnerable position of coming out as trans. During my time at social work school, I never came out as trans to any of my clients. What a very new experience to have my trans identity—once obvious—be suddenly invisible. There was both relief and grief, hand in hand. Relief that I could move more easily through the world, free from the jarring feeling of being called "she" and "ma'am," and grief because I never wanted to be a man, I never felt like a man, yet there I was, with the world receiving me without question as male.

Unfortunately, my dad died during the summer after my second year of social work school, and I proceeded to take the following year off from the program. I knew I had to do something to make some money, and at the time I had a nonbinary friend who was working as a preschool teacher. They assured me I could get hired as a substitute even without any experience, and I did! This job truly changed my life and the course of my career. I fell in love with being a preschool teacher.

It was also during this year off that I finally made the tough decision to have top surgery, seven years after coming out, seven years after thinking so strongly it was something I'd never do, and three years after starting testosterone. I felt a lot of ambivalence but knew I couldn't go one more summer binding my chest in the heat and humidity, and I felt increasingly self-conscious about my chest. As someone who loves swimming and the outdoors, the discomfort of binding for so many years was enough to tip the balance.

Although many people feel an immediate sense of relief and rightness after surgery, for me it took months to emotionally adjust to my new body—far longer than the physical healing process. Even now, nearly ten years later, I can still find myself missing my old chest sometimes, and even laughing with certain friends about how we wish Velcro boobs were possible. However, I can also say with the utmost certainty that I don't regret my decision one bit. It has brought me peace, ease, and affirmation in so many ways.

Despite returning to social work school and receiving my MSW degree from Smith, I chose to continue pursuing early childhood education. When I entered my first lead teacher position three and a half years ago while living in Portland, Oregon, I felt bold enough to start the year using they/them pronouns. These pronouns that had been tickling my curiosity for the previous decade finally felt common enough in my community that I knew I wasn't going to be alone. In fact, it felt like most everyone I met in Portland used they/them pronouns. I finally felt safe enough to give them a try. It helped immensely that my coworkers and the administrative team were so on board, as were so many of the families I worked with.

I also continued to surprise myself by leaning into my feminine side. I had never had a femme phase growing up—I'd been a tomboy and had rejected makeup and other things associated with being a girl. But everything changed when expressing my femininity meant that people perceived me as a feminine man rather than simply a woman. I don't think I knew until it was happening that it was something I was interested in exploring. It was fun to discover that side of myself, and it helped me feel more visibly queer and genderqueer. While the children I worked with were still learning what pronouns were, I felt free to be myself and express myself with them. There I was, a preschool teacher—beard, lipstick, nail polish and all.

Young children truly are the most loving and accepting beings. After working with preschoolers for ten years now, I've been fortunate enough to have taught several trans and gender creative children. How beautiful to be a trans teacher and to get to offer love, support and validation to these kids and their families. I truly believe that the impact of seeing oneself reflected in others, especially those who are older and in leadership roles, cannot be underestimated. I only wish I had been so lucky to be taught by trans people when I was growing up.

It's been sixteen years now since I came out to my family as trans and although the first few years were a challenge, for the last decade my gender has pretty much felt like a non-issue. My father, who was sixty-six when I came out, was the most compassionate and open of anyone in my family.

My mom and siblings, meanwhile, were painfully resistant to my needs and didn't put much effort into using the right name or pronouns for years. Despite their struggles, however, my family's love for me was unwavering and for that I am deeply grateful.

Sadly, my mom died in September of 2021. Since her passing, it's been interesting to find myself back in a place of needing to address my gender and pronouns with my sister and brother. I knew they/them pronouns were something my mom was never going to be able to understand or use, so I waited until her passing to talk with them. Despite my pronoun request not coming as a shock, I am once again facing their resistance and slowness. I know it is a change that will take effort and practice on their part. It will take intention, attention, and care. And while I continue to navigate these frustrating family dynamics, I feel happy to have settled into my present and ever-growing genderqueer identity, finally using pronouns that clearly reflect who I am!

I cannot express how happy and proud I felt when I heard from Peggy that she was going to expand the traveling exhibit—which she and her codirector at Family Diversity Projects, photographer Gigi Kaeser, had already enlarged—into a full-length book about trans and nonbinary people and their families. It has felt awesome and inspiring to reconnect with this project, sixteen years later, and to see this book become a resource that I wish I could have had when I was coming out. My hope is that this book finds its way into the hands of trans and nonbinary youth, their parents and guardians, teachers, doctors, clergy, and politicians. I am so grateful for all the hard work that has gone into putting this beautiful book together, especially to the participants for sharing their truths, joys, and vulnerabilities. Our stories can save each other's lives.

Angelle Eve Castro and Family

Angelle. Photo by Jill Meyers

Angelle Eve Castro (*she/her*)

sister, daydreamer, friend

I've known for as long as I can remember that I am trans. There's one memory I always find myself returning to, probably my earliest recollection of anything relating to gender expression. I was very young—it must have been before even starting kindergarten. I was with my family and a family friend at an indoor gym where parents would bring their kids to play.

The friend was a girl a bit older than me, someone I looked to as a role model. She and I were in a room that was all about letting kids use their imagination. There were stuffed animals, different make-believe sets, and, most importantly, a chest full of all kinds of clothes. Sifting through that chest, I was mostly unimpressed with its contents until I pulled out a long, flowy dress. I was captivated by it. I put it on and it fit perfectly. I can remember the joy that welled up in my heart. I loved who I was in that moment. I danced around that room and felt so free I could've sworn I was flying.

But there was something awry about that happiness I was feeling. Something forbidden, even. I was a boy, after all. I would eventually have to leave that place and leave that dress behind, leaving freedom behind with it. I couldn't let that happen. The next thing I remember is hiding in a closet behind a wall of stuffed animals. In the darkness of that moment, I determined that this feeling was something to keep hidden. And so, I did, or at least I tried to.

While growing up, there were always times when I couldn't hide those feelings. On the first day of kindergarten, I met a girl named Annie and was jealous that she had such a feminine name. In second grade, I shaped my handwriting to be like the handwriting of the girls in my class. In third grade, I had my makeup done for the class play, and I jumped around unable to contain my joy. The truth about who I am would reveal itself to me continually. But these events were few and far between compared to the constant reminders that I was assigned the role of boy. I was often questioned by the guys around me, "Why is your handwriting so girly?" The joy of having my makeup done was snuffed out when an older boy asked me why I was so giddy over a little makeup. My mom would often lament about how she wished for a daughter but birthed only sons. Instances relating to gender always left a bitter taste in my mouth.

In middle school, when puberty struck, my bubbling internal conflict reached a boiling point. How could I be so unmistakably feminine, yet the world around me insisted that I be masculine? Desperate for answers, one day I scoured the internet searching for something to explain why I felt the way I did. Why do I feel like a girl on the inside? Am I a girl trapped in a boy's body? I learned about gender dysphoria and finally was able to put a name to the uncomfortable feeling I'd experienced my entire life. But I knew little to nothing about transgender people. I knew that being transgender made me very different from everyone else, and it scared me. It just reinforced the idea that being trans was something to keep hidden.

Throughout middle school I ended up telling a handful of people the truth about my gender, all of whom were girls in my grade that I had grown close to. I was surprised when all of them were really kind to me about it, and I found a little bit of reprieve knowing that I wasn't completely alone with the knowledge of my true self. Even so, it still felt like a secret that I couldn't fully share. In private with my female friends, I felt somewhat like I was one of the girls, but I was still stuck being a boy everywhere else. I distanced myself from these friends to protect myself from the pain of feeling that way. I went back into the closet.

The feeling that my transness was a deep dark secret was magnified one day when a heated argument broke out in the comment section of a social media post. One of my old friends was arguing with a newer friend who I hadn't come out to. I was trying to mediate the situation but was showing an obvious bias for my newer friend. My old friend, someone who I had trusted to keep my secret safe, then commented, "Why don't you go put on some makeup?" My already anxiety-ridden heart dropped into my stomach. Being trans was so awful, so worthy of shame, that it was literally being used to blackmail me. And not only that, but it was working. I messaged her, apologizing profusely, swearing that I would stop defending my new friend if she'd delete the comment and not expose me. I cried myself to sleep that night.

In the following months I became severely depressed, so much so that I was suicidal. I started to see my transness as a curse. The way I saw it, being trans had only brought me suffering, and there was no reason to believe that anything would change. There were many nights I didn't sleep at all. I would stay awake trying to figure out how to kill myself painlessly. I didn't want to suffer the pain of death, I just wanted it all to end, to slip quietly into the night and never again deal with this curse.

The people around me could tell that there was something deeply troubling me, and I ended up telling a few of my closest friends that I was feeling suicidal. My concerned friend group hatched a plan to cheer me up.

One day at lunch, a group of my friends and classmates all stood up in front of the table where we were eating. They said that they knew I had been feeling down lately and that they wanted to lift my spirits. All together they sang me the song "Count on Me" by Bruno Mars. Wherever all those friends are now, I hope that they know they saved my life that day. I still go back to that song during times when I'm feeling down, and it revives me the same way it did then. Although they weren't aware of the real me, there were people in my life that I didn't want to let down. I decided I wanted to keep living, even if I couldn't reveal who I was inside.

I gave up trying to express my transness and instead just leaned into being the "me" that people expected. It was just bearable enough that I believed I could make a life that way. I pushed on in this state for years. High school and the years after graduating were a blur of creating new ways to convince myself and everyone around me that I was a man and I was happy that way. But I wasn't. I was never happy about who I had become or who I was becoming.

> **❝ I am still transitioning. I'm happier than I could've possibly imagined in my wildest dreams. Every day I wake up, and I'm more myself than ever before. ❞**

I had people in my life who I loved and people who loved me. Still, it didn't feel like I was receiving any love at all—only the person who I had become against my will. I didn't allow myself to think about my past, and I also couldn't seriously consider my future. Regardless, I stepped forward tentatively into the uncertain future awaiting me.

Two years after graduating high school, in the fall of 2018, I moved away from my hometown of Amherst, Massachusetts, to Boston to start college at Benjamin Franklin Institute of Technology. I had never really wanted to go to college, but I was deeply drained from living in the home where I grew up repressing myself. I was ready for a change. It also brought me closer to my girlfriend Grace, who had moved away the previous year for college. I wasn't surprised when I immediately started to struggle in my classes. Bottling up my emotions and my identity had taken its toll on my desire to learn.

One invaluable outcome of moving away for college was that I had no shortage of time alone with my thoughts. Those long days and nights of pondering brought me to a point where I was finally able to consider my issues with my identity. Realization dawned on me that I was struggling so much because I had been repressing my true self. I resolved that my gender dysphoria was never going to go away unless I faced it head on and dealt with it.

Now that I had acknowledged and begun to understand the feelings that I had kept repressed for so long, I had a choice to make. Would I continue trying to keep my identity a secret to protect myself? Or would I accept the fact that I was transgender and move forward in authenticity, finally admitting to myself and the world who I have always been?

It took some time to reach a conclusion, but in the end, there wasn't a decision to make. I needed to live as authentically as possible. I accepted the fact that I was transgender and set my sights on taking whatever steps were necessary to relieve myself of dysphoria. It wasn't going to be easy, but it was, without a doubt, the only path that would lead to true happiness.

I wasn't ready to come out of the closet quite yet, but I started trying to prepare myself for that eventuality. An old but familiar uneasiness took root in my heart. Would the people in my life accept me for who I was and support me in my endeavor to become the person I had always kept hidden away inside of me? I wasn't 100-percent sure that they would, and it held me back from doing what I knew needed to be done. One day in October of 2019, something was able to push me off the edge of uncertainty upon which I stood. It was a newly released song from E ve, a Japanese artist who had quickly become my favorite from the days I spent listening to them while pondering myself. Their songs often describe the feelings associated with going through the motions of a dull and unfulfilling life—feelings of trying to drag on aimlessly or putting on an act to be more digestible to the people around you. The music was always relatable to me. But this new song hit me somewhere deeper than any had before and came at a time when I was waiting for a sign to lead me in the right direction. The song is titled "Raison D'être," literally meaning "reason for existence" in French. Every word rang true for me.

I seized the courage that built up inside me, ready to tell my truth to the world. Over the next few days, weeks, and months, I slowly came out to people who were close to me. First came my girlfriend, Grace. She was one of the people that I was most anxious about telling since she was closer to me than anyone else. I knew though that she had to be the first person I told. At this point we had been together for over four years. We had grown together and helped each other through everything.

On the day that I resolved to tell Grace, I was a nervous wreck. It had been ages since I last told anyone I was trans, but the pain I had associated with having people know was still fresh in my mind. I drove to Grace's apartment, ready to lay bare the truth about myself but scared for what might come of it. When I arrived at her place, I was practically mute. I knew I wanted to tell her, but I couldn't get the right words to come out of my mouth.

When she gently inquired what was on my mind, I forced myself to say that I had something to tell her that might affect our relationship moving forward. But no more words would come. I ended up typing up a sort of coming-out letter on my phone. She read it and took a moment to process. The silence felt like hours. After a couple of minutes, Grace said that she supported me and wanted to be with me no matter what. We cried together, our tears a mix of catharsis and uncertainty about what the future would hold for us. But at least we would get to experience that future together.

Moving forward from there, I decided that I was going to repurpose the letter I wrote to Grace and edit it to fit whoever it was I was coming out to. It's hard for me to voice my thoughts coherently, but when I can write them down it becomes much easier for me to make sense of what's happening in my head. Coming out to my loved ones didn't seem like such a daunting task once I realized I could do it in writing.

A few weeks after I told Grace, I sent the revised letter to my mom. I spoke about how she had always been aware that I was depressed but didn't know that the reason was because I was repressing the fact that I was trans my entire life. A few more weeks passed, and I sent the letter to my Lola ("grandmother" in Tagalog). She was helping me pay my way through college, but I had decided that I wanted to drop out of school and focus on my transition. I told her that my heart wasn't completely devoted to school, and that transitioning was more important to me than getting a degree.

Then I sent the letter to my three brothers that I grew up with. I told Tyrell, Isa, and Sammy that I would never want to lose the love that we shared, and that I hoped they would accept me for who I truly am. And they did. Everyone I came out to accepted the truth about my identity and supported me wholeheartedly. Deep down, I think I knew that they would all love me unconditionally. Coming out to everyone else was a much more harrowing proposition. It was going to take some time until I was ready to do that.

At that point I was ready to start transitioning, even if not everyone knew the truth about me yet. Around the beginning of 2020, I started seeing a new doctor who specializes in trans healthcare. I learned about what transitioning entails, both the social side and the medical side. A whole array of medical procedures and therapies that would target my gender dysphoria and help the perceived version of my identity match the version of my identity that I had always experienced on the inside.

While I was preparing myself to start the long process of transitioning, the Covid pandemic flipped our world upside down. Because everyone was quarantining from the rest of the world, I got to begin my transition very privately. In late April of 2020, I began hormone replacement therapy. As I started undergoing the changes that came with HRT, only a handful of the people closest to me knew. I had a lot of time to think about who I wanted to become and what steps were necessary to achieving that ideal.

I created my new name during this time: Angelle Eve Castro. I knew I wanted to keep the prefix "Angel" from my first name. It was passed from my grandfather Angelo to my mom Angélica and then onto me. When I discovered the name Angelle, I loved how unique and feminine it was. It matched exactly who I envisioned myself as. My middle name Eve comes from E ve, the artist who helped me reach so many conclusions about how important it is to let my authentic self shine through. I took my mom's last name, Castro. The real me was beginning to take shape.

About a year after starting my transition, I was finally ready to tell everyone the truth about my identity. I got to reintroduce myself to the world: "My name is Angelle Castro, and I am a transgender woman." The world smiled back at me in response. I received overwhelming support from the people in my life. There were a few individuals who couldn't bring themselves to fully understand what I had gone through and who exactly I was. But most of the people in my life were willing to accept my truth and loved me all the same, if not more. The real me was finally getting the love she deserved and had fought tooth and nail for. I was reborn in every sense of the word.

More than a year has passed since then. I am continuously learning new things about who I am as a person, things that I never had the chance to express before starting my transition. It's incredibly liberating to be seen as the woman I've always been but wasn't always able to express. The bonds I have with the people close to me are truly strong because they love me for me. And just as importantly, I love myself fully and authentically. I love who I am and who I am becoming.

My hope is that, in time, the world will come around to realize that transgender people are who they say they are. Full stop. Anybody who is suffering from gender dysphoria deserves to receive the treatment that is so often held from us.

There are many systemic injustices that affect people who belong to racial, sexual, and/or gender minority groups. Trans people, especially trans people of color and especially trans people, face nonstop discrimination for simply existing. But trans people, in all our strength and all our authenticity, refuse to give in to the walls of cruelty that are constantly closing in around us.

I'm not quite sure what direction I want to go in life. What is wonderful, though, is that I have a life that's entirely my own, and I get to decide what to do with it. I'm grateful for all that I've gone through, good and bad, because the sum of my experiences shaped me into the woman I am today. It's so important that people like me get to live a life expressing themselves authentically. The world is a better place when trans lives are uplifted.

Angélica & Angelle. Photo by Jill Meyers

"Mom, I have something to tell you that I've been holding for a long time. . . ." I can still remember seeing my second-born Angelle's long text. Before I even started reading through it, all the possible scenarios ran through my mind.

Angélica Canlas Castro (*she/her, them/they*)

mother, social justice educator, certified Revolutionary LOVE coach

When I got to the part of Angelle's text where she came out as transgender, time stood still. I stopped breathing as she described in one short paragraph her lifelong journey of hiding in the closet for fear of not being accepted and loved for who she really is. When I finally came back to the present moment, I felt my heart break—not for me but for her. I couldn't fathom what Angelle had endured holding this sacred secret.

I imagined that time was standing still for Angelle as well, and that she was holding her breath waiting to hear if her mom—the woman who thought she birthed a boy 21 years ago and had spent years raising this boy into a "fine young man" who was off to college doing what "he" was "supposed" to be doing—could find it in her heart to simply accept her child and keep loving her.

For me, there was not even a moment of hesitation or a question in my heart and mind whether I could accept Angelle. In fact, I loved her even more! After all, to me, she was the same beautiful person I birthed into this world, the same joyful person I watched run through grassy fields picking flowers for me, the same animated person whose contagious belly laugh filled any room, the same thoughtful person who cared so deeply for anyone and everyone connected to her, the same sensitive person who cried when she fought with her older brother over a video game. To me, this was a reintroduction of who Angelle had known herself to be—a woman, a sister, a daughter—my trans daughter!

" What a gift I have been given these last few years to truly get to know my daughter, the real Angelle! I have watched with joy as she continues to blossom into the full expression of her authentic self through her art, writing, playing, makeup, jewelry, dresses, and long, curly hair. "

I thought about the many nights she cried herself to sleep as I sat by her bedside, rubbing her back and asking if there was anything I could do to alleviate her pain. I went back to times where her eyes looked lifeless as she would talk to me about struggling in high school and wanting to drop out. I recalled my pep talks reminding her that she didn't have it that bad and it could always be worse, not knowing the full scope of what she was holding. And now I had a chance to do better, a second chance to be a mom to my amazing child.

I quickly texted back a response so Angelle knew that I fully supported her coming out and that my love for her would never change. I meant every word of it. I felt so honored to know that my child trusted me enough to come out to me, and I wanted her to know that I didn't take her vulnerability and trust lightly. I gave her a moment to read my text response, then I followed up with a call. We cried together as I told her how proud I am of her courage and resilience.

I remember saying to Angelle, "I don't want to make this about me at all, but I regret not creating a space where you could have felt like you could be your authentic self." I knew I had tried to be inclusive. I raised four sons, or so I thought, so when my children would talk about someday having a girlfriend, I would always say, "or a boyfriend, or whoever you decide to be with." I wanted them all to know that I would love them whether they were gay or straight. Angelle told me it was just that she had not come to terms with accepting herself as trans, so she couldn't imagine anyone else accepting her either. And although there's truth to that, I now know I could have done so much more to create a space where Angelle would have been welcome to come out as a trans girl as opposed to a gay boy. My unintentionally oppressive ways of being created limits to what Angelle could openly and honestly express to me.

Watching Angelle's relationships continue to flourish is life-giving: her longtime partner Grace, who lives up to her name; her three brothers, Tyrell, Isa, and Sammy, who keep her close, loved and protected; her cousin Dechaunte who is her best friend and who she has always looked up to; and her entire friend and family network. They have all been her biggest supporters and her sustenance through her liberation journey.

I had already committed my life to being a social justice educator due to my own and my family's lived experiences around racism, sexism, misogyny, classism, ableism, and ageism. I was born in the Philippines and at eight years old my family immigrated to the United States as diplomats. I began to experience oppression almost immediately, particularly racism, classism, and sexism, in spaces and from people I didn't expect it from, like in church and from various religious leaders, close family, and friends.

My children identify as multiracial as I identify as Asian and Hispanic and their fathers identify as Black. Sadly, I have been a witness to their experiences of trauma and oppression from a very young age. And although trans oppression is quite pervasive in our current climate, I look to Angelle as one of my supersheroes. Her coming out has fueled my commitment to educate myself around trans oppression and to help create inclusive communities where we can all thrive. I can honestly say that my children have been my biggest source of inspiration for my work, especially Angelle. She has taught me more than she will ever know about choosing oneself!

I began using both she and they pronouns several years ago for my own reasons as I continued to explore and be open to my own learning and expansion around social justice. I was teaching and advising on a college campus at the time, and I began to see all the different and expansive ways that my close circle of friends and my myriad students and colleagues engaged thinking outside the gender binary and gender norms and embraced gender fluidity and ways to be gender nonconforming.

To say I admire Angelle is an understatement; I have immense love, gratitude, respect, and admiration for her courageous soul that exudes her truth; her generous heart that she can now truly wear on her sleeve; her bright spirit that fills the world with much needed light; her unburdened laughter that transforms everyone around her; her brilliance that she gets to fully explore and express; and her unapologetic transness that liberates minds and hearts everywhere. I am so proud of my trans daughter, and I am ecstatic for the world to see and experience what the embodiment of revolutionary love looks like.

I t was clear when Angelle and I first got to know each other that she was someone who would be by my side for a long time. We first met each other singing the Pokémon theme song in the backseat of my best friend's car. We

Grace Bertrand
(*she/her*)

social worker, daughter, friend

got to know each other watching our favorite childhood movies, visiting the snapping turtle at the pond by my house, and making each other laugh so hard over the stupidest things. She was more than the person I was dating through high school; she was an instant best friend, my perfect match.

Through all this joy, though, I also saw an Ang who was extremely quiet at times, especially when we were with other people. It's hard to describe, but there were many times through high school where I would see Ang walking through the hall in school with her bright pink headphones, seated around our friends, or even with me and her eyes would be missing her soul. She has a certain twinkle to her eyes that not all people have. It's like when you catch her eye, you remember a little happy secret you have, or she's reminding you of a happy memory. Often back then, that spark wasn't in her eye. I chalked it up to the fact that she was shy, that high school is a stressful time, or just that she was putting on a serious act. I also struggled with depression and anxiety and figured that the pain I was sensing was something like what I was feeling.

Angelle & Grace. Photo by Clare Bertrand

However, when I spent time with Ang alone, we got to know each other better than I've known anyone. She has been my ultimate companion. She has listened to all worries and concerns I've told to her and supported me even when I couldn't vocalize them. Every important person in my life has loved Ang. She is simply lovely to be around, joyful, knowledgeable, hilarious, eager to learn, and extremely kind to everyone. She is the best person I've ever met.

In college we started to play the next part in our lives. Going to parties, dating the way society told us to, dressing the way our friends did, and generally not feeling super comfortable until it was just us. At that time, I started to have thoughts about my sexuality. It's hard to explain how I realized I may be gay. I thought that I would've just known and that it would have been super obvious, but it wasn't.

I grew up in a super accepting house, I learned my brother was gay at a young age, and I had many adults and friend's parents in my life who were gay. I loved many gay people and knew that it was a joyful and beautiful thing. Despite this, I had followed the rules set up by society and played the part asked of me and lived as a straight person. As I got older, though, it became easier to think for myself and really analyze my feelings before I could suppress them. I realized that to fully know if I was gay or bi or whatever I was, I would probably need to try dating a woman. This was terrifying. I was absolutely in love with Ang, and there was no way I was going to leave the best part of my life just to check to see if I was gay. I told no one.

> **"** *Angelle has a certain twinkle to her eyes that not all people have. It's like when you catch her eye, you remember a little happy secret you have, or she's reminding you of a happy memory. Often back before she came out as trans, that spark wasn't in her eye.* **"**

When Ang came over in one of her off moods, it was not completely out of the blue. She was struggling with her mental health, and I was happily the person who could hold her and kiss her until she felt better. I felt like a sponge that could kiss, talk, and hug away her sadness. It was a meaningful job, and I took it seriously. She did the same for me.

That day, Ang took my phone and began to write in my notes app. Had she found someone else? Did she want to move back to western Massachusetts, or even farther to California, and break up? I began to cry as she wrote the note, anxiety tearing through me as I feared I was about to lose my very best friend, my soulmate. As I read her letter, I instantly began to feel peaceful. This was not any of the bad options I had thought of at all. I was not losing Ang. I was gaining Angelle.

It was scary of course. I knew that as a Black trans woman she would not be safe in many spaces. I knew people would judge her. However, I knew I would keep loving her forever and ever. That was not scary at all, and it made the moment happy for me because I knew she was finally telling me something that she must've held onto for so long. That's when the questions began. Millions of them. They'll probably never stop. We ask each other everything. We give full, big answers, ask follow-up questions, and sometimes change our minds weeks or months later.

I revealed to her later how I had been questioning my own sexuality. A while after she came out to me, I realized how obviously gay I had been; I had been dating a woman the whole time! She empowered me and I empowered her as we grew and loved together. I love Angelle more than anything. Her journey has been one of the best parts of my life and I feel so lucky to get to know her more and more every day. One of the best parts has been seeing the sparkle in her eye stay there. Of course, there are moments or days where she struggles to get the sparkle back, but now we can talk openly and sponge up any sadness until the sparkling Ang is back.

Sammy, Angelle & Isa. Photo by Jill Meyers

When Angelle came out, I was aware what transgender meant. I have friends who are trans and my favorite tattoo artist, Ruby Doom, is trans.

Tyrell (*he/him*)

brother, son

66 *The world needs more love and less hate. Angelle embodies that love every single day.* **99**

We live in world where transphobia and racism are rampant, to say the least, and the fact that my sister overcame all of it and is still here is a testament to how strong Angelle is. On my worst days, she's always been there for me no matter what. She's literally my Day One. Angelle's heart is bottomless, and she's loved me unconditionally and everyone around her and that love goes both ways.

I was fifteen when my sister Angelle came out to me and my family. At first, I honestly thought it was a weird joke because of how out of left field it seemed. But as I read the text she sent us, I realized that she was serious. My shock turned to sadness as I realized how alone she must have felt for the last twenty-one years. Because we grew up in the same community, I had an idea of all the transphobia she must have internalized growing up.

Isa Castro-McCauley (*he/him*)

basketball player, son, brother

The dynamic between a brother and a sister is a bit different than that of two brothers, so Angelle's transition has taken some getting used to. Over time, I have become more and more proud of the woman Angelle has become, and I'm so happy that she is able to fully love herself now.

I told her that my love for her would not change and that I fully supported her transition.

After Angelle made her transition public, I was able to have conversations about it with friends and family. But when someone that everyone already loves so deeply transitions, that love doesn't go away. I have seen nothing but love and support for my sister since she came out.

When my sister Ang came out to me a few years ago, I was surprised but I also wanted her to know we were there for her. Looking back, I wish I was more careful with my language, because before I knew Ang was transitioning, I would use words like gay in a way that was attempting to be humorous.

Sammy Castro-McCauley (*he/him*)

student, brother, son

I haven't really encountered any bullying or harsh judgment about having a trans sister. In fact, most people are very understanding about it. I admire Ang because she lights up any room she's in and, to me, that is very admirable.

I think it's important to recognize that everybody is their own person with their own journey, so it always helps to show more compassion toward those around you.

Myles Kaleikini Markham

Myles. Photo by Celeste Burns

(*he/him, they/them*)

social engineer, producer, problem solver

I'm a transmasculine nonbinary person who uses he/him or they/them pronouns. I was born in 1990, the last of three children in my family. From a very early age my family knew that although I was being raised as a girl, there was a lot more to my gender story.

My father was Native Hawaiian and Japanese along with some German, English, and Jewish heritage. He worked in the hospitality industry, which is what brought him to Minnesota where he met and married my German and Swedish mother about a decade after the laws forbidding interracial marriage were overturned by the Supreme Court. My parents moved to North Florida, where they became evangelical Christians, and that's where they raised my brother, my sister, and me.

Throughout my childhood our family attended predominantly white churches, and I participated in congregation-based programs like Sunday school and Wednesday night bible study classes. In these churches, folks were never outright hostile or discriminatory, but I also never saw families like ours and I certainly never met other people like me. We were a mixed family living in a very segregated community. Despite how loving and open-hearted both of my parents were, in the absence of any kind of representation, it wasn't difficult to internalize the message that religious, racial, sexual, or gender identities that didn't fit neatly into a box were to be seen as abnormal and even morally flawed.

I thought if I had a personal conversion to Christianity, this could make life easier for me. Being officially designated as a "child of God" could, I thought, help me escape all the ways I felt like an outsider and potentially "fix" what I believed was broken in me. There was nothing more I wanted as a kid than to simply be treated like everyone else, to be "normal," to be considered "good," and to do what I could to make the world a better place.

I became an honor student, a serious athlete, and a devoted church youth group leader. I grew to love studying the Bible and church history, and in time viewed myself as a part of God's mission to the world. Much to my great misfortune though, I was beginning to dig deeply into my evangelical faith just as adolescence came barreling toward me.

While being a teenager can be tumultuous for anyone regardless of gender identity, for a trans or gender nonconforming person, puberty can feel closer to a death sentence. It wasn't that I hated or had a problem with my body per se, but I didn't feel like I had much, if any, control in the story my body was starting to tell. While my parents never pressured me to conform to a particular kind of femininity, that pressure came instead from the church ministries that were a big part of my life. Spiritual approval and acceptance became more important than anything else, and as a result I jumped through the hoops that were presented to me.

Whether it was agreeing to participate in "ex-gay ministries," working for Southern Baptist summer camps for little or no pay, or training to become a long-term, cross-cultural missionary, I was always held to a different standard of disclosure, transparency, and accountability. I agreed to meet with pastoral counselors, mentors, and peer leaders under the pretense that I would share the most intimate details of both my past and present. I consented, believing that somehow the pain and humiliation would shame me into maintaining a straight and narrow path.

With time, I developed an anxiety disorder, depression, autoimmune issues, and skin pigmentation problems, and I saw the decline in my physical and mental health begin to affect everyone around me. However, the more LGBTQ+ people I met, the more I realized that this wasn't just a "me" problem. Similar symptoms weren't just showing up in LGBTQ+ people; they were showing up in our parents, siblings, cousins, uncles, aunties, and grandparents too. I began to see that for so many of our families, our vital connections to one another were being frayed and sometimes completely severed because of theological fears turned into church policies and then deemed orthodoxy without any room for question.

When I finally trusted God enough to let myself see and feel the pain that came from that belief system, I couldn't unsee it. Eventually, my conscience just wouldn't allow it any longer. In 2013 I came out, at that time, as a gay woman. Having lost all my professional connections, given I had only worked in conservative Christian organizations until that point, I went straight from graduating from bible college to working full time in LGBTQ+ education and advocacy.

My life became marked by the significant loss of family, friends, and my church on one hand, and on the other, the relief that comes after having a heavy yoke, at long last, broken. Slowly, I started to see what I was going through as a kind of resurrection and that on the other side of my sorrow, there was joy and freedom. I felt the permission to be stretched further spiritually when I stepped outside the dominant narratives about who evangelical Christians told me I should be. I searched out liberation theologies and used my dad's East Asian and Native Hawaiian lineages as sources of learning about God as well. I found a different way to be Christian and a different way to be human. I built back much of what had been lost and began to feel safe to peel back more layers of my identity.

Despite becoming fully affirming and supportive of the trans people I knew, it still took me years to accept my own gender identity. A part of this was because the way the transgender discourse was presented to me was rooted in Western and dualistic notions of gender. For example, transgender as a term was defined as what happens when someone "crosses" genders, which assumes that there is something—a binary—that everyone who is trans must cross. I didn't entirely resonate with this concept or the limited ways I saw trans identities represented in film and media at large. Even the term nonbinary, while closer, still left me wanting.

> **These days I'm not so interested in talking about the intersection of transphobia and racism and the trauma that comes from that as much as I'm interested in thinking about the intersection of gender euphoria—meaning the joy, delight, and pleasure that is to be found in and through the experience of gender diversity— and antiracism.**

This changed, though, when I started to learn more about the gender systems in Indigenous communities, especially within my own Native Hawaiian lineage. In traditional kānaka maoli communities, people who experienced gender diversity were described as māhū, which means middle. Historically the people who were māhū had a sacred role in maintaining the presence of all the ancestors and making sure their legacies lived on through teaching, storytelling, and other cultural customs.

Along with learning about different kinds of "betweenness" to talk about gender, having several difficult therapy sessions, and wearing out my friends and family with countless late-night conversations, at twenty-seven years old I was finally able to name an experience that I had known to be true for most of my life. It was this revelation—I'm a transgender person.

I didn't know what it would be like moving forward or what words I would eventually use to describe myself, but at that point I didn't care about finding a new box. I was too relieved to have finally found myself, period. Since then, embracing my gender identity and faith have been a communal effort. My mentors, my friends, my church, and my professional colleagues have all been a part of reminding me of who I've always been and calling me into who it is possible for me to become.

This doesn't mean that the last three years have been easy. I know my family still struggles with the feeling that I "took" someone or something away from them. I've also had to spend a huge amount of time on the phone self-advocating for my health care. And I've watched lawmakers and news pundits throw the identities of trans people around like it's all a political game. Yet, I can honestly say that I'd go through these challenges day in and day out for the rest of my life if it meant I could continue to share the health, wellness, and peace I've begun to feel. I'm so proud of our beautiful and resilient trans community, and I'm proud of myself.

What I would say to my teenage self is something like, "Myles, the sacrifices you are making of your personal health, safety, and wellness to preserve the comfort of other people in your life will never truly help anyone. You are doing nobody any favors by shrinking yourself down and conforming to the dreams that other people have for you. The best thing you can do for yourself and for others is to be honest, compassionate, and genuine. Above all, you can't be true to others if you can't be true to yourself first."

I'm not entirely sure what the difference is between "activism" and the natural result of trying to live a life that supports the health, safety, and wellness of the people around me and the land we get to live on. Professionally, I've served as a community organizer, live event producer, educator, consultant, and writer in the areas of racial, reproductive, and LGBTQ+ justice and have spent most of my career doing this in Christian contexts. Right now I split my time between implementing the community engagement strategy for the documentary Pray Away about the history and continuation of conversion therapy and the "ex-LGBTQ" movement; working for Presbyterian Disaster Assistance, a disaster and refugee response organization; leading workshops on faith, gender identity, and Bible interpretation and theology; and serving on the board of a nonprofit ministry called Transmission Ministry Collective that's dedicated to the spiritual growth and leadership development of trans, nonbinary, and gender nonconforming Christians.

I've been learning more about what it means to embrace my various ethnicities. Learning more about my Native Hawaiian and Japanese ancestries has opened me up to new ways of thinking, of knowing, and of being in my body. I've heard this practice described by some as "re-indigenizing" oneself and one of my favorite ways to do this is through surfing. While mainstream surfing often replicates the racist, sexist, and dominance-based values of broader society, the origins of surfing couldn't be more different.

For centuries, Pasifika—notably Native Hawaiian people—expressed the playful and recreational dimensions of their relationship with the ocean through wave-riding. Surfing put riders into communion with the ancestors and reminded the riders to respect all of nature and honor their responsibility to protect the ocean.

Out in the water I smell and taste the salt, I feel the weight and pressure of the waves, and I'm reminded that I am a creature among many other creatures. In the ocean waves, I feel close to my elders who have passed away. I feel close to myself. I feel present. Above all, I feel safe and known in a way that I don't ever experience on land. Surfing to me isn't a sport so much as it's a healing modality. It's one of the main ways I've learned to love and trust my body, and that feeling is something I hope everyone gets to experience at some point in their life.

TAYLOR and SZN ALXNDR

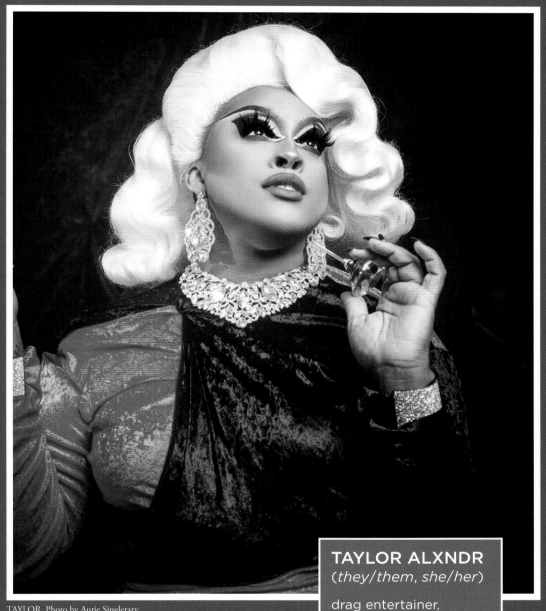

TAYLOR. Photo by Aurie Singletary

TAYLOR ALXNDR
(*they/them, she/her*)

drag entertainer,
mother of the House
of ALXNDR

I was born in a small town called Griffin, Georgia, located at the very edge of the metropolitan Atlanta area. I was raised there on a 400-acre cow farm, surrounded by multiple generations of my blood family. I moved to Atlanta in 2011 to attend college at Georgia State University.

In terms of gender identity, the most accurate and popular descriptor for how I identify would be agender. However, I feel as if my gender identity is more nuanced than that. Terms like ungendered or degendered or post-gender make more sense in terms of how I navigate in the world. Racially, I identify as Black and Indigenous. Religiously, I don't subscribe to any faith.

Very early in my life I knew I wasn't cisgender. Around the time that I started coming to terms with my sexuality, I also started questioning and challenging gender as a social construct. It wasn't until I went to college and started taking courses in gender and sexuality studies that I found the language to describe the thoughts and feelings I had been living with for a long time.

When I started to come out as nonbinary, I was surrounded by a lot of people navigating that same path. We were all very young and very new to being in spaces where we could question what we had been taught. I was incredibly fortunate to have had that launching pad and support for my burgeoning nonbinary identity.

In my gender journey, I've also been incredibly lucky to be surrounded by people who affirmed me at every stage I went through. Whether it was changing my pronouns or changing my labels, there were always people—friends, colleagues, and my chosen family—who were willing to lend an open ear. They understood that I was in the process of becoming myself while leaving behind what our society told me I was supposed to be.

In today's world, I think there's an elevated understanding of what being trans or nonbinary means. I don't think this level of understanding was this present or visible ten years ago when I was coming into myself—and of course, there was even less understanding before then. A lot of the movement toward trans liberation and visibility has been pushed forward over the past ten years by us young folks and our access to the internet.

I've always been a more effeminate person in every aspect of my life, so growing up I encountered many people who were critical of my expression—how I spoke and how I walked, et cetera. Having lived my entire life as a visible and proud Black person equipped me for when I started to come into my gender identity and faced harsh remarks and negativity. I always just brushed their negative comments off—they never caused me to dim my shine. Trans elders I've spoken to over the years have always called it "your essence," and they've told me that nobody can take your pure, true essence away from you. I've also been told by the elders that all trans people have their own essence and shine, and that cisgender people try to take it away from us because they're jealous of how free and unlimited we are in our ability to be fluid. Learning this made me even more confident in who I am.

Personally, I know that being a trans or nonbinary person is not a choice. However, why should it matter if it were a choice? If someone were to choose their gender identity, would that choice make them worthy of being discriminated against or harmed? Whenever I encounter the conversation about whether being trans is a choice, I always turn the conversation on its head. I begin questioning the person who has said this to me, and I ask them when they "decided" to become who they are. After all, why should my gender identity have to be biologically inevitable, i.e., that I was "born this way," for my gender to be respected and given an equal place in this world?

> *The more that we liberate and expand gender identity, gender expression, and gender roles, the more everybody—trans, nonbinary, and cisgender people—will be free. And yet, as much as we fight for trans liberation, we must not forget that included in that is also the elimination of racism and anti-Blackness. Without both happening at the same time, there is no true form of freedom and liberation for trans folks.*

I believe that gender is a social construct that we all fail at. There is no such thing as the perfect man or the perfect woman who display and perform all the right roles and characteristics of these constructed gender identities. Those who try for this so-called perfection often enact harm or neglect on themselves and on the world around them.

True trans liberation and safety in this world looks to me like an expansion and proliferation of rights and services that have historically been denied to us. It looks like access to competent and fair healthcare. It looks like school systems making all schools a safe space for trans and nonbinary students to exist free of fear and to learn just as their cisgender counterparts need safety.

Our justice system must learn to respect and honor the identities of trans people and do everything to protect them—which means a complete overhaul and rebuilding of our justice system! We must eliminate the current prison industrial complex, which historically has discriminated against incarcerated trans folks. A safe world includes the complete separation of church and state and making sure that all organized religions becoming inclusive of trans folks of faith. I think a societal understanding of trans folks will lead to the greatest and most immediate changes. This has yet to happen.

The advice I would give to trans and nonbinary youth coming up in the world is to give yourself the space and time to become who you are. This is not a race. This is not a competition. Contrary to what the world has told you, this will be an ongoing journey throughout your life. Give yourself some grace. There are millions of people just like you across this world—now and throughout history. Anyone who tries to tell you that you are wrong or invalid is both uneducated and hurting on the inside.

For anyone who exists at the intersection of being both Black and trans or nonbinary, I simply think that the marginalization and oppression that we face are compounded. If you look at the statistics of incidents of violence for white trans folks, you often see double or triple the number for Black trans folks. People often forget that oppressions overlap and intersect. As much as we fight for trans liberation, we must not forget that included in that is also the elimination of racism and anti-Blackness. Without both happening at the same time, there is no true form of freedom and liberation for trans folks.

I began getting involved in activism as soon as I came to Atlanta to attend college. I cofounded Southern Fried Queer Pride, a queer and trans arts and community organization based in Atlanta, to uplift Southern queer and trans communities. We've sponsored annual festivals, protests, gallery shows, dance parties, stage productions, town hall discussions, and so much more. Most of my work revolves around fighting the narrative that being from the South means you must have a terrible existence as a queer person. A lot of my activism is in direct defiance of that notion, and in turn uses being from the South as a launching pad for community change and growth.

Around the same time that I began getting involved in community organizing, I also began getting involved in drag performance. I went to my first drag shows as a first-year college student and found myself entranced with

SZN & TAYLOR. Photo by Robin Rayne

the power of the art form. I threw myself out there as a performer in my second year at Georgia State, starting in local bars on amateur nights. I started producing my own shows, which were different from a lot of local shows in that they were variety shows featuring a range of drag performers and other performance artists. Over the years my craft has grown and the number of shows I have produced has also grown. The year 2022 marks ten years of being a drag performer, and I have so much more creativity to bring into the next decade of my work.

The House of ALXNDR is not only my drag family but also a chosen family of people who brighten my day and bring me joy in so many ways. We are a hodgepodge group of amazing artists who, though incredibly different in our personalities, come together to be there for one another. Whether it's navigating depression, job loss, relationships, gender identity, or hardships that we face trying to be entertainers in an ever-changing city, my drag family is the family I can depend on when I need an open ear or a shoulder to lean on.

As the mother of the House of ALXNDR, I'm always opening my door and my heart to my drag children whenever they need anything. I feel very lucky to be trusted in this position.

SZN. Photo by Aurie Singletary

I'm first-generation Ethiopian American, born in California but grew up and lived in Georgia most of my life. I identify as bigender and for that reason I use both he and her pronouns. I still associate with my masculine-presenting identity; however, I do identify as a woman as well but just not in a traditional sense.

SZN ALXNDR
(*he/him, she/her*)

drag entertainer

> **" My transness is kind of unique and unfortunately it isn't really on the radar. "**

I'm a proud member of the House of ALXNDR family. I'm rather distant from my biological family. My drag family is my chosen family! Being part of this family means I have the space to grow, love, live, and learn as a human being and still stay true to who I am at my core.

Kylar William Broadus

Kylar. Photo by Joy Flanders

(*he/him*)

lawyer, civil rights activist

I was born fifty-eight years ago to my parents, William and Fannie Broadus, in a little town in the middle of Missouri called Fayette. Sometimes I hide my Missouri twang very well and most people assume I'm from a metropolitan area because I learned very early that some people thought you were stupid if you were from a rural area.

I spent my whole childhood in Fayette in the same house, which my father built himself—he worked by day and built the home we grew up in by night. Both of my parents always had a main job and then multiple other side jobs, but they always put my sister and me first. When I was born my father was forty-five and my mother was thirty-five, and back then it was unique for a family to have children so late. In fact, my mother almost died giving birth to me because she was a very thin woman, and I came out over eight pounds. I felt blessed to be born to my parents because they loved me unconditionally. Like my parents, I've worked hard my entire life. I had my first job when I was five years old, which is why I know the value of work ethic.

My parents were people of the civil rights movement. And honestly, whether or not we want to call it the Jim Crow era, they were the descendants of slaves. They both had extremely hard lives. They grew up with no new clothes; they would wear the same outfit for a year or longer and at most they'd get one pair of shoes a year. They told me about cutting cardboard to make soles for their worn-out shoes. These were not made-up stories to make it sound worse than what it was. My father became the head of this household in eighth grade, and he had to provide for the entire family. My parents did not teach my sister and me to be victims but to be workers and the creators of our own destiny.

As I grew up, people would say I was a lesbian because I always looked and dressed like a masculine child. My father would cover me so I could avoid wearing dresses. Then when Sunday would roll around, it was the only day of the week my mother would make me wear a dress because we grew up in the buckle of the Bible belt. There was no getting away from going to church on Sunday, but it felt horrible to me because I had to wear that dress. You'll never see a picture of me smiling on a Sunday. My little cousins would be going, "Why you wearing a dress, Kylar? Ain't you a boy?"

My parents tried hard to protect me from the world. On schooldays my mom left early for work thirty miles away, so dad would let me change up the frilly outfit my mom had laid out for me to wear before going to school. I couldn't have asked for a better father. I adored both my parents, and I tell everybody that I was both a daddy's boy and a mama's boy. They're gone now. But you know what? They commune with me every day. When I write a speech, guess who enters my spirit and soul? Both my parents are always right there with me!

When I was coming up, I heard many of my father's stories about the military and how he was treated, and then how he was treated as a Black veteran and not being able to use his GI benefits because he was Black. He served on foreign soil and many white people want to minimize the impact of what Black troops did during World War II. We learned about their contributions much later without the whitewashing of history. My dad never carried animus or hate but he made the best life he could for himself and most of all for his family.

My dad was working at his many office jobs at night, and emptying the trash was my duty because I wanted to do my part. Eventually I worked up to dusting. I was so excited to get assigned a new chore because I felt I was learning a strong work ethic while contributing to our family and society. That worked well as a kid, but it got me in trouble with my health as an adult because I had learned how to be a workaholic. It's both a bad thing and a good thing because I believe in doing every job well, whether it's sweeping or mopping the floor or doing a legal brief.

My grandfather was Catholic, so I did a lot of stuff with the Catholic Church and my parents decided to join the Second Baptist Church. The white Baptist Church was called the First Baptist Church and the Black Baptist Church was called the Second Baptist Church, and those labels are still used today across our country. Neither of my churches bashed gay people at that time that I was attending them, but people in the congregations would come up to my folks and say, "Oh, I see your son is with you," even though everyone knew my parents had one older girl and one younger girl—me.

There were times I would be watching the national news with my father, and I got very uncomfortable and tense when a story about Christine Jorgensen or about the "Gay Movement" came on. I didn't say anything at all, but I must have realized that the first transsexual woman to become a widely covered public figure was someone like me and the movement meant something to me. In hindsight, my dad never blinked an eye or ever made me feel uncomfortable.

I knew my father could read me because I'd go on truck runs to unload twine with him and my sister. I remember being five and this guy said,

"Oh, I see you brought your son with you." This is when I first knew I had an ally because Dad would say yes and keep moving along. He never said a word to me. He never judged me. He even brought me to hang out with his buddies at the barbershop after it closed. Who would take their girl child to a barbershop? Though we never discussed it, and I didn't have words for it, it was obvious my dad knew something was up with my gender identity.

At age twelve, I found a *National Enquirer* with the Billy Tipton story. He was an American jazz musician and bandleader who had lived as a man for most of his adult live. After his death, friends and family were surprised to learn that he was transgender. I ripped out the article about Billy Tipton and I kept it hidden away, like a Playboy magazine some boys would hide under their mattress. I hid it in my house because this was my only access at the time to trans literature. There were a few short articles in *Jet* magazine that mentioned Black trans folks, but only a couple of lines at most.

In middle school, because of the hormonal shift of puberty, I felt like I was in the wrong locker room with the girls. I didn't look at anyone, and I didn't want anybody to look at me. It was so uncomfortable, to the point where I began to become isolated. The school counselors noticed and called my parents. I didn't feel like I fit in because I didn't like what the girls were doing. I wanted to play football with the boys, but I couldn't keep up with them anymore, which I used to be able to do before my hormones shifted. The school recommended that my parents take me to a mental health facility. And you know what a nightmare that was back in the 60s, because then they were doing electric shock therapy. The other complication is that I was a Black child, so the institutional and structural barriers were there to prevent any support.

My mother trusted the school counselors, and she took me to a mental health center. My memory of this remains as vivid today as if it happened yesterday. After the first meeting for testing and assessment, I came out obviously traumatized by the experience. Immediately Mom took me under her wing to protect me and pulled me close to her and away from the white doctors. She was nobody to mess around with, and she very politely told them, "Thank you very much for your time, but my husband and I will take care of this at home." We left the hospital, and she took me out for a hamburger and ice cream and brought me home. Thank God, my parents were not about to have their child go through any of that mess. They were very bright people and didn't want me undergoing shock therapy because they knew it wasn't the answer.

I distanced myself from my peers and concentrated on my studies. It was only music that kept me alive. I understand when LGBTQ+ kids and kids of color find something that they can concentrate on like theater, it keeps them going on. Music was that for me. That's why I had connected with Billy Tipton; the article about him kept me alive. I literally came home and read it every day after school. It was my real world inside my head.

We trans folx of all races and ethnicities need to love each other and work together. If we don't show each other how to love each other, then why should other people love us?

After graduating from high school, I went to Central Methodist College, a small liberal arts school where they had a great music program. I was a brass player. I started on cornet, and then played the sousaphone, the baritone, the tuba, and finally euphonium. I played in any kind of band that was going on. Music has always filled my soul. As a kid, I had been so enamored by music that I drove my mother and father crazy, playing horribly loud music in the house. But they let me do it. I ended up majoring in music in college and planned to focus on becoming a professional musician, but my trans journey took over. I set aside my career in music to pursue civil rights law.

When I went to law school, I found this great therapist who was a lesbian and wasn't transphobic. I also came out to my MD, a cisgender straight woman, and she was phenomenal. I had been going to her for a while and I said, "I need to tell you something, Doc." And you know what? After I told her I was trans, she grabbed my hand and said, "Honestly, I know absolutely nothing about gender identity, but you know what? We are going to figure this out together." From then on, she had my back. She helped me walk my walk. I am forever grateful and indebted to her.

I went to law school at the University of Missouri in Columbia and there were lots of racial problems there, as there still are. I was still very quiet then because I hadn't come out publicly, but it was clear to everyone that I was different. Sadly, I wasn't yet able to fully be me until I got into trial practice class. One of my professors said, "Wow, anybody that can stand up and do all this on their feet is a born trial lawyer." After that, I began to feel more confident about myself.

I didn't officially transition until my late twenties and early thirties, which was early in my timeframe of the arc of the trans movement. I flew back and forth to the University of Minnesota's gender program. At the time, you needed to do two years of living in your authentic gender identity before you could access any medical interventions. It was called the "real life test." I explained that I had been living as a man for many years and had letters from my doctor and therapist to support me. They said they would reduce the timeframe to one year. When I came out as a trans Black man, my life was in danger every single day because nobody knew much about trans people, especially where I lived and where so many people carry guns all the time.

Others within and without the LGBTQ+ community labeled me as a butch dyke because it was convenient for them, but people didn't understand that I never felt like a butch dyke or a lesbian. I could never use the women's restroom or go into the women's locker room at the gym without women running out yelling, "There's a man in there."

Some years later, after working for a large law firm, I got a job at a large financial corporation. My coworkers were totally fine with me wearing a suit and they helped me tie my ties and gave me great support. After some years, I decided to hang out my own shingle and do my own private law practice. I started on the local level in Columbia, Missouri, trying to get the human rights ordinances passed there, which took more than ten years.

I still practice law, I still do activism, I still do public speaking, and I still do whatever it takes to make a buck. That's what I learned from my parents. They would say, "If you can't make a buck one way, then you've got to make it another way." I was doing quite well financially for a while. When I was a business law professor, my white students would comment if I was driving a nice car, because it was unusual for a Black man to have money.

I began to work nationally and internationally to help make the current trans movement in the United States more visible. Then I worked on building momentum in the fight for equal treatment for trans people under the law. A group of us came together in New York City and decided we would start by working to get local governments all around the country to pass laws protecting trans people. Then we would go on to get the state level. Our hope was to get enough power to get a national bill passed. I believe in inclusivity, which meant bringing as many people and representation as possible to the table.

Besides helping trans people negotiate with their employers about how to stay at work and educate employers about how to support their trans employees, I began to work on the national policy level, including the Matthew Shepard and James Byrd Act and ENDA. I also helped with national litigation about marriage cases and many legal battles involving trans issues. I continue this work today. I've just received the Spirit of Justice Award in Boston from GLAAD and I am included on the Robert F. Kennedy Foundation Board for my advocacy and legal work.

With all my visibility, I've had my share of death threats over my career. I am blessed, but I knew from the beginning that when I undertook this work my life might end early. I'm thankful that I've lived this long. I've always said that I'm a Southern gentleman because that's how my parents taught me to act. They always taught me that karma will come around, though they didn't use the word karma. They would say to me, "God will take care of that situation, so you don't need to lash out at people." Many people are amazed that I'm not vindictive. Anger only kills you. It really does. So, I never lash out even when I witness extreme racism or transphobia. I just leave at a certain point because my time is so much more valuable. I'd rather move on and do positive things.

My family includes my sister, Marsha Mae, and my nephew, Christian. They support me by believing in me and encouraging me to work on behalf of others to make the world a better place. They love me unconditionally. What could be better? Both Marsha Mae and Christian came with me to the distinguished alumni ceremony at my alma mater where I was honored for my contributions to society. It was touching for all of us, and it felt wonderful for us to be together since my sister and I had recently lost our last parent and my nephew his grandmother. It was our first event without one of our parents in attendance.

I'm a proud Black American, and I remember the first time I went into a church to talk about being Black and trans, I was scared to death. But when I broke it down to humanity and what the right thing is to do, people got it. Unless we people of color and LGBTQ+ people band together to do this fight, none of us is going to win. LGBTQ+ people are not out to hurt anyone, nor are people of color. Until we can come together and stop the fighting, we will never move forward.

Burwell/Burns/Alexander Family

Josef. Photo by Patrick Jervis, Jr.

Josef Wolf Burwell
(*he/him*)

physician associate,
humanitarian

My awareness of being trans happened twice in my life: initially when I was only three or four years of age, and then again at age 55. The lengthy time in between was spent suppressing my pervasive sense of being male and generally trying my best to fit my female body into situations that felt "just masculine enough" to ease my emotional distress. Now I like to say that being a trans man is the least interesting thing about me!

When I was in preschool, I expressed myself as a little boy. I called myself by a boy's name, Joe Jeff, and whenever I was given the choice, I wore clothes from the boys' department. Wearing a dress to church was a unique torture for me, and I would begin ripping the dress off as soon as our car pulled into the driveway back home. I only played with other boy, and judged girls to be no fun, unpredictable, and fragile. The boys I played with at that age didn't seem to care about gender so long as I could keep up with them, and I could!

Upon entering public school in 1965 in Winston-Salem, North Carolina, I refused to join the other girls in recess games. Remarkably, my first-grade teacher allowed me to wear a pair of shorts under my dress. Back in those days, girls were required to wear skirts to school and wearing pants was not allowed. Thanks to that teacher, I joined the boys in playing football, baseball, and basketball and I excelled among the boys at all these games. I absolutely loved getting dirty and sweaty. I continued these joyful activities every year until junior high. I was in my element for those thirty minutes of daily recess at school.

I continued to want more than anything to become a boy. This is what I wished for when I blew out my birthday candles and what I prayed for at church. I wondered if I could make a trade of sorts, and in my mind, I would bargain with God—hoping that if I gave up my above average reading skills as a second grader, maybe God would allow me to awaken as a boy. The wishes, prayers, and deals I tried to make with God went unanswered for a long, long time.

My masculine gender expression was not accepted by my mother, who wanted me to "act like a lady." I was constantly being told by my mom, "Girls don't do that!" The sad thing is that whatever Mom was telling me to stop doing—sitting without crossing my legs, climbing trees, or removing my shirt in public—were all completely natural to me. As I got older and more mature, I began to suppress my male gender expression and I tried to act more like a typical girl. By puberty, I tried to become friends with girls who were my peers, but this challenge was complicated by a new mystery—

I felt attracted to girls! Back in 1972, I didn't understand sexual identity any more than I understood gender identity, and there was no one I knew to ask. I didn't even know what questions I should be asking.

My mother, Helen, a no-nonsense Hungarian immigrant, was a charter member of the church I was born into. She had converted from Catholic to Baptist because when she was a non-English-speaking, starving child in West Virginia, the Baptists had fed her and her siblings when no one else would. I was raised in this Baptist church in Winston-Salem, North Carolina, and I truly hated being at church because it took away from my outdoor play time and gender roles and attire were firmly set in stone.

The typical church schedule for my family was all morning and all evening on Sunday, all evening on Wednesday, nightly Revivals in the summer and fall, two-week summer Bible camp, and an annual out-of-town church convention. It sure felt like a lot of church! My mom was so dedicated that we were never, ever late for any service. You can imagine my mother's shock when I declared at age 15 that I would no longer attend church. My siblings had all gone off to college or beyond by that time, so it was just my mom and me and my long-distance truck driving father. He didn't attend church, choosing to spend the time when he was at home hunting small game or drinking beer.

It's an extreme understatement to say my announcement that I wouldn't go to church anymore was not well received by my mother. I probably could have shared any adolescent misdeed like a car crash, unintended pregnancy, or alcohol-related arrest, and it would have been welcomed compared to, "I won't be going to church." Mom was so angry! She threatened me in all the ways a God-fearing person has handy, such as with eternal damnation and suffering. Then she threatened me in all the ways that most mothers have handy, such as a lifetime of house chores until I "get out on my own."

I quickly opted for promising that I would have a meal on the table for the entire family by 12:30 p.m. every Sunday and do a variety of chores I already did anyway. This was far better than eternal hellfire, and even though I had never spent more than ten minutes in my mother's kitchen, I had unfounded confidence that I could cook for seven relatives who always dropped in for Sunday dinner. My first attempt was less than stellar, but one of my older sisters invited me to her place for cooking lessons. I produced many more Sunday dinners. My confidence grew and I ultimately learned to put a decent meal together. It was worth the effort because I never had to go back to church!

In an apparent effort to take charge of something in my out-of-control life, I very nearly stopped eating during puberty. This was a conscious effort to make my breasts smaller; it also had the unforeseen benefit of causing amenorrhea—which means that my periods stopped. The physical consequences, of course, were devastating to my health. By the time I weighed only ninety-three pounds, I didn't have the energy to run up and down the basketball court, a game in which I had consistently won recognition. I no longer had clothes that fit properly, having lost a quarter of my body weight. I was ill, and I was in complete denial about having an eating disorder.

> *In the seven years since I came out as a trans man, I have experienced a lifetime of change. . . . I've felt gender euphoria—the opposite of gender dysphoria! My wishes and prayers from fifty years earlier when I was a child were answered by medical science and perseverance. It has all been worth the wait, the challenges, and the mysteries!*

Anorexia was not a word used among non-medical folks at that time. My mother was called to the school, and my track coach, who was also the Athletic Director, gave me an ultimatum: Weigh at least 103 pounds by spring or no more high school sports for me. He required me to eat cafeteria meals at his side and there were weekly weigh-ins at his gymnasium basement office. It was a struggle, but his method was successful. I survived and ran track for the school. A few years later, I graduated from high school in good health and at a normal body weight.

The summer after high school graduation, I had my first relationship with a young woman. I thought being a lesbian was the entire explanation for the sense of difference I had felt since I was very young. Of course, as I know now, this was not the entire explanation. Lesbian relationships came easily for me, but they ended just as easily. There was always something missing, and I couldn't identify the issue. It felt like there was a pebble in my shoe that I could never shake out. I saw other lesbians who seemed to embrace their sexual orientation, but I couldn't get my head around it.

It took an extended period of not having a girlfriend in my life to allow me the time for introspection. Because of migraines, I had stopped eating gluten products or drinking any alcohol. No wine, no women, no good food. A previous girlfriend called me by a new nickname, "Monk." But truly, I was heading into a big change; I just didn't know what was coming.

My initial paid summer work as a teenager in the 1970s was mowing lawns and being a mechanic in a bicycle shop assembling new bikes. Then I became a lifeguard, then an EMT, then a soldier in the US Army, then a certified emergency physician assistant. None of these jobs were considered traditional jobs for women—in those decades, they were done almost entirely by men.

For two decades prior to my transition, I competed in Ultra Competitions on different continents around the globe. Ultra-Marathon events are considered 100+ miles in length when running, or 200+ miles in length when cycling. Arguably, the miles of training and competition were a useful distraction from my undiagnosed gender dysphoria. Decades had passed since my anorexia, coming out as a lesbian, and a lifetime had passed since I had played exclusively with the boys in elementary school.

I was alone inside a tiny trauma unit in Northern Iraq, where I was on call for medical emergencies. I read the pages about reclassifying "gender identity disorder" to "gender dysphoria" in the *Diagnostic and Statistical Manual of Mental Disorders* (DSM) several times.

At long last I saw an explanation for my entire existence, for the difference I had always sensed inside of me, for the pebble in my shoe. Finally, I knew who I was, and I knew there was a way to become my true self. I cried because I had a diagnosis! I cheered because I had a diagnosis! I wasted no time getting a plan in place.

Within weeks of my return from Iraq to my home in Phoenix, Arizona, I found a competent physician to begin my medical transition. This is when I first felt gender euphoria. I just needed to explain this miracle to my extended family.

My parents were no longer living by this time, but I'm the youngest of five siblings, and I wanted to let them all in on this important news. They had each, over time, accepted me as a lesbian, but this was going to be an entirely new coming out story. I really didn't have the language of advocacy that a trans activist, or even a knowledgeable trans person, might have acquired over time. Even at 55 years old, this was brand new to me.

By the time I returned to North Carolina, I was three months into my medical transition. Except for a slightly masculine haircut, there were no real physical changes yet. My siblings' reactions were as varied and individual as they are. To be clear, they are all well-educated, well-read folks, but their education and literacy had not included extensive transgender awareness. Well, neither had mine until about six months before!

One sister immediately grasped the concept as it applied to me personally. She responded by saying, "Of course! This explains so much about you!" One brother also gave a wholehearted, "Good for you, Josef, this is great news," immediately using my new name. At the other end of the spectrum, my oldest brother declared that he would never call me by the new name I had chosen for myself. He proceeded to spend two hours explaining my gender expression as "me just being me," which he said does not require a "sex change." In between were two other sisters who were somewhat noncommittal. They had questions, and the questions were not how we all hope allies might sound. For example, one sister said, "Why do you have to change your name? I'm the one who named you." And the other sister asked, "Why are you doing this at your age? Why can't you just be happy as a lesbian?"

Over the years, the noncommittal sisters have become true allies. I think they just needed to see the changes and the real happiness it brought me. The stubborn brother has indeed begun to call me by my name, possibly because using my female birth name in front of other people would seem patently ridiculous.

My transition has brought me inner balance and peace. It also brought me the ability to enjoy a healthy relationship with my wife, Tamira. I met Tamira through our social justice activism. A mutual friend thought we should meet, not with a romantic alliance in mind but simply to network our forces for good. We met at a fundraiser that I was producing for Trans Spectrum, and she had been nominated for an ally award. The running joke between us is that she didn't win the ally award that night, but even better, she won my heart.

Legal changes to protect trans people are essential. We need real teeth in the actual practice of providing equal opportunity for trans people in the workplace. We need legislation that allows us to play sports in our expressed gender. Legislation that follows through on health insurance to cover behavioral health and medical and surgical transition is also crucial. In addition, it is so important to make trans healthcare, specifically medical transition, a part of medical education for all licensed clinicians.

In 2000, I founded Peacework Medical, and I feel privileged to be a part of something bigger than myself that brings meaning and purpose to my life. We are a primary care medical home mainly for undocumented LGBTQ asylum seekers, many of whom are also seeking gender care. Nearly all our patients have been held in ICE detention cells on our state's southern border, and many have horrifying stories of physical and psychological abuse related to misgendering. With our medical records proving that an individual is in fact transgender, their asylum cases are strengthened. Dozens of our clients have won residential asylum in recent years in collaboration with the ACLU, Trans Queer Pueblo—a local social justice organization, and our medical support at Peacework Medical.

Our completely volunteer team is intent on keeping our patients healthy. Many of our patients have never experienced primary care responsibly done. But we are committed not only to providing excellent support during gender transition, but also to preventing the common lifestyle diseases before they take hold—diabetes, hypertension, and coronary artery disease.

Peacework Medical is also growing the next generation of humanitarians since most of our volunteers are at the beginning of their careers. Until gender care is taught in medical schools, this is one of the better options for clinical training. I lecture extensively on this topic by invitation, and this is also a tenet of my nonprofit's mission.

An entirely separate area of activism I engage in is peer support. Trans Spectrum of Arizona is a peer support group in Phoenix for all folks under the trans umbrella and our allies. I've been a board member and a group facilitator since 2015, and I currently serve as Outreach Coordinator. Peer support is remarkably meaningful and effective especially in the early period of one's transition. I've heard new participants in our groups remark repeatedly that they had never seen so many trans people or felt so normal until finding us. For me, it's been like a home base where I feel like one of the guys among many other trans men. Allies benefit greatly too; their journeys are equally unique, whether they are friends, parents, children, or significant others of trans and nonbinary people.

In peer support groups, I've often heard broad assumptions about relationships in the trans world. These assumptions are sometimes made by folks who are not in relationships when they begin to transition. I've heard many trans men say, "A straight woman won't be interested in me." But labels are mythical! The more trans people meet their allies, all kinds of assumptions begin to fade. Nowadays, the number of young people identifying as trans or nonbinary is growing exponentially, and by joining this wider community, they have far more knowledge, power, and influence.

My advice to trans and nonbinary people is advice I have given to myself repeatedly: Believe in yourself and respect yourself for exactly who you are. Ask questions, listen to answers even when they seem to conflict, keep exploring and learning, and be flexible and patient with your evolving self.

Tamira Burns
(*she/her*)
humanitarian

I'm a cisgender woman, the mother of a transgender son, and the wife of Josef, a trans man. My journey as a trans ally started with my ex-wife. I identified as a lesbian and spent fifteen years in a committed lesbian relationship. Seven years into our relationship, we were married in New Mexico when the Superior Court clerks of New Mexico rebelled and started issuing marriage licenses same-sex couples before same-sex marriage was legal in all fifty states. It was a joyful, historic event!

When I was still married to my wife, our daughter started the journey to become our son, Ryan. My assigned-female child had been playing male cosplay characters since about age 8 and had come out as queer at age 12. This was not surprising as what was called "gender-bending" was common in the cosplay community. It was a good place to practice being someone else and seeing how a different gender identity or sexual orientation felt while being "in character." I had a lot of cosplay kids over at my house because it was a safe place for them to be who they were. I was already familiar with binders, packers, and silicone breasts long before I understood what being transgender really meant.

My wife worked as a crisis counselor at "Camp OUTdoors," an Arizona LGBTQ+ summer camp where our kid went to their first sleepaway camp

Josef & Tamira. Photo by Patrick Jervis, Jr.

at age twelve. Over the next two years, the routine was for me to drive both my wife and child up to Prescott for camp, then turn around and bring them home about five days later. We always stopped for dinner, and I was gifted with the excited, affirming stories and revelations from my happy, exhausted campers.

When my kid was fourteen the ride home after camp was different—it was silent and lacked the usual excited chatter from either my kid or partner. We pulled into our usual restaurant. My wife and kid sat across from me in the booth looking serious. My wife began by saying, "Our child has something to tell you." My kid had tears in their eyes and the words that came tumbling out were, "Mom, I want to be called Ryan and from now on I'm using he/him/his pronouns."

I felt like the world had stopped moving. For me, this had come from left field, or so I thought. I couldn't speak for a few minutes. My head was racing wildly trying to find an appropriately affirming response at odds with the slam of internalized fear I was feeling. I blurted out something like

"You know I love you and support you no matter what." I then excused myself to the restroom, where I had an ugly cry meltdown.

For all my open and affirming acceptance of any kid that came through my door, I had no idea how to process that my "daughter" was a boy. All my attachment to the feminist ideal of passing on the mantle from mother to daughter came crashing down. I wanted to support Ryan, but what if it was a phase? Or if not, how could I keep him safe as he transitioned? All these thoughts and more kept me frozen in grief in a public bathroom stall, wondering how I was going to ever go back to the table. My wife eventually came to coax me back. Poor Ryan was devastated and thought he had somehow broken me, or that I didn't really accept him. We took our food to go and made the long drive back home in uncomfortable silence. This is how my journey to being a trans ally began.

In the weeks after the big awkward "Coming Out" at the restaurant, we started the adjustment phase of moving from using my child's birth name to calling him Ryan and changing she/her pronouns to he/him pronouns. Despite my honest efforts, it seemed that my brain would not fully cooperate. I could see how hurt Ryan was whenever I slipped up. The loving and close "we can talk about anything" relationship we'd had was now tense and distant.

Ryan chose who in the community could be told and who could not. It was hard to keep track, and the rules changed a lot, as rules from teenagers often do. The adult friends and family who were let in on the change, amazingly, were all great with Ryan's new name and pronouns. Someone suggested I change his name in my phone contact list and add Ryan's pronouns, so every time Ryan called or texted me, his new name and pronouns would come up. This is advice I pass on to the parents and partners of trans folks to this day.

The cosplay kids just rolled with it, as they do, and really helped me and my wife to get the hang of it. They also helped Ryan be more patient with us. I overheard one conversation that went something like this: "Ryan, why do you think your mom is your adversary? She's always been the mom everyone comes to for advice. She's known you the longest, and it takes older women time to adjust. Be nicer to her." Ha! I was now seen as an "older woman." Yup. Forty-one must have seemed ancient to Ryan's friends!

When my wife and I tried to get Ryan into counseling, we found out that there weren't any therapists in the Phoenix area who worked with trans kids or their families. Together, we worked up a presentation about transgender, nonbinary, and gender nonconforming people and trotted it out to the social work and psychology community at every conference we went to over the next five years. We learned more and more about what trans and nonbinary meant, and about the lack of access to health care that pervaded the trans community. I started working with communities of faith to start programs to keep trans kids safe and healthy. I counseled many families in these faith communities who had trans kids, knocking down the Biblical excuses to abuse and abandon their children.

> **" What this world needs now is education, education, education! I want transgender and queer issues to be part of every sex education program and all medical training. "**

My wife came out as a trans man in the last three years of our relationship. I really came around to loving him for who he was, but unfortunately, he worried that I would never be able to see him fully as a man. We separated and he filed for divorce. This was an important time in my life that tested my ideas about gender and sexuality. While the divorce broke my heart at the time, ultimately, it gave my ex the ability to grow into the man he wanted to become. We remain very good friends to this day, and I am still an ally for him and adore his new wife.

Enter Josef Burwell. The ink on my divorce papers was not even dry when I found out that I had been nominated as "Trans Ally of the Year" through Trans Spectrum of Arizona, a peer support group for trans individuals and their families and loved ones. I had not been out at a public event since my ex and I had separated two years prior. The event where the winner of the Trans Ally of the Year award would be announced was a fancy dress Winter Gala event. Talk about nerves! I ordered a dress online, praying it would fit, and it did. I grabbed my bestie James, who is a tall and beautiful nonbinary human, and off we went to the gala, all dolled up.

Although I was not the ultimate winner of the Trans Ally award, the couple who did win were so deserving! I enjoyed myself and caught up with many folks I had not seen for a while. I'm an introvert, however, and my social battery ran down quickly. I wanted to get home to a nice cup of tea, but I had made a bid on two beautiful art items in the silent auction. I had the best bid on one, and went to pay for it, when the person in charge of the auction said, "The person who bought the other part of this set hasn't come to pay. If you can wait another fifteen minutes until we close, you can have it for your bid amount." I was standing near the back of the atrium, introvert in full quiet mode—clutching my piece of art to my chest while trying not to be noticed—when my dear friend Isaac came running up to me, literally jumping over a small sofa to get to me. He said, "Tam, have you met Josef Burwell?" "No." "You have to meet him! You two are doing the same humanitarian work with border justice and trans causes!" I was so tired, I said, "I'm so done, sweetheart. Can you just get his business card? I swear I'll call him." "No," said Isaac, "Wait here, I'll go get him." Off Isaac ran. "Never stop a Jewish trans guy on a mission," Isaac had told me many times. I took a deep breath and straightened my shoulders. Guess I was going to have to meet this Josef guy.

Isaac returned with Josef and made introductions. Josef took my hand and I looked up into the bluest eyes and the kindest, most handsome face. The earth shook. Uh oh, I'm in trouble! Then he handed me his business card, "Josef Burwell PAC, Medical Director, Peacework Medical." I thought, "Oh crap, soooooo out of my league!" I brought myself back to earth, and we made plans to meet over coffee the following week. I grabbed the matching piece of art and my bestie and ran out the door.

Josef and I met for coffee that week and found out that we really were doing the same work. As we were getting ready to leave, I agreed to come see what Peacework Medical was all about. At some point, he moved from the couch beside me onto a steamer trunk coffee table across from me to face me. He took my hands, and we talked and talked. Coffee turned to lunch; lunch turned into a walk. Oh my! I snuck out to text Isaac, "I'm so smitten! Help!" He texted me back a smile emoji. Josef walked me back to my car and asked me if I'd come to dinner with him in two days. Which, of course, I did.

Wine and firelight outside under the stars! Josef fed me all the things I loved that he could not possibly have known about. We talked and talked. Finally, he said, "Will you stay tonight?" And I did. He made me lunch before I left for work the next day. And the rest is history. Josef and I have a beautiful friendship, share a solid shared humanitarian mission, and have an epic romance. Five years in, we got married, and we will celebrate our first wedding anniversary this fall. My husband still takes my breath away every day. Today, I run Peacework Medical with Josef and work with Trans Queer Pueblo in their border justice program as the voice of medical reason in asylum hearings. This work is my passion.

I want folks under the trans umbrella to have universal access to legally changing their name without a hassle from a transphobic clerk. I want name and gender markers on IDs to be easier to get and not require letters from doctors about gender surgery. I want more healthcare professionals and surgeons who work with the trans community to start using an informed consent model. There is no need to have letters from mental health providers when a person's lived experience is clearly that of a trans or nonbinary person. Gatekeeping at all levels needs to be universally stopped.

Within five years of starting to advocate for better care in the social work world, clinics in Arizona popped up that specialize in transgender mental health care and there are ways of getting hormones through telemedicine. More and more companies are allowing gender-affirming surgeries paid by insurance, and gender-affirming surgeons who once only took cash are now signing up to take insurance. There are peer support groups in many major cities around the country. Medical schools are adding trans healthcare into their curriculums, and trans health professionals are being invited to lead grand rounds and special training groups to teach about trans health.

In the four painful years of the Trump administration, when LGBTQ+ rights were shredded and vilified daily, the reaction of many organizations and philanthropists was to throw money and time into the community to help create safer places and access to care for trans and nonbinary people. In the years since the 2016 election, more grant money for trans causes has become available than ever before. There are decent folks who realize that the only way to make sustainable change is to create it from within. They may not be comfortable marching for trans rights, but they have power and the cash to make life better for those who are marching.

I'm a deeply spiritual woman, an ordained minister, and part of the Arizona Interfaith Society, where I've been blessed to be able to help change hearts and minds of some of my interfaith colleagues. I also facilitate open conversations where we bring trans and nonbinary folx into congregations to tell their stories and take respectful questions from parishioners.

Sadly, I feel that some Christian denominations are so toxic for people who are LGBTQ+ and/or people of color and that it seems like no one can get through to these homophobic, transphobic people. I consider myself non-denominational. I'm registered as a fill-in minster with the United Church of Christ, which is a social justice denomination that leans left and seems to find value in my teachings.

My hope is that trans and nonbinary youth will have access to support wherever they live. Studies show that just one adult ally can reduce the suicidality rates of trans or nonbinary youth to the levels "normal" for the general age group. More than anything, I hope that young trans and non-binary youth can find affirming friends to help get them through their rocky times. More and more parents are coming around. More and more churches and schools are creating open and affirming safe places to worship and study. For every place of fear or hate, there is an equal place of love and help. May love and acceptance flourish!

Ryan Michael Alexander
(he/him)
creative, resourceful, mad scientist

I've found that transgender people will either have already known their whole life that they were this way or would find out much later, after a series of gender dysphoric (or even euphoric, if they are lucky enough) episodes. I was the latter in this scenario. Before my realization at age sixteen, I suffered compounding dysphoria as early as age six without understanding what it really meant. I am twenty-seven now, and couldn't be happier with my transition.

My family held given names in a certain high regard. Not to mention, they were incredibly proud of the unique name they had given me. Inevitably, there was going to be some friction around my changing it. By trying out my new name in a game of Pokémon: Emerald, which I hid on an incredibly old Game Boy Advance in my backpack, I was able to privately wear and test out my identity in a controlled environment. Laughably, I chose a pretty common name to replace the old one. It really works for

Tamira & Ryan. Photo by Patrick Jervis, Jr.

me, and I don't usually have to worry about spelling my middle name anymore.

When I came out to my mom, there was a lot of crying and open sadness in the beginning. My mom informed me that she needed time to process the grief. I understand, logically, that people need time to grieve over sudden losses even if they don't necessarily relate to literal death. However, it was exceptionally hard to have this happen while I was still present and very much alive. I felt the implication that my transitioning had "killed" her only daughter, and anger that she couldn't accept me despite being so entrenched in the LGBTQIA community. I felt like a ghost inhabiting a corpse, watching people cry about my death and unable to act while my mental state silently deteriorated. Fortunately, my mom and I always had a fine relationship, despite the rough patches. Over time, being able to share openly as myself has greatly improved our communication, and her relationship with Josef has made us able to relate on a pretty cool, unique level.

My advice to parents of trans or nonbinary kids is to say: if you feel the need to grieve about a transition, please do so privately. Your child is counting on you to support them as a parent, which means that they will internalize your behavior and blame themselves if you lash out.

Remember that their transition is about them, not you. Respect the pronouns of your child *and* their friends. Yes, they will notice.

Being young *sucks* no matter how you identify. For a trans kid life can seem insurmountable, but believe me when I say that you *can* survive this. Moving forward takes compassion and forgiveness that only you can give yourself. External validation, while nice to have, is best when you are able to accept it sincerely. Know that you are not alone in this vast world. If not for yourself, there is always someone or something out there worth surviving for.

> **It was hard for a long time, but I managed to stay alive this long! Since that wasn't always a guarantee, I embrace my survival with gratitude and hope that it can inspire those like me to thrive.**

Sarah McBride and Family

Sarah. Photo by Sansskruty Rayavarapu

Sarah McBride
(*she/her*)

state senator, aunt, daughter

I've known that I'm trans for as long as I can remember. I didn't always know that there were other people like me, but my earliest memories are of me praying that I would wake up the next day as myself. When I was separated in line at school from kindergarten on, I always had this longing to stand in the girls' line.

I think a lot of LGBTQ+ youth grapple with existential questions that most people don't grapple with until they are well into adulthood. When I was young, I certainly grappled with questions such as: What is a life well lived? What does it mean to live an authentic life? What does it mean to live a fulfilled life? For a while I felt that a meaningful life was simply a life of professional success—of change-making and making other people in my life proud. I also thought that the only way to do those things was to remain in the closet. From a young age, I kept my authentic self buried deep inside of me because it seemed like my dreams of finding love and doing work I loved in a community I loved were all mutually exclusive with being out as trans.

I got involved in politics after I started volunteering for campaigns here in Delaware. Because of my own experience as a trans person living in the closet, politics became an outlet for me to create the changes in the world that I thought would fill the void in my life. I also felt that if I could help create a world where other people could live openly and authentically, perhaps I could almost live vicariously through them.

In many ways, my interest in politics stemmed from my sense of loneliness and my fear that there wasn't space for someone like me in society. But when I started reading about American history, I found hope in the history books. While no one like me had ever made it very far within those history books, what became clear very quickly was that history is the story of advocates, activists, and a handful of courageous elected officials bringing people in from the margins of society into the circle of opportunity. And while the trans community had not yet been the direct beneficiary of that support, examples of that kind of community change in the past provided me with a lot of hope.

I think one of the challenges when we talk about gender identity is that people who aren't trans often have a difficult time wrapping their minds around what it feels like to be trans and in the closet. The closest thing I can compare my old life to is a constant feeling of homesickness, an unwavering ache in the pit of my stomach that I knew would only go away when I could be seen and affirmed as myself. But as I got older and had opportunities to make changes in communities I loved, including as the student body president at my university, I saw that even those positive experiences didn't fill the void in my life. In fact, they accentuated and amplified it. The homesickness grew greater, and I thought about my gender identity every single waking hour of every single day.

I began to realize that I was watching my one life pass by living as someone I wasn't. It was with that increasing pain and with some of the courage and confidence that I had gained in college that I realized that you're never going to make everyone happy and that even the negative things people say about you aren't the worst things in the world. With those insights, I decided to come out to my parents on Christmas Day in 2011. I know that not everyone has the privilege or safety to do so.

My mom talks about how we are oftentimes thinking the same thing. And it's true. I'll bring up an idea or she'll bring up an idea about what we want to do on the weekend, and we are thinking about the exact same thing. When I was home from college that Christmas holiday, she felt that something was bothering me. I wasn't planning on coming out that day, but she essentially asked me what was wrong and so, without planning to do it, I told her that I was transgender.

I've always known that I lucked out in the parent lottery. At the same time, I knew that my news would be incredibly difficult for my parents. But I also was lucky that I never had to fear that at the end of what I knew would be very difficult conversations, my parents wouldn't be there to love and accept me. I knew they would stand by me.

That first day I was intentionally very patient with my parents, even though we aren't the most patient family. I don't want to suggest that it was perfect or without conflict. What was most important, though, was the level of grace that we extended one another through those early months. Inevitably, there were going to be moments where we weren't patient, moments where either my parents or I said something a little harsh. We recognized that we were all bringing a lot of fear and feelings to our conversations. But even when we lost our temper or got upset, we knew we had to continue to extend grace to one another.

When you come out, you've been bottled up for so long that you want nothing more than everyone in society to affirm who you are. So in those first few months and even years after coming out, you're so hungry for that affirmation that when someone doesn't say the right thing in the right way every single time, it can hurt a lot. I think it's important for the families of trans people to understand that when their trans offspring get upset at their mistakes, it's because they are so hungry for that love after a lifetime of never experiencing it as their authentic selves.

On the flip side, for trans people, it's important to recognize that you've had however long, fifteen, twenty, thirty years, to come to an understanding of who you are. It's not news to you when you come out, but in most cases, it is news to everyone else. My parents didn't have twenty-one years to come to terms with my gender identity as I did. And so that meant that they were going to go through a lot of the same emotions that I had gone through over the years. And yes, that included for my parents a sort of process of grief. Truthfully, in many ways, my journey to coming out was a process of grief as well. I grieved the future I had imagined. It was only in accepting that I might be giving up my dream future that I was then able to accept myself.

I came out publicly at American University at the end of my junior year by writing an op-ed in the student newspaper and simultaneously to my wider world of friends on Facebook. I got a lot of attention for this in the media and was featured in national outlets. Despite my fears, the responses I got on campus and off were almost universally messages of love, support, and celebration.

Before coming out, my volunteerism had led to internships and, eventually, jobs with a charismatic and compassionate elected official named Jack Markell in his successful campaign to become governor of Delaware. I also was privileged to intern and eventually work for Beau Biden, the now-late son of President Joe Biden, during his successful campaigns for Delaware attorney general.

Because I had entered college with enough extra credits from advanced courses in high school, I had the choice to either graduate early in December of my senior year or take the first semester off. I wanted to try to intern at the White House, so I decided to take the first semester off. It was the first time that I applied under my chosen name rather than my birth name. Having worked in Delaware politics with Jack Markell, our now former governor, he was exceptionally helpful to me by writing a letter of recommendation for me. In fact, asking him to write that letter resulted in me coming out to him because I wanted him to write the recommendation under my chosen name rather than under the name I had used when I worked with him.

When I told Governor Markell the news that I was trans, he didn't skip a beat and he said he wanted to make clear to me that he and the first lady of Delaware were right there by my side and that they loved me and would do anything to support our family as we started this next chapter.

> " The early messages we get about gender stereotypes and about how boys and girls are supposed to act come at us from every direction—parents, peers, social media, television. Even before I knew that there were words to describe my experience, I somehow knew that it was something that I needed to keep a secret. So I kept all these feelings inside of me. I've heard it said that it's hard to be what you can't see. "

I'd always been interested in interning in the White House, and my formative years in politics took place in the lead-up to the 2008 election. Barack Obama's campaign was an almost euphoric experience for an idealistic, hopeful young progressive Democrat. For me, Obama's election was monumental and having the opportunity to work in the White House with him was my dream job.

I was interviewed for my internship in the White House Office of Public Engagement by a gentleman named Gautam Raghavan, who is now the head of personnel for the Biden administration. At the time, he was the LGBTQ Outreach Director for the White House, and he interviewed me about three days after my Facebook and op-ed posts about being trans had appeared. Since American University is in DC, he had read the coverage about my public coming out. Within three months of coming out publicly, I was walking into the White House with my new ID reflecting my name and gender as my authentic self. There had been two trans men who had interned at the White House in the Obama administration prior to my time there, but as far as anyone knew, there had never been a trans woman walking those halls.

The Office of Public Engagement is what they call the front door to the White House because it manages engagement with different stakeholders and constituency entities. Whether it is women, African Americans, Latinx and Hispanic communities, labor, LGBTQ+ youth, small businesses, seniors, you name it . . . if it's a constituency group, this office engages with them all. In a White House run by Barack Obama, a former community organizer himself, our office was exceptionally important to him. President Obama knew that it was our office that ensured that the policies of the White House was informed by the people impacted by those policies, particularly the marginalized.

Every day we invited groups into the White House, many of which had never been invited there under any previous administration. We would talk to them about what the administration was doing to improve their lives, but also to hear from them about what more we needed to do. Some of those meetings were with cabinet secretaries, and a lot of times those meetings were with President Barack Obama, Michelle Obama, Vice President Joe Biden, and Jill Biden.

I'm so grateful that I had that experience as a White House intern as my authentic self. To be welcomed every day as an out trans woman into that historic building—that symbol of our democracy, a place where every avenue of society converges—was truly amazing. It certainly didn't seem possible to me growing up, so the act of simply walking through the door to the White House was the personification of our progress.

I started working in the White House just three months after marriage equality passed in the Supreme Court. President Obama had come out in support of marriage in May of 2012, and I got there in the fall of 2012. It was the point in the administration at which they had finally found their footing on LGBTQ+ equality and began to lean in publicly in a way that they hadn't before. I was outside the White House on the night of the Obergefell decision on marriage equality when the White House was lit up like a rainbow, with throngs of people celebrating outside the gates. Photographs don't do it justice. To see the White House lit up like that, it felt that everything is possible. I still believe that nothing is impossible!

President Obama always supported marriage equality privately. I think, however, that his daughters' fervency and passion made it a situation where he, like so many other politicians, could no longer look his children in the eye and continue a public position that went counter to their family's values. I think that is true across the country. So often it is young people who have opened their parents' hearts and minds to LGBTQ+ equality. And what was true for my generation on issues of sexual orientation is true with this generation on issues of gender identity. For most teens, gender identity and sexual orientation are not issues. Adults are making it an issue.

At the White House, my approach to advocacy was to say that I was a safe person for anyone to ask any questions and I'd answer them. Frankly, just being present made a huge difference. Many people didn't even have to ask me questions. They were able to realize the humanity behind an issue that was previously abstract because they were walking the halls with a trans person; they had become friends with a trans person.

With the experience and the renewed hope that this experience provided me; I went on to advocate for nondiscrimination protections for the trans community in Delaware and then, eventually, became the national spokesperson for the Human Rights Campaign, the nation's largest LGBTQ equal rights organization. In doing that work, I saw that state legislatures are the place where the rubber meets the road on public policy. They have the potential to be laboratories of democracy for bold ideas that meet the scope and scale of the challenges we face. I felt that elected office was where I could make the most amount of change.

When I ran for the Senate in Delaware, I ran as someone who was not only trans but who had been working in trans advocacy for a decade. The presumption that I was running to solely work on trans rights was predictable. It felt absurd to have to keep saying, "I'm not running to be the transgender state senator. I'm running to be the health care and paid leave senator." I don't think any other person of another identity would have to say that so explicitly. A woman would not have to say, "I'm not running to be the pro-woman senator." I think it's a demonstration of inherent bias that a trans person must make that so clear. The good news is that I don't have to do that anymore because the breadth of work I've done speaks for itself.

Even some of my Republican colleagues have told me that I have proven to them that I'm not here just to work on one issue. But you know what? Being trans is important! I am bringing the trans perspective to the table, and it's important for me to do that. Diversity in government is not a luxury. It's a necessity in a healthy democracy where everyone has access to all parts of our government, including serving in public office. It's also a practical necessity because you can't craft effective solutions for diverse communities if you don't have the full diversity of those communities in the conversation.

Beau Biden would always say, "Life has a way of intervening when you make plans." And that has been true at every step of my own life. Even five years ago, I never would have anticipated the life experiences that I've had over the last ten years. What I've learned is that the only way to ensure that there are opportunities to grow and to do what you love is to do as good of a job as you can at any given moment. The rest will fall into place.

What's happening across the United States right now is incredibly scary. There are times where I have a crisis of hope and wonder whether it's all worth it or whether there's a path out of this. But I think about a couple of things. The first is that in my own life and in my work, I have seen change occur. No one can tell me that we haven't made progress.

Progress doesn't always happen in a linear fashion. It is often two steps forward and one step back, and, sadly, it's a big step back right now. But at every point in the LGBTQ+ movement, it has been by taking on the biggest challenges that we take our most significant steps forward. Once those conversations start within the public, things change. So, yes, they have their next wave of attacks and it's going to get bad, and it might get even worse before it gets better. But if we continue to fight and to have those conversations, equality will move forward.

I am so grateful that I am trans. And I'm so grateful for the journey my family has had because in many ways, if not for the hardship and the difficult conversations that have come from our family's journey, I don't think we would have been able to meet the ensuing challenges with the same resolve and ability.

Indeed, being trans introduced me to the man who would become my future husband, Andrew. Andy, as he was known, was a trans man about three years older than me when we met fighting for LGBTQ+ equality. He was brilliant, kind, and, most importantly, goofy. We quickly fell in love, but just as it seemed like we had a world of possibilities before us, he was diagnosed with cancer. We put everything we had into his treatment, with him as the patient and me as his caregiver. But when it became clear that his cancer would ultimately take his life, we decided to get married. We were able to do so just four days before the love of my life passed away.

What I want to tell young trans and nonbinary kids is that there is no one way to be trans. You are the best expert on who you are and what you need to be happy, healthy, and safe. And don't let anyone else tell you different!

Sarah, David & Sally. Photo by Sarah McBride

Sally McBride
(*she/her*)

retired high school counselor, LGBTQ+ rights activist

When I worked as a high school counselor, before having my own kids, I thought I was very intuitive about young people, particularly teenagers. Despite that, many years later, I had no clue, nor did my husband, that my oldest son, Sean, was gay, and that Sarah was a trans woman. No clue whatsoever!

When Sean came out to me and Dave during his first year of medical school, we were shocked, blindsided, and, most of all, worried. My first response to Sean was, "We love you! We respect you, and we want you to do whatever makes you happy in life," but I was very concerned that Sean would be discriminated against and defined solely by being gay. Dave's biggest concern was that he wanted grandchildren, but Sean reassured him that he also wanted children. Dave and I already knew a lot of gay people who had good lives, so it was far easier for us to accept that we had a gay son than eight years later when Sarah came out to us as trans. I'm not particularly proud of my first response, but let me just say that Dave and I knew right from the beginning that we would love Sarah and do whatever she wanted us to do to support her transition. At the same time, I was so scared for her safety and worried that she would be discriminated against at every turn—far more discrimination and danger than I had imagined Sean would face. For those reasons, the moment that Sarah told me that she was transgender, I literally fell on the floor devastated. I felt like all of Sarah's hopes and dreams and my hopes and dreams for her were shattered.

Back when Sarah came out, the only transgender role model that we knew about was Chaz Bono. Besides him, we knew very little about what it even meant to be transgender. So my husband immediately googled the word "transgender" and found the website for the National Center for Transgender Equality and together we began to educate ourselves. One of the statistics that David saw right away was that 40 percent of transgender people attempt suicide. But when they have a loving and accepting family, that number goes way down. We took that to heart.

After our initial response to Sarah's coming out, we talked nonstop for five solid days, and she answered every question Dave and I could think to ask her. Sarah was so patient with us, even when I said to her, "Do you really have to do this?" She replied, "Yes, I have to do this. This is me. This is my authentic self." Even after hearing Sarah's words, I asked her, "Can't you wait?" She was finishing her junior year in college as student body president, and I thought it would be easier for her to come out after graduation a year later. She said, "This is who I am. I've known since I was five years old. I cannot waste another second."

Our physician son Sean made an appointment five days later for Sarah, Dave, and me with one of the leading transgender adolescent psychiatrists in the country in Washington, DC. After three hours of intense interviews with Sarah and Dave and I separately and then with the three of us, the doctor told us, "Yes, your daughter is transgender, and she will be able to realize her dreams. She has no behavioral issues, and DC is a very safe place to be for a white transgender person." That doctor was the first person who gave us hope. Two weeks later, we were in touch with two other families with transgender daughters who were over thirty. Their children were happy and healthy and fulfilled, and they were both loving, close-knit families. Talking to them gave us even more hope.

I would never equate my child coming out as transgender with the death of a child, but at first, I felt like I was losing my child. When I said to Sarah, "I don't want to lose you," she responded, "Mom, you're keeping me and gaining Sarah." She was so right, but it took me some time to get there. I must admit I went through some of the stages of grief—first, denial and then anger because I felt like a victim, until gradually I reached full and total acceptance.

Sarah's two brothers were overwhelmingly supportive of her. Whatever she needed, they were willing to do. I had an Aha moment when Sean called us and said, "I'm not worried about Sarah. I'm worried about you and Dad. How are you doing?" I said, "I'm feeling sorry for myself." Then I added—and I can't believe I ever said this: "How many parents have both a gay and a transgender child?" At that time, Sean was doing a fellowship for medical school, and he was working in a hospital with pediatric brain tumor patients. He said, in the kindest way possible, "Mom, what are the chances of having a nine-year-old girl with a terminal disease? Your child is healthy. Your child will live." That was a powerful moment for me.

Within a week of that conversation with my son Sean, Dave and I arranged for Sarah to start seeing a psychologist to help make sure she was happy and healthy emotionally. And Dave and I also saw a psychologist to make sure that we were also healthy emotionally and could be as supportive as possible.

Dave and I began to tell our friends individually or in small groups with Sarah's approval. I have a wonderful close-knit girlfriend base and I wanted to meet with all of them face to face because my feeling was that I was taking them on a journey alongside my journey. I wanted to give them the right information because there are so many misconceptions and stereotypes out there about being trans. I encouraged them to ask me every question they could think of and not hold back. Dave told his law firm colleagues and together we told our church friends from our progressive Presbyterian church.

After coming out to a friend and to her family, Sarah started telling people at American University, including her professors. In fact, Sarah came out in a very public way in an op-ed she wrote for her college newspaper and on Facebook on the last day of her junior year at American University. I have to say that the response from her friends and community was amazing. Because I've been very involved as a community activist and Dave was a lawyer, we know a lot of people in our community. The response to us and to Sarah was equally amazing. We couldn't have done it without the widespread support we received as a family.

Fast forward to now. If someone had told me eleven years ago that our family would be where we are today, I would have told them, "You're crazy!" It has been the most incredible journey, and our daughter is making a real difference in the world. As for me, six years ago two other moms and I started a support group for parents of transgender and nonbinary youth that we call PTK Delaware. We are still going strong! More than 300 families have come to us for at least one meeting. One of the most rewarding things for me is to see parents come to their first meeting. Some are crying, and some are just so frightened they

> *If your child is coming out as trans or nonbinary, not only has your child probably been struggling with who they are for a long time, they've kept this knowledge inside for a long time. They need your support and love. Parents who have teenagers coming out to them are especially challenged because not only are their kiddos often dealing with gender dysphoria, but they are also in the throes of puberty. Even without gender issues, the teen years are a difficult time. It is especially important to support your LGBTQ+ kids during those volatile teen years.*

can't talk. However, it's clear that by taking that first step to come to a meeting, they are trying to make sure that they are providing their children with everything they need. Many parents who come to our group don't know what it means to be transgender or nonbinary. Many of the stories break your heart, and to witness these families go from confusion and fear to a healing acceptance of their children makes me feel like I am making a difference. To hear that their children who were depressed and suicidal are doing better is the best feeling in the world. PTK provides a safe and nonjudgmental space: we provide support and education to parents. For example, if a parent uses the wrong pronoun, we give them suggestions about how to handle that: i.e., just apologize and correct yourself. We suggest to parents that they can practice correct pronouns on their own. We tell them to put their child's new name and pronouns in their phones. Most importantly, we tell the parents to give themselves grace. It's so helpful when other parents reassure newly struggling parents that they've reacted in the same ways and tell them how they dealt with the situation.

The Gender Identity Nondiscrimination Bill was introduced in the Delaware legislature in the winter of 2013, and Sarah was able to arrange her schedule senior year in college in DC so that she could come to Wilmington to advocate for that bill. Dave and Sarah and I went down together every Thursday for a couple of months to advocate, and the bill passed! We wanted to do that with Sarah because we thought it was important for the legislators to see a loving and accepting family and to see an amazing young woman with resiliency, intelligence, courage, and competence.

Advocating for this bill was one of the hardest things I've ever had to do. To sit and listen to the opponents of the bill calling transgender people freaks and spouting lies claiming that if this bill passed, men would dress as women to go into female bathrooms to accost children, I almost lost it. It was so devastating. But the bill passed, and because of that, it was one of the best things I've ever done.

That is where our support group comes in because it's a nonjudgmental space—a space where we give information. For example, if a parent uses the wrong pronoun, we give them suggestions about how to handle that: i.e., just apologize and correct yourself. We suggest to parents that they can practice correct pronouns on their own.

There are so many things I love about Sarah. She loves being an aunt and playing with her five nieces and nephews. I so admire her strong desire to help others and improve their lives. She is so good at listening to all sides of an issue and then building consensus toward a final solution. She is truly making a difference in people's lives. Her courage and resiliency amaze me. Sarah has carried being a change agent one step further into her phenomenal career, and in thirty-one years she probably has had more experiences and lived life more fully than most people do in a lifetime. Sarah had big hopes and dreams from the time she was eleven years old, and she is realizing them. She doesn't just sit by and talk about things. She gets things done!

When Sarah came out to me and Sally it was a complete surprise, and I didn't even understand what the word transgender meant. When I told that to a reporter years later, she didn't believe me. That is how much things have changed in the years after Sarah came out.

David McBride
(*he/him*)

husband, father, lawyer

I did react with more fear when Sarah came out to us as transgender than I did when Sean came out as gay some years earlier. I thought then that the difference was that I knew and respected many gay men who were happy people and successful in the legal profession. But when Sarah came out, we didn't know any transgender people who could serve as role models to allay our fear. As a first step, we reached out to our former pastor—who then was serving a church in New York City with many gay members—to see if he knew of any transgender members in his church. He did have a transgender woman congregant whose parents lived near us. We met with them, and they told us their story and their daughter's story, and it was reassuring.

When I first spoke about Sarah's transition to a few of my friends, I was candid about my fears, questions, and confusions, but I also told them about the suicide statistics and the difference accepting parents make in the lives of their transgender children. I told our friends we wanted Sarah to live and have as good a life as she could have had if she were cisgender. Framed in those terms—and they are the reality—I think there are very few parents who, knowing those facts, would choose differently. Only transgender people feel gender dysphoria, so it is difficult for some cisgender people to understand the feeling or to believe it is something inherent. But if parents and other family members can learn to understand the real pain of gender dysphoria, they can begin to understand some of what their children are going through.

> **"** When I googled the word transgender, I learned a little about the meaning and a lot of frightening information about the discrimination that transgender youth suffer. One website reported how the incidence of suicide dropped dramatically if the family was accepting and even more if the community was accepting. That determined how I would respond and how I hoped our community would respond. We were not disappointed. **"**

Juliette, Sarah & Sydney. Photo by Sarah McBride

The hard part for parents who believe that God will not love their transgender child is that they feel like they must do everything they can do to try to "cure" their children. I think the crucial fork in the road to acceptance is whether you believe that being gay or transgender is a choice you make rather than a biological/psychological fact that you cannot change. My education on that point came years before my son Sean came out as gay. A gay friend, responding to my question to him of why he decided to be gay, asked me when I decided to be heterosexual. Of course, the moment he asked me that question I knew I had never decided to be heterosexual. It just was who I am as I began to experience sexual attraction to girls and women.

Several months after Sarah came out to us, she expressed a fear to me that I might never love her as much as I had loved her when she was my son. Of course, I denied that was the case, but the truth was that I wasn't sure how I would feel. Now I think of Sarah as having always been our daughter. My memories of her before she transitioned are fading, and the memories of her life since she transitioned are so vivid and significant that they have crowded out almost everything else. That is a big change from the first year, when I missed the child I had known as my son.

Until Sarah met her future husband Andy, I did continue to fear that she would never have the opportunity to love or be loved. When I was walking Sarah down the aisle of her rooftop wedding to Andy, I realized at that moment that I loved Sarah even more than ever. Now when I think about Sarah as a child, my memory makes her into the little girl she always knew she was. She has become Sarah in my past and present.

I suppose what I admire most about Sarah in all her roles is her courage, her honesty, her intelligence, her patience, her calmness, and the fact that she still likes to come and stay with us on the weekends. I love how she can laugh at herself and at us with equal warmth. I think the best thing Sarah has done is to give hope to other transgender individuals, their parents, and families, just as that Pennsylvania family and their daughter did for my wife and I long ago.

Sean McBride
(*he/him*)

dad, sibling,
oncology physician

When I came out as gay at age twenty-one, my parents were entirely understanding and supportive. In fact, I imagine it went about as well as it could have. As a gay man, my philosophy when it comes to gender identity and sexual orientation has always been that you embrace and love everyone for who they really are.

After Sarah came out to me, my relationship with her didn't change in any material way. We were always close and shared a deep love of history and politics. If anything, we became even closer, and because I'm a doctor, I spoke with her frequently about her gender-affirming care.

I've never experienced any bullying related to Sarah. If anything, Sarah's gender identity and career have received unadulterated praise from my friends and colleagues. They're always impressed when they hear I'm the brother of state Senator Sarah McBride. I've always been impressed by Sarah's inimitable intelligence, equanimity, and progressive pragmatism.

My husband of twelve years and I live in Brooklyn, and we have three wonderful kids: six-year-old twins—a boy and a girl—and a two-year-old son. They're our everything! Our kids know Sarah as Aunt Sasa. She's very

> **It is truly a gift when your sibling shares their truth and reveals their core self to you.**

involved in their lives, talks to my daughter all the time, and shares a deep bond with all three of my children. I'm sure in the future we'll explain to them that some folks are born with anatomy that matches their gender identity and some aren't, and for those who aren't, they sometimes must take some extra steps to be seen as who they actually are.

As a physician at Memorial Sloan Kettering in New York City, I work to ensure that my LGBTQ+ patients feel comfortable revealing their true selves to me and asking the sometimes unique questions that they may have related to their healthcare. This is my form of activism.

There are close-minded individuals in our society who constantly look to erode the fundamental rights of their fellow citizens. The wages of their sins of intolerance cost our country dearly. I hope that people of good will at all levels and branches of government recognize that scapegoating serves no one and see clear to love their neighbors as they would themselves. I hope that embracing that simple solution will lead to political practices that protect all LGBTQ+ people.

I'm the middle child of the three McBride siblings. When I was twenty-three years old, my older brother Sean came out as gay. I was in my first year of law school at the

Daniel McBride
(*he/him*)

father, brother, attorney

time and Sean was in medical school. It's been a long time, but I remember the phone call when he first told me he was gay. I immediately told him that I would love and support him no matter what. My mom and dad probably deserve credit for raising all of us siblings in a way that taught us to be accepting of all people.

There is an eight-year difference between my younger sister Sarah and me. When we were little, as was my duty as a big brother, I picked on Sarah. As we grew older and matured, particularly me, we became friends. Sarah and I had a good relationship before she came out. Although I expected the relationship to change after Sarah came out, it honestly didn't. I quickly learned that regardless of gender, the person I knew and loved remained the same.

I have a three-year-old and a two-month-old baby. The three-year-old is getting closer to the age where we will have the discussion with her. When it comes time to have that conversation, I have a great resource who will be able to help me formulate a plan—that resource being her Aunt Sasa.

The slogan "family first" isn't conditional. Friends come and go, but family will be there no matter what—as long as you are there for them. If someone turns their back on a family member because they are LGBTQ+, then they have no spine in that back. If you are so worried about what people may think or say that you let it affect your relationship with your LGBTQ+ sibling, then you should sit at the kids table at Thanksgiving and keep it down while us grown-ups talk. I'm not an activist, just a loving brother.

> **When Sarah came out as trans, I wanted her to know that I would have her back no matter what because we are family.**

I've always admired both of my siblings. Sarah and Sean are both incredibly smart and have always been extraordinary at whatever they do, ever since they were very young. What I admire most about both of them is that they are humble and have great senses of humor—which includes being able to laugh at themselves.

What I admire most about Sarah is her willingness to really listen to opposing points of view. She understands that there can't be change without some level of compromise. That is what I love about Sarah as a person, as a politician, as a sister, and as an aunt to my girls. She will do what she believes is right, regardless of the reaction.

Jozeppi Angelo Morelli and Chris Mohn

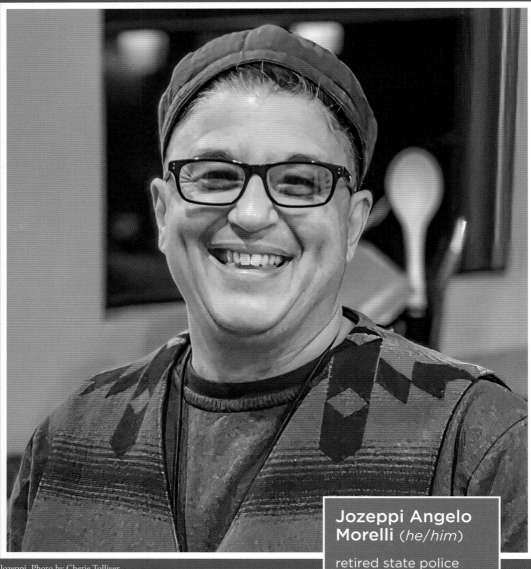

Jozeppi Angelo Morelli (*he/him*)

retired state police investigator, activist, public speaker

I'm a retired New York State police investigator and federal agent, and I was a first responder at the World Trade Center disaster on 9/11. I currently live in what I call rural white America, in Sedona, Arizona, which is on the sacred soil of the Yavaipai-Apache nation and the Hopi tribe.

I was raised as a girl with white privilege by white adoptive parents in a traditional Italian Catholic home in New Jersey. On May 25, 2021, I underwent gender-affirming surgery at the age of fifty-four. I had always felt awkward in my body as a kid, but I thought it might be because I was a transracial adoptee. I gravitated more to traditionally male sports rather than the sports that girls were allowed to play back then. I focused on being the best athlete I could be and spent very little time connecting with other classmates except in sports venues.

I knew in sixth grade that I liked girls, but I didn't have words for those feelings. Only boy/girl relationships were talked about in my school. It wasn't until college in the late 80s when a female friend handed me the book *That's Not What I Meant!* by Deborah Tannen that I began to understand myself. Most of all, I recognized how much I thought like a man. I still had no language or idea what transgender was, so I concluded that maybe I was a lesbian. I had hidden relationships with women and fake relationships with men to satisfy my family.

I lived as a lesbian for years, but I always felt more like a man than a woman. However, I didn't give my gender or sexuality much thought because I was so focused on my job. Now I know that I had built a wall of distractions to avoid facing the truth about my gender identity.

I studied criminal justice and psychology in college so I could follow in the footsteps of my law enforcement family. I was offered a job as a state police investigator in the early 90s and I took it. New York City, here I come! In the 1990s I was assigned to a federal task force at the World Trade Center. On the morning of September 11, 2001, I stopped near the Brooklyn Bridge to pick up bagels to bring to work and received a call telling me that a plane had hit the World Trade Center and that there were two others missing in flight.

I immediately ran to my uncle's office at the Kings County District Attorney's Office to get him out of Brooklyn. His office overlooked the Manhattan skyline, and we saw the second plane hit the second tower. Everything seemed surreal, as though time was happening in slow motion. After that, I was directed to help get a fire truck in Brooklyn to go directly to the World Trade Center. I stayed in Brooklyn, attempting to guide fleeing people and their vehicles to safety. The fire truck went over the bridge and never returned. All the firefighters on that truck died that day. I drove over the bridge, witnessing horrific sights as the twin towers collapsed. It is a day and time that still haunts me even twenty years later.

I was disconnected from myself after September 11th, and certainly felt that no one who hadn't been there could relate to me. Grief and despair were always present, not only for the lives lost, but also because I felt that no one would know the truth of what really happened. It is interesting to me how suppression of the truth has shaped this country in so many ways, especially for marginalized communities. My Catholic faith, my upbringing, and my job all taught me that silence is the best practice. It has been a challenging journey to unlearn some of that.

It wasn't until 2009 when I met an awesome Black trans woman at work that I even began to comprehend that I might be trans too. She talked to me about gender dysphoria—the distress felt due to the mismatch between someone's personal sense of their gender and the gender assigned to them at birth—and told me her personal story.

That definition does not begin to describe the soul-searching, gut-wrenching, turbulent, compartmentalizing process that many gender non-conforming people go through, including myself. For me and many others, it was a time of not knowing, then wondering, and finally accepting the reality that you were not born into the right body for who you know yourself to be. You think and fear you are going to be rejected, lose your job, your partner, your family, your God, your friends, and your life as you know it. You go to a place of heaviness and grief until you have the courage to confront it and risk losing it all.

I wasn't ready yet to take that leap, so I chose again to live in silence. I'd been wearing men's clothes for twelve years and engaged in relationships with women playing a traditional male role, but I diminished the importance of gender identity. I asked myself repeatedly, "What's in an identity?" Obviously there is a lot, because suppressing my authentic self was soul-crushing!

In late 2011, I finally started taking steps toward claiming my real identity as a trans man. I legally changed my name to Joey and started asking people to call me Joey. (It was only after my gender-affirming surgery that I legally changed my full name to Jozeppi Angelo). I also started reading up on testosterone. I discussed my feelings about transitioning to male with my doctor, but not with anyone else. At that point my health was deteriorating, most likely because of exposure to chemicals on 9/11. I had difficulty breathing, liver disorders, and bad migraines. I was afraid I might die, as had some of my 9/11 colleagues, before I had the chance to be me.

I was so nervous, but also excited, when I finally had the courage to take testosterone. Unfortunately, I had to stop taking it rather quickly due to my 9/11 health issues. I was devastated and decided to just go through the motions of living. My health continued to take all my energy. I had a few mini strokes and was diagnosed with polycythemia. Feeling unwell was the norm for me, and doctor appointments filled my calendar.

During this same period, I was beginning to question the relationship between the police and marginalized communities. I felt particularly uncomfortable in my professional role. I was dating mostly women of color. The Trayvon Martin case turned our squad room into an "us versus them" atmosphere. I stood without hesitation with my Black and brown colleagues. There was no doubt that white supremacy existed in my workplace and that some of my fellow police officers expressed these racist beliefs openly at work. This shook me to the core. The continuing deaths of my Black and brown siblings at the hands of my law enforcement siblings and my growing awareness of the murders of trans women, particularly Black trans women, left me feeling confused, emotionally detached, and overwhelmed.

During this time, I was encouraged by a friend to attend a Revolutionary Love conference at the Middle Collegiate Church in the East Village of Manhattan. I was told that this conference connected the concepts of love and justice in many different areas of life and that it would give me a deeper understanding of intersectionality among marginalized communities. Attending this conference changed my life! I listened intently to the many speakers who expressed their passion for equality and justice, and I was very intrigued by Middle Collegiate Church's multicultural diversity. I loved the energy I felt in this church, and the ministers were fully committed to justice work. I became an actively involved member of the church.

I now call the senior minister, Rev. Dr. Jacqui Lewis, my big sister. She is a strong Black woman who has a heart as big as this world, and she has compassion and wisdom to match. Rev. Jacqui encourages me to use my voice to speak out about gender issues and creates a safe space for me to share my story. It is she and other strong, unconditionally loving, and God-centered women who have helped me be the man and activist I am today.

One Sunday night I sat in a pew under one of the beautiful stained-glass windows, a place I often gravitated to. I looked up and written on the window was the date June 6, which happened to be my Nana's birthday. She had been my best friend and died at the age of ninety-two shortly after 9/11, which had added to my feelings of emptiness and sorrow. Sitting in the pew that night, I knew that this church had called to me and that I finally had found a place of peace inside myself. When Middle burned down in 2020, I sobbed. In that building, I had learned about and felt unconditional love and truly understood that this trans man has a seat at God's table.

I retired from law enforcement due to my deteriorating health and three years later, I made the decision to move to Sedona, Arizona, because Western medicine wasn't working for me. I knew that my Middle Collegiate Church family would always be with me even after I moved.

When I arrived in Sedona, my lymphatic system was shutting down and I had tumors in all parts of my body. I began working with my naturopath practitioner and went through a two-year, grueling, roller-coaster healing journey incorporating a plant-based Indigenous diet and detox methods with ayurvedic practices. Early on in this journey I recognized that my own healing required me to connect to my gender identity. My mantra became, "Honor the body I'm in, and love and be the man I've always been inside."

I spent my first year in Sedona focused entirely on my physical health, trying to stay alive and heal from my 9/11-related diseases. I didn't connect with many people during this period and when I began to, it was challenging. I was often misgendered, sometimes purposefully. I would repeatedly request that others use he/him pronouns to describe me, and I spent a lot of time and energy educating people about using correct pronouns even in my LGBTQIA2S+ community. I didn't realize how hard it would be for me or other trans people to be accepted and affirmed there.

It was my connections with my Indigenous identity and communities that sustained me during this time. For years, aware from adoption records that I was partly Indigenous, I had sporadically learned about history and

Grandmother Roanna & Jozeppi. Photo by Cherie Tolliver

connected with other Indigenous people. Living in Sedona, near them, I could immerse myself in that part of my identity. I learned, listened, and leaned into my Indigenous spirit, honored to be guided by several Indigenous elders. They all supported me through the growth of my Spirit Walk, toward acceptance and adoption into the Hopi family. Grandmother Roanna Jackson adopted me into her family, the Hopi Sand Clan, in 2021.

My Hopi siblings gave me the name Flower Rock, which is a three-tier boulder that guards the First Mesa of Hopi Land. Mysteriously, flowers bloom from this rock every spring. Valencia, my Hopi sister, says, "Only a bulldozer can move Flower Rock, just like Joey." Grandmother Roanna gave me the name Snake Warrior. Snake medicine is powerful, primal, healing, and transformational. My Hopi family sees, welcomes, and accepts who I am. We have never talked about my transition. We continue to share deep heart experiences and conversations.

As my health continued to improve, after a year in Sedona, I became involved with our local LGBTQIA2S+ organization. We held a transgender summit for the whole state of Arizona. I was the emcee at this sold-out event! During this summit I became vividly aware of the intersectionality of race, sexual orientation, and gender identity. I was also reminded of the lack of understanding and support for the BIPOC community, who experience most of the violence, housing and job discrimination, and homelessness.

Misgendering, microaggressions, and macroaggressions toward me and other gender nonconforming folks continued. For example, one gay white man often remarked that my voice wasn't deep enough. He would sit in his office at work and talk openly to others about me. Another gay white man repeatedly called me "she" whenever he was talking about me to other people. I continued to request that these men use my correct pronouns and respect my trans male identity, but they never did. The only person in Sedona I shared these experiences with was my therapist. The emotional damage was taking a toll on my body and my heart.

I never imagined experiencing harassment from white gay men in their sixties. However, I've since learned from personal experience and from other trans people that the cisgender lesbian, gay, and bisexual community does not always understand or affirm the trans, nonbinary, and gender nonconforming community, a division that needs to end. In the past few months, I've realized that Sedona is not a welcoming community. It has been the continued presence of my friends, Indigenous family, and faith community that has kept my spirits up.

We are currently experiencing anti-transgender legislation all around the country. The propaganda pushed by legislators, religious leaders, and parents is not based on facts and is blatant discrimination. My personal hope lies in our youth. I've witnessed some amazingly courageous trans and nonbinary youth activists and I've asked them to join me in using our voices together to undo damaging anti-trans legislation. Young folks are speaking up and taking their protests to the streets, to courtrooms, and to social media, where they are creating queer-positive peer groups and online communities. They are determined to disrupt the stifling environment that so many transgender and nonbinary youth are living in today.

When I started my healing journey, I blamed my bad health completely on the 9/11 toxins. That was only partly true. My healing process taught me that 9/11 was just a part of the iceberg within me. I had buried truths about the emotional, mental, and physical abuse I had experienced as a child from a sibling and the impact my parents' inaction had on me. Choosing to be silent, building walls, and suppressing all these truths for decades almost cost me my life. If I could say anything to my younger self, it would be, "Breathe. You will be safe and in control of your life when you get older."

I haven't said much about my immediate family or relationships because I've always kept my private life private due to my job and because of the lack of acceptance from my family. My relationship with my mother was always challenging and complicated. In recent years, despite my frequent requests, she refused to call me Joey. However, just before she passed, she gave me a great gift. I flew east to see her right before her death. When I sat down at her bedside, she was sleeping. I touched her and said "Annunziata, che fai," Italian for "Nancy, what are you doing?" I had always greeted my mother this way on the phone because then she knew it was me.

> " I believe it's our duty as adults to encourage young people and give them platforms to speak truth to power. Even though many young trans and nonbinary people are resilient thanks to the creation of positive peer groups and online communities, we adults need to take more responsibility to help create safe, affirming spaces to allow these youth to just be kids and thrive. We need to listen and learn from them. "

Surprisingly, she opened her eyes and said, "Hey, Joey." And then she closed her eyes. Those were the last words she spoke to me. I sat quietly by her side filled with emotion, holding her hand. Her caregiver was shocked. "Oh, my gosh. Your mother told me that she would never call you Joey." I felt deeply touched that my mom had finally recognized me as the man I am today. Her son, Joey.

My family today is my chosen family. I have Pastor Jacqui Lewis from Middle Collegiate Church and Chris Nelson Mohn, a special friend who I met before I transitioned. I have also coparented a few multicultural children in different stages of their lives. I recently had the honor to officiate at my chosen daughter's wedding. I also have my Hopi Indian family in

Arizona whom I honor by supporting them financially and helping their children strive for a better future and education.

I met Chris Mohn in 2013 on the Living Legacy Pilgrimage, a trip to famous civil rights sites. She and I sat at the same table the first night. Every day for the next weeks, we processed what we were witnessing and how it was impacting us. We also began to share our personal lives and continued to communicate after the trip. Chris and her partner visited me in Brooklyn, listened to my law enforcement stories, went with me to Washington, DC, for the National Peace Officer Memorial week, and visited me in Sedona twice to witness my life with my Indigenous community and to support my transition. I visited Chris in Massachusetts right after my mother's death in New Jersey. Chris is and will always be a part of my chosen family.

As for me, at long last I've become the man I always knew I was. I feel like a man. I am a man. All is finally well and whole with my soul. I live by the philosophy that everyone, including myself, wants to be seen, heard, loved, and affirmed. If I can do anything to facilitate that kind of life for any trans or nonbinary person of any age, I will. I hope those of you reading my words will join me in the challenge and joy of creating compassionate, safe places that honor diversity and equality, places where no human must live in the margins of society.

Chris Mohn
(*she/her*)

retired teacher, parent, Unitarian Universalist

I met Joey before his transition when we both went on the Living Legacy Pilgrimage. This tour was founded by the Unitarian Universalist minister Gordon Gibson, to meet the people, hear the stories, and visit the sites that changed the world in the Civil Rights movement. Not only were Joey and I re-energized in our commitment to racial justice, but we also became friends.

Since then, I have witnessed his journey to accept and become his true self, a queer man, and a passionate advocate for the trans community, locally and nationally. However, that is only part of his story. His professional life as a (now retired) law enforcement officer and his Two-Spirit

Chris & Jozeppi. Photo by Erik Mohn

Hopi family life, for example, are also significant, sometimes conflicting and challenging, parts of his identity. He is committed to bringing people with different understandings about these identities together to hear, see, accept one another, to bridge divides, and to work together for justice for all.

As a Unitarian Universalist, one of my Sources of wisdom and the one that is most important to me is "Words and deeds of prophetic people which challenge us to confront powers and structures of evil with justice, compassion, and the transforming power of love." Joey and many of my adolescent students in the LGBTQ+ community are such "prophetic people" for me because of the way they live their

> **" Joey is a remarkable human being! I am profoundly grateful to be part of his large and diverse chosen family. "**

lives. Their stories of survival, authenticity, courage, creativity, and persistence inspire me to be present for truth telling, companion the "othered," and dig deep for my own authenticity, courage, creativity, and persistence for myself and in the service of others.

Ava Berkofsky and Megan Auster-Rosen

Ava. Photo by Simran Malik

Ava Berkofsky
(*they/them, she/her*)

cinematographer

Most people thought I was a boy until I was around eleven years old. At that point, my parents started to have more of an investment in me being perceived as a girl, so they began forcing me to wear girl's clothing. I grew up in an image-obsessed family; my mom was a model and fashion person. My dad was a fashion photographer.

It was hard for me to explain to my parents, who were my authority figures, something that I couldn't quite articulate myself. I felt much more comfortable being misgendered as a boy. I really did. But I was also very anxious about other people finding out that I really was a girl. When you do get found out, it can feel embarrassing for everyone.

I fought wearing girl's clothing as best I could, but my mom told me that if I wanted my allowance or to have any freedom on the weekends, I had to wear a skirt three times a week. I quickly figured out that if I just put shorts and a T-shirt in my book bag that I could jump behind some bushes and change halfway to school, and then put the skirt back on before I got home at the end of the day.

I only recently started identifying as nonbinary. Literally the only thing that changed is that our culture at large has found language to describe something that has always been true for me. In the queer community, it has been understood for quite some time that there are lots of different gender identities along a wide spectrum, just as there is a sexual orientation spectrum. So, for me, it wasn't a big revelation when I changed my pronouns.

I think nonbinary is a more accurate descriptor than being called androgynous, or at least it takes on the question of gender a little bit more directly. In my opinion, gender is completely made up. It doesn't exist. Sure, there's a sex that you are born with that is defined only by your genitals. But gender itself is just an idea, and it's a very strong idea that many people are very committed to. However, it is just a concept. It is not real.

It's amazing to finally have a baby because I've wanted a family for so long. After Megan and I got married, I realized that I could finally have a child. I knew that we'd have to find a donor and that I didn't want to be the parent who carries the baby. I was open to adoption, and I was researching it more and more. Megan was open to adoption as well, but she decided to try and get pregnant first. And it worked!

We named our baby girl River. I think that once River becomes a more conscious being, we will have a conversation to discuss the concept of gender. We'll explain to her that we went with the default pronouns of she/her as we didn't want to deal with using they/them pronouns because it's annoying to constantly be correcting people. After all, River has me as a parent, so she'll learn quickly what nonbinary means as soon as she understands what male and female mean in our culture.

Before River was born, Megan and I had decided her name was going to be Lou Martine Berkofsky. Martine was for Megan's grandfather and Lou was short for Lupe, which in French means wolf. But when Megan was giving birth, it was a forty-two-hour long, very harrowing process. Every time Megan would push, the baby's heart would slow down and getting our baby out of her body was hellish. River had the cord wrapped around her neck twice during the birthing process. She had such force and strength that when she was finally born, I got a strong image of a flowing river. After we went home and contemplated it for a while, we decided to call her River.

I told all our friends: Don't give us girl clothes. Don't give us boy clothes. Just give us cool clothes. Despite our instructions, Megan's mom just can't stop giving her girly outfits. She's got a compulsion. It's interesting to me and Megan how even an incredibly progressive feminist can't stop gendering our baby with clothing that is so stereotypically female. Even though Megan's mom knows that we're not going to put River into a tutu, period, she bought her a tutu! I mean, someday River might get to the point in her life where she wants to be a ballerina, and then she will get a tutu and that's fine with us. We'll get her whatever she wants, but she gets to choose. She doesn't get "assigned" a tutu at six months old.

As a nonbinary person, it's inaccurate to refer to me as River's mom. I'm not a mom; Megan is River's mom. I use the word Baba. I am a parent and I like the sound of Baba as my title. In various languages it means "father," "holy man," and "grandmother." We need more words than mother and father to describe being a parent because being a parent doesn't only come in two genders.

I feel like I should correct people more often when they misgender me, particularly by calling me a mom. like when our pediatrician referred to me and Megan as River's two mommies, but there's only so much I can do. I wish we had celebratory terms for people who live outside of the gender binary. I want a word for being River's parent that affirms my identity. That's why I like Baba. It's a fun word, and it will come to River's lips easily. It's not Mom. It's not Dad. It's Baba. It feels like me. I figure when my kiddo gets older, my title may change and if so, we will have fun figuring it out together.

Being a director of photography for television and film is what I've always wanted to do since I learned what the job was. In the past few years, I was nominated for two Emmys for my cinematography work on the HBO series *Insecure*. I've also been nominated for an American Society of Cinematographers award, which is an even bigger deal to me. I love being on set. I love the physics of the camera and the light and the bodies and all of that. My job is amazing because it's constantly asking me to be creative technically and artistically.

> **" Nothing changed when I claimed the label of nonbinary to describe myself. There was no gradual or sudden discovery of my place on the gender spectrum. I'm the exact same person as I've always been. I've always been nonbinary; there is just a word now that describes who I am with more authenticity. "**

In my profession I work with 99 percent straight people and 90 percent men. It has been helpful, not only at work but in my whole life, to assert my authentic self. I work with big crews of men and I'm the boss. I choose to work with people who are just good, lovely people who treat me with respect, regardless of how they feel about my gender presentation. I interviewed a gaffer the other day who asked me my pronouns. Since most straight people don't have a concept outside of the binary of male and female, I was so pleasantly surprised that I said, "Who are you? Where did you come from?"

Traditionally in the cinematography world the guys are very manly men, and when I show up to lead the film crew, my presence is usually questioned. I often deal with distrust for a while and then eventually, everyone chills out. I've had issues with my crew members calling me "Ma'am." I can't stand that. I'm working with men over sixty and they're like, "Yes, ma'am." And I'm like, "Please don't call me that." I had to talk to this one guy who is nothing but respectful to me other than he can't stop using that word, "Ma'am." When I took him aside, I told him it felt disrespectful to me. I said, "I understand it comes naturally to you, and, to you, ma'am is a term of respect. But I've asked you so many times now not to use it that it feels like I can't work with you if you're going to continue to do this." Then he started crying and told me about his trans nephew. I said, "That's great, but I want you to stop using this word that feels like sandpaper against my skin." I was probably the first or maybe second non-male director of photography he'd ever worked for in his forty-year career. He felt terrible. But even after that conversation, he couldn't stop calling me Ma'am. He's hardwired.

Right now, I'm still working and traveling around the United States to shoot films or television series, but my happiest time is when I'm home with Megan and River. All our friends say that we're very lucky because she's an easy baby. She is so sweet, and she thinks everything is funny. River has a great personality—she's really engaged and makes a lot of eye contact. There's this book that I often read to her about barnyard animals, and when we get to this page where I make the sounds of the animals, River looks up at me like she's ready to hear the sounds and she smiles. She already knows that it's her favorite page in the book.

Megan Auster-Rosen (she/her)
clinical psychologist

I'm married to Ava, and I identify as queer. Everyone assumes that I'm straight because I don't present as a stereotypical queer woman. In fact, I never got bullied for my sexual orientation when I was growing up because I didn't look a certain way that would have been a tip-off to people. I work as a clinical psychologist both in a hospital setting and in private practice, but I also have a background in theater and writing.

> My goal is to support Ava through whatever process helps them feel most comfortable and embodied in their identity. And, as a parent, I want to make sure River will feel safe expressing who she is and that she will feel loved and cherished by me and Ava for her entire life.

I'm the biological mom of our six-month-old daughter, River. I wanted the experience of being pregnant but ultimately I found it very physically uncomfortable. It was very important to Ava that the donor be someone known and Jewish, so we found an old friend of mine who lives in Australia, and we flew him and his partner to come stay with us for several weeks. Damon is a Jewish bisexual artist, and his partner is a South Korean artist. They are the loveliest people you could ever meet.

Ava, River & Megan. Photo by Simran Malik

Our daughter has three names, River Martine Berkofsky, and they are all gender neutral. It took Ava and me a long time to figure out her name after she was born, but it was never going to be a gender-specific name. We had five days after taking her home from the birth to come up with the name for the hospital to put on the birth certificate.

As a psychologist I think a lot about how our identities shape us, and that when people are made to fit into an identity that doesn't feel right, it creates a huge amount of stress that can result in lifelong struggles. What is happening across our country right now is terrifying—for example, the "Don't Say Gay" bill in Florida, and all the different ways that people are being forced back into the closet. I hate to say it, but I strongly believe that suicide rates are going to increase significantly if people aren't allowed to express who they are.

Ben and Bedaura Haseen

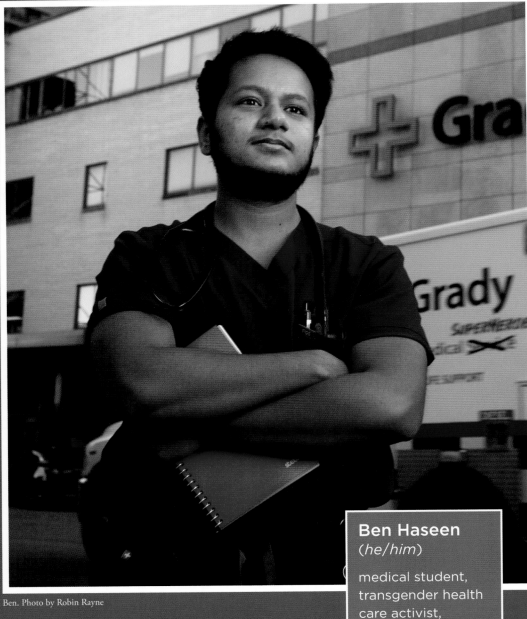

Ben. Photo by Robin Rayne

Ben Haseen
(*he/him*)

medical student,
transgender health
care activist,
researcher

I'm twenty-five years old, and I think I'm the
only Bangladeshi American Muslim transgen-
der medical student in the United States. I was born with my identical
twin sister, Bedaura, in the city of Dhaka in Bangladesh, and our younger
brother came along a few years later. My sister had a learning disability

growing up and because of limited resources in Bangladesh, she couldn't continue her schooling. My parents really wanted Bedaura to go to elementary school, so they decided to immigrate to America.

When we moved to the United States, we lived for four years in Queens, New York, in a neighborhood where there was a lot of gun violence. After someone was shot right below our apartment window, my mom had had enough. When I was around nine, my parents packed their bags and we moved to Georgia. My mom has never felt comfortable working in the United States because of the language barrier so she stays home. I think her English is great, honestly, but she feels very nervous talking to people in the outside world. My dad was a taxi driver in New York City, and in Georgia he drives for Uber. Our family has lived very simply in blue-collar neighborhoods throughout our entire lives.

Around the time we moved to Georgia, I started having crushes on girls. I was assigned female at birth, and I wasn't interested in boys like all my other friends were. When I was around ten years old, I learned what it meant to be a homosexual and to my dismay I started to think that maybe I was a lesbian. I had a great deal of internalized homophobia because my Muslim faith and the culture I was raised in told me that I shouldn't accept gay people.

While I was growing up, I always dreamt that I was a boy and never felt comfortable wearing girls' clothing. When I got my first menstrual cycle, it was psychologically traumatic. I know that most girls don't enjoy having a period at first, but for me, it felt like I was dying on the inside. I never put two and two together until, many years later in college, I figured out that I had been experiencing gender dysphoria for a long time.

In my last year of middle school, I realized I had to stop escaping from my feelings and acknowledge my attraction to girls. I started coming out as a lesbian to my closest friends and all of them took my news well. They all said that although it was surprising, they accepted me for who I am. When I came out to Bedaura, she said, "I love you for who you are, and that's it."

Unfortunately, Georgia in the early 2000s was not the most accepting place for queer youth, and as more people in school heard about my sexual orientation, I started getting bullied a lot, verbally and physically. I was still closeted with my parents, and my life at school continued to get worse to the point that I was suicidal.

I knew I couldn't talk to my family, and even my friends didn't really understand what I was going through. I was close to one counselor in high school, but I didn't know if she liked LGBTQ+ kids. I took a chance because I was so desperate and knocked on her door. I was crying and I told her everything that I was going through, and thankfully she was incredibly kind and accepting. She became my guardian angel! I'm incredibly grateful to her. Finding that one person saved my life.

At sixteen, I was volunteering at a local public library and one day a little girl around six suddenly came up to me and just stood there. Without warning, she smacked me on the middle of my chest and yelled, "Why do you have breasts?" It was kind of hilarious. This child was rude to me and hit me, but for some reason, I was oddly appreciative of her. I felt like it was the first time anyone had ever given me a gender-affirming gesture.

Around that time, my mom went through my phone one morning, and she found out that I was talking romantically to another girl and confronted me about it. I was in such a low place in my life that I just gave up and told her I thought I was a lesbian. My mom didn't take it well and basically told me I had to go back in the closet or else! She even mentioned conversion therapy, which really scared me because I had heard a lot of scary stories about that. I ended up going back in the closet, and I was miserable again for another two years.

Finally, when I turned eighteen and went away to college, so much freedom came into my life. I began to explore myself and relationships, and that's when I first started to build my queer community. I had my first long-term relationship with a woman, and as I got more and more comfortable in my skin as a lesbian, I began to realize that it wasn't just my sexual orientation that was different, but also my gender identity. I discussed my gender questions with my then-girlfriend, and she was super accepting. She told me, "If you are trans, I'm going to support you all the way." Even though our relationship as a couple ended, I'm incredibly grateful for her understanding and kindness during that pivotal time in my life. She pushed me to go see a therapist, get a gender dysphoria diagnosis, and start hormone replacement therapy.

When I started my medical transition, my mom started to notice my physical changes. Six months into my transition, I sat down to talk with her. She said, "When you were growing up, you were always such a miser-able kid. You never smiled in photos. You would cry almost every day. Now I see you are smiling. You are happy. You have so much to live for and you have so much passion in you." My mom realized that I was a much, much happier person being who I truly was. She said she was sorry for what she had put me through when I first came out as a lesbian. (And my mom almost never apologizes for anything!)

I thought my dad was going to be the harder one to crack because he's a very traditionally masculine man in a lot of ways. But when I came out to him as trans, he said, "Well, it's weird, but I will learn to adjust." My brother and sister have always been very supportive. They've really been my back-bone, and they helped me have the courage to come out to my parents. Of course, it was hard for my sister to rewire herself to think she has a twin brother instead of a twin sister. She had taken it much easier when I had first come out as lesbian. Bedaura and I looked exactly alike up until we were about thirteen, and then we started looking a little different. Of course, people assume we are fraternal twins now.

At this point, my whole family here in America has accepted me, which makes me feel so hopeful. And surprisingly, my family in Bangladesh accepted me even faster than my family here. As people get more and more exposure to what it really means to be a trans person, most people realize that we are not a threat.

While I was in college, I was also doing a lot of research trying to figure out what I wanted to do with my life. I got a job working in a research study at Grady Hospital, the largest trauma hospital here in Atlanta, inter-viewing men who had lived through traumatic pasts. One of the men I was interviewing told me about his early sexual trauma and then he said some-thing that changed my life. He told me, "You're the first man I've ever felt comfortable sharing so much of myself with. I really hope you become a physician." His statement was the catalyst that led me to pursue medicine as a career.

Around the same time, Bedaura was diagnosed with lupus and was in the hospital for about a month. She had some good doctors, but she also had some terrible doctors who were incredibly mean to my parents because they were immigrants and didn't speak perfect English. The experience of seeing these doctors talk down to my mom and dad made me feel like I had a responsibility to become a good physician who would make all people comfortable.

I chose to go to Morehouse School of Medicine here in Atlanta and during my first year of medical school, I began my medical transition. I'm in my third year now, so I'm almost three years into my transition and I live fully as a trans man. My entire medical school class has witnessed my transition up close, and since then, I've been doing a lot of advocacy work about being a trans man of color in the medical system, both as a provider and as a patient.

I've had so many trans immigrants message me on social media and say things like, "I've never felt validated by someone in the medical field until I found your social media profile and saw the work that you are doing." I've started a YouTube channel where I talk about being a trans man and discuss the importance of easy access to medical knowledge for all trans and nonbinary people. I've also been able to connect through Twitter to a bunch of trans medical students around the country who are doing the work of changing medical curricula. Right now, I'm working on a podcast about making trans health care knowledge accessible to all med students. We are collectively working together to make medicine more inclusive.

I've given talks about transgender health needs at Emory University School of Medicine, where I received the huge honor of leading grand rounds—something that's almost never done by a medical student. Usually, grand rounds are led by a physician who is an expert in one field, and they teach other physicians in other fields about their work. I was also invited to the South Asian American Policy and Research Institute to talk about the health disparities of being South Asian and transgender in the American medical system. I recently got asked to be a reviewer on a LGBTQ+ health article for *The Lancet*. It is one of the most recognizable scientific health journals in the world! I'm finally being recognized for my expertise in this field.

When I was growing up, I didn't have anyone to look up to and I definitely did not know any trans doctors, so it is my goal to continue to be visible regardless of what I'm going through at what time in my life so that other people can know that this is possible and something that they can strive for.

Most of my classmates have been super supportive. Many of them immediately started using my correct pronouns, but there have been a small handful of students who have said awful things behind my back. One student told another classmate that I'm just a girl pretending to be a boy. I confronted him and told him he can't say those kinds of things, especially as a future physician. He took it well and apologized. In fact, he felt incredibly guilty, and I think he took the criticism to heart.

I don't usually tell my patients that I'm trans, but I wear two pins on my white coat—one is the trans flag pin and the other has my he/him pronouns. If the patient is queer, they immediately open up to me. If a patient doesn't know what the pins mean and doesn't mention them, we just go on with the exam. I haven't yet felt the need to come out to any of my patients, but I imagine I'll do that at some point in my career. One queer woman came into a vaccination clinic looking incredibly nervous because she was afraid of shots, but her fearful expression turned into a smile and her eyes brightened up when she noticed my pins. It was great that this patient felt better knowing I was queer friendly.

> **"***I made a conscious effort to be very upfront about my gender transition from female to male in medical school because a lot of trans people in my community say that they haven't really been treated well by the medical system. I wanted to expose the next generation of doctors to what it means to be a trans person and to the fact that we are all deserving of respect and good care.***"**

For the last two years, I have been invited by the Health Careers Opportunity Program Academy at Morehouse School of Medicine for Black and brown disadvantaged future medical students to teach body diverse and gender inclusive applied anatomy! Teaching is one of my passions and I love the opportunity to show off being Professor Ben! And the best news, I just passed my last licensing exam for medical school! Dr. Ben Haseen coming soon in 2023!!!

On a personal level, after my first long-term relationship ended, I wanted to find community. I was the only trans person I knew, and I was also the only trans Muslim South Asian person I knew about. When I searched online for "transgender Muslim Americans," the name Feroza Syed showed up. I found out that she also lived in Atlanta and was an activist—what a small world! I immediately went to a talk that she was doing about bisexual health, and as soon as I showed up at the event, Feroza and I locked eyes. It was almost like a fairy tale. We were the only two South Asian people in the room, and I just looked at her and she looked at me and we smiled. After the event, Feroza introduced me to many other LGBTQ+ Muslims. That's how I reconnected with my religion and my ethnic community.

Working with Feroza to do community building with queer LGBTQ+ Muslims and South Asians has really reignited my passion for being an out and proud trans South Asian American Muslim! As I've started to come out within the more traditional Muslim community, people are getting to see me as the person I am, rather than seeing me as a sinner. I believe that they are slowly coming around.

Because of my online advocacy work, I get a lot of death threats and I've had terrible things said to me. I've even been called a child molester because I'm trans. And as a brown Muslim trans man, I worry about my safety, especially at airports. TSA always goes through my bags more carefully, and when I go through the scanning machine and the TSA folks don't see male body parts, they often start asking me a lot of questions.

There is so much violence directed at trans women of color, especially Black trans women. One of my neighbors, a transgender Latina woman who lived two miles away from me, was murdered recently right outside her apartment. I want to help in some way to make the world safer for BIPOC trans people.

My advice to younger trans and nonbinary kids is to find your people. Those people don't have to be physically present to be there for you. There are so many wonderful groups available now. There's one group called Desi Rainbow Parents that is an inclusive LGBTQ+ group for South Asian kids. There are even a lot of very good children's television shows that are trans inclusive, like She-Ra and the Princesses of Power. I've watched all the episodes, even though they were made for children! She-Ra has positive trans and nonbinary characters, which is amazing to see. When I was ten years old, where was She-Ra?

I will continue to fight for the rights of trans kids everywhere and I will always have their backs. When I was growing up, I didn't have anyone to look up to and I didn't know any trans doctors, so it's my goal to continue to be visible regardless of what I'm going through in my life. When people ask me what I want out of my life, I have a simple answer. I want to be remembered by my patients when I'm no longer here. I want them to say, "Ben was a kind doctor and he cared about me."

Ben & Bedaura. Photo by Robin Rayne

Bedaura Haseen
(*she/her*)

college registrar's assistant

My identical twin sister is now my twin brother, Ben. He is five minutes older than me. When Ben and I were little and throughout elementary school, we wore matching clothes all the time. We used to play together with Barbies but at the same time, Ben wanted short hair and to wear jeans, not dresses. My mom was good with him and let him cut his hair short and wear the clothes he preferred. Our classmates and teachers didn't have any trouble telling us apart because Ben was always the gifted student on the honor roll, and he dressed like a boy. Ben was kind of an ideal kid. I was in the shadows and most people only knew me because they knew Ben. I always had to compete with Ben, but now I'm so grateful because the competition helped me push myself to succeed in school.

Not many Muslim scholars speak about transgender people. I know in Bangladesh there are a lot of transgender people, and they are accepted. When Ben came out, everyone in our family here and in Bangladesh accepted him. My dad's family is from a small village where they don't even have electricity and they accepted Ben! What I do know and believe is that everyone should be happy about what God gave them. I truly accept that idea. Right now, it's hard for me to drive because of my slow reaction time from my health problems and I could be unhappy because all my friends are driving. Instead, I say, "This is what God gave me. Maybe there's a good reason for me not to be driving."

Ben is always busy with his medical school, and we don't talk much when we are apart, but when we get together, we have a great time. Sometimes we go hiking or dine out or go to museums together. I'm happy for the work Ben is doing right now, especially his advocacy work. I have faith that he is helping a lot of people already and I am positive that he will be a great doctor in the future.

> **If someone Muslim came out to me as trans, I would say, 'Thank you for coming out to me. If you think you are a terrible sinner, you aren't. You are just like me.'**

Ben has an immense amount of positive heart, often more heart than someone who is praying all day. For example, if you compare a Muslim woman who wears the hijab but doesn't fulfill the five pillars of Islam—which include charity and submission to God—to a woman who doesn't wear the hijab but does fulfill the five pillars, you can see that being a loving person is the most important thing in life.

In my final year of college, I came out to my best friends that my twin sister had transitioned and become my brother, a trans man. One friend who also follows Ben on social media said, "There's nothing wrong with that. I still love you and if you need anything, just call me." In fact, all my friends thought it was cool and they are all very supportive of Ben.

I don't miss having my twin sister because when Ben transitioned, I didn't lose my sibling. I didn't lose Ben! When we were both girls our parents were more protective of us when we went out just because we were both girls. Now I can go out more freely. When we were both girls, day trips were fine, but now I can plan an overnight trip because Ben will be with me.

The thing I admire most about Ben is that he seems like a tough person on the surface, but underneath it all he is really kind. If he gets mad at me, the next day he'll buy me a box of chocolates. He's got one of the softest hearts I know, but you really must know him to know that.

When Ben came out, my mom was nervous because there are hate crimes all over the United States, even in liberal states. Now that Ben is doing advocacy work, Mom will say, "Why is Ben trying to be so public like Bill Gates?" Other than that, my mom is less concerned with Ben being transgender, but she's concerned that he has distanced himself from the Muslim faith. I try to comfort her, as there is a verse in the Quran that says that whenever God wants someone to have faith, they will have faith. God probably wanted me to have faith, so I accepted Islam fully. Maybe it will take Ben more time. God doesn't just give faith to you—you must work for it.

When Ben first came out to our mom, I was right there. Ben called and told her, and Mom cried and asked him a lot of questions because she was curious. She said, "What is happening with my daughter?" Then Mom and Ben decided they were going to tell my dad on the weekend when Ben was coming home for dinner. My mom tried her hardest to keep the news in, but she just couldn't and she was crying when she called my dad to tell him about Ben. My dad was a very strict father, so I was nervous about how he would react. Instead of being upset, to my surprise, my dad was laughing and happy. He called Ben, and they had a good conversation. There has been no conflict between my dad and Ben about him being trans. My dad then called all his relatives in Bangladesh and started telling them, and they were all accepting.

Love and support are the most important things anybody can have; it's important for everyone to love their trans family members. In India there are a lot of trans people who are looked up to as they embody the two spirits of female and male joined together. As far as my relationship with Ben, God taught us how to love all people. It's not for me to judge anyone. The only person in the universe who can judge is our creator.

I love Ben as my brother just as he is. Being trans has never changed our love and never will. We will always be twins.

Ben McLaughlin and Krysten Ella Lobisch

Ben. Photo by Jill Meyers

Ben McLaughlin
(they/them)

mental health clinician

I was born in western Massachusetts thirty-one years ago and I've lived here my entire life. Like many, my queer and nonbinary journey began long before I had the language to describe my experience. As I look back, I feel like the signs were all there, buried under anxiety, expectations, and an environment that didn't inspire courage or vulnerability.

Growing up, I never really embodied traditional masculinity. I was always a sensitive kid—socially anxious and quick to cry, which were two things I hated about myself because they made me easy to bully. I was also short and scrawny, which gave people the impression that I was too weak to fight back.

My parents were very achievement-oriented and cared a great deal about what other people thought of them and their family. My mother had a hardline stance on non-normative aesthetics. Tattoos, piercings, and what she called "extreme" hairstyles or hair colors were viewed as an impassable barrier to success in society. In general, nothing in our house ever felt like a "small deal." My father had a temper and my mother tended to catastrophize, so benign things were quickly blown out-of-proportion.

Suffice to say, our household was not a place where it felt safe to struggle openly with any issue. I became terrified of under-performing or getting into trouble at school because I knew it would lead to a blowout with my parents. My sense of self-worth became tied to my achievements, my ability to please others, and my need to be perceived as "smart." It was a fragile defense mechanism that killed the joy of learning altogether and destroyed my motivation. Instead of developing good academic skills, I coasted on natural talent and creative cheating methods.

Today as a mental health clinician, I can look back and say I was experiencing executive dysfunction and can understand the ways that trauma and anxiety interfere with problem-solving. I'm also roughly the same age that my parents were back then, and I feel a much greater empathy toward them now that I can understand the pressures of holding a life together. I think a lot of their anxiety about their children succeeding was an extension of their own anxieties about themselves.

I consistently felt out of place around boys my age and struggled to engage with the culture of adolescent masculinity. It became a toxic, paradoxical relationship—I was often confused or disgusted by the way my peers would act or talk, yet I still felt intense pressure to appear "manly" and conform to peer pressure. Unsupervised peer spaces were the worst. For a long time, there was a kid on my school bus who would harass me and my younger brother daily. I would typically read quietly on bus rides; he would force his way into my seat and swat my books out of my hand. When that stopped getting a rise out of me, he started pushing up against me, moaning my name, and groping me. Every day, he started with his usual routine: leaning in and touching me inappropriately. One day, I snapped in a big way and ended up pushing him into the window of his bus seat. He never touched me after that.

Gym class and the locker rooms were similarly stressful. I was not necessarily bad at sports, but the traditional gym sports tended to favor competitive people with better physical abilities. And if there were ever an environment that fostered hypermasculinity in boys, it would be gym class. The gym teachers were outright negligent regarding what went on in the locker room. Guys would "pants" each other, snap towels, kick open the doors to bathroom stalls, and trash the belongings of people they didn't like. There was also a popular prank called "party-boying," where a group of people would crowd around a person shouting, pelvic thrusting, and waving their arms. I think people really underestimate the impact of those behaviors on those of us who are consistently the target.

I had two friend groups—my school friends and my weekend friends who lived in another city. At school, I was well established as an awkward, nerdy kid. My closest friends were generally girls because I felt more comfortable around them and didn't feel the same hierarchical social pressure that I felt with guys my age. Conversely, my weekend friends were almost all boys from out of town who knew me as an adventurous person. I was still awkward by all accounts, but I felt empowered as a part of our Gooniesesque social group. We would climb trees, jump fences, fight, stay out late, and create mischief. I'm thankful for those weekend friends, because those experiences were essential to building the meager confidence I had as a teen.

I still struggled with unnamable feelings about myself. The alpha male of my weekend group was athletic, good-looking, and popular. He espoused a hypermasculine and homophobic worldview, and his assertive personality made him difficult to question. If I tried to defend someone he was criticizing, he would jump to question their masculinity, sexuality, and intelligence. I would watch as the others in the group would nod their heads and agree with him. It was almost always easier for me to agree rather than defend my views.

I learned to perform whatever self was needed to avoid conflict. For instance, I'm drawn to characters in the media who are ostensibly male but embody non-normative traits like long hair, soft features, nonviolent and gentle dispositions, or flamboyant and/or "overly" emotional personalities. When emo culture first became a thing, I felt immediately drawn to it. Unfortunately, both my school friends and weekend friends were metalheads who scorned emo music, so I pushed myself toward more "acceptable" music choices.

By high school, I was depressed and having trouble focusing. Twice I had tried to talk to my mom about my mental health—once about feeling depressed, and once about whether I might have ADHD. My mother didn't want to hear it. She questioned what I "could possibly have to feel depressed about." She outright derided my thoughts about ADHD, as I had been earning straight A's on almost every report card. I left both conversations feeling invalidated and defeated.

I was dating my first girlfriend, and we had been having a tense conversation via text message because the relationship wasn't working out. At one point, she said that she liked me, but could only really be happy with a woman. This bugged me immensely. I was already struggling with feelings of inadequacy, and this triggered a cascade of negativity. I didn't feel connected to my masculinity, but simultaneously hated myself for feeling envious of others' femininity. The greatest barrier to my own self-acceptance was the daunting prospect of dismantling the old and inauthentic "me" that had been built in the minds of others. When I first learned words like bisexual and androgynous, they bounced around in my head for weeks as I concocted stories and characters that flirted with these ideas.

College ended up being a pivotal period in my awakening. For the first time in my life, I was living in a new area, around new people, giving me the freedom to decide who and how I would introduce myself to others. I was also in a much more diverse environment; hundreds of microcosms of culture that were refreshing and different. I made a conscious decision that I would be different too.

My first year in college I got involved with Live Action Role Play (LARP), a large-scale storytelling game that blends play combat and interactive theater. LARP is immersive and improvisational, and in its best moments it causes you to become someone else. It started as a hobby but became a space that challenged and empowered me. In real life I was undergoing incremental changes, slowly reshaping the old me into a new me. In LARP, I could switch the entire medium of my existence.

The first time I ever came out, it was to someone I barely knew. He was a student at a neighboring college, a friend of a friend. It was an unremarkable moment; he asked if I was bisexual, and I said that I was. I had been asked "Are you gay?" many times before but had answered truthfully that I wasn't, even though I knew that these people were really asking, "Are you some kind of 'not-straight' person?" So, when I was asked if I was bisexual, it was the first time I had felt seen as someone on a gradient. It was a small moment, but it felt like I had let out my breath after holding it for a long time.

> " Throughout my process, the people who love me have embraced my changes immediately and unconditionally. There is a Taoist concept— wu wei, or "effortless action"— that I see in parallel to my transness. I want a person to experience their gender effortlessly, without external pressures or motivations. I want trans people to discover themselves on their own terms, and for us to live in a world that allows the vulnerability that is necessary for growth. "

I began at last to develop both a sense of queer identity and a queer community. I watched people answer questions about themselves and found the words to ask myself some of the same things. Through self-acceptance, I began to experience love in more broad and nuanced ways. I formed relationships that fell into fuzzy categories between "family," "friend," and "lover." Some of those relationships continue to enrich my life, nearly a decade later.

I also met members of my queer community who were very rigid and doctrinaire. I remember being part of a discussion about "outness." One particularly outspoken member of that group was insistent that everyone needed to be out, drawing on Harvey Milk's philosophy of visibility as a means of activism. I understood the basic premise: if we, as queers, are not making ourselves seen, then the problems we face will never be recognized or addressed. To this person, all non-straight and non-cis people had a duty to be out.

I didn't agree with this way of thinking then, and I still don't agree now. If I had the awareness then that I have today, I might've fired back with Black feminist writer Audre Lorde's famous quote, "Caring for myself is self-preservation, and that is an act of political warfare," but at the time I felt insecure in my fledgling queerness. I tried to offer a rebuttal but was reminded, as someone who wasn't out, that I was still an outsider in these discussions. Unsurprisingly, I didn't hang out with those people after that conversation. My university campus was huge, and I had already found a core group of people who accepted me wherever I was in my journey.

My senior year, I took a class called Psychology of Gay, Lesbian and Bisexual Experience, which focused on the ways individuals and cultures experience non-heterosexuality. We covered a wide range of topics like identity development, stigma, and gender roles. I began to see my adolescence through new eyes, which changed the way I saw my current self. Although the class wasn't explicitly about trans topics, gender was discussed in parallel to relationships and attraction.

The class had a section on the ways gay, lesbian, and bisexual people are viewed in various cultures, which was a smattering of recent and ancient history, mythology, and politics. It was an enlightening class. One week we explored blended genders and third-gender identities. Initially, it was something I couldn't wrap my head around. My understanding of the world was still very concrete: gender was objective, gender was biological. But as we discussed it, we narrowed down on a question that didn't have a perfect answer: What is the difference between being "feminine" or "masculine" versus being a "man" or a "woman"? Is an identity an immutable category that simply "is," or something that needs to be enacted?

I remember feeling angry. I had believed, like many, that chromosomes and genitals tell you what you are, and that you should live up to that biological imperative. I rejected the idea that gender could be anything other than immutable, but I couldn't rectify my thinking with my own experiences. If my genes made me intractably a man, why would my preferences or mannerisms strip me of my masculinity? Conversely, if those mannerisms were what determined my manliness, then why should my physical features matter at all?

A quote by an unknown author says: "You do not have a soul. You are a soul. You have a body." I think these are important words for any person who's ever felt at odds with their body, whether they are trans, disabled, or dysmorphic. Our true inner self is not distinguished by our bodies or by how we are perceived by others. As one of my favorite authors, Antoine de Saint-Exupéry, once wrote, "It is only with the heart that one can see rightly. What is essential is invisible to the eye."

I was never very spiritual during my adolescence, and I was actively opposed to organized religion because I viewed it as another prescriptive, exclusionary system. I am still not religious, but queerness has allowed me to access something akin to spirituality. In a freshman-year astronomy class, I learned about binary star systems—stars that orbit one another, sometimes so closely that they can't be perceived as separate from a distance. I started thinking of my soul in a similar way, a reframing of my compartmentalized selves.

When the term Two-Spirit was brought up in my Psychology of the Gay, Lesbian, Bisexual Experience class, I felt an immediate resonance. As a white person, the term Two-Spirit will never be an identity that I can claim, but that moment of exposure to the term was the first time I saw the possibility of my gender as an interplay of multiple forces rather than something monolithic. Later that week I dreamed that my different souls were floating in a vast, pre-soul nebula. They formed and reformed like celestial bodies, orbiting each other before blinking out of existence. The souls of my gender(s) are a part of that internal constellation, alongside the souls that are genderless, or even nonhuman altogether.

I first started self-identifying as nonbinary five years ago, but I didn't use that language publicly until about a year later. I've always had a contentious, self-conscious relationship with my own gender identity, and have questioned whether my own self-perception is valid and whether my identity is a "real" identity versus an aversion to masculinity rooted in gender-based trauma. I do experience significant dysphoria around my body and facial hair, so I'll probably get electrolysis or laser removal if I can afford it. I don't intend to seek hormones or surgery at this time, but that may change as my self-perception changes.

My domestic partner, Krysten, was the first person I talked to about my nonbinary identity, and that moment came after months of reflection. Krysten was incredibly influential in my opening up. She's the type of person to bare her unapologetic soul to the world: stubborn, blunt, genuine, and loving. We often tease each other over our differences; she is loud where I am quiet, impulsive where I am hesitant, straightforward where I am roundabout. She can be pushy, which is frustrating, but her pushiness also can move a person toward honesty and exploration. What you see is what you get with her, and that inspires me to try to be the same.

Krysten, as a queer trauma survivor herself, is never the person to tell another who they are. She might ask questions about your past, your process, and your privilege, but she doesn't question you. I have trouble believing in the idea of unconditional love, but my relationship with her feels about as close to it as it gets. We have a nontraditional relationship. Most notably, Krysten and I are polyamorous; she and I were both seeing other people when we first started dating and went into our new relationship with transparent expectations. She and I, both as individuals and as a couple, maintain a variety of different relationships; all parties involved are aware of each other, and each unique relationship is honored for what it brings into our lives. It's incredibly liberating, in that no one person bears responsibility for being another's "everything." Polyamory makes you think about love in terms of abundance rather than scarcity.

For a trans or nonbinary person, our gender disclosure is the ultimate act of vulnerability. I held my own gender in secret for years before I transitioned my presentation and pronouns because the insecurities of my youth still permeated the way I navigated my adult life. I knew that I was nonbinary but could see how trauma had distorted my relationship with my gender and worried that it somehow lessened my truth. Just as I had been excluded from masculinity, I was worried that I would be excluded from "nonbinarity" as well.

If you look across culture and history, you can see a hundred different ways to understand masculinity and femininity. I've heard people argue that queerness and transness are a "fad" or a "phase." So, what if they are? Every human on the planet goes through phases; our new self grows like ivy over the cracked edifice of our old self. There are some people who will experience their gender consistently throughout their lives, and others who will see it evolve alongside every other aspect of themselves. Both are valid. Impermanence doesn't make a thing any less real.

To date, I haven't come out to my parents or other adult family members. Both of my brothers know my full truth and my cousins have some understanding, but otherwise I've kept my family on a need-to-know basis. I imagine some of them have suspicions, as I've been consistently vocal about my support for LGBTQ+ rights and have become much more gender nonconforming in my appearance over the years.

If they have suspicions, however, they apparently have not felt the need to ask, and I have no intention of starting the conversation. At this point in my life, I'm not even sure if I believe in the idea of coming out, because it feels like a social obligation on behalf of straight/cis society to name myself as "different." It's assimilationist; why should any person need to declare their identity for the sake of another? I have no intention of coming out, but I have decided that I won't conceal or compromise myself either. People can see me as a person, or a label, or an affront to God for all I care.

In 2018, my mother died of a heart condition that runs in my family. I was working on my master's degree at the time, and that sudden loss nearly derailed me. Time and distance had changed us both. The sharp edges in our parent-child relationship had rounded out as I became an adult, and that allowed us to relate to each other about the things we'd always had in common.

Mom died without ever learning the truth about me, and while I maintain how I feel about coming out, I still regret that I denied her the opportunity to get to know me. When we hide ourselves away, we protect ourselves from rejection and simultaneously deny the possibility of acceptance. She had always wanted a daughter, and I'll never know if a nonbinary offspring would have been enough. Mom's death was really the final tipping point for my gender expression. After her funeral, I started growing my hair long and switching up my wardrobe. I inherited Mom's jewelry box, and her pieces brought me gender euphoria and a sense of closeness with her.

Transitioning my outward presentation brought changes, of course. I've gotten a few quips about needing a haircut from some members of my biological family, but for the most part they seem to accept my appearance as another one of my quirks. My work environment and coworkers have all been accepting, even if not all of them get it. Some people have outright mistaken me for a woman, especially since face masks are ubiquitous in healthcare settings right now. Even though I use they/them pronouns, it puts a smile on my face when a stranger refers to me as "she" by mistake. One time, I had a stranger say, "You go, girl," before turning to me and then fumbling, "I mean . . . guy? Person?"

Even if we were to eliminate gender-based bigotry in society, an unlikely prospect at best, society must still recognize that the traumas and losses of that bigotry are carried by the survivors and their descendants. I would like to see society acknowledge those wounds and empower people to heal.

I don't believe that people grow up so much as they grow outward. Every experience we have reshapes the lens that we use to see both our past and future experiences. We add layers onto layers, like paint on a canvas. When I think about myself, I don't think in terms of boundaries and fractures. It feels more like a palette; I see each moment as its own composition and recognize that not all compositions require an entire spectrum of colors. I also recognize that every composition is a process of visions and revisions. As Antoine de Saint-Exupéry once said: "To live is to be slowly born."

I turned thirty-seven in 2021, and it's taken me this long to really feel like I'm a whole person. I grew up in a tiny rural town in northern New Jersey that was incredibly insular and intolerant of difference. Even when I was a young child, my parents were never supportive of the things that were most important to me, and they are only peripherally involved in my life now.

Krysten Ella Lobisch
(*she/her*)

educational advisor, teacher

I came out as bisexual at fourteen, as soon as I learned the word, as I've always been terrible at pretending to be someone I'm not. If to be my authentic self I had to be an outcast, I decided that I would make that sacrifice. And after I came out, I did feel extremely isolated. There were no other "out" teachers or students in my small high school, and no student or local community organizations for LGBTQ+ youth. I was immediately branded "weird" by almost everyone and avoided at all costs.

One of the first things I did after I came out was to cut my hair very short because that was the only template for being a queer woman that I knew about, and I thought somehow having short hair would make me recognizable

Ben & Krysten. Photo by Jill Meyers

to other queer people. I saw Ellen DeGeneres had short hair, and she was practically the only lesbian role model in the media. It's great that kids today have so many more visual representations of queerness in all its diversity.

Once I felt more comfortable in my queer identity, and I was surrounded by queers of many different kinds, I discovered there were ways to perform queer femininity. I love the creativity women can easily have with their looks; I love makeup, colors and patterns, earrings, cute shoes, and all the accouterments of being traditionally feminine. I find it empowering to present as femme. It bothers me when nontraditional expressions of womanhood—like having short hair, being straightforward and opinionated, or not wanting children—are framed as invalid.

It's not always possible for queer people to be out safely, but I feel that if we are, it's important that we use our platforms to speak out loudly and often about issues of concern for us. If people aren't aware of the injustices happening around them—on a personal, visceral level—they will never be compelled to make changes. There are individual minds that need to be opened.

We will never get 100-percent support from the public—or we never have in history—but we don't need 100 percent. We just need enough people to believe in and work toward "justice for all" to make powerful waves.

I am hopeful in working with young people that we're starting to see a cultural shift where queerness is becoming less marginalized. I find in youth activists a healthy level of suspicion for binaries, systems, fixed rules, and categories in general. They are very curious; if they can't find a good reason for a so-called norm, they want to know whether it should be changed. I hope that kind of determination and curiosity will lead them to ask tough questions of the people in charge and to demand change. It's imperative that we begin to build legislative bodies that are representative of the many identities of people they serve, including the working class, Black and brown folks, people with disabilities, and queer folks.

> **" Queer love is one of the most powerful forces I've ever witnessed because there are no templates—it gives so much opportunity to create your own adventure. "**

I feel so lucky to have my new job in a high school in Springfield, Massachusetts, working in the guidance department. One of my students called me a "mental health teacher" and I like that job description. I act as an advocate and mentor for the students to help them learn leadership and self-advocacy skills, make positive choices for the future, address academic concerns, and develop their social and emotional growth. I deal with heavy issues every day because upwards of 90 percent of the students in our district are trauma survivors, but it's incredibly rewarding to be the adult in their lives that I wish I'd had at their age.

When I teach my first class of each group of students in September, I make sure to come out as queer to every single one. I don't want any student, especially not marginalized students, to feel like there's no adult on their side or no one who will listen to their concerns. In my first month at this job, about twenty students came out to me. Some of them tell me I'm the only adult in their lives who uses their correct name and pronouns. I know all the statistics about how much more susceptible queer youth—and queer youth of color in particular—are to mental illness and suicide when they lack adult support in their lives. I don't want any of my students to feel the despair I felt as a teenager.

My parents say that they love Ben, but they don't really want to know the entire story of who we are. Ben is an amazing human because of their identities, not despite them. I got into a major argument with my parents during Christmas a few years ago when I was explaining the concept of gender-neutral pronouns to my nieces because Ben uses they/them pronouns. My parents wanted me to stop talking about it, but I refused. Sometimes cis straight people think every aspect of being queer is about sex. I couldn't get through to them that I was talking about grammar. We haven't seen one another face-to-face as a family since that argument.

I've known since childhood that I didn't want to have children. I told Ben that when we met, so it was never an option for us. But I've always found incredible emotional comfort in the presence of animals. For a long time, it was just me and my three rescue cats, Tao, Toast, and Chainsaw. All my cats adopted Ben as "Dad" almost immediately after Ben came into my life; Ben is amazing with animals and children. In May this year, we adopted a rescue dog, Rusty, a two-year-old Golden Retriever mix who is now in the final stages of becoming a certified therapy dog.

I'm tremendously proud of Ben for the growth I've seen in them in the past seven years. It's been beautiful to watch Ben feel more at home with themselves and their queer and nonbinary identities over the course of our relationship. When I first began dating Ben, they identified as bisexual but not yet as nonbinary. Back then they dressed like an average college guy, in mostly dark colors, and I used to tease them about that. Now they have a lovely, colorful wardrobe! They wear jewelry and hair accessories and cute shoes and makeup, and they seem so much more comfortable in their own skin. Sometimes we even trade shoes and clothes since we're almost the same size.

When we met, I didn't know that Ben's gender identity would become more feminine, but I've tried to support Ben's transition as much as possible. When Ben began using they/them pronouns three years ago, it took me a little while to get them right all the time. If Ben decides they want hormone therapy or surgery in the future, I'm sure we'll figure that out too. I encourage any change that helps Ben to feel more like their true self and I'm so glad to be along for the journey.

Fresh Lev White and Haia Sophia

Fresh Lev. Photo by Haia Sophia

Fresh Lev White
(*he/him, they/
them, love*)

Buddhist meditation
and mindfulness
teacher, love and
compassion activist

I'm a fifty-nine-year-old Black trans man who engages in both Buddhism and Judaism as my main spiritual practice. I live on the unceded territory of the Huchiun land currently of the Lisjan Ohlone People, aka San Francisco's East Bay. From a young age, I remember feeling genderfluid. "Masculine female" was the term I began using to describe myself in my late teens. When I look back on my life, I didn't experience being born in the wrong body. I have never experienced anything being wrong except for the way we humans have been conditioned to put everything and everyone into boxes.

When I was a kid, my mom worked hard to make me more feminine. After exercising to Jack Lalanne in the summer mornings, she would teach me these etiquette moves like how to walk with a book on your head while not swaying your arms. She taught me to hold a glass with my pinky out and to always cross my legs when sitting. Because she made it into a game, it was fun for me, but nothing really stuck.

When I came of age to take a ballet class, I fought and resisted until she allowed me to shift to tap class, where the boys were. I remember really wanting to be a Boy Scout Cadet, but I was put into the Brownies. I managed to get kicked out by stealing all the pretzels and then hiding with them in the schoolyard during the Brownie meetings. Whew!

I grew up in New York City, where everything moves fast, and I grew up early. One thing that was always consistent was the masculine energy that lived inside me. One day I was playing doctor with a boy and discovered that we had different body parts. It didn't really faze me that much, as I still felt like a boy/girl. Unfortunately, I continued to have fights with my mom about not wanting to wear dresses. My mom was also really into outfits, and she would dress me in cute Dutch, Asian, or Latin style dresses. (It took decades for me to realize that African designs in formal settings were and are threatening in our society.) I hated how I felt in dresses and girl's shoes! In addition to having to be more feminine, being African American in my family meant you were always dressing up to prove your worthiness. I was only allowed to wear dress pants, skirts, and pressed blouses to school. I was never allowed to wear jeans and t-shirts like my friends, which was crushing and messed with my own self-esteem—I wasn't allowed to be authentic.

From a very young age I was attracted to females. You know how with little boys and girls, adults might say, "Oh, look how cute they are together." When I was five or six, the adults used to say that about the boy across the street and me. He was a cute boy, but I remember how the girl down the street made my face turn red and my heart race every time I saw her!

I was a very fortunate foster youth. My foster mom became ill when I was around seven years old. At the age of ten I was asked if I wanted to be adopted by her and her husband, my foster dad. It was a no-brainer for me. Along with another foster youth, I was gratefully adopted. Sadly, my foster mom died four months later. Before she passed, we left our house and moved into an apartment in a sweet location with new schools and lots of grassy areas. No mom, new home, and new school. It was a lot for a young person to take in, especially a transmasculine youth.

At age eleven, I had already kissed a girl. I remember having crushes on Diahann Carroll, Rita Moreno, and Barbra Streisand. I didn't understand my young crushes, but I sure felt them. I remember watching Flip Wilson in drag at a really young age and loving Flip as Geraldine! I was attracted to femininity, but I had no desire to be feminine.

By the age of eleven, my period came one day while I was jumping rope. I had some resistance to menstruation because I felt like my body was betraying my vision of myself. Growing breasts and having to wear a bra was a similar experience. I didn't not want to be me; I was just more than a girl, and these two aspects of puberty put me in boxes I didn't really fit in. When I was around fourteen years old, peer pressure really came in and friends really wanted me to wear makeup. I didn't want to, but I let them do my face. That lasted for about a week before I decided to make new friends.

What I remember about my attractions to girls was that this kind of attraction wasn't modeled anywhere, so I didn't think it was acceptable. By the time I was around fourteen, I had also dated a few boys because that was "normal" for a girl, but my dream was that if I had to get married, I'd have daily luncheons where I could spend time making love to the other wives.

When my adoptive mom passed, two things impacted my life. One is that I never saw my dad cry and I wasn't encouraged to cry either. "Hush, hush!" was often the response to my tears from the adults in my life. It just wasn't part of what we did in our family. The other thing is that Dad got lost in a bottle. Pretty much every adult I knew as a kid drank, and now my own father was choosing drinking over parenting. By fourteen, I was going to bars using a friend's sibling's ID myself.

My exposure to the queer scene, unfortunately, came through going to bars and parties where alcohol and drugs were easily available. By the age of sixteen I dropped out of school, partly because of the depression after my mom died and partly because nobody was available to help me with my ADD or my dad's alcoholism. A Twelve Step support group like Alateen would have been so helpful to me then, but it was never suggested. I grew weary of cutting classes, reading the required books, and acing the tests. I loved learning, but at this point school felt like an inconvenience for someone who needed to be moving all the time. I left school for good in ninth grade.

In June of my fifteenth year, I walked to the subway in the north Bronx to take the A train to the New York City Gay Pride celebration. I felt real young then, and I was! It was probably an hour and a half-long journey but there were so many friendly, exuberant queers on the train that I felt safe.

At this point in my life, I still believed that being gay was an abomination as my mom was a Christian who often offered homophobic Bible quotes when I was growing up. Once I came out as queer, I felt I had given up any connection to G-d or any spiritual presence. Once I got to the parade, I remember thinking that if I ever stepped into a church, I would probably melt like the Wicked Witch in *The Wizard of Oz*. But as we got close to marching past St. Patrick's Cathedral on Fifth Avenue, I was amazed! I saw a hundred or more priests and clergy on the front steps of this huge cathedral waving and cheering us on. My heart cracked open. It was one of the most beautiful experiences in my life! In that moment, I understood that Love was my creator. Since then, I haven't used the word *God*. Instead, I've used terms like *Love, Spirit, Universe,* or *Creator* whenever I've offered gratitude or prayer.

Although I was part of the LGBTQ+ community, the word *lesbian* never worked for me. When I came running out of the closet at age fifteen, I identified as a baby-butch and continued to describe myself that way into my early thirties (well past my baby years, LOL). By sixteen, I gradually transitioned into only wearing men's clothing. At that young age, I went to a gay club and—long story short—I got a job as a bouncer. I told my dad about it, and he allowed me to borrow his suits and taught me how to tie a tie three different ways. We never talked about my sexuality. We never talked about my gender. We never talked much at all, and yet he was supportive to me—finally—in this realm. Unfortunately, he passed the day before my twenty-first birthday from alcoholism.

I was often perceived as male—my size, energy, and gender presentation earned it. One evening I got off at a subway stop on my way to my job at the club, and as I was walking, I passed the "ladies of the evening." All of them taunted me sweetly and I smiled shyly but proudly and kept walking. One night they discovered that I was butch because I had my jacket off and they saw my breasts under my shirt. Once they recognized me as a butch dyke and not as a young man, they would come to the club when it closed at 6 a.m., take me out to breakfast, and walk me back to the subway station because it was in a dangerous area. A couple of weeks later, I learned that some of them were trans women. I've been very fortunate to be escorted through my life by angels, and they were some of them.

When I first heard the word *queer*, in the 1970s, I was so excited! As bell hooks said, "Queer is not about who you are having sex with—that can be a dimension of it—but queer is being about the self that is at odds with everything around it and has to invent and create and find a place to speak and to thrive and to live." Back then I identified my gender as butch, my sexual orientation as gay, and my whole self as queer.

I became the first popularly known drag king in D.C. back in 1987 when I was performing and raising money for the National Gay & Lesbian Task Force, which at the time was supporting people living with HIV. I remember performing before the late and great Urvashi Vaid and her life partner Kate Clinton—such an honor. After saving money working at Lambda Rising and then Food for Thought, both in Dupont Circle, I soon found myself on the way to California. A few years in, at the age of thirty-two, one day in my San Francisco apartment, I was wearing a black t-shirt, my favorite black Levi's, and my brown work boots. I remember looking in the mirror and thinking, "Oh, my God, I found me! This is my look!!" Then a voice in my head said, "But you're not a man." I realized how rarely I looked in the mirror and how much I experienced myself as male.

I never fully rejected my female body; in fact, I loved my body. My problem was always with how the world perceived me, not with how I saw myself. After this revelation, I began diving deeper into feminism, through reading and listening to others' ideas. I was a bouncer at women's clubs, and I joined the San Francisco Dyke March Committee, which I pushed to support all women's causes, while centering on queer women and lesbian rights.

Around age thirty-eight, a straight cisgender female friend, after we had kissed on a previous night, said, "Can I ask you something?" I could tell she had something serious to say, and I said, "You can ask me anything." She then said, "Are you trans?" I kind of lost it. I was like, "No, I'm not trans!" My rejection of that identity was very strong. Because the majority of the trans people I knew were trans women who were struggling to survive—like the women who picked me up from the club when I was a teenager— I didn't believe that I had earned the title of trans. I didn't have a connection to nonbinary and transmasculine communities at that time either. I was out of touch. I surely had some research and reconnecting to do!

> "I don't feel that I was born in the wrong body, but my authentic identity wasn't being seen in our society. When I talk to teens about the diagnosis of gender dysphoria, I remind them that there are way more than two genders. The dysphoria is with our society! Yes, we are required to use the gender dysphoria diagnosis to get hormones prescribed, but we do not have a disorder. We are living into the fullness of this human experience, and we are fine just as we are!"

Even though I already knew that I wanted to have top surgery, I still didn't see myself as a trans man until I realized that I'd always been transgressing gender. I began questioning myself almost every day for the next ten years. My first question was: Do I feel I'm not butch enough? And my second question to myself was: Am I a misogynist if I transition from female to male?

I had heard rumors that if you were living as a woman and you transitioned to male, you would become a violent misogynist. Patriarchy is insidious, even for female-identified folks. Of course, these ideas of who a trans man was also came from the anti-trans lesbian, gay, and bisexual community, and they had some influence over my thinking at the time. Ultimately, I discovered that these rumors were lies; that a man's personality is not born but created. Fortunately, I had beautiful and gentle cisgender male and kind trans men friends who modeled what was possible for me.

At the relatively youthful age of forty-eight, I started taking testosterone. My spirit was ready. My body was ready. I inhaled all my learnings from being female and took them with me! The hardest part of my transition was that once I started taking T, mentally and emotionally I was fully there as a male, but the rest of the world wasn't seeing me that way. I would go to a supermarket and the cashier would say, "Thank you, Miss." That freaked me out before I transitioned, and then after taking T, it was a hard blow to my self-esteem. I stopped shopping in places that used formal greetings.

When I was still being misgendered often, it felt embarrassing and was the most challenging period in my transition process. Then, because of my genetic makeup, it took me three years to grow a beard. On the rare occasion when I'm misgendered now—and it happens even with my beard—I don't need any apologies for being called "Miss." I respond by saying, "No problem. There's nothing wrong with being female and I'm just putting out some feminine energy today."

When I transitioned, my name was Fresh, and I would tell people that my pronouns were "he or anything kind." I've always felt gender-expansive even when I was pushed into a box called "man" by the queer and trans community. When I'm called "he," I feel like my masculinity is being seen and I celebrate it. Currently, I enjoy my comfort with my masculinity, which I experience as both masculine and gender-expansive, as it's always been. I'm exploring more of who I can be in a new relationship with a cisgender woman who enjoys the soft and harder sides of me.

I'm so lucky to have this healthy body that has protected me and others from harm. I cherish and honor the privilege of having been labeled female at birth. I don't regret it at all. It was a gift, and something more expansive would have been ideal! You can learn to love all of who you are, including the person who managed to stay alive and got you to who you are now, no matter their gender.

My gender and spirituality have grown together. I've appreciated all that I've gained from my understanding of Christianity, Judaism, Taoism, Buddhism, Shamanism, Wicca, and paganism. In the 1980s I discovered a book by the late Vietnamese Buddhist Master Thich Nhat Hanh, and through his teachings I learned to be present in each moment. This continues to be my work—being present with everything just as it is from a loving and compassionate perspective.

I started practicing Buddhist meditation and was soon invited to teach teens and adults, which helped me to expand my understanding of Buddhism and the responsibilities of being a spiritual leader. In 2013, I began the Bay Area's first Trans and Genderqueer Meditation group in my living room. Our focus there was as much on connection and sharing experiences as it was on practice. Two years later we moved to the East Bay Meditation Center in Oakland, California, a place where BIPOC, justice, accessibility, and community are centered around Buddhist teachings and wise activism. I created the first Transgender and Ally Day Retreat at Spirit Rock, a well-known and beautiful Buddhist retreat center in Marin County.

One person on a retreat I was leading was sitting on their meditation cushion and sobbing. I asked what was happening and they said, "This world is trying to erase us." In time, in my response to their pain, I spoke to the entire group about where LGBTQIA+ people are now and where we were twenty years ago and forty years ago. Even in these very hard times for trans people, it's important to recognize everything that we have achieved. I shared that it's because of our achievements and visibility that we are receiving pushback, and that we have much better tools than our transcestors had to stand up and push back. They will not erase us!

Of course, LGBTQ+ people still experience hate crimes and terrible violence, especially in the BIPOC community, but we're moving in a positive direction rather quickly, considering the long history of homophobia and transphobia in America. And no, it doesn't always feel or look like progress is being made, nor does it mean that we're satisfied with our progress. Far from it! However, there are now inspiring trans and nonbinary actors in film and on television like Laverne Cox, Scott Turner Schofield, Dominique Jackson, Elliot Page, and the first openly trans Emmy award winner, Michaela Jaé Rodriguez. And we have trans folks in higher levels of government such as Undersecretary of State Admiral Rachel Levine and Delaware State Senator Sarah McBride. Visibility matters! Many trans people around the country are fighting major court battles against their schools and workplaces. The transphobic oppressors are fighting harder because we are making bigger and broader gains. Don't give up! Find an organization you can support, just like so many of our trans ancestors did before us.

My Buddhist practice, my current connection to my loving Jewish community, and Al-Anon support me with healing my childhood traumas. As a member of the East Bay Meditation Center and Kehilla Synagogue, I have the honor of being with a community of mostly BIPOC folks at each space. And when I walked into the arms of Kehilla Synagogue, I had no idea the head rabbi was trans or that I'd be joining a Black trans Torah group led by a Black rabbi. I'm just walking my path.

I have learned to create family most of my life, as my foster family and I separated. I love them; we are just not the same people. The woman who long ago asked me if I was trans has become part of my family. There are also people I call cousins who took care of me after my top surgery, and exes who remain dear who also saw me through my journey in some way. And I have a buddy, Ace Morgan, who has called me "brother from another mother" for years. He's a trans brother who supported me through so many of my changes and encouraged my healing. In 2021 I found my closest earth/blood relatives. My biological cousins are just fabulous! I also learned that my biological sister, who I never met and had passed in just 2017, was also queer.

Looking back in my own life, I've been offering LGBTQIA+ ally trainings for twenty years and I've worked directly with trans folks as a counselor and coach for the past fifteen years. The teachings of the Buddha offer a path that helps us to choose to live more wisely, and for me that includes generosity of time and energy. Judaism offers connection, food, prayers, and music that brings such joy.

I've also talked to a lot of teens and young adults who are struggling with their gender identity. The most essential thing I try to get across is that they are worthy of love. I tell them that whoever/whatever created us knew exactly what they were doing. I want them, or you, to connect deeply with themselves and feel who they are. They are enough. *You are love, dear ones!* Each inhalation of breath says you are meant to be here. Love yourself. You are worthy.

I walk in the world perceived as a Black male. The more I practice loving myself and having empathy for all that I've gone through, the more I heal, and the more I attract more loving and beautiful people around me. And speaking of love, I'm also dating someone special, Haia Sophia. She sees me, honors me, and loves me. We each feel seen and loved and I couldn't be with her if I hadn't done my healing, self-love, and anti-patriarchy work. It is lifetime work, yes, and so worth it!

Fresh Lev & Haia. Photo by Cody Young

Haia Sophia
(she/her)

nurturer, small business owner, dreamer

I'm a white-presenting cisgender Latina who was born in Hollywood, California, in the glorious 1970s. I was raised in the Catholic church by a Latina mom, so one can imagine what that means in terms of my experience of my body and my sexuality. I've identified as bisexual since my late teen years, but I'm considering identifying as pansexual. I have spent most of my adult life in love relationships with cisgender heterosexual men. When I met Lev, I was looking to reconnect with a queer community and my own queer identity.

I've always been attracted to masculinity in my partners, but I hadn't had the opportunity of dating a trans man. About a month before meeting Lev, I had a brief conversation with a friend of mine about the possibility of having a romantic relationship with a trans man and heard myself saying that I was worried that I would offend a trans man by misgendering their body parts. My friend suggested that I simply ask what they call their parts. I immediately thought: "Why haven't I always done that?"

When I first met Lev, it was pretty much love at first sight. I'm not sure how I felt so comfortable in all this newness, but I do know that it had and has everything to do with who Lev is as a human. His open, loving heart is the space that I knew I could rejoice in. Since I met Lev in a queer space—mostly filled with dyke-identified women—I guess I assumed from the outset that he was trans. I don't remember thinking about it either way. I'm so thankful for the bold space of that night.

We are new! We've just been in our relationship for five months, and it's getting real. We met at my friend's Thanksgiving dinner party, which Lev calls a "Dykesgiving." In our relationship, Lev and I are often very playful with each other. He is my lover and my buddy. We both delight in the natural world, good food, and music. Also, we both are committed to spiritual practice. I've been attending some Jewish services with Lev as well as attending my Quaker meetings.

> **"I hope that everyone who needs to talk finds someone as wonderful as Lev to be in conversation with."**

I became a mom fifteen years ago and my daughter Delilah is everything to me. To my delight, she has really opened and warmed to Lev's company. She recently took the opportunity to get to know him better by using Lev's story as a basis for a school project. My family of origin doesn't live in the Bay Area and therefore hasn't met Lev yet, but I've told them about him and shared photos.

My best friend has met and loves Lev almost as much as I do. She keeps asking to spend more time with us. Also, the mutual friends that initially introduced us are part of our circle and I'm so happy to be together with Lev in community. In my last relationship with my ex-husband, we had very separate social lives and this is the opposite experience—I love it!

Dee Dee Ngozi Chamblee

Dee Dee. Photo by Robin Rayne

(*she/her*)

executive director,
activist/advocate,
consultant

I was assigned the male gender at birth in the rural South in Conyers, Georgia. I am a trans woman who has a heterosexual orientation. I am Black and Baptist. Oprah Winfrey is my television mom, as she taught me how to be the strong Black woman I am today.

I always felt like I was a girl, and I was attracted to boys at the early age of five. At age six, I had my first kiss with Phillip, a boy in first grade. He pushed me gently up against the wall and nailed a quick, juicy kiss on my lips. I was in heaven. I floated back to my seat in class and was in dreamland the rest of the day. During that weekend Phillip and his twin brother were swimming in a local lake and both got caught up in a riptide and drowned. I was devastated that my first love was dead. I went to the funeral home, but I couldn't bear to stay but a minute. I didn't dare share with anyone that Phillip and I had kissed.

My dad didn't understand me, nor did my ten uncles who all drove race cars and drag raced. On most any day our front yard would be filled with these greasy men working on cars. I had an Easter basket that I used to carry around as my purse and the uncles would be looking at me funny and asking my dad what the matter with me was. My dad would laugh and tell them to pay attention to what they were doing and leave me alone.

My mother was a different story. One day while my mother was at work, I found a green corduroy dress and put it on. I was in heaven! I danced and floated out to meet my mother as soon as she pulled up in the driveway. I was so excited to show her my dress, but I was stopped dead in my tracks when I saw the look on her face. It looked like smoke was coming out of her ears and thunderbolts out of her eyes! From that moment on, I shut down anything about expressing my female identity.

My aunt had ten sons who would come to visit a couple times a year. I overheard her ask my mother about me. She said, "Why is he so peculiar?" I didn't know what peculiar meant so I asked my mother. She said, "Shut your mouth and don't ask me any more questions."

There were two trans men who lived across the street from my grandmother, but she couldn't stand looking at them carrying on and dancing in the neighborhood. Hearing what my grandmother said about her trans neighbors made it clear that I needed to shut down even more. I learned not to move around too much in front of other folks because I had a very feminine body and way of moving.

I was bullied for being gay when I was in high school, but soon I started to fight back and began to receive a reputation. I started to become more open about my sexual orientation in the way I dressed, and I began to have emotional crushes on white boys. Every year I'd pick a different boy to have a secret crush on. In my later years in high school, I joined the drama club where I found a friend named Todd. We became close and both of us worked in the school library. One day Todd told me there was a club where people like us dressed in women's clothing. I was so intrigued that I skipped school and went to that club. I was in heaven again!

At the time, my home was becoming unbearable as my mother was very abusive emotionally, verbally, and physically. I decided to run away from home and started living on the streets. Being homeless led to survival sex work, prisons, depression, alcohol, and drugs. My epiphany happened when I found out God loves me just as I am and does not hate me. I read about the Eunuchs in Isaiah 56.3: "I will give them an everlasting name that shall not be cut off."

I met NY DJ Ron thirty-two years ago at a club called Marquette. This club was known all over as "The Club." In that era, people like me were called drag queens, and on any night, people would come to see all the fabulous costumes we wore. We would parade all up and down Martin Luther King Boulevard. When I first saw NY DJ Ron at the Marquette, he was spinning records and had everyone out on the dance floor. From that moment on, all of us girls loved it when DJ Ron was working. We would dance until the sun came up, and then run like vampires from the sun. Usually, we would hide our boy clothes in the bushes and retrieve them in the morning, changing in a gas station bathroom before catching the bus to go home. Sometimes my home was an abandoned building or a rundown rooming house. Sometimes I'd go to my mother's very nice middle-class house, but I didn't like staying there because I couldn't be myself there.

NY DJ Ron changed my life. He took me off the streets, and I became a housewife. I had a white poodle named Poon Poon who didn't think he was a dog. One day me and Poon Poon decided to take a walk up to the store and when we got to the corner, I saw that there were a lot of young drug dealers standing around the store. We were trying to make our way through the crowd, but when one of the men spotted us, he yelled out, "Here come the sissy and the sissy dog." This guy had a small rottweiler. He let him off the leash and this dog was coming for us. My little Poon Poon turned into a pit bull, and he whipped that dog's butt! The men started laughing at their friend, saying that a sissy dog had beaten up his dog. From that day on, Poon Poon and I walked those streets with no problem.

My husband moved us out of the hood into a nicer neighborhood, where we were welcomed. Soon I knew everyone, or rather everyone knew of me as Ms. Dee Dee. I had the best parties with a mix of many different types of people. Sometimes a few partygoers would end up spending the night in our house, and in the morning, I'd fix a big breakfast and talk with them, listen to their problems, and give motherly advice. Some of them started calling me Mother, but I felt I was too young to be a mother. My chosen family, or House, as we call it, was just beginning.

During this time, I was going to the clinic because I had been HIV-positive for ten years. While waiting for my appointment, I'd go outside and care for the people coming in—pushing wheelchairs, singing church songs, and praying with people. I loved it! One guy who worked in the clinic called me over to his van and said, "Hey Ms. Dee Dee, do you work down here?" I said, "No, Mister Jimmy, I just like helping people." Jimmy said, "I got a job for you."

> **"I would encourage all trans youth to seek a spiritual connection. There you will find all the answers to your questions—why you are who you are and what your destiny is in this world. God loves you just as you are."**

I had never had a job as my true self, Ms. Dee Dee, but soon after Jimmy and I talked that day, I was working at my own desk right in the front entrance of the clinic. On my first day on the job, I put on my best pantsuit and caught the train to work as Ms. Dee Dee Chamblee. When I got to the front door the Holy Spirit stopped me and said, "Look across the street." When I looked, I began to see memory flashes of me jumping in and out of cars on that very street. I collapsed right there on my knees and thanked God for saving me.

I went to the head administrator at the clinic because some of the staff members were still using my old name. She suggested we have an in-service staff training on cultural competency, and together we trained the entire staff about how to treat trans people. At the training, she informed them that they could no longer be disrespectful and that it would be grounds for termination. The next day when I got to work, the staff were opening doors for me and saying, "How you are you doing this morning, Ms. Dee Dee!" Overnight, the atmosphere of the clinic changed.

From then on, I started doing cultural competency training for many other local organizations that served my trans community. I knew my trans friends needed services, but they didn't have safe access because they were often misgendered. It hurt the trans women when they were called he or mister while looking like Diana Ross.

I knew that education was the key because once the staff members were educated, they couldn't play dumb. They could no longer say things like, "I'm not one of them, so I don't know whether to call them a man or woman." I taught these workers that it's easy to ask folks how they want to be addressed. No big deal.

Gradually I began to teach these workshops all over the country at universities, colleges, and conferences. All along the way, I gathered more young people who called me Mama Dee Dee. Now I have so many children around the country that I can't remember all their names, but I can remember their spirits. The spirit is the real part of a person and that is what we are doing in our family. We are each expressing our spirit—what's on the inside.

All my trans and nonbinary children know that I am supposed to be a part of their lives—their chosen mother. I love them into loving themselves! Some of them were runaways and I took them in and, if possible, helped them mend their relationships with their families. Some were able to return home after their family took some counseling with me and understood how to treat them and respect their gender identity.

Our families are the people who choose to love us, not because of bloodlines. We create our own families to love and nurture us if we can't get that from our families of origin. My chosen family consists of me—also known as Mama L'Amoure—my husband Pappa NY DJ Ron, our daughters Pearl, Kleopatra, CoCo, and Vanessa, and our sons Pastor Sean, Cash, Dean, and Jamel. They all call me Mama now, as do another 150 folks scattered across the country. I taught them that they are all originals, as there has never been anyone like them ever created. I tell them all, "Just because you were born a trans person, don't think that there is something wrong with you." I teach them to come into the consciousness that God loves all of us and that we were born this way for a reason. No one is an afterthought because God doesn't make mistakes. God loves all of us unique creations just as we are.

I'm very excited about the future. In 2011, President Obama honored me as a "Champion of Change," and I was invited to the White House where I had dinner with President Obama and First Lady Michelle Obama! And with President Biden speaking out to the trans community saying that he has our back, it makes me feel optimistic that things are going to get better despite the hate rising against people of color and LGBTQ+ people.

Sometimes your family of origin must go through a mourning period of letting the old person die to receive the new person—the one who was there all along but who they never recognized. Sometimes parents feel jealous because you are living your own life. I wondered why my mother wasn't proud of the life I was making for myself. When I was invited to the White House, nobody in my entire family had ever gone to the White House, no less to have dinner with the President of the United States. When I told my mother about it, she only grunted and said in a low voice, "That's good," without really meaning it.

That's all I got from my mother whenever I told her about one of my accomplishments, not to mention my marriage, which has lasted longer than any of my sisters' or hers. That is how I came to the sobering revelation that my own mother was jealous of me. I had humbled myself because I believe what God says about the importance of honoring your father and mother, so I had gone along for quite some time with her misgendering me. Eventually I had to push her to stop it because I'm not a child anymore. It surely has been a journey, but I kept praying and loving my mother despite her shenanigans. She has finally started to call me Ms. Dee Dee. Hallelujah! It pays to pray. Prayer is my superpower!

My local chosen family usually meets me at Tabernacle Baptist Church every Sunday. I found this church by chance. When I first heard Bishop Dennis Meredith say that the church's duty was to love and accept transgender folks, I was shocked! I had never seen a Black pastor talk about us in this manner, and I was so impressed that I joined his church and helped create the first transgender ministry in a Baptist church. After church my daughters and I usually go out to a family dinner at a restaurant, or I cook at my house—spirit food to help us conquer the week ahead.

Pearl Styles, Vanessa Pemberton, Dee Dee Chamblee, Kleopatra McGlothin, Kendra Render (CoCo). Photo by Robin Rayne

Mother Gladys, the president of the women's board at church, asked me to join their board meetings. I was nervous when I went the first time. When Mother Gladys left the room, all the other church mothers surrounded me and asked, "Why are you here?" I replied that I was there to be a mother to the children who are thrown away because they aren't understood or respected. I said, "Transgender children are God's children too!" When Mother Gladys came back into the room and realized what was going on, she made it plain that she had invited me to come and join their group, no questions asked. If you go to an affirming church, you will find love, courage, and respect for yourself and others. Remember that the Holy Spirit is always there to help and guide you along your journey.

My most important advice to the trans youth is to step out and don't be afraid to be yourself. We elders have opened the door for you to come into your destiny. Come in! There is love waiting for you.

Rhett Bolen and Family

Rhett. Photo by David J. Spear

Rhett Bolen
(*he/him*)

high school student

I'm eighteen, a high school senior, and I'm a Two-Spirit trans man. I'm half Salish Native American, half African American, living in the Confederated Salish and Kootenai Tribes of the Flathead Reservation in St. Ignatius, Montana, a small town not far from Missoula. From my backyard I can see the beautiful Rocky Mountains.

I live here with my mom and stepdad and Zion, one of my two older brothers. My oldest brother, Comfort, has his own place, and YaYa, my mother's mom, lives by herself down the road about a five-minute drive away. We are all members of the Salish tribe. My biological father is a Black man who lives further away.

My memories of my childhood are a bit hazy, but my earliest memory of anything related to being transgender happened in elementary school. I was seeing an in-school counselor, and I remember saying something to her along the lines of, "Man, I feel like my life would be much easier if I was a boy." I wasn't thinking I was trans because I had never even heard that word. I was just thinking, "Man, it would be cool to be a boy."

My first actual discovery that there was such a thing as an LGBTQ+ community happened in fourth grade when some of my classmates began to talk about it. Until then, I hadn't known that there were people who weren't straight like my parents, and that there was a huge queer and trans community of people around the world who supported each other.

I began vocalizing to my friends that I liked both boys and girls. I thought girls were pretty and I also thought guys were pretty. And when I told my friends, they all said, "Yeah, yeah, yeah. Me too." However, when we asked questions about sexual orientation in school, our teachers didn't want to talk about it with us. So, my friends and I figured that we were going to have to find out for ourselves. We did research online and we finally understood ourselves to be part of something bigger. There was a whole LGBTQ+ community around the world. To have had that conversation about LGBTQ+ people in a school setting would have been so helpful. The fact that these trusted adults wouldn't tell us anything felt so alienating. Personally, I felt like something was wrong with me and that I had to hide who I was.

When I started questioning my gender, I was in fifth grade. My early childhood thoughts of wishing I could be a guy began to grow a lot stronger. For example, whenever I was playing games online where you could dress up your avatar, I always chose a boy character and dressed him in masculine outfits. My mom says that as soon as I could pick out my own clothes, I immediately stopped dressing in dresses and skirts and girly stuff. I was so much more comfortable wearing shorts, pants, more boy-like clothing. In fifth grade, I started acting more boyish, or what we called tomboyish. I didn't really think I was trans at the time because I still didn't really know what transgender meant. I just assumed I was a tomboy, and I remember thinking, "I can settle for this. I can live like this."

From when you first learn to talk, certain ideas are ground into kids' minds. "Oh, you're going to be a heartbreaker," or "Oh, you're going to get all the girls." I think it is blatantly wrong to grind these ideas into children's minds when they are so young. Those messages affected my mental health severely. From a very young age I started feeling isolated because I felt like I had to hide. I became a very anxious kid and was much less talkative and much more reserved. From fourth grade to sixth grade, I was an all-F student.

But then came sixth grade! I started asking my friends to try using different pronouns for me, not only she/her pronouns as they were using at the time, but also he and they pronouns. I guess I was trying things out and discovering myself. I ended up really liking it whenever any of my friends used the pronoun they or he. Basically, I liked anything that wasn't feminine.

Toward the middle of sixth grade, I told all my friends that I thought I was trans and I wanted to be a boy. At first, I felt too scared to tell my friends I was trans because I'd heard many stories about things going bad when people came out. But nothing really changed when I told them. It all went well, and I was very thankful for that. I think they were all so accepting because they were also discovering themselves. I still know some of those friends to this day. One of them also came out as a trans man! Even to this day, throughout my transition, I haven't really experienced anything bad or negative. I know I'm very lucky and I'm very grateful because I know it isn't like this for everyone.

After a year and a half of being out to my friends and nobody else, I told my first actual adult—my eighth grade English teacher. She came up to me in private and said, "Hey, I heard some kids calling you a boy." I thought I was in trouble, and I was really, really scared. But instead of being mad at me, my teacher asked me what my pronouns of choice were! That was the first time an adult had genuinely asked me that question. I sat there for a second and began crying. She comforted me and was so nice and caring that I told her I went by he/him pronouns. Then she asked me, "Is there a name you go by?" She helped me feel comfortable being who I was as a person. I couldn't be more grateful to this day for her support. It was just that little spark I needed!

At the time I went by the name Michael because it was a character that I liked in the musical Be More Chill, and I had been called that name as a nickname before I came out. Later, I changed my name because I wanted to choose a name that fit me better. I chose Rhett because it seemed like such a unique, raw name, a little like both of my brothers' names—Zion and Comfort.

> **"I say this to the younger ones like me who are on this gender journey and to the older people as well: you are allowed to take as long as you need to be you. Never stop discovering yourself."**

The day I came out to my mom, I was having a terrible breakdown due to depression and anxiety. I missed the bus, and I texted my mom at work to tell her that I couldn't go to school and then came out to her in a text that said, "I'm a boy." It was very emotional, and my mom left work to come be with me. When she got back home, we sat down on the couch and talked and talked. I told her I wanted to go to the same private tribal high school she had attended— the Two Eagle River School—and she said yes. Not only did coming out improve my mental health, but it also improved my grades too. I became able to vocalize more and get the help that I needed. I was in one of the best places I'd been in for a very long time. I'm still there!

When I got to Two Eagle River School in ninth grade, there were multiple teachers and multiple students who asked me, "What are your pronouns? Oh, and what name do you go by?" It was just such an open-minded, caring community. I was so incredibly grateful to be able to live in my own skin comfortably and for everyone to be so kind. It made me feel human, for lack of a better word.

Over the years, I've moved further and further through my transition. When I first told my mom about being trans, she told me that she didn't ever want me taking hormones. She said, "That's too big of a step." Now, four years later, I've been on testosterone for about two months. I'm so grateful and it wouldn't be possible if it weren't for my mom. My mom has become one of my biggest supporters, and I sure do love her. I have so much gratitude that she has supported me and helped me get to where I am with my transition.

Rhett & YaYa. Photo by David J. Spear

My grandmother YaYa has always supported me 100 percent and I love her dearly. We are super close! YaYa has had a hard time with my name, just remembering is all. She has always been kind and has taught me how to be the same—yet she is the farthest thing from a pushover!

From day one, my stepdad, Alfred, was so positive. When I told him I was trans, he immediately said, "You do you! I love you. You are great." And I love him for that. He is absolutely the sweetest, most caring, kindest person I know. He has been such a great support to me. Both of my brothers have also been very supportive. At first my biological dad was very opposed and didn't support me, but over time he has gotten better. I can say with confidence that he is supportive now, and I'm so proud of my dad for going through those changes and accepting me, because I understand from a parent's perspective how hard it can be.

I want to say something important to parents of trans and nonbinary kids. My mom was supportive right away, but she was scared for me. I understand that she just wanted to make sure that I was okay. It took her some time, but she ultimately realized that she wasn't losing her daughter and that I was still her kid. I wasn't going anywhere. I loved her. And over time, she became more open-minded about me taking hormones. When she realized that being trans is who I am, and that it is permanent and not a passing phase, she became a lot more willing to help me on my journey. I hope you will do the same with your kid.

Just as it's hard for a kid who is discovering themselves to be trans or nonbinary, it is also hard for parents when their kids come out. I've heard multiple parents say that it feels like they are losing a kid. I've even heard a few parents say that it feels like all their efforts raising their child were going to waste. But that's not true! You raised this kid. They are still your kid, and you are going to be in their life if you are supportive and love them and learn to accept them. It is very sad for me to see parents who tell their kid that being trans or nonbinary is not allowed in their home. No matter what you say, it's not going to stop your kid from discovering who they are. You are just going to push them away from you.

Like my parents, most of the Salish tribe members on my reservation don't really care too much about gender. Everyone here has been very supportive. Even at powwows, where there are fancy dancers and chicken dancers, the dancers are usually separated by gender. But if there's a boy who wants to fancy dance with the girls, the leaders are going to let him. And if a girl wants to dance in a traditional dance for males, they are allowed to. If you have the right outfit and you meet the requirements, go ahead and dance! Powwows welcome everyone.

I haven't encountered much negativity about LGBTQ+ people on my reservation or in nearby towns. I only had one experience when I used to work at our local grocery store. People always see me as a cisgender male, and one day a man came up to my register to pay for his groceries and started saying how much he hated the gays and how nowadays all these kids are trying to come up with new genders. He was completely unaware that he was talking to a trans man. All I could say was, "I don't think you should be sharing your opinions here now." The man got mad at me and complained about my terrible customer service. I usually forget that people who are rude and transphobic exist because everyone on my reservation has been so supportive of me. Even when I originally went to apply for the grocery job, I told the boss my name and my pronouns. He simply responded, "It's nice to meet you, Rhett. You're hired."

Sadly, queer people of color can also get harassed in the wider LGBTQ+ community, which is very upsetting to witness. Our community should be a safe place for every one of every race. Our queer community is where it's at today because POC LGBTQ+ folks had the guts to stand up for not only themselves, but for everyone. A lot of people think it was gay white men who started the Stonewall uprising, but it was Marsha P. Johnson and Miss Major and other POC trans women who were the ones on the frontline.

I would like to help the youth of the LGBTQ+ community. There have been multiple times when I've done what I could to help other young people, even inviting a few to stay in our house for a while, which my mom supports too. I like to give people the resources they need to help themselves.

Currently I identify as pansexual or omnisexual. I have a long-distance partner who lives in Mississippi, and our first anniversary is coming up in a few days. They are on the nonbinary spectrum, and they are still discovering themselves. As of right now they identify as a genderfluid boy who uses all the pronouns with a preference for he/they. Just watching them learning to be comfortable in themselves has been inspiring.

I want to say to trans youth who don't live in a safe situation like mine but who still want to come out, please take your time! If you are genuinely not in a safe place, you do not have to come out! When you come out is your decision alone. Make sure you have a plan, because I've had friends who came out impulsively and were kicked out that very day by their parents. Of course, I never want to discourage people from coming out and being able to live as their true selves. But please just make sure you have a safe place to go. It's great living openly, but the most important thing is to be safe.

To younger people who are just starting to discover themselves, don't feel bad about trying on different labels or different identities. Explore yourself and keep exploring yourself to find what makes you feel the most comfortable. If you stick to a name or certain pronouns for a while and down the line they no longer feel right, please don't be scared to change your mind. You are still discovering yourself and you are allowed to take as long as you need to do that.

Rhett & Glenda. Photo by David J. Spear

I'm the mom of three wonderful sons, Rhett, Comfort, and Zion. I live on the Confederated Salish and Kootenai Tribe reservation in St. Ignatius, Montana. There are around 8,000 registered tribal members living here along with people of all races. My family has lived here all our lives.

Glenda Pierre
(*she/her*)

parent, credit repair worker

I didn't know that Rhett was trans until one day when I was at work, I got a text from him. I thought right up to that moment that Rhett was a girl, but in the text, he said that he was a trans boy. I still get emotional talking about this even now because it was very hard for me. I had to educate myself and ask questions because I literally didn't know anything at all about being transgender then.

It turned out that Rhett hadn't told me he was trans for several years because he was scared that I wouldn't want anything to do with him. My own child! I was shocked and sad that Rhett would think that way. Gosh, it wasn't even a possibility in my mind. No matter what, I would never, ever turn my back on any of my children.

My husband Alfred and I have been together almost thirteen years. He's been a huge part of all three of my kids' lives because their biological dad was absent for a long time. Alfred really stepped in and accepted them all as his own children. Alfred helped me get to a place of accepting Rhett because Alfred accepted him the moment he came out.

I did feel grief for a while after Rhett came out because I felt like I was losing my only daughter. I had to retrain my thinking so I could get to the place where it was okay in my heart. I'm totally accepting of Rhett now.

I still do get upset with myself because I didn't see signs that Rhett is trans, and I often ask myself what did I miss? How did I miss it? I'm a parent. How did I not know? That still makes me more upset than anything. But after I knew, I looked back at certain things and was like, "Wow, okay." I thought back to when Rhett used to wear dresses and pigtails, but then there was a time when he refused to wear pink anymore. He would say, "I don't like that color. I don't want to wear a dress." At first, I'd say, "Well, you're wearing it!" Rhett wanted to buy clothes in the same stores that his older brothers bought their clothing. He only wanted boy clothes and to wear black and gray and other dark colors. Finally, I was like, "Whatever!" That was around five years ago.

> **"I didn't lose a child—I gained a son! Now I'm so fortunate that I have three wonderful sons. I want each of my children to find their happiness and if Rhett is happy, then I'm happy."**

There is another trans boy on our reservation and he was the only actual transgender person I had ever heard about. He came out to his family just a short time before Rhett came out to me, so I reached out to this boy's mom, Mary. She and I had a long conversation and shared many tears. Even though she had totally accepted her son, when she talked about the memories it was still emotional for her like it is for me. Now, whenever I want to know things, she's the one I reach out to. On our reservation, most people are quite open-minded. I haven't heard anyone say anything negative about Rhett. My sisters and my mom are all okay with it, and Alfred's two children both fully accept Rhett. I love everything about each one of my kids. My Rhett has a big heart, and he loves to help people and he does what I ask—he's respectful to me and Alfred. Animals love Rhett. They all just go to him, which is awesome. Rhett is a good kid all around. All my boys are good kids.

Two months ago, Rhett decided to start to take testosterone. I knew nothing about hormone treatment, but my new friend Mary gave me the information I needed. We had to find doctors and a therapist, which took about a year, but luckily the doctor and the counselor are both very supportive of Rhett. If any parent ever asks me for guidance in the future, I will happily support them just like Mary helped me.

Zion, Comfort, Rhett, Alfred, Glenda. Photo by David J. Spear

W hen my stepson Rhett came out as a trans man, it didn't bother me at all. When I grew up my mother's best friend was a trans woman, so I had been around trans people. The only hard part for me was the name change, as it was difficult to remember to call him by his new name at first. I still catch myself saying "she" sometimes, but I'm working hard to get it right.

Alfred Woodcock
(*he/him*)

college student

For the past three years, I've been a full-time college student learning about our Salish history, and language program at the Salish Kootenai College. When Rhett told me he was a boy, I said, "I love you no matter what." I admire Rhett's persistence in all things. That boy gets things done! I love laughing and joking around with him. He's an all-around fun kid.

I'm the eldest brother in our family. I'm twenty-four and I live close to my family in my own place. On the Flathead Reservation, we are among the last people of a dying race. I used to be Christian, but I don't go to church anymore. The older I've gotten I have become more interested in science. I know that there is probably something bigger out there, but I know it isn't some bearded white dude living up in the clouds.

Comfort Bolen Jr.
(he/him)

caregiver for elders

> *People are not born with hate. People are taught to hate.*

I've always been supportive of my baby brother Rhett. When he told me he was trans, I was like, "Yeah, that's cool. If that's who you are, I'm supportive of you. I'll be here with you every step of the way. Whatever makes you happy, that's all I care about."

If someone doesn't like LGBTQ+ people, it can be very difficult to change their mind. People are not born with hate. People are taught to hate. That's the only way it happens.

When Rhett told me he was my brother and a trans man, I said something like, "You do you and I'll do me!" I'm in big support of Rhett. He is awesome. We support all kinds of people in this house. I say to everyone I know, "Do what you want to do and if it makes you happy, then by all means, pursue it." I couldn't have been happier about having another brother.

Zion Bolen *(he/him)*

brother, son, gamer

> *My kid brother can make me feel positive when I'm in my darkest of places. It's truly a beautiful thing.*

I was in a relationship with a trans man for about a year when I was younger. I'm glad that I had that experience as it made me more knowledgeable when Rhett came out. I simply don't understand why a cisgender sibling would reject their trans sibling, because that seems so petty and selfish. It would be like me saying to Rhett, "I know you don't feel comfortable in your body because you know you aren't a girl. And I also know that you are constantly feeling anxious because of this; however, I would rather you feel awful than for you to live openly as a boy." No, that's just obnoxious! I love my little brother. I love his positivity overall.

Feroza Syed and Family

Feroza. Photo by by Robin Rayne

Feroza Syed
(*she/her*)

real estate broker, activist, motivational speaker

Ever since I can remember I've always been a girl, or what the world calls female. One of my earliest childhood memories was while visiting family in India at around four years old, and my cousin grabbed her mother's dupatta (shawl) and wrapped it around her like a sari. I quickly copied her by doing the same with my mother's dupatta, only to be scolded. My mother said, "You can't do that!"

This strong reaction told me that my mother had noticed me dressing like a girl and that she didn't approve, and nor would others. From that day on, I began a long journey of hiding who I was, hiding girl toys from my parents so they wouldn't take them and only being able to be myself when alone in my room.

As I continued to hide my true self for years and years, the pain and realization that I might never live my life authentically settled in. Growing up in a conservative Indian Muslim family, I started to believe my only way to proceed was either to come out and dishonor my family or save them some shame and kill myself. It's crazy how a child's mind works, isn't it? And so my initial coming out, as it were, came after a suicide attempt.

My mother promised me that we'd find a way to deal with my belief that I was a girl and made me swear that I'd never try to kill myself again. My parents never went to any kind of support groups or had any knowledge about how to deal with my situation, but fortunately they found a therapist for me who specialized in gender dysphoria. This was one of the best things that could have ever happened to me. The therapist affirmed me, told me I wasn't alone, and introduced me to a youth group that helped save my life. Years later in college, I transitioned and began to live as the woman I always was. Because I was privileged to rarely be misgendered by cisgender people, my appearance initially helped me stay safe.

I say "initially" because although I was allowed to blend into society because I appeared to be a cisgender female, it also caused issues for me when it came to disclosure. Over the years I have been raped, spit on, choked, and thrown down a stairwell, always at the time of disclosure to men that I was a trans woman. I was also bullied in school, teased, and thrown up against lockers. I lost most of my extended family due to my decision to transition. Using religion as their justification, many people in my Islamic and Indian community turned their backs on me.

My immediate family wasn't a cake walk either. I'm so grateful for my two brothers Arif and Abid, who have always supported me uncondi-tionally. My chosen family has always been there for me, including several friends from my youth—Mia, Jeshebeab, and Adrian have been staples in my life. Also, my ballroom community, the Haus of Balenciaga, and the South Asian queer community have been my support teams.

People often ask if being trans was a choice I made, to which I always respond, "And so what if it is? All humans deserve the right to live their lives unapologetically and authentically." People get unnecessarily hung up on how others dress, who they date, and what they do to their body, which are all things that have nothing to do with how you choose to live your life.

> **" Being trans is only part of my experience as a woman, a daughter of immigrants, a Muslim, a person of color, an aunt, a daughter, and a sister. I have many identities and they intersect in so many ways. "**

I personally choose to live my life with empathy and kindness.

Over the years, my immediate biological family has really come around. I'm very close now with my parents, as well as my siblings and their wives. I'm blessed to have six wonderful nieces and nephews, and I love spending time with them. I've also in a sense replaced my extended family that I lost years ago with my chosen queer family, which has continued to grow over the years.

I believe that all monotheistic major religions have positives and negatives, and the negatives can be terribly harmful. Many LGBTQ+ folks are forced to choose between their very existence and their religion because many of us are taught that our existence as a trans person is an unforgivable sin. I believe faith is a very personal thing and that our relationship with God is ours alone. Most prophets from all the major religious traditions were kind and empathetic humans who aligned themselves with the most marginalized communities of their time.

Since my second coming out as trans in 2018, I've continuously worked to help improve my community in any way possible. I've worked with organizations like PFLAG and Desi Rainbow Parents to help parents and their queer children find the ability to be accepting and live authentically. When I first came out four years ago, Ann Miller, the volunteer director of PFLAG's Gulf Region, reached out to me. She was running one of the only children's youth support groups and she asked me if I could facilitate this group. I said yes immediately because when I was young and suicidal, I went to a group called Youth Pride that saved my life when I realized for the first time that I wasn't alone. Getting support when you are young is crucial, life-altering, and life-affirming!

I'm an activist and currently sit on the LGBTQ Advisory Board to the mayor of Atlanta and I'm the Trans Affairs Committee cochair for that board. I'm also on the national board for the LGBTQ+ Real Estate Alliance and locally I sit on the board for the Trans Housing Coalition, an organization that houses primarily Black trans women. I've also spoken at dozens of schools, public events, and universities.

Often people think that being visible in and of itself isn't activism for our community. I disagree. I think being visible is a form of activism provided you are helping inspire, educate, and motivate your community and those outside of it. I am constantly sharing information on my social media.

I'm a successful businesswoman and top producer at the luxury brokerage Atlanta Fine Homes Sotheby's International Realty. I'm also a daughter, sibling, loving aunt, and a supporter of everyone in my chosen family. I like to consider myself one of the South Asian aunties to many of the young adults in our LGBTQ+ community.

Through my work with the Trans Housing Coalition, I've seen how the hardest hit are often marginalized communities when it comes to housing. For that matter, BIPOC people have it hard in almost every aspect of society in terms of access to healthcare, education, employment, and violence committed against them. And Black trans women are the most marginalized of all. Despite being the ones who have been leading movements for change for our queer community for years, it is appalling that these people who have done so much for us are the ones who are left behind.

My intersectionality has meant that I've also experienced racism, Islamophobia, anti-immigrant xenophobic sentiment, and other forms of marginalization. Though all these experiences are different forms of oppression, they're all ultimately based in hate. Whether it was in my youth or as recently as enduring all the hate from the Trump administration, I've lived my life from a place of love while trying to change people's perceptions of my marginalized communities.

I look forward to a world in which the binary is broken down to the point where our youth can present as they wish from any age. I think ultimately, I and so many others from our age group could have been saved from so much trauma in our youth if we were allowed to express ourselves authentically.

Many people don't personally know a trans person and they don't realize that the things they are hearing about us are false. For example, when a trans woman athlete has been on hormone therapy for two years, there is no biological advantage anymore regardless of her physical presentation. As far as the fear that trans people will attack women in public bathrooms, incidents of sexual assaults are predominantly by cisgender white men. This is a fact, not conjecture.

As time proceeds, I'd love to see the transgender, nonbinary, and gender nonconforming community have easier access to legal name changes, gender markers of their choosing, and easier access to adoption. Healthcare, housing, and education are human rights and often our community is not afforded the same access to them. I have socioeconomic, racial, and passing privilege, amongst others, which have allowed me to overcome many of the obstacles people in our community face.

Abid Syed
(*he/him*)

father, rapper, business man

I was young when Feroza told me that she was a trans woman, and it didn't really affect me or my relationship with her in any way. I guess I always kind of expected it. I loved her the same and I was always supportive of her. Back then, I just wanted her to be happy because I saw her go through a lot of tough times, as most people weren't as supportive as I was of her transition.

I will always support Feroza! We are still as close as ever. We speak daily and she and I always lean on each other for advice. We also goof around to the max. I know I can always count on my sister for anything I need, and Feroza feels the same way about me. I admire Feroza's perseverance and commitment. When she makes up her mind to do something, it will get done!

I hope that changes take place that will allow trans people to have the same rights, access to education, and work opportunities as everyone else.

Abid, Feroza & Juweria. Photo by Robin Rayne

Watching my sister grow and accomplish all that she has done has been amazing. Feroza did it all on her own and made it against all odds. I'd like to see those odds change for her and for other trans people who follow in her footsteps.

For the most part, my friends have been completely accepting and supportive of Feroza. Birds of a feather flock together, so I guess most of my friends were of the same mindset as me. There were a couple of instances where someone tried to pick on her or me because of her gender identity, and they were dealt with!

My sister, Feroza, is probably the most affectionate and caring person I know. The Syed siblings all have big hearts, but Feroza's heart is the biggest.

I have always defended Feroza, whether it was with family, strangers, or friends. An example is when I got married in India, our parents and other members of our family tried to tell me why it wasn't a good idea for Feroza come to the wedding. I told them that I could care less if anyone else showed up or not, but I wasn't going to get married if my sister wasn't there. Feroza attended, of course, and we all had a wonderful time.

Our kids refer to my sister-in-law Feroza as "Aunty." Feroza is the "fun one," and they love to hang with her anytime. I'm married to Feroza's brother Abid, and we have two sons, ages eight and ten.

Juweria Syed
(*she/her*)

mother, real estate agent, instructional designer

Feroza always looks after them and is our first go-to as a babysitter. She is always thinking of our boys, buying them gifts, and making delicious sweets and snacks for them. I have a super close relationship with Feroza, myself, and we do a lot of things together. She's part of my day-to-day life because we work together as realtors at the same firm.

> **I'm so glad that my sister-in-law has love and support from her family. She certainly has mine!**

Parker Glick and Ericka Miller

Parker. Photo by Robin Rayne

Parker Glick
(*he/him*)

disability rights
advocate, home
chef, photographer

I identify as a trans disabled man. I was born in Korea thirty-three years ago and adopted as a six-month-old baby by a family in America. I'm one of three adopted children in our family of seven siblings. Fun fact: I was born with my disability, arthrogryposis. Essentially, my joints contract so I can't walk, and my arms don't go up above my head. I blame that on my biological twin. I always joke that I must not have paid my rent in the womb, so my twin decided to kick me out early. Then, a couple of years ago, I was in a car accident, so I also have an acquired disability—traumatic brain injury. Disability can happen at any point in anybody's life.

I like debunking the idea that disabled folks don't understand the concept of gender identity or sexual orientation. I came out a couple times—the first time as a lesbian when I was in college. I guess we all have our phases of getting to know who we are! My mom wasn't really a fan of my first woman partner so when we broke up, my mom was relieved. Maybe she also hoped that I would "quit" being a lesbian.

After learning from social media about what it meant to be transgender, I eventually came out as a trans man a short time before I turned thirty. Since then, I've been transitioning by using testosterone gel. It's been an ongoing journey for my family as well as for me. I do take into consideration that my transition is also a transition for my parents and siblings. It's not been all smooth sailing, but I appreciate the efforts they are all making. My next oldest brother has a dark sense of humor, and he told a bunch of jokes when I come out as a trans man. Honestly, I found his humor very comforting!

On social media it's no secret that I'm a trans man, so when I met Ericka, I didn't have to say anything about my gender identity. Before she became my girlfriend and we fell madly in love, I always put it in my dating profiles online because it's not something that I wanted to hide. I've been told that at first glance, I can "pass" as male—not that passing has ever been my goal—but I wouldn't want someone I was dating to assume I was a cisgender man. I would want them to know I'm a trans man so that they could decide right away if it's comfortable for them to date me. The same is true about my disability. I always put photos of me in my wheelchair and never try to hide the fact that I've got shorter arms and whatnot. I'm totally aware of how many labels are attached to my name. Because I'm an Asian man, certain situations have brought up the unfortunate xenophobia in our nation against Asians, especially since Covid. Sadly, prejudice is alive and well.

I recently worked with the Georgia Advocacy Office. It is the state protection and advocacy agency to ensure that all Georgians with mental and physical disabilities are protected against neglect, abuse, and exploitation. My primary role was as an employment advocate. I worked with individuals to help them advance in their careers, acquire assistive technology, and organize their state benefits. I really enjoyed doing this work, and I never felt so appreciated at a job.

My coworkers were all wonderful people and none of them had a problem with my transition. Some folks knew me prior to my officially coming out as trans and, naturally, they were still dealing with their own transition issues—for example, remembering to change my pronouns. I always have tried to be gracious when people make mistakes.

When I saw new clients, if I wasn't misgendered as female, I didn't feel like I needed to come out and tell them that I was a trans man. I only came out as trans if I was comfortable that the client was in the LGBTQ+ community because we live in a very dangerous world. It's unfortunate that I still have to say to my friends, "Please don't tell anybody that I'm trans. It's not your business to tell. It's for my safety!"

> *I believe that visibility and representation are essential to make sure that equal rights and accessibility are available for all.*

I try to take everything with humor. For example, I'm a person who uses personal care attendants daily. It's a very intimate and vulnerable relationship, so I always need to consider when to come out. It's gotten me into some predicaments, such as the time I was getting ready for a job interview. One personal care attendant didn't want me to dress in the masculine attire that I requested and stated that if I didn't wear a dress, I wouldn't get the job. People just need to be better educated about trans and nonbinary people.

People also need to be taught about disability awareness. When I found an LGBTQ+ church, the community there wasn't educated at all about disability. I had my name tag on, but I was constantly getting called "Buddy," and people kept running around trying to do things for me. The situation was incredibly infantilizing. Many people with disabilities are angry, but not because we are disabled. It is because there are so many obstacles in our way which make many things inaccessible to us.

I feel like my disabilities have been a little bit more of a challenge for me to deal with than being trans simply because we live in a very inaccessible world. I'm not able to get transportation in the evening so I can go on a date. I'm often not able to pull open a door to a restaurant or a hotel room by myself because they are too heavy. I'm grateful, or rather fortunate enough with my trans experience, that being a trans man hasn't been a huge barrier in my life.

Here is my advice to parents with trans kids who are just coming out: Please don't bombard them with too many questions. This whole coming out process is a long journey. When I first said I was trans, my mom asked me what that meant. I didn't have a clue how to explain it to her.

Why are we still thinking in gender stereotypes and binaries? Why are there gender reveal parties for babies? These parties should only be for trans folks so that we can come out and celebrate our transitions. That would be cool! Stereotypes for gender roles truly demean the existence of nonbinary people. How can parents continue to get rid of these stereotypes? It's not so hard. Your daughter wants to play with trucks. Well, why not? Your son wants to wear a dress. Well, why not?

For people who want to be trans allies, "Do your own research. If you want to be an ally, one of the most important things you can do is to ensure that you're considering us when you're voting."

> **Ericka Miller**
> (*she/her*)
>
> disability rights advocate, executive director, baker

I was born with spina bifida and I'm a wheelchair user. I also have other invisible disabilities, mostly with my mental health, and hydrocephalus, which is fluid on the brain. I met Parker at a conference in DC where we marched with a group to meet with our state legislators on Capitol Hill to lobby for disability equality and legal protections. I used air tires for this march, which was up and down hills in my manual wheelchair. However, I was very fortunate because I had already started chatting up the nearest stud, who happened to be Parker. Parker helped me navigate up to Capitol Hill, as his chair has power and was easier on me as I was trying to push up a giant hill. I swooned the entire way.

After this first meeting, Parker and I didn't develop a solid friendship right away. Over the years, it just seemed like every time I was single, Parker was dating someone, and every time Parker was single, I was dating someone. It kind of went that way until the beginning of this year when we were chatting one day by text, and he asked if we could talk via video chat.

Ericka & Parker. Photo by Robin Rayne

When I called Parker, he asked me point blank if I was flirting with him. That was just the beginning! Parker and I are ridiculously new as a couple, but we're both so into it. And we've known each other for about six years now, so it's been a long time coming. We're making up for lost time and we've decided that we are going to live together very soon.

I identify as a queer bisexual woman, and I've only been officially out to my family for two years. I struggled with the concept of bisexuality because I had a really hard time with heteronormativity. For a while, I really thought I was straight because that was what I was supposed to be.

When I dated my first girlfriend in tenth grade, neither of us were out. She was a social butterfly, and her mother was very involved with the PTA at our high school. It was clear that we had to be secretive about our relationship. On Valentine's Day I bought roses for every single one of my female friends so that nobody would know that I was getting a flower for my girlfriend.

For the first thirty years of my life, I was terrified that my family wouldn't accept me. It was only when I moved from Florida to Rochester, an incredibly queer-friendly city, that I felt comfortable in my LGBTQ+ community.

I was suddenly comfortable to come out to my friends, my coworkers, and my disability community, and I was very proud of being out. I boldly went to all different kinds of clubs and events, and I was very happy.

But when it came to my family, I was still so scared that I wouldn't be accepted. I've dealt with a lot of biphobia in my life, but I was fortunate that both of my parents were okay with it after I revealed my sexual orientation to them.

> *When I came out, I honestly didn't know if I would lose my family or not. So, when my community and my family said that I was brave, it felt like thirty years of pressure to hide disappeared in a moment.*

When you can't come out, it feels like you are hiding away a piece of your soul. I had to decide if I was going to continue to be unhappy or just let it out of the box and deal with what happened. When I came out, I honestly didn't know if I would lose my family or not. So, when my community and my family said that I was brave, it felt like thirty years of pressure to hide disappeared in a moment. It was like a balloon being released to float free! However, I also understand that the fear is real for many young people who are debating coming out.

If you aren't comfortable coming out, you don't need to say anything right now. I know that it's crushing and horrible and it shouldn't be that way, but your safety is the number one priority. If you do have a support system outside of your family, such as a teacher at school or a relative or a friend—a person where you can get love and support, or possibly even someone who might take you in if you were to get kicked out of your home—then do it. It's so important to me that every single queer youth stay alive to live their best life. My door is always open!

Anjali Rimi and Naga Gouri Devi

Anjali. Photo by Cody Young

Anjali Rimi
(*she/her*, *they/them*)

community leader, immigrant, Kinnar Hindu

I realized I was transgender as an eleven-year-old still living with my family in India. It wasn't a new feeling, but rather something I came to fully express; beginning with telling my mother I felt like a flower waiting to blossom. My mom replied that she knew and understood, but feared that it wouldn't be possible in a world that would never see me as anything other than a boy.

Even as an adult, my memories of the trauma I encountered in childhood are still vivid: The violence, abuse, and scorn I endured at school when I came out as a trans woman at fifteen. My father beating me black and blue. My mom to this day remaining steadfast in her love and support even as everyone else in my world walked away. Although coming to the United States for grad school gave me the opportunity to fully express myself as a woman, it also made me a victim of a hate crime. The next few years pushed my authentic identity back into the shadows until I could begin fully transitioning at 25.

> **" I want politicians to know that trans people aren't political pawns or caricatures, we are human beings worthy of respect and dignity. The most abhorrent sin of all is attacking trans kids for political clout, something too many politicians are doing today. "**

When I was growing up in 1980s India, most people weren't even familiar with the word *transgender*. There were no LGBTQ+ support organizations. However, there were numerous communities encompassing eunuchs, intersex, asexual, transgender, and other gender non-conforming people that were known as Hijra. Hijras themselves often preferred the term *Kinnar*, referring to mythological beings skilled in song and dance. Despite centuries of tradition associated with these folx, most South Asians did not view them as worthy of respect or dignity.

Overcoming the hate and prejudices over the past forty years has been a tumultuous journey, both in society and within my own family. It tested the limits of my father and brother's capacity for love, understanding, and tolerance. My mom worked hard to protect me from their abuse and push them towards true acceptance. Eventually they did realize I can live a respectful life in society, reaching milestones in education, career, and community as a fully out and authentic trans woman.

Of course my journey is still in progress, and the path is rarely linear. I was fired immediately after beginning estrogen treatment while living in San Francisco in 2003. This and other instances of severe discrimination pushed me back into closeted life for another decade. After once again being outed at work, I decided to live as an openly trans woman ever since.

I always knew that my existence was a manifestation of Yellamma, a goddess worshiped in several South Indian states who is revered as the mother of the universe. Also referred to as Maa Bhavani, she is a beautiful, shining patron goddess who protects her many Kinnar devotees. Amidst the struggles I faced during transition without the support of family and society, my centering in the female divinity of my Hindu traditions helped me survive.

Hinduism has a vast corpus of history and tradition that celebrates the beauty of existing as a genderfluid and gender-expansive person. My Hindu faith gives me strength because I know that I am the *ansh of ardhanarishvara*—one who receives the blessings of Yellamma and the benevolence of Bhavani and Shakti's child. An *ardhanarishvara* is the combined form of the Hindu deity Shiva and his consort Parvati, encompassing both the divine masculine and divine feminine. For those who can see me for all of me, I refer to myself as a woman of trans experience. When I'm not in safe spaces, I am perceived and refer to myself simply as a woman.

We need humanity to understand and acknowledge that our obsession with the gender binary results in an incomplete and intolerant worldview that directly harms trans people. We need to dismantle the laws and prejudices that target trans people, whether in the United States or throughout the world. We can learn from traditions like Hinduism to decolonize our minds and employ religion as an asset in our struggle for trans liberation.

Like many trans people, my existence has made me a target of violence. I've endured as a child being bullied in school, and as an adult facing a torment of online abuse. Nevertheless, I live without fear because my soul is free and I draw strength from my faith, community, and chosen family.

The pandemic magnified the marginalization, isolation, and discrimination trans, Hijra, and other communities endure throughout the world, particularly in India. While I don't personally live in fear as an activist, I like many trans people have learned to prioritize pragmatism and safety wherever I go. I seldom travel alone and am careful about engaging in accountability conversations with transphobes. As a victim of attacks due to my brown skin and trans Kinnar gender identity, I am even more conscious of my safety in the United States than I am in India.

When I'm misgendered, I assess the situation in order to understand if the act was an innocent mistake or a conscious attempt to be hurtful. In the case of the former, I treat it as an opportunity to educate, foster, and allow for learning. For the latter, I fight back and aggressively assert my rights as a trans woman. When I see others getting misgendered, I will intervene to keep trans people safe.

As cofounder and president of Parivar Bay Area, America's only trans-led, trans-centered South Asian LGBTQ+ queer organization, I work to advance our mission to build a community of light, love, and acceptance, a community that celebrates South Asian queer transgender intersectionality. Leading this grassroots organization of so many powerful trans warriors has been an honor. Within the past four years, we launched the largest grassroots relief effort across India during the second Covid-19 wave, held more than forty global events, and raised almost half a million dollars. In addition to my work with the South Asian diaspora, I work to fight to dispel transphobia everywhere through my work with Trans PULSE Canada, San Francisco Pride, Harvard Medical School, and numerous BIPOC queer/trans centering organizations in my local community. I am fighting for economic justice, liberation, healthcare equity, and social inclusivity for all trans and nonbinary people.

This is a crucial fight for ourselves now as well as to allow future generations to be able to live authentically in their gender identity while enjoying the love and support of their families and communities. And to that end I welcome anyone, trans or not, who shares this dream to join us.

I am a trans woman as well as an immigrant, rape survivor, trained chef, community leader, daughter, Hindu, and corporate professional. My identity is and always will be intersectional. This existence gives inspiration to some, though I have discovered it can also be quite intimidating to others.

Leading Parivar Bay Area and working in community, my dream is to materially change how the world sees South Asian trans Hijra people like myself and allow us to control our narrative and demand a seat at the table. I want South Asian LGBTQ+ folx to feel confident in expressing their identities and to embrace their forgotten heritage of trans Hijra acceptance and equity. Most of all, I want to save trans queer lives.

Naga & Anjali. Photo by Cody Young

Naga Gouri Devi (*she/her*)

retired teacher, mother

My name is Gouri, and I was brought up in India. When I gave birth to my two children, I was very proud. I thought for many years that I had two sons. By God's grace, the youngest is actually a girl, but I don't mind. I feel proud.

When Anjali first told me that she was a woman, I kept asking myself, "Why, why, why did this happen?" It was very difficult for me to digest at first. My husband was against it and would always say his *son* must be a boy and get married and have children. That is our custom. My mother, father, and elder brother still ask me why my younger son isn't getting married and why he says that he is a girl. My husband and I have drifted apart because I am proud of Anjali but he is still ashamed. He has abused me because of my support for Anajli. Because of this, I don't live with him anymore and instead live with my daughter.

Yes, I felt very bad when Anjali came out. But as a mother, I couldn't help but love and support my daughter after seeing the pain she went through. I wanted to help her grow into a beautiful, educated, and healthy woman. There were many steps that Anjali had to walk. I wanted to be at her side.

Being a trans or nonbinary person isn't a bad thing. It is in our culture and in Hinduism. There's nothing to worry about and nothing bad in it.

> **Lord Vishnu also changed his gender and became a woman and then became a man. If our gods can change their genders, I decided that I would always support my daughter being a transgender woman.**

When Anjali told me she wanted to transition, I thought, "Why try to stop her? This is her life. Boy, girl . . . this is Anjali's life." I told Anjali, "Whatever gender you are, you should live as that person. I am with you. I am always with you. Even if your father is against you, never mind, I am with you."

Parents must support their transgender children. Don't be against them and deny the affection every child needs. Please support them and help them build a good life. Otherwise, they will be shattered. They will be very anxious and suffer an unbearable loss. That pain will make it hard to gain anything in their lives. Parents need to support their children and give them all the love they can give.

Elliott Bertrand and Family

Elliott. Photo by Alyssa Botelho

Elliott Bertrand
(*he/him*)

college student,
singer, stage manager

I'm eighteen years old, and I'm a trans man. I was assigned female at birth, but I always knew that something wasn't right about being labeled female. The first time I started exploring my gender identity was in middle school.

If you looked back at my middle school Google search history, I'm sure you'd find several tabs from when I was googling "gay," "transgender," "LGBTQ+ identities," and several videos on YouTube about queer people sharing their experiences. I cycled through many different labels and identities during that time, but none of them stuck with me for very long. I tried demigirl, nonbinary, genderfluid, bigender, and many others but none of them fully fit me. I shared my search for my identity with my group of friends, and although they probably didn't understand it, most of them supported me. The few that didn't support me decided to just ignore that part of me, and we drifted apart in time.

I asked for my first binder at the beginning of my freshman year of high school. I don't think my parents thought that it was anything more than me just wanting to hide my chest, which I'd always wanted to do even before I started questioning my gender identity. I cut my very long hair that was hanging down to the middle of my back into a shoulder-length bob, and then finally to a short pixie cut. I changed the clothes I was wearing from somewhat girly t-shirts to button-downs from the men's section. Slowly, I began to realize that what I had been feeling all this time was simple: I'm a boy. For a while, I wasn't ready to let myself truly grasp that fact, and I think that was why I went through so many different identities.

The first people I came out to as trans were two of my closest friends and I was able to try out a few names and pronouns with them to find which ones felt right. I also tried out different names and pronouns online. I came out to my mom and dad mid-freshman year after I had settled on the name Elliott and he/him pronouns. I wanted them to know right away because I was very sure that my name wasn't going to change.

It was very hard for me to tell my parents, and I cried the entire time. I wasn't afraid that they would react badly, but I didn't want their view of me to change. It took me a while to get the words out. My dad guessed that I was coming out as a lesbian, which was a good guess considering my recent changes in appearance, and I laughed because it was kind of the opposite of what I was about to tell them. Once I got the words out and said, "I'm a trans man and my name is Elliott," my mom and dad were totally accepting, though they kept messing up my name and pronouns for a while. I knew that they weren't doing it maliciously, but it still really hurt. Once my parents understood how much they were causing me pain, they tried harder to get my name and pronouns right. To get help for our family, we set up regular appointments with a local therapist who specializes in working with trans people.

I also came out to my grandparents on my dad's side around that time. They seemed a little confused, but eventually they adapted to the change and told me that they loved me no matter what. With my grandmother on my mom's side, the coming out process happened later and was less well received. At first, I thought it went okay, but she did many hurtful things. I was close to cutting her off because of everything, but she finally realized the pain she'd been causing me. It was a slow process, but now my grandmother has made the change and supports me, even if she doesn't completely understand.

> **Even if someone's exploration of their gender is a phase, it's important to allow them to explore and express themselves to see what feels right instead of forcing them to conform and repress their feelings.**

After I came out to my family, I knew that I wanted my friend group and certain teachers at my school to know. I was in a play at the time portraying a female character, so I was worried that the change would be weird for the other kids in the cast. One of my closest friends who knew asked me if I wanted her to tell the entire cast. I said yes because letting other people spread the news was so much easier than trying to tell every person myself. That night at rehearsal, my castmates came up to me and confirmed what my new name and pronouns were, and they all made the change pretty much instantly. It was awesome to have that support backstage when I was stuck playing a woman onstage.

When I started transitioning socially, I wanted my theater teacher and my choir director to be the first teachers to know. Theater and music are a huge part of my life, and I thought coming out in those artistic worlds would go well. My theater teacher was very accepting, but my choir director was a different story. When I came out to him, he wasn't outright mean, but it was obvious that it was something he didn't like. He refused to call me Elliott, giving an excuse that it was the name of a relative who had passed, and instead gave me the nickname "Bertie" based on my last name Bertrand, which I didn't like. At the time I was willing to let it go because it seemed better than outright transphobia. In retrospect I know that even though it wasn't blatantly obvious, his actions were transphobic and hurtful.

I was in the women's choir, but the director changed the name to treble choir to seem more inclusive. However, when he explained the reason for the change to the class, I felt I was singled out as the reason the name had to be changed. He pretty much outed me, which made me very uncomfortable. I also learned from a friend that during a choir concert, someone had asked the director's wife why the name of our choir had been changed. She said, "It's because of those guy/girls thinking they are special."

The last straw was when the choir director's behavior caused me to have an anxiety attack during class. All his microaggressions had finally gotten to me, and I told my parents about what had happened that day after I came home from school. I was moved out of the class as soon as possible, and the school administrators investigated. In conclusion, they said that they had no findings of misconduct, likely because the administrator conducting the investigation was homophobic.

The choir director let me know that he was willing to let me come back if I apologized for the miscommunication. We were far past apologies by then, and I realized that if I stayed at my school, I would have to be around him to do the activities that I loved or give up theater and choir altogether. That's why my parents and I decided it would be best for me to transfer to the other high school in town. It was a difficult decision to leave all my friends, but ultimately that decision led to a lot of new opportunities for me. Everyone at my new school welcomed me with open arms, and I've made some of the best friends I've ever had.

At my new high school, I became the publicist for the thespian troupe and I've been in multiple shows. Navigating choir and theater during my voice change after starting to take testosterone was a little awkward, but I had my awesome choir director, theater director, and voice coach to help me through it.

Even though I was out of my original high school's environment, our battle in response to my mistreatment by the choir director there was far from over. My parents and I were frustrated that the administration's investigation went nowhere, so we took the issue to the school board. For a while, I was too afraid to speak and advocate for myself and my dad did most of the talking. We believed that the district's nondiscrimination policy lacked the clear, strong language needed to protect trans and nonbinary students.

In the first meeting, we expressed our frustration with the results of the investigation. In the second meeting, someone decided to show up to oppose me and my family. A "formerly lesbian" pastor took time out of her day to publicly embarrass, antagonize, and misgender me. The school board members did absolutely nothing to stop this woman as she berated me during her public comment time. I had to leave the room sobbing because I couldn't take it anymore. I know she intended to tear us down and convince us to stop fighting, but it only sparked me and my parents to keep up our fight for better treatment of trans and nonbinary youth.

It would take fourteen months and countless public meetings, rallies, and new school board members to finally get the words "gender identity" added to the school's nondiscrimination policy. The whole process was hard on me, and I wanted to give up so many times, but I knew I couldn't because my story and my fight would encourage other students to stand up for themselves.

We had a ton of support from friends, students, teachers, and other people in our community. Throughout all of this, my parents evolved from being just supportive people and quiet allies to being activists and advocates for the LGBTQ+ community in our town and beyond. Even though the battle was a roller coaster of emotions, backlash, and controversy, it was worth it to make sure that other students like me would be protected.

To parents who don't accept their LGBTQ+ children, I feel sorry for you. You have chosen your ideas, something that you can change, over your own child, who can't change who they are. I hope someday you realize the pain you have caused and repair your relationship before it's too late.

To young trans and nonbinary people, just know that the problem isn't you or who you are. Ignorance is everywhere, but it's important to understand that hatred toward you is never your fault. It can be difficult navigating negative environments, but when your family supports you—whether it's your family of origin or your chosen family—you'll have everything you need. Not everyone will accept you, but the people who truly matter will.

I think ignorance and hate stem from a lack of education early on, so young students must be taught about sexual orientation and gender identity in ways that are appropriate for their age level. Currently, there has been a lot of anti-gay and anti-trans legislation being put into motion by homophobic and transphobic politicians. We need to be able to combat this, and the best way to do that is to stop it at the source. If we had more representation and allies in local, state, and national government, we could stop these bills from getting as far as they have. This will take a lot of work from very dedicated people, but I believe that it's possible.

Randy Bertrand
(*he/him*)
husband, father, protector

I'm Elliott's dad, and I'm proud of being part of his life journey. There wasn't a single "aha" moment when we saw that Elliott was struggling with gender issues. Jennifer and I could look at him and say he was a typical tomboy, but there was nothing that really stood out as a watershed moment when we noticed a drastic shift in his identity. I do recall in middle school where Elliott began talking about some of his friends identifying as pansexual and slowly alluded to possibly being pansexual himself.

I was incredibly conservative, and Elliott knew this. I think he was just testing the waters to see if I would accept him. I had no idea what pansexual meant, so I asked. The way he described it—probably watered down for me—was that he didn't confine his love to any specific societal norm or gender. Seemed fine with me, so, no big deal.

In eighth grade Elliott started cutting his hair shorter—still feminine, but much shorter than other girls his age. Then there were trips to the library where Elliott's book choices became more focused toward LGBTQ+ issues. My mind started to put two and two together. I began to do online research, and most of the parental advice centered around accepting and allowing the teen to be in the proverbial "driver's seat," so I didn't say anything to Elliott.

Early in Elliott's first year of high school, I felt I had a clearer picture: short hair, holding hands with an out bisexual friend at school, purchasing and wearing a binder to minimize certain features. I was convinced: Elliott was a masculine or butch lesbian.

Jennifer, Elliott & Randy. Photo by Alyssa Botelho

Elliott's coming out was a moment that our family talks about often. I remember Jennifer and I were in the master bedroom chatting about something when Elliott came in with a very serious look on his face and said he needed to talk to both of us right away. Keep in mind, he was fourteen years old at this time, with a very conservative Army veteran father, so I can't even imagine the courage Elliott needed to have conjured up to face me. I look back on how I held myself as such a tough and stern father and wonder if he held off telling me important life details because of his fear of my reaction. Either way, the information he needed to share with us this evening was too much for him to hold alone any longer.

I'd like to say I just sat there and listened while Elliott came out, but I can't. Thinking I had all the answers, I stopped him mid-thought and said something to the effect of, "I think I know what you are going to tell us. You're a lesbian, right?" I felt like I needed some validation of my gaydar— the ability to spot LGBTQ+ people. He almost chuckled his answer to my question, saying quietly, "No, I'm not a lesbian." So, then I was even more confused. I knew my kid. How could I be wrong?

Elliott was standing there a little teary-eyed and I was scared to hear what he was going to say. I don't remember verbatim what words he used, but it was something like, "I believe I should have been born a boy. I'm transgender." I was more than a little shocked at his statement, but something clicked in my head. Perhaps it was something I had read about in my research on LGBTQ+ teens. I looked him in the eyes and replied, "Okay. I assume you want to use he/him pronouns?" I knew that the best path for parents was not to question but to affirm. I really didn't know what I was saying, but I knew that my future relationship would be shaped by how I responded to this incredibly personal detail about Elliott's life that he had decided to share with me.

> **When your child comes out, never ask, 'Are you sure?' Never say, 'You don't know what you are talking about.' Never say, 'You are too young to know.' And never say, 'This is probably a phase.' Your child knows 100 percent more about the subject than you do. A great question to ask is simply, 'How can I best support you?' This allows your child to be in the driver's seat, right where they belong.**

After Elliott came out as trans, we made his first appointment at the University of Florida Gender Clinic. Up until that point his transition was only social. He was chomping at the bit, while I was a little more careful and calculated. When we called for an appointment, the earliest we could schedule one was over four months away. Elliott was incredibly disappointed, but I was relieved to allow a natural pause in the process to adjust and reflect on the journey.

Ironically, we received a call a few days later that there was a cancellation at the clinic, and they had an opening in just over a week. So much for my goal of taking the longer, slower road of transition. I realize now that my desire for a transition process that proceeded slowly was only for my comfort. I made it about me, and now, several years removed from that event I can truly say that Elliott's transition was never about me.

The night of the January school board meeting, as the self-described ex-lesbian pastor started speaking, I rose from my chair and executed an about-face, turning my back to her and to the board members. It took about fifteen seconds, but then something amazing happened. Other members of the audience saw what I was doing and understood why. One by one, and sometimes in small groups, most of the audience stood up and turned their backs on her. I never asked anyone to do this. Many believe I put the audience up to this, but even my own family didn't know what I was planning. This was my silent protest, but a great number of amazing people showed solidarity for our family's fight and stood shoulder to shoulder with us.

With the growing support of the Flagler County LGBTQ+ community, we decided to shake things up a little at the February school board meeting and hold a pre-meeting rally outside the Government Services Building to show students that we supported them. Of course, the "Good Reverend" showed up with her group of less than ten supporters while around sixty people showed up in support of our cause. What amazed me was the number of kids who shared stories of bullying and discrimination and how they needed these protections to feel safe in schools.

An amazing and unexpected thing happened that night. The state of Florida had some newly enacted legislation which necessitated changes to the district's nondiscrimination policy. As part of the changing of any policy, there was a minimum thirty-day period where citizens could provide edits to the policy before the board voted on adoption. This was the opportunity I was looking for. A chance to add the words and compel the board to vote on it.

Something else was lurking in the background that would shape how our efforts would continue: Covid-19 and the ensuing lockdown. In late February, with the Covid-19 pandemic reaching across the world, the state of Florida entered a state of lockdown. Everything was closed, including public meetings like the school board general meetings.

I don't think I slept more than four hours a night in March 2020, as I scoured the internet for as much literature as necessary to support our efforts. I compiled a list of the districts in Florida that already provided protection for students who were trans or nonbinary on the basis of gender identity through their nondiscrimination policies.

The nondiscrimination policy came up for vote in April. There was a single motion to adopt the updated protections, but the remaining four board members just sat there and did not provide a required second for a board vote. I was devastated! The motion died right then and there. All my efforts and the countless emails sent to board members showcasing all the new evidence I had encountered, and the cowards wouldn't even bring it to a vote!

I'd love to blame the board members for their apparent cowardice, but learning a little political savvy was in order here. There were elections being held for multiple board seats that year and with an incredibly conservative voting base in Flagler County, it wasn't surprising that board members didn't stick their necks out on a policy that might cause them to lose votes and possibly the elections. What were we to do? We would shift our efforts to supporting candidates who would support our cause.

The LGBTQ+ community of Flagler County endorsed the two candidates who most closely aligned with our values. Once the polls closed, I kept refreshing my phone to see what direction the school board election was headed. In the early evening hours, I saw that the two board members we supported were elected. This gave us the needed vote to second the motion to compel a vote if the nondiscrimination policy were to be brought up again.

I'd love to say that the school board ruling we successfully fought for marked the end of our struggles to protect local trans and nonbinary kids, but that would be a lie. Over the next year, we saw numerous attempts at the local, state, and federal levels to eliminate and erode the tenuous protections that LGBTQ+ youth have. I also know that just because there are words in a policy, it doesn't mean that our kids are safe. We have witnessed numerous attempts to ban queer-themed books and censor teachers and parents who support LGBTQ+ kids in our schools. There have been times we have felt isolated only to find so many other families through PFLAG who were following a similar path. PFLAG has offered us an opportunity to connect individually with other people unlike many national or state-wide advocacy groups that don't have the bandwidth to offer this type of individual support. PFLAG offers a community where you can share ideas and I've come to love and respect all the members of my local group and the national organization as a whole.

Elliott is doing well and is supported by me and his mom, but there are so many kids who don't have family support. I want these kids to be heard and to feel some hope—hope is a powerful thing and can save lives. Those who can't live their authentic lives right now need to see that there are people out there fighting for their right to live safely.

Dear parents of LGBTQ+ children of all ages, the first step is to listen to your children. Your child isn't obligated to share any information with you, so their choice to share such a personal aspect of who they are should be treated with the respect it deserves. It is not the responsibility of anyone in the queer community, including your children, to educate you. They'll have a lifetime of continuously having to educate others, so the least you can do is seek out information on your own.

If you don't understand, do the research. I'm not talking about seeking biased information on social media—go to your public library and get a book. Ask a local PFLAG chapter for some resources to help answer questions. Go to one of their support groups online if PFLAG doesn't have a chapter near you. Your kid seeing you reading a book or an article about how to support them will speak volumes about your commitment and love.

It's too bad kids don't come with an owner's manual, but if they did, it would be a million pages long. The most important thing to remember is that the moment before and the moment after your child comes out to you, they are still the same person. Some things may change like pronouns, first names, or choice of clothing, but they are still your children, worthy of your love and protection forever. Our work as parents is never done!

Jennifer Bertrand
(*she/her*)

stay-at-home mom, retail associate, LGBTQ+ youth advocate

I'm Elliott's mom. I was born in the 1970s and raised Catholic. I consider myself a Christian but not religious, although we baptized our children in the Lutheran Church. I believe we will all be judged when our time comes, and I intend to be judged on my kindness.

Early in my childhood I knew my uncle Danny was gay. I didn't really know what it meant, but I knew the word gay, and I knew my uncle Danny was a fun guy. I saw him mostly at family events—reunions and weddings—because he lived in California, and we lived in Georgia. Danny passed away about a year before my youngest child was born and if the baby were a boy, he would have been named after Uncle Danny.

Little did I know that I did have a child with the middle name Daniel; I just wouldn't know it for almost fifteen years. Elliott Daniel is now in college and about to embark on a whole new journey, even more of a journey than these past three years have been since he came out as a trans man.

Elliott as a child was, to put it mildly, a pistol. I can remember the only way to get Elliott asleep for a nap as a baby was for him to fall asleep in his swing, and I learned to take the quickest showers in history. He was a very active baby! He was always very independent, always wanted to do everything himself.

When he was six, Elliott was diagnosed with bilateral permanent hearing loss, proving that for the previous year, he really couldn't hear us instead of pretending not to hear us. Parents of the year, right here! Oops. He compensated for not being able to hear by reading anything he could get his hands on.

We moved down to Florida and Elliott went to a new elementary school, where he was a cheerleader and played on the soccer team. Elliott had long wavy hair during his entire childhood, but in middle school he asked me to get it cut off into a pixie style. He compromised with me and went shoulder length and then went to a pixie cut a month after that. His hair, his choice! He started asking for more masculine, comfortable clothing and we got it for him. Elliott asked for a binder before entering high school and we got it for him. We were surprised, as we didn't know what a binder was, but Elliott had done his research and convinced us he would wear it safely.

In Elliott's freshman year, Randy and I could see he was struggling with something. Honestly, I thought he was going to tell us he was gay. He was very emotional, even to the point of crying, as he told us he was pansexual. He explained to us that he didn't care what gender a person was but how they made him feel. It made total sense to us. He was relieved that we were okay with that, and I could literally see some of the weight lift off his shoulders.

About two weeks after that, he came and asked to speak to us privately again and was emotional once again. He could barely get out the words to tell us that he felt he had been born into the wrong body and identified more as a male than a female. He was so worried that we wouldn't accept him for who he truly is and would deny his reality.

I'll admit it, I didn't fully understand at first and it took time for me to wrap my head around what that meant. He asked us to start calling him by a different name—he had already chosen his name after trying out a few names with friends, as he had been out to them for a while. He asked to be called Elliott, or Eli if that were easier for us. Also, he wanted to start going by he/him pronouns.

I asked Elliott what had changed from two weeks earlier when he had come out as pansexual. He responded that he had hoped to make things easier for us! This wonderful, quirky child was worried about making things easier for his parents all the while worrying himself sick that we wouldn't accept him.

Randy and I began to honor Elliott's wishes, correcting each other when we slipped with his name or pronouns. Elliott also gently corrected us. We changed Elliott's contact information in our phones so that we could see his chosen name whenever he called and get used to using it more consistently. My husband began diving into anything he could get his hands on to read and better understand how we could help support our son. Elliott's older sister accepted him immediately. That's the younger generation for you!

Elliott wanted to keep his transition private for the time being and we followed his lead. We initially asked Elliott to wait until he was eighteen to make any permanent changes, like making his new name his legal name or going on hormone therapy. But as time went on, we could see how this waiting was negatively affecting him. We also realized that as his sister was graduating high school that year, our extended family needed to be told, as some family members were coming to the graduation, and we didn't to deal with any negative responses at the celebration.

Elliott was able to tell one set of grandparents in person as they spend time in Florida each year. We helped Elliott through coming out to them, and while it was more difficult for them to understand what *transgender* means, they love their grandchild deeply and promised him that they would honor and use his name and correct pronouns. Sometime later, his grandfather admitted that he didn't understand what made Elliott decide that he was a boy, but the relationship with his grandchild was very important to him and he didn't want to lose that.

I wish I could say it went as smoothly with my mother; my father had passed away two years before Elliott came out. My mother struggled initially, and it got way worse before it got better. I won't go into details, but at one point, we had to explain to her that if she continued to disrespect Elliott and use his former name, or deadname, we would have to decide how to proceed. That was a wake-up call, and three years later it still isn't perfect, but it's so much better.

My three siblings initially insisted that we explain why and what it meant instead of doing some reading and research on their own. This caused friction and wasn't easy. They did refer to my son as Elliott right from the start, but anytime they asked about him and I tried to explain, they immediately went to their refrain: "We don't know enough about it to understand, so we won't comment." I finally just stopped trying. It was easiest for everyone.

In October of 2019, Elliott asked us to take him to River City Pride in Jacksonville. Though we didn't know what to expect, we thought, "Hey, we can do this for our kid." Just wow! We immediately saw the weight of what was happening with the investigation at school drop off Elliott's shoulders. I have never in my life seen so much love, color, and acceptance in one place. There was absolutely no hatred, no opposition. Just the pure joy of people living and expressing who they are. I wore a "Free Mom Hugs" t-shirt, and I've never ever given out so many hugs in my entire life.

The woman who opposed us at the December school board meeting was a local "ex-lesbian" pastor. She held a sign that read "Stop lying," and for her entire three-minute public comment explained that she lived her earlier years as a lesbian and activist, even ran a magazine for the queer community, but eventually found her way back to heterosexuality. Then she proceeded to call my husband and me child abusers and confused parents of a beautiful girl who needed to be regarded as such and was way too young to be making those kinds of gender identity choices. The school board members sat there dumbfounded, allowing her to say those horrendous things about us. One of the members even thanked this woman for her comment and for being at the meeting.

My husband got up to speak and simply asked them if the school board members still felt their policies were good enough. My son, who does not like to speak in front of anyone, came back in and spoke about how he knows himself better than anyone and asked them to please protect him and other students like him. I have never been prouder of anyone than I was of my son!

During the next couple of months, there was a rather lively atmosphere at the school board meetings. Peaceful and happy gatherings on our side, loud and aggressive opposition from the other side. I saw students get up and proudly represent themselves and other trans students who were afraid to speak out. I saw members of our community come out of the woodwork to stand with us and some who spoke out against us with so much hatred. And then Covid hit, and everything went into lockdown. Meetings were moved to virtual, and the board voted down adding gender identity to the list of protected categories by four to one. The one pro-trans voter on the board had spent some time researching the subject and realized that not all students were represented in the nondiscrimination policy. She requested more time for them to review the information, but she was voted down.

> **Our child challenged everything we were brought up believing. I've always tried to be the person that accepts everyone, no matter the color of their skin or their sexual orientation. It wasn't until my own child came out as trans that I, in my late 40s, even realized that gender identity and gender dysphoria existed. I'm grateful to my son for opening my eyes.**

Randy and I began campaigning for new school board members, as it was an election year. Two seats were up for grabs, and we were able to help flip one seat to a candidate with more of an open mind, someone who would at the very least listen to what we and others had to say and weigh all options before voting.

At some point, we had declared that our son was the face of our campaign, my husband the voice, and myself, the heart. By the time gender identity was voted on again in December of 2020, the face, voice, and heart were all losing hope, but we all vowed to keep going.

That meeting was torture to sit through and wait until the vote came up. At that meeting, a student member of the school board was given a chance to speak. She presented a community petition that well over 500 parents, students, and community members had signed in support of adding gender identity to the protected groups. The entire petition effort was student-led.

When the board members called for the vote, you could have heard a pin drop. Complete and utter silence. Three votes for and two against were cast in favor of adding gender identity to the nondiscrimination policy, protecting an entire class of children in our schools from ever having to endure what my son and our family endured. If not for the rule of no cheering, probably 75 percent of that chamber would have erupted into applause. Instead, we ugly-happy-cried and celebrated after the meeting adjourned. It was over. We and our supporters and fellow warriors had convinced enough of the board members that they needed to do better.

During this campaign we've met so many people, way too many to mention, who have become family. Someone told me during this battle that "the blood of the covenant is thicker than the water of the womb." I immediately wrote that down and still look at that quote every single day.

One new friend created a social media group so that we could all keep up with all the goings-on of the school board and our case. This group has grown into having over 600 members. Together, we have marched and paid tribute to the victims of the Orlando Pulse shooting on the fifth anniversary of that tragic event. We are growing stronger, and I can't wait to see what this year brings.

We now have so many fantastic people in our lives who are chosen family. Countless kids view our house as a safe place where they can be who they truly are and be respected for being themselves. We are not perfect, but we are trying.

The principal who didn't bat an eyelash at welcoming Elliott to his new high school was sadly lost to Covid-19. He didn't live to see the vote go in our favor, but we know that he knows. His physical presence and support are missed every single day.

In January of 2021, a friend from across the state and I discovered that we both had LGBTQ+ children. She reached out to me to tell me she had started a PFLAG chapter in their community. Despite the pandemic, they continued to grow their chapter and were recently recognized as the PFLAG chapter of the year. She asked us if we would be guest speakers at one of their virtual meetings and tell our story. Randy and I happily obliged and as result, discovered an entire new family. My friend invited us to participate with their group in Tampa Pride and we had a blast. It's amazing to see my child's eyes light up when he sees what might be possible in the future.

I wish people could see what acceptance and support of these kids can mean because the alternative is too horrible to even think about. My child, and so many others like him, are the same people they've always been. They just want their outsides to reflect their insides. Who doesn't want that?

My son Elliott has such a bright future; I can't wait to see what he does. As a mom, of course I worry that someday he won't be accepted—which is probably inevitable. I do know, however, that Elliott has the skills to handle himself and come out on the positive end of whatever life throws at him.

Ted Rau and Family

Ted. Photo by Jill Meyers

Ted Rau (*he/him*)

organizational
consultant

I was raised as a girl in Germany in a middle-class family with four siblings. I met my now ex-husband Jochen in Germany when I was only nineteen years old, fell in love, and a few years later, we got married. Soon after, I gave birth to our first daughter, Helena, and our other four children followed along.

I came out as a trans man four years ago: first to myself, then to everyone else. Answering the question "When did you know you were trans?" is awkward. Two answers are true at the same time: always and not until right before I came out. It turns out that I was in total denial for a long time. I thought other people were trans, not me. As time went on, I started to have conversations about my gender identity with my partner and close friends, but I held on to my belief that while I felt like the trans people I knew, I couldn't possibly be trans myself.

I had two breaking points; the first happened when I googled "How do I know that I am transgender?" In my search, I found the "button test." Here's how it goes: if there was a button you could press, and it would turn you irreversibly into the other gender with no social repercussions, would you press that button? I immediately felt angry because the test seemed so stupid. I thought to myself, "Wouldn't every woman press the button?" Then I asked myself, "Wait, are there women who actually want to be women?" I know it sounds hard to believe, but I had no idea. I assumed that hating being a woman was what every woman felt.

The second breaking point for me was when I said "I'm transgender" out loud for the first time. A close friend of mine was married to a transgender guy and was pressuring me to speak to him. When I finally dared to call him, I immediately started crying. He was great and waited for me to calm down. After several minutes of crying all I could say was, "How on earth can I reconcile all the years of not acting on my feelings?" He said something that I'll never forget: "Instead of beating yourself up and asking yourself why you didn't have the strength to come out, why don't you marvel at how powerful our society has been in keeping you silent?" That opened the door for me. I was able to forgive myself for denying my gender identity for so many years.

Everyone around me was supportive when I came out except my parents, who took a while to come around. In fact, the things they said at first were the most hurtful responses that I heard throughout my transition. Things like, "You will never look 'real' or be 'real' because you weren't socialized as a boy. You will never be accepted by men or women and therefore you will live your life all alone. You will traumatize your children and break up your marriage. The male hormones will make you aggressive." I guess my parents were worried and that's how their fears came out, but their statements hurt me badly.

My parents eventually came around. My mom saw me for the first time post-transition shortly before she died—her first reaction was surprise and pride that I looked good as a man. It took my dad more time to get used to me and find peace with my transition. He told me, "When you were a young girl, I figured you'd grow up into a woman. But I guess girls can grow up into men!" Perhaps I would have changed a few words in that sentence, but it was one of the sweetest things I'd ever heard from him.

My husband Jochen took my transition well. We had already separated, and I had fallen in love with my neighbor Jerry and moved in with him right across the common from my house. A few years after our separation, Jochen and I got divorced.

My kids took a moment to adapt to my transition, but they were all fine. Their reactions differed in the ways one would expect given their respective ages and personality differences. Some were a bit disoriented for a while. My hormonal transition was easy for them because they saw me every day and my looks changed gradually. Of course, my physical changes were much more dramatic for people who hadn't seen me for a year!

It took a while to figure out what the kids would call me. I didn't want to put my kids through awkward situations on the playground, so they switched to calling me Ted instead of Mom or Dad. Yet even that is not always so easy. For example, I remember my then twelve-year-old texting me: "My friend's mom just asked me who would pick me up, my mom or my dad, and I didn't know what to say because I can't say 'My Ted.'"

The kids go back and forth between my ex's house and my house, a one-minute walk across the common. Jochen lives alone with the kids, and I live with my cis male partner, Jerry. Fortunately, Jerry is bisexual, so he was fine when I transitioned from female to male. We had to renegotiate a lot of things, but our relationship wasn't very gendered in the first place.

My kids love to tell new people that our family includes five children and three dads. Unfortunately, they take more heat than I do, and it's sad for me to see them being bullied because of who I am. At the same time, I also know they are proud and happy for me and, for some of their friends, our rainbow family is cool! I guess I get some credit, especially among the teens, for being unconventional.

I am a much happier person now that I'm living as the man I always was. Before my transition, I used to wake up every morning with headaches. It was a ritual: get out of bed, take ibuprofen, go back to bed, and wait till the medicine kicked in, and then go about my day. My headaches stopped right after I came out.

Germany hasn't made it easy to change my passport from female to male. It's still in progress! Whenever I travel for work internationally and need to use my documentation outside the United States, I get pulled out at every checkpoint. The most difficult border crossing was in Germany, where I was passed on to supervisors who wanted to see each of my documents repeatedly. I guess a trans man traveling alone with five kids made them nervous!

> **Once, I was talking with some women who were sharing their birth stories. Since they didn't know I was a trans man, they assumed I had no clue about anything birth related. It was weird because I had given birth more often than any of them.**

Since I've changed my name in the United States but not yet in Germany, traveling outside this country isn't easy because I never know which name to put on a form. For example, when I fly from Massachusetts to Germany, I'm entering the wrong name in one of the countries either way. When I originally asked for help from a lawyer on remotely changing my name and gender in Germany, their response was that it might be easier to become a US citizen so I can get an American passport with my correct gender marker. I do worry about legal issues in the future for trans people in America, which is one reason I'm not becoming a US citizen yet.

My work is teaching consent-based governance, a governance system used in many cohousing communities. The teaching videos and webinars that I made when I was still presenting as female are still around on the internet, but they are slowly getting outnumbered by my new videos as Ted. It was quite funny, as people sometimes referred to the person with my old name and appearance in the video as a different person. Many folks assumed that we are siblings because we look similar and have the same last name. Sometimes I tell people; sometimes I just let it go.

The discussion about trans people using bathrooms is short-sighted. Take me, for example. When people hear that I am trans, they are blown away because I pass as a cisgender guy. Can you imagine what would happen if I walked into a women's restroom? It wouldn't make any women feel safer in there. If people can only use the bathrooms of their assigned sex at birth, we'd have a lot of male-looking people in women's restrooms. Is that what women want? Playing devil's advocate here, that practice would make it even simpler for cisgender men to go into women's bathrooms because it wouldn't be an unusual sight anymore to see male-presenting folks there.

I've spent years watching gender dynamics from both sides. Given the circumstances, I had the experience of being raised as a woman which shaped me to become the person I am today. I've been taught, like most girls, to be nice, kind, and to prioritize the needs of others above mine. I've spent years resenting overly confident boys and men. So, yes, sometimes I don't fully fit into the "man" box, and I am very skeptical of some behaviors that I witness in many men. It's good for me to have the trans man box to account for that difference. In fact, I started wearing earrings because I looked too much like a run-of-the-mill cis heterosexual man for my own taste.

I'm also highly critical of some typical feminine behaviors. For example, when I used to go to the library with five moody kids as a mom, I knew that other moms were judging me. I know that is true because I've been privy to conversations between moms. Yet if I walk in the library as a man with the same grumpy kids, everyone celebrates me for being such a great dad who takes his five kids to the library!

A woman recently confided in me she'd had a late miscarriage. I lost a child, too, in a stillbirth, but I couldn't say anything because I would have had to say, "I know what it's like because I'm trans and I birthed six children and one of them died." That's not a conversation you can have easily, since I look like a cis man! The fact that I'm never misgendered anymore creates an inevitable distance between me and other moms, even though I've had thirty-seven years living as a woman and eighteen years as a parent.

Jerry & Ted. Photo by Jill Meyers

Jerry Koch-Gonzalez
(*he/him*)

organizational consultant

Ted's transition began two years after we started living together. It took a while for him to shift his perspective from wishing he had been born a man to realizing he had always been a man. As he committed to transitioning, Ted had a lot of anger at what he called "the lost years." For me, I was lucky to be bisexual and I moved easily along with Ted during the early stages of his transition. The middle period was harder. In my mind, his journey absorbed a lot of his attention and I felt lonely until his transition was complete. Ted is now confident in his male body, and he looks great to me.

Ted and I have been together for six years. There was remarkably little tension among the kids when Ted came out. It made a huge difference to our family that we were living in a supportive community and that we had all witnessed a beloved young neighbor go through a female-to-male transition before Ted did. Becoming the secondary adult in his kids' lives has been both wonderful and the hardest thing I've ever done. The depth of my relationships with the kids goes by birth order. I'm closest to the youngest three.

Of course, I'm aware that in the wider world there is a lot of transphobia and fear of transgender people that can turn into violence at any moment. There is always a risk to be out for all LGBTQ+ people, and there are places where Ted and I can hold hands in public and places where we would never do that. Being in this book will make us more visible, but the contribution we hope this book will make far outweighs the risk, as it will help make the world safer for Ted, our extended family, and so many others. The real dream we have is that gender identity and sexual orientation will become non-issues.

What people need is to find ways of spending enough time together so that assumptions and stereotypes get replaced by actual experiences with real human beings. It is only then that we can realize that we are all seeking to meet the same universal human needs and that we are inevitably all interconnected.

Jochen Rau
(he/him)

father, engineer, software developer

My ex-wife Ted and I moved to our home in cohousing with our four daughters and then had Emil a year later. Three years later, we separated and got divorced a year and a half afterwards. We all still live in the community so our five kids can go back and forth easily, which has been beneficial for all of us. The divorce was difficult at first, but it wasn't that devastating to the kids since we lived across the street from each other.

> **Being trans is not just a feeling; it's way deeper. It's an identity and suppressing it can cause great suffering.**

Our older four kids had already dealt with a lot of change in their life when we moved from Germany to the United States and the divorce was just more change for them, so they were quite resilient. In any case, when Ted transitioned, there wasn't a lot of stress for us or in the cohousing group because we already had one kid transition in our community. Our cohousing community is a liberal bubble in a liberal bubble in Massachusetts. We were just incredibly lucky to end up here.

Every family is different, and it's hard to step out of what you've been taught for generations. If I were giving advice to an unsupportive family, I would be gentle and try to make them aware of the suffering their lack of acceptance could cause their trans family member. That's the guide as far as I'm concerned. I'm a Unitarian Universalist and we believe it's important to minimize the suffering of others and to increase their joy.

Helena Rau
(she/her, they/them)
high school student

When I first heard that my mom was transitioning to male, many people told me that they were sorry I was losing my mother. But I never lost anybody. You don't lose your trans family member because they've always been that way. Yes, my "mother" label for Ted is gone, but my mother is still who Ted was. He gave birth to me and that can never change.

When I describe my family to my friends, I usually say I'm eighteen, the oldest of five siblings, and I have three dads. Then I wait for them to guess how two of my three dads could both be my biological parents. It's quite a fun game.

I identify as pansexual, and I go by she/her pronouns. But I'm also transitioning into using she/they pronouns because I personally don't know who I am 100 percent. I'm part of the LGBTQ+ community and I came out to my friends more than a year ago and to myself, maybe two years ago. My family responded very, very well. I think they kind of already knew and they were very accepting about it. My friends were also accepting, so I've never really had issues with coming out.

You must listen to what the person who is transitioning wants to be called. There was a time when we couldn't use he/him pronouns for Ted in public because people would have been confused as he didn't yet look the way people thought a man should look. But that changed as Ted started to use hormones and other medical treatments.

Having three dads is not much different from being in any other family. Mostly it's just funny, because you have to put different names on each one so you don't confuse them all. Like, Dad, Dad, and Dad doesn't work. But Dad, Ted, and Jerry work just fine.

Sophia Rau
(*she/her*)

high school student

I'm sixteen and I have two bio dads, one step-dad, and four siblings. Having so many siblings can be difficult because there is only so much attention to go around. Having two dads who are my biological parents has made no difference in my life. It's totally normal for me at this point. I usually tell my friends something along the lines of, "I have two dads and a bunch of annoying siblings!"

I'm bisexual and a cisgender female. I have come out to people casually over the last year. It really was never a big deal, since a lot of my friends are also LGBTQ+. I don't talk about my sexuality at school much because I want to avoid negative reactions that some people may have if they knew. But the truth is that most people know that I'm bi already, which I'm perfectly okay with. I haven't heard anything homophobic from people at school, at least not to my face, and most people at my school are supportive of LGBTQ+ rights. I'm not in a GSA, but I try to voice my support for queer rights as much as I can to let people know I'm a safe person to come out to when they are ready.

> **The most important thing to realize is that trans and nonbinary people are who they are whether you approve of them or not. Why wouldn't you just want them to be happy if they are simply being who they are inside?**

I want other teens to know that being trans or being in my family is not as different as they might think. At first, I was in denial about Ted's transition, and it took me a while to switch over from "Mom" and she/her pronouns to "Ted" and he/him pronouns. But I've noticed that after his transition, Ted and I have become way closer. It's hard to get to know someone well who is not living as their true self!

One of my favorite things about our family is that we all have the same sense of humor and wit. I think it was easy for all us kids to support Ted because of how much happier he is now that he can express himself the way he wants to. I also think it is important to realize that Ted has always been a man, so nothing has really changed except how we refer to him and what he looks like. It's not like we were going out and getting our nails done together and now all he wants to do is go to Home Depot!

I'm thirteen and the middle child in our large family. When Ted came out and transitioned from female to male, honestly the most important thing for me was to make sure Ted felt comfortable. The hardest part for me was switching from saying "Mom" to calling him Ted or Dad. It took a bit of time to get used to it, but we all got comfortable with it. When Ted went through the physical changes, we all supported him, and we were all very excited for him. The surgery was a big deal. You can clearly see the difference between when Ted was seen as a woman and now. He is a lot more comfortable and more himself.

Antonia Rau
(she/her)

middle school student

I did get bullied two times because my dad is trans. A few people said things like, "Oh wow, it must be really weird to have three dads," but I knew that being trans wasn't fully accepted in society yet so I just accepted that some people would say things like that. I just ignored their comments. I think the bullies gave up after a while because I didn't react the way they wanted. They wanted me to get mad, but I didn't get as annoyed as they hoped I would.

❝ Transitioning is just becoming publicly who you have always been. I believe Ted's transition improved each one of us in our family and has helped us all to be ourselves. ❞

What I most like about our family is that we all are very different. We all have different interests, but we all fit together, and we have multiple things that we all do. Sometimes we just wake up and do art together for an hour or we watch shows together. We go on camping trips with my dad, Jochen, and we do a lot of family things like trips to lakes with Ted and Jerry.

Personality-wise, Ted has stayed the same. For example, in public you don't see many dads hugging their kids, but in our family it's a completely normal thing. Ted hugs us all the time and we hug him. Some people are still weirded out that our family is so affectionate, and we hug each other all the time and we share everything.

People need to understand that having a parent come out as trans doesn't impact the family as much as they might think it would unless the family members are not accepting. If you have an accepting family, it's not going to be much different than it was before. It's like another stage in life, like if someone in a family grows up and moves away. You lose a little part of them, but they still have their same personality, and you still can stay close, and you gain a lot more too. It's important that people understand that all of us kids still love Ted exactly how he is.

Julia Rau
(she/her, they/them)

middle school student

If I was trying to explain my family to someone, I would say I used to have a mom but now my dad is trans and he likes the way he is, and I also like the way he is.

I feel like people should be able to be who they are without being judged, even if a boy wants to wear so-called "girl's clothing" or if a girl wants to wear "boy's clothing." Some people think I'm a girl but then they look at my baseball cap and they think I'm a boy. But if they look at my eyes, they will think I'm a girl.

> " I like my family because we are different from many other families, which I think is a very good thing. Most families have a mom and a dad, but my parents figured out who they are, which is good. "

I'm like a puzzle piece that I'm holding and trying to find where it goes. I've been bullied because other kids can't always tell if I'm a girl or a boy. I sometimes feel like I can't fit anywhere. I like to play basketball because I get a lot of exercise and I feel great when the ball goes in the hoop, but at my school I'm the only girl playing basketball during recess. Some kids have tried to make me feel like I don't belong anywhere. I want to figure out who I want to be, too, so I won't feel as lonely as I usually do now.

When someone bullies me or someone else, I say, "Why does it matter to you? What's your problem? Why are you making fun of me? Are you trying to be cool or are you trying to hurt me?"

Ted and Jerry are a great pair because Jerry really understands my dad Ted and helps him figure out his way through life and how he's going to represent himself. I call Jerry "Jerry Berry" or "Jerry Bear," and I call Ted "Teddy Berry" or "Teddy Bear."

If a kid asks me if I have a mom, I say, "No, I don't have a mom. Is there anything wrong with that? Should I change my family so you can think I'm cool?" I'd rather not be cool and have my family just as it is. I like having a family that is different from other families.

back: Jochen, Emil, Antonia, Jerry, Helena; front: Sophia, Julia, Ted
Photo by Jill Meyers

Emil Rau
(*he/him*)

elementary
school student

I'm the youngest kid in our family and the only kid who's a boy. I have four sisters. At my school, there are girls who always play with trucks in the sandbox when we go out to the playground, and lots of boys do that, too. It's really cool how boys and girls play with trucks, not always girls playing with dolls and boys playing with trucks.

I can explain the trans flag, which is blue, pink, and white in the middle. The white stands for being trans or nonbinary and the blue stands for boys and the pink stands for girls.

Anna and Riley Lange

Anna. Photo by Robin Rayne

Anna Lange
(*she/her*)

deputy sheriff,
parent

I was born fifty years ago in Atlanta, Georgia. My family of origin consists of my mom and my dad and my older brother. My ex-wife and I had a son, Riley, who is eighteen, and he and I spend a lot of time together.

At such a young age, I remember thinking I should have been born a girl, but I played typical boy games and I loved sports. As I got older and went to high school, there were things about me that I realized weren't stereotypically male. However, no ray of sun ever tapped me on the shoulder and said, "Hey! You're female!"

My sense of disconnection with my assigned gender got more apparent to me as I got older, but I still couldn't put it into words. At first, I thought, well, maybe I'm a cross-dresser, as I liked wearing women's clothing. Sometimes I thought that maybe I'm just gay and haven't accepted it. You have so many emotions that you go through when you're trying to figure out your gender identity. Of course, we didn't have computers or the internet when I was younger, so I didn't know there were tons of other people who felt exactly like I did. I'd go through this cycle of exploring those feelings and then putting them away out of shame.

I continued my life as a straight man, but after marrying my wife, my feelings of gender discomfort were getting stronger to the point that I was getting depressed. I started doing some research, and when I read about transgender people, I said to myself, "Well, that's pretty much me right there." I came out to my wife and told her of my lifelong struggles with my gender identity, but that I wasn't sure if I was going to transition or not. She was supportive at first, but it placed a heavy burden on our marriage.

When I was still married, I confided in my brother that I was trans but that I probably wasn't going to transition. He said if I didn't tell my parents, he was going to tell them. Both my wife and I begged him not to say anything. I told him I was not planning on transitioning right now as I was still trying to come to terms with everything. He gave me an ultimatum to tell my parents by this date or he was going to tell them. He ended up outing me to my folks.

It was devastating for me because he was my best friend, someone I trusted and looked up to. After he outed me, our relationship hasn't been the same since. My parents wanted to have a big family counseling session, so off we went to Atlanta and had one session that was awful. However, on the positive side, the therapist told my brother that he had done the absolute worst thing by outing me to my parents. The therapist tried to make my brother and my parents understand that if a person feels the way I felt about my gender identity, no one can change it.

The relationship with my wife also did not survive. We ended up divorcing a few years after I confided in her. I could not be the husband she wanted me to be, but I was going to do my best to be a good dad to my son. A few years after I was divorced, I was hit by a car while I was riding my bicycle. I sustained some pretty bad injuries, and I remember being angry that I wasn't killed.

It took a year to heal physically, but mentally I was in bad shape. I was drinking alcohol daily, whereas before I wouldn't drink on the days I had my son. One day, he looked up at me and said, "Dad, you sure do drink a lot." That moment will forever be etched into my mind. What kind of example am I to my son? It was a wakeup call but one I needed. I realized just how depressed I was, because wishing you had been killed by the car that hit you isn't exactly the healthiest of thoughts.

I always promised myself that if my depression reached the level that I was considering suicide, I had to explore transitioning. I realized I had reached that point. When I accepted the fact that I was transgender and there was nothing I could do to avoid it any longer, I crumbled to the floor and sobbed uncontrollably. My life as I had known it was about to be turned upside down. Every day I told myself, "I'll find some inner peace one day at a time."

Once I started hormone therapy, the first thing I noticed was a sense of calmness about me that I had never known before. That's when I knew that transitioning to female was what I absolutely needed to do. I was finally looking forward to waking up every day.

When I divorced, we split custody of Riley half and half. He was around eleven when I came out to him that I was transgender. I explained it in a way an eleven-year-old could understand. The first thing that Riley said to me was, "Can I ask you a question? Are you going to act weird when we go to the grocery store and it starts raining? Are you going to worry about your hair like Mom does?" I started laughing and said, "No, I think we'll be okay! That's not going to happen." Now several years later, I freak out like his mom, but I'll never admit that to him. His only other concern was being bullied at school. A valid fear for sure, and I felt bad he should even have to worry about that.

When I came out to Riley, I tried to reassure him that I was still going to be the same person for the most part. Your job as a parent is to give your child security and confidence and to make them feel like things are going to be okay. Even when you're terrified, you try to convey that it won't always be easy, but in time, it will feel better. I think Riley realized that I wasn't going anywhere.

The younger generation, even here in Georgia, just kind of roll with the punches. I've met several of Riley's friends and being trans is just not a big deal to them. Riley still calls me Dad at home. But if we are in public, he calls me Mom to avoid other people's confusion. I have not forced Riley to call me any specific name and I wouldn't unless we were in a dangerous situation for him or for me.

Quite a few years before my transition, I graduated from Auburn University in criminal justice and started working in law enforcement. Law enforcement isn't exactly the most LGBTQ-friendly community! In fact, it is a very transphobic and homophobic environment in the middle of Georgia, where I work as an investigator in the County Sheriff's office.

There are no legal protections here for trans people, so I was very thankful when I came out at work that I didn't get fired immediately. In Georgia, your employer can terminate you at will for "no just cause" because transgender people are not a protected class. I first came out to a human resources person because he's a lot younger and I thought that he would have a better understanding of some of my rights.

I asked our human resources person if he would come with me to tell my boss, a sheriff in his eighties, since I felt he could answer some of the questions the sheriff might have. Where I work, nobody knew a transgender person personally until I came out, so there were a lot of misconceptions about what it means to be trans. Literally, there are no policies or guidelines at the agency to help a trans person navigate through their coming-out process. I was told straight out that I was going to have to have thick skin to get through it. I was advised, "Don't let it get so bad that you feel like you have to sue us!" My personal belief is the main reason I wasn't terminated is because they didn't want to be sued.

The sheriff gave a verbal order saying that nobody should mess with me or they would have to answer to him. But when he addressed my whole division, he said twice that he didn't believe in the whole concept of being transgender. Unfortunately, that set the tone for other people. Once they realized that the sheriff wasn't going to do anything to protect me, it opened the door for a lot of the things that happened.

In law enforcement, there's a lot of joking and camaraderie. If you make a mistake or do something stupid, you're going to get called out on it. That's just what we do. When I came out, I expected that I'd get picked on a little bit. That would have been fine by me, but some of my coworkers, including supervisors, crossed the line. I started feeling like I had a target on my back coming into work. I felt that if I made one mistake, that would be reason enough to get rid of me.

> **My county must have spent a million dollars already fighting against covering trans health care. I just can't believe that they've been willing to spend that much money when they said that finances was one of the main reasons they denied my claim. They've spent far more defending their case than it would have cost them to cover my surgery.**

On the other hand, I have some supervisors who didn't have any issues with who I am. In fact, most people at work, once they realized my personality wasn't going to change, didn't have any issues with me being transgender. They are not going to vocalize their support for me, but it was clear that me being trans didn't really affect them as long as my quality of work remained the same. The only time I've ever received a complaint about being trans was when I was working a homicide and the suspect's mother complained about me. It felt awful because I was just trying to help this family.

When I did officially transition, my parents were the last people to find out. I knew if I had told them first, they would have given me a hard time about telling the folks at work. I was sure they would have said, "You're going to get fired if you come out," and I just didn't want to deal with their negative advice. Transitioning was stressful enough. When I did finally come out to my parents, I told them that I'd been taking hormones for over six months and that I had already told my boss and coworkers. They were shocked to find this out.

By this time, I had kind of patched up my relationship with my brother, but when I told him I was in the process of transitioning, he said, "I just don't really see where our relationship is going to go." I told him, "I'm comfortable with who I am. You're the one who has the issue." But every time I tried to talk to him about who I was, he would say, "Hey, I want to read some scripture to you." I just didn't want to hear it. Finally, I said, "You either accept me or you don't. Every time you call me, you try and belittle me to a point that I'm just done with it. You don't have to like what I'm doing, but you can respect me enough to treat me decently. When you can do that, you can call me." Since then, we talk very rarely, and when we do, it's just small talk.

Since then, both of my parents have made a lot of progress. They both use my chosen name now; pronouns are still a little iffy sometimes but at least they're trying. I am thankful because there are parents still out there that turn their back on their own children. I still have a good relationship with my parents. I see them quite often, and I talk to them probably every other day—more so with my mom than my dad, but I still get along with my dad. They're not very religious, but they are both very conservative politically. It can be frustrating to see them back a candidate who is voting for and advocating for legal ways to discriminate against the LGBTQ community.

My dad used to be the county commissioner. One time he told me, "I have local constituents, so I can't pass any laws in the county to protect LGBTQ people." That's Georgia for you! Even same-sex marriage wouldn't be recognized in Georgia had it not been for the federal government passing the Marriage Equality Act.

I sued the county about health insurance coverage for my medical transition. Turned out that there's an exclusion in my work health insurance policy for transgender health care. When I discovered this, I did some research and found a clause in my policy that said that Blue Cross Blue Shield could amend the policy to be equal to the applicable federal law. So I was thinking that since Obamacare had passed, it has been illegal to discriminate against trans people.

I called the insurance company to see if I was covered and suggested that maybe they hadn't given me an updated policy plan. They told me I was covered for gender reassignment surgery! Then I contacted the surgeon that I had chosen and had her office call because physicians deal with insurance companies all the time. I wanted her office to verify that I was covered, and they were told I would be. I flew up to New York and had my medical consultation and was given a surgery date. After the consult, the doctors are required to send the official pre-authorization form to the insurance company, and that's when I got turned down. My insurance company said I wasn't covered because of the original exclusion.

I told them that I wouldn't have flown to New York to see this doctor had she and I not been told that I was covered. My only option was to appeal the decision, but thankfully the hospital in New York City has an LGBTQ liaison who works for them. Not only did I send my appeal letter to the insurance company, but I also sent it to the doctor and to the LGBTQ liaison. They read it and said that they knew someone who could possibly help me. Until then, I felt powerless because if you appeal these cases directly to the insurance company, you have no voice. I didn't have the resources to afford an attorney, so how was I going to fight it? I desperately needed some legal help, and that is when I was introduced to the Transgender Legal Defense and Education Fund (TLDEF). In 2019, we started litigation with their help.

My lawsuit became very public. Everybody around here knows about it. And most of the people that I work with point blank told me that I was going to win my case. It baffles me that the sheriff's office fought this because cases very similar to mine had been won or settled in the courts across the nation. Nobody from the county government or Sheriff's Office was willing to stand up and publicly say to just add trans healthcare and be done with this. I believe their thought process was, "Heck no, we ain't paying for that and you aren't going to tell us what to do in our county."

The day I found out I won my case, I was at home packing for an out-of-town tennis tournament. My attorney called and asked if I had a few minutes to speak. I told him sure, that I was on vacation and at home and had all the time in the world. That is when he said, "Let me be the first one to congratulate you for winning your case!" I just started bawling and couldn't even speak for what seemed like forever. After nearly four years since I was denied gender-affirming care, this nightmare was finally going to be over. Not only would I be able to receive trans healthcare, but so many others in the Southeast would benefit from this decision. It was a huge victory.

The defense from Houston County and the Sheriff's Office as to why they denied this healthcare coverage was cost to the taxpayer since our healthcare plan is self-insured. Their research stated the procedure I was seeking would have a one-time cost of about $26 thousand. I was shocked to learn the county had spent close to $1 milllion defending their stance. The real reason they have fought this case is pretty evident.

The elation of winning the case was overshadowed by the possibility that Houston County and the Houston County Sheriff's Office would appeal the decision. A judge has now ordered a jury trial to determine if the county and sheriff's office intentionally discriminated against me. A trial was held and a jury of my peers found that there was intentional discrimination and awarded me $60 thousand. The judge also ordered an injunction forcing the county to remove the transgender healthcare exclusion. I have a surgery date of December 15, 2022. Even after the verdict, the county has filed an appeal and ask the court for a stay in the injunction. It is a race to see if I can have surgery before a decision is made by a judge to grant the stay.

On a positive front, I started playing tennis three years ago on a local women's team and my teammates have been super supportive. One team here tried to get me kicked out of the league, but what's great about the USTA is they have a fair play all-inclusive rule. So regardless of whether I'm trans or not, I'm allowed to play. So here I am, and my teammates have really stuck up for me. Even opponents that I've played against have been fine. I've lost some tournaments, of course, which certainly helps as no one on an opposing team can say that I have an advantage when their team-mates beat me!

Our area is very conservative, and my son Riley didn't know any other out LGBTQ+ people when my lawsuit first became public and made the news. I think a lot of the pushback that he got was from his friends' parents talking about it. And then it trickled down to him because at that age when parents speak, most kids will kind of mimic what they say. Riley got picked on a lot at his middle school because of me. That was certainly tough for him and for me.

Over the years, Riley has been growing very strong and seeing his work ethic makes me proud. And most important, my son is a very kind person and he's growing up to be a fine young man. Whatever Riley puts his mind to, he will do well at. My son has had my back since day one. I feel kind of like it should be the other way around; I should have his back.

After all I've been through, I'd like to tell young trans and nonbinary youth: you're going to be okay. Obviously, if you're getting kicked out of your home by your parents, that's a whole other world that I never had to experience. I can't give you advice for that. But don't spend your whole life worrying about what people are going to think or say or do about you. At the end of the day, no matter what anybody has said or done to me, I finally have found peace within myself. And that's the most rewarding thing that you can give yourself.

Anna & Riley. Photo by Robin Rayne

Riley Lange
(*he/him*)

high school student

At first when Anna, who was my biological dad, came out to me about being trans, I didn't know a whole lot about it. I was in seventh grade at the time. We were sitting at a kitchen table, and I was kind of shocked because I'd never been around anyone trans before. Honestly, at first, it was scary, and I didn't know what to do. I was worried about getting picked on because I had been picked on before for other reasons. Over time, I relaxed a bit.

The main reason that I was so scared at first was that I thought that my dad was going to be gone from my life, but that wasn't the case at all. A father figure is often seen as passing down morals about how you treat people and helping you to develop your character. But Anna does that with me. What I admire the most about Anna is that she has never failed to be my guide.

I'll put it this way: People are going to say stuff and make fun of you, but you just have to deal with it. At first, I didn't really understand, and I would get mad when people would say things and pick on me about Anna being trans. But as I moved through school and through the years, there was a group of close friends that I stuck with, and they understood and are just awesome about it.

> **What I admire the most about Anna is that she has never failed to be my guide.**

When someone comes out, you find out who your real friends are. Even if your family rejects you, you need to find that group of people—or even one person—who supports you and stick with them. Maybe it's different up North than it is down South, but I mean, people are going to say stuff, maybe especially down here. But as I said, you've got to have tough skin, and eventually people mature, and they'll just stop talking about it.

I had a few teachers I knew would not agree with Anna's transition. And then I had teachers who were very supportive and told me that they were there for me if I ever needed their help. One of my teachers surprised me. I thought she was very conservative because of the way she taught, and I wrote an essay for her class about how my dad had impacted my life. And this teacher pulled me out in the hallway the next day, and she said that my essay made her cry and that she had learned a lot from what I wrote.

Some of Anna's friends became like a second family to me. We would go over to their homes for gatherings, and it felt good to be surrounded by people who understood. Truthfully, when she came out, it opened my eyes to a lot of amazing people and a lot of amazing experiences.

I decided to tell people instead of keeping it a secret because I didn't want Anna to not be able to come to my school functions or my sports games or anything like that. It was a hard decision to tell people, but I think it's the right decision because if you keep it a secret, down the road, it's going to blow up and then everyone would freak out about it. I think that if you tell people casually, you might hear, "Oh, I already knew that and it's not a big deal."

Anna and I like hanging out together at the house. We've gone hiking together since I was little, and I've started on the Appalachian Trail with her. We spend a lot of time together on the trails and we go rafting down rivers. We both like being outdoors. I wrestle and, like Anna, I play tennis.

Right now, I'm taking a college class in US history where we are studying the antebellum period in the South, and I find it fascinating. I think all these political efforts to ban critical race theory or information about LGBTQ+ people in our schools are completely wrong. Everyone deserves to know the truth. Everyone deserves to know the real history of our country and how awful it was and continues to be for many people.

There should be laws protecting LGBTQ+ people because it's unfair to discriminate against them. Anna's lawsuit has been going on for a very long time, and it is very stressful for her. I can tell, and I don't like seeing that. Anna is a strong person to get through this. I don't think I could do it.

Anna spends her life, especially with her job, trying to help people. She helps the people who are against her lawsuit and try to hurt her. I admire that she continues to help all kinds of people. I think that's a great thing.

Robert Williams and Family

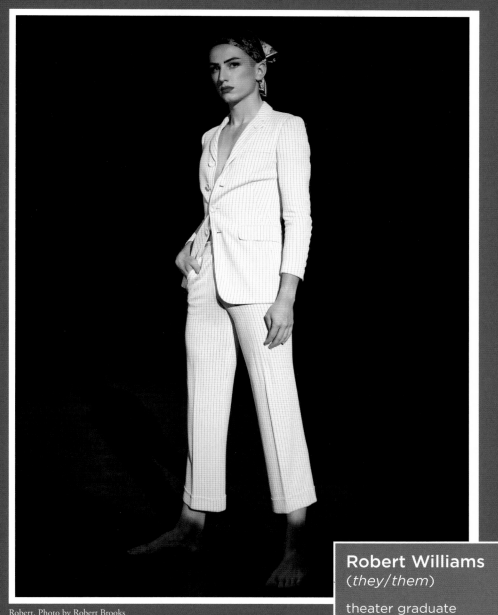

Robert. Photo by Robert Brooks

Robert Williams
(*they/them*)

theater graduate
student, drag artist,
activist

In preschool and in kindergarten, whenever I was asked what I wanted to be when I grew up, my answer was always the same. I would say decisively, "I want to be a girl." I would fawn over princesses and strong women in cinema and onstage and I wanted to be just like them living freely in my femininity.

Of course, whenever I said that I wanted to be a girl, my teachers looked at me with disgust and told me that it was not possible for me to grow up to be a woman. I confided my dilemma at school to both of my parents, who gave me free rein to live in my feminine euphoria at home, playing with Barbies and wearing dresses I would borrow from my sister or making my own haute couture gowns out of bedsheets and towels. Outside of the house, I would feel hurt that folks didn't understand me and meet me with the same embrace my parents did.

My mother always told me the best anecdotes about strong queer figures from the art world like *RuPaul's Drag Race*, and she would tell me about some of her close friends who were queer. Thanks to my mom, I had a window into a world of folks who lived unapologetically and knew I wasn't alone in my experience.

My earliest memory is from preschool, when the teacher sent me to timeout for playing with "girl toys." I thought, "Why am I being punished when I'm allowed to play with these toys at home?" Often I would find my sister on the playground during recess, as she would allow me to play with her group of friends. I felt safe with her and comfortable around her friends, and together they would protect me from the playground bullies who loved to pick on me.

In junior high and in the first two years of high school, my church friends gave me the most support to embrace my femininity. I'm fortunate to have attended a liberal Episcopalian church. During the school week, I cloaked myself in a false community, But I felt such relief knowing I could be my full self in Sunday youth groups and at weekend camp retreats. They gave me the strength to carry myself through the school week.

During my time at Mississippi School of the Arts, a residential art school for high school juniors and seniors, I became comfortable sharing my queer identity as there were so many other queer students living freely around me. I found a safe environment to dive deeper into who I was, peeling back the layers of protection I had surrounded myself in for so many years as a survival tool. But something still didn't seem right. I knew I was queer. But I also knew for certain that the gender assigned to me at birth was not my own. I kept this knowledge private, not yet having the full knowledge of what it meant to be a trans person.

In August 2018, I moved to New York City to finish my undergraduate degree in theater at Marymount Manhattan College. That summer I continued to question my gender. I felt somehow obligated to fulfill the gender assigned to me on my birth certificate, but I always felt that my image of myself was incomplete.

When I arrived in New York City, I began to experiment with they/them pronouns. At first, I was scared to even tell folks that I had switched my pronouns, feeling a sense of "imposter syndrome," as if those pronouns did not belong to me. My friend Nyesha allowed me freedom to explore, always encouraging me to discover new facets of myself. We held long conversations with each other about the intersectional politics of gender and the ever-evolving understanding of gender. Those conversations gave me clarity and, day by day, led me further to embracing who I am: a transgender nonbinary person.

One summer night after leaving a trans nonbinary group at the LGBTQ Center of New York City, I got off the subway and felt the need to call my parents. The first time when I came out to them as queer, it was like pointing out the giant elephant in the room. Even though I wasn't worried about their reaction, as they had expressed love for exactly who I am my whole life, I had never spoken about my gender with my parents. This evening was a little different. As soon as they answered the phone, I blurted out, "You two know I'm nonbinary, right?" It wasn't a request, it wasn't a declaration, it was a check-in to make sure that they knew what I knew about myself. I wanted us to be on the same page.

There was no resistance from my parents, only questions to me about how I wanted us all to move ahead. I informed them that my pronouns were they/them and that I would like them to use these pronouns from then on. We ended the call there, and I felt at peace and grateful that my parents accepted me through every part of my gender journey. My family still slips with my gender pronouns from time to time, but they always apologize and correct themselves. I understand that it is hard to break old habits. As much as I was adjusting to being an out trans nonbinary person, I had to provide grace for their adjustment too.

After I came out, my mother got very involved in her local PFLAG group. My mom was always an ally to queer folks, but she wanted to expand her knowledge about trans and nonbinary people. She swiftly became active, working with other parents whose younger children had recognized their authentic genders at an earlier age than I had.

My main advice for parents of trans, nonbinary, and gender-nonconforming children is to take the time to understand them. It's okay to be afraid, but don't let the fear of knowing who your child really is deter you from maintaining a loving relationship with them. They are still the same person. The only difference is that they have found a place of gender euphoria in themselves that they want to share with you. Meet them there!

When I returned to college in the fall, I informed my friends, who I hadn't seen all summer, about my *coming into* my actual gender identity. This is how I like to frame it, as I never had to *come out* because I was born queer and transgender nonbinary. I just had to *step* into it. I was filled with gratitude that every single one of my friends embraced me for who I am.

I thrived at college, as I felt comfortable being myself with my friends. A couple of trans and nonbinary and queer friends of mine even started a theater troupe called "Biscuits & Queers" to tell our stories about growing up queer in the South. We never mounted a full-scale public performance, but we held monthly art nights in a friend's apartment.

I fell in love with the spectacle of theater at a very young age and was infatuated with old Hollywood starlets like Bette Davis, Ginger Rogers, and Julie Andrews. So, of course, I wanted to emulate them onstage. But, of course, I was met with the same thing repeatedly when I would try out for roles in our school shows: I was too effeminate, too goofy, I couldn't sell a heterosexual love story, yada yada yada.

When I moved to New York, my goal was to obtain a degree in theater history and performance text and dismantle the binary gender system in terms of educational acting practices and the American theatrical canon. We already had queer stories, but I wanted to see what elements of drag could teach us. I was fascinated by the birth of drag in ancient Greece to prevent women from performing onstage. Over the years, drag evolved from a tool of the patriarchy to a tool against the patriarchy, with queer folks employing it as a way of challenging gender norms. With my theater degree in the field of dramaturgy, my plan was to work on projects building bridges between audience members and what they saw on stage. In my cabaret works, this meant showcasing a vast array of what constituted drag and what constituted gender.

My theater practices go hand and hand with my activism. After a few brutal years of anti-trans legislation and dysphoric stories in the news, I knew I wanted to create stories of gender euphoria to uplift trans and nonbinary folks. As important as it is to remain involved in the political process, it's also important to take care of my community because merely existing as a trans nonbinary person is an act of resiliency all on its own. My intention is to get a doctorate in performance studies to further expand my theory about trans drag performance. With this degree, I intend to work either in a higher education setting or as an artistic director of a theater to continue to expand what gender looks like onstage and in theatrical works.

With regards to my personal life, when I think about what a future long-term relationship with a partner looks like for me, I don't really have a clear picture in my head. If I meet someone, sure I'm for it. In the meantime, I have an abundance of love from my family and my friends, who I consider my chosen family. With or without a long-term partner, I know I have folks in my life who love me, so I don't feel alone.

I definitely want a child in the future. Not the near future, but in the future for sure. I'd even go for a single parent situation. I know my future child would have many aunties who will love and adore them, and I'm certain that my chosen family members would immediately become a big part of my child's life.

Slowly through the years, I've expanded my community. By doing so, I can now live fully in gender euphoria. The sense of belonging to a community has allowed me not to hide from myself. Gender is an ebb and flow. Gender evolves over time and can shift depending on how one sees oneself.

Trans, nonbinary, and gender nonconforming folks are not experiencing a "phase" or latching onto a "trend." We evolve in the same way all kinds of folks change over time. It's important to keep in mind that although we are currently a topic of public debate and highlighted in the media more than we ever were, this doesn't mean we are a passing fancy.

I think it's important for folks to understand that everyone needs time to figure out who they are. I certainly wouldn't want to dismiss someone who is sharing a part of themselves they recently discovered or acknowledged. Have patience, have humanity, and have compassion for trans and nonbinary people navigating who they are after years of living with an identity that was not their own.

Trans and nonbinary people cannot be placed in a box designed to fit in a cisgender binary system. It is important to introduce language that protects and recognizes us in legislation, but the end goal is to get to a place where gender is not a category that constrains us. Trans and nonbinary youth deserve the same opportunities as their cisgender counterparts. By creating environments where trans and nonbinary people are made uncomfortable in terms of using bathrooms and playing sports at school, we only further damage what could be a healthy environment for young folks to grow in.

> " Dismissal of trans, nonbinary, and gender-nonconforming people is trying to erase thousands of years of our existence. Our earliest documentation was in ancient Egypt! Our identities are not new, only new to those who have become aware thanks to mainstream media drawing attention to us. "

These efforts to protect trans and nonbinary folks are not for their benefit alone; they also aim to create a space for cisgender students to understand they live in a world with a wide array of folks. It is crucial to have education about our existence, it's crucial to create spaces where folks have equal and equitable opportunities. These changes will carry forward into everyone's adult lives; people will have better knowledge of the intersectional web that connects us.

My advice to young gender nonconforming folks is that there is no rush to find your authentic gender label. There is no rush to have a definite answer for family and friends. Figure out who you feel most comfortable with. Start there. Relationships built on trust will further support you in your gender journey. I know that in some scenarios disclosing your real gender identity to your family can impact your safety. If this is the case, find an ally you can lean on. Know that you are not alone in this experience, nor do you have to experience it alone. There are more folks like you than you think. You might be surprised by who you find along the road. Keep an open mind, and most importantly, do what will serve you best in your gender journey. Enjoy it, don't rush it.

Scott, Tracy & Robert. Photo by Carla McDonald

W hen I was pregnant with my first child, Tabitha, I was put on bed rest and, as a result, watched a lot of daytime television. I have held on to a memory of Bob Saget as a guest on Regis and Kathie Lee. He was asked about the news that he and his wife were going to be parents and did they know yet if the baby was a girl or a boy? His response was that it didn't matter because they had already decided to raise their baby as a girl. It was a quick laugh, a one-line joke, but I've thought of it a lot over the years. Most people do raise their children in a very gendered way, and I often wonder whether Scott and I did this with both of our children?

Tracy Williams
(*she/her*)

PFLAG Board member, activist

As an explanation for my world view, I sometimes tell people that I was raised by radical feminists. I do this in a light-hearted way, but there is a bit of truth to it. I have three sisters and my father would be quick to tell us that he wanted all his daughters to have every opportunity he was afforded. My father volunteered for the local NOW chapter and my mother still has the first issue of *Ms. Magazine*. My aunt, my father's only sister, went to

New York as a single woman to become a television producer in the early 1960s. I thought all women could do this. It didn't seem odd at all. With that as my background, I too, wanted my second child, Robert, and their older sister to set whatever goals they wanted. Tabitha was interested in sports. Robert loved theater and fashion. Scott and I worked to encourage both of our children to follow their passions.

Up to Robert's second-grade year we lived in South Carolina, and I knew Robert was not interested in the same things as other assigned-male-at-birth kids in their class. Robert was not going to have a favorite NASCAR driver or play baseball or soccer, and Scott and I were fine with that. Initially, I thought it was because Robert and Tabitha were only eighteen months apart and spent so much time together. Tabitha was social and wanted friends to come over. Robert did not have many close friends but hung out with Tabitha's friends. Again, it didn't seem too out of the ordinary, but I knew something was emerging under the surface.

We moved to Mississippi when Robert was going to enter third grade. New school. New opportunities to make friends. They still did not have a lot of close assigned-male-at-birth friends. I began to think that Robert might be on the LGBTQ+ spectrum, and I was preparing for the day when Robert was ready to "come out." Scott was too, I think.

Not long after we settled in Mississippi—a longer process than usual, as Hurricane Katrina created some hurdles for us all—Robert began to exhibit anger issues. We attributed that to the trauma of moving, evacuating, being homeless and temporarily homed, and moving again. We connected Robert with a counselor, which helped, but Robert was still dealing with some internal struggle. On a walk when Robert was twelve, they confided in me that they were gay. I accepted their statement as a matter of fact and thanked them for letting me know.

Before Robert came out, I had what I thought was a good bit of experience with the LGBTQ+ community. My mentor when I was a teenager was a local gay Memphis artist named Charles. I took his art class and I adored Charles and his sexuality didn't affect me at all. Later, I studied art in college, where I was in contact with many gay professors and students. When Scott and I were in South Carolina, we were members of an Episcopal church that was led by a gay priest, although I don't think he was officially out. The youth leader at the church was a lesbian. All this to say, I felt comfortable with gay people from early on.

About a year later, Robert recanted their statement that they were gay. During their teenage years, Robert was often angry and lashed out at me. As much as that hurt, I attributed it to continued internal wrestling with their identity and just being a teenager. I suspected the recanting of the coming out was not genuine.

Robert next came out at about age sixteen, after they had been away at Mississippi School for the Arts. The disclosure was in the form of a written letter and was quite emotional. I was so relieved that the internal struggle was going to begin to resolve for Robert, and Scott and I were both very accepting of the news. Robert seemed scared, and I was almost offended by that. It was as if they were expecting Scott and me to respond in a negative way or to be angry. I remember thinking, "Is that what Robert really thinks of me?" I discussed it with a gay friend of mine from church who assured me that Robert probably didn't think of us that way, but that it was a very emotional event and for me to just be grateful that Robert trusted us to love them. Neither Scott nor I were surprised or caught off-guard by the announcement, and we have continued to love Robert for who they are.

In 2003, when Rev. Gene Robinson was consecrated as the first openly gay Episcopal bishop, all our Episcopal church friends were thrown into turmoil. I remember feeling proud of my denomination as I had always loved the progressive stances of the Episcopal church, but so many opinions and emotions were swirling around me that I decided to seek counsel with a priest. This priest was the rector of a congregation that had a very high percentage of LGBTQ+ parishioners.

I was thankful that Fr. David Upton was willing to meet with me one-on-one and answer all my questions. I wanted the church to be affirming and inclusive, and I also wanted to know from someone with a seminary degree how scripture is used to judge the natural loving response to gay people. Fr. Upton debunked all the Old Testament passages that were being used to exclude and marginalize LGBTQ+ people. He reaffirmed that God is love. And that God loves all of creation and He wants all of us to respond to each other with love. That was all I really needed to know regarding Bishop Gene Robinson or anyone gay.

Robert's coming out as nonbinary years later was a little more difficult to digest. Scott and I didn't have much experience with trans folks, and I certainly didn't know the term nonbinary until it became part of our family experience. I had to do my homework, for sure. The adjustment to the new pronouns has been a learning curve too—it was having to undo a twenty-two-year habit. It has been a journey for me, and I want more than anything to honor the person Robert is.

> **" I've often said to parents of LGBTQ+ children that their religion, if it is rooted in love, will affirm and support their family. I then tell them that if their church is using scripture to shame, exclude, and marginalize their family, it's time to find a more loving church. "**

I first heard of PFLAG from a couple at our church in South Carolina. They had a gay daughter and told me about attending PFLAG meetings as a way of learning to support her and be better allies in general. I didn't have a need for the organization at the time but filed away the information. Flash forward to living in Mississippi and knowing I had a gay kid. Scott and I both went to a PFLAG group meeting and met the families and core group of members. I became friends with a trans woman and a family whose kid was going to transition. Nothing was theoretical anymore. I knew my kid and other kids were going to be helped by this group. I have stayed a part of it ever since.

In the past few pandemic years, our PFLAG chapter has made online connections with the Gulf Coast Pride events and the Gulf Coast Equality Fest. We take these opportunities to let families know we exist and that we are here to help them. We provide resources if they need to know about gender-affirming doctors and counselors, and how to talk to their school systems. I have been a Gulfport PFLAG boardmember for about two years now. Staying active with my PFLAG chapter is one thing I have committed to doing. Our group will continue to stay visible in the community and to make sure that the school guidance counselors have our literature to share with students and their families.

Scott and I are both proud of the person Robert has become. They have a passion for everything they do and have taken steps to advance their knowledge in so many areas. I love that they were self-assured enough to go to a residential high school so that they could more fully immerse themselves in theater. I love that they found a way to study theater in New York. I love that they have goals and work toward them. I love that Robert always stands up for other nonbinary folks and speaks out about gender identity.

About a year ago I was on a video call with alumni from my college sorority. I found myself in a breakout room with alumni from the 1960s. One of the women was telling her story of her life after college and spoke about her years of being married to a man and raising children, then getting divorced and her subsequent marriage to a woman. She told us that she is in the happiest chapter of her life. Before the call was over, she said, "Your children are not confused. Listen to them. They know who they are."

Scott Williams
(*he/him*)

reverend, parent, activist

Robert was a good-natured, smart child who enjoyed playing with their older sister, Tabitha. They both loved to play with dolls, and I never thought much of it. In my view, it was feeding their creativity. The summer before their junior year in high school, I noticed that Robert was acting differently and would snap at me and Tracy during almost every conversation.

After this happened several times, I called us into the master bedroom. I asked Robert what was going on, why was Robert so cross with us? After a few moments Robert tried to talk but was unable to. They started to cry and wrote something on a piece of paper and handed it to me. It simply said; "Dad, I'm gay. I love you." I told them to stand up and I asked, is that what this was all about? I told Robert, "You are my child and I love you." Big hugs! It turned out that Robert had been terrified that we would throw them out of the house as had happened with some of their gay friends. Robert was so much calmer after coming out to us and being accepted and loved. I felt the same when Robert came out as nonbinary some years later. I still have slips with pronouns, but I accept Robert unconditionally and they know that.

Jesus put it well: "Love your neighbor as yourself." Unfortunately, prejudice is learned at home, so to counteract it, I continue to communicate to government representatives and school boards. I believe we cannot let down our efforts and constant communication in a respectful way is the best strategy to get the message out.

Robert always appeared to know what they were going to do. When they were a young teen, they read a book about Walt Disney and said to me, "That's what I want to do, and I can to it better." Robert finished their undergraduate degree at Marymount Manhattan College, where they were in the top 5 percent of their class It will be fun to watch where their career goes. Robert is very responsible for a twenty-four-year-old and is determined to move their career along. It's a wonderful thing that they love what they do. Not many people can say that.

> **My most important advice to other parents who have LGBTQ+ children of any age is to just love them. Listen to their story about their gender and sexual orientation journey. Do not begin spouting scripture to them to make your point!**

My experience has been that some denominational beliefs are based on certain scriptural verses and not the entire biblical chapters. Using single verses from the Bible takes the quotation out of context. I would ask people to read the entire chapter with an open mind, pray about it, and see if God speaks differently to them. I believe with God's help, anyone can open their heart to understand that all of us are God's children, made in His image, and loved by Him in *agape* love. I deeply believe that God loves everyone, no matter who they are in any shape or form.

Lana Patel and Family

Lana. Photo by Diane Bondareff

Lana Patel
(*she/her*)

daughter, artist,
tenacious

I identify as an Afro-Indo-Caribbean trans woman born in New York City. I was born male on the outside, but I was always female on the inside. It just took time for me to align my body with my brain. I started my transition back in 2006 at the age of seventeen.

I was only three years old when I realized that I was a girl. I was in bed wearing a red shirt and it hit me that I didn't have the anatomy of the little girls I grew up with, and I wasn't allowed to have long hair or wear girl clothing. I owned my newfound revelation that I was a girl, but my family kept forcing me to adopt a masculine identity that felt foreign to me.

When I was around nine, my stepfather was watching the Jenny Jones talk show on television one day with my little brother and me. There was a Black gay couple on the show and my stepfather said, "Those guys deserve to burn in hell. These are the kind of people that I'm trying to protect you and your brother from." His words scared me to death and etched themselves deep in my brain. I knew right then and there that living as my true self would be nearly impossible.

I grew up hearing popular Jamaican dance-hall music, and all the rampant homophobia in the lyrics told me clearly that I wasn't accepted by my culture and community. The music was so infectious to dance to—until I allowed the words to register with me. The fact that musicians who openly sang about killing gay people were celebrated and given awards was terrifying to me.

Growing up, I researched and watched everything related to gender, whether it was about adolescence for cisgender kids or the rare program about trans youth. The encyclopedia became my best friend, and I learned about how trans folks at that time were treated through the mental health system. Being trans was considered a mental disorder. Through my self-education, I had learned about various gender identities and understood that I was a transsexual—the medical term for being a transgender person back then. I was thirsty for knowledge but didn't know what to do with all I was learning. I did know that I would need parental consent to proceed with a medical transition.

I came out when I was twelve to my eighth-grade teacher in an essay about what we did during the past summer. I had discovered my sexuality while watching *Queer as Folk*. While it helped me figure out my sexual orientation, this TV show lacked representation for transgender people. I had no idea how to navigate my gender identity at that time, so it seemed easier to deal with my sexuality. When I told my teacher, she was super supportive and connected me with the school counselor who helped me come out to my mom. My mom did not take it well, and she was the one to tell my extended family.

When I officially came out to my entire family, it was September 2001, right when 9/11 happened. There was so much going on in the world and so much going on with me. My being the first LGBTQ+ member of the family was a challenge for everyone. I was a trans teen of color in the South in an area that believed in conservative religion so deeply that there were churches on nearly every street. The LGBTQ+ community didn't have a safe haven there and my neighbors liked it that way. Luckily, my best friend was amazing and so accepting. She and her family were such incredible allies, and their support really helped me in the beginning.

My family was not receptive to counseling or support groups. Well, we went to counseling one time when I first came out, but we never went back. I think a PFLAG group would have been very beneficial for my parents as they could have used peer support, and I plan to encourage them to go now. Being Caribbean immigrants truly shaped the way my parents see the world and how they see me. Because homophobia and misogyny are rampant in the Caribbean, both of my parents were taught at an early age that you are supposed to hate anyone outside of the cisgender/heterosexual "norm." This made my early upbringing hard because I was worried that I would be disowned the moment I came out.

My mom and dad responded to my coming out almost as badly as I thought they would. It was a very tough conversation that led them to shaving my head without my consent and being forced to live pretending to be a boy for the next year. I felt a lot of shame in the beginning, and I needed to do a lot of healing. Many years later, after my medical transition, my parents realized how important it was to accept me because they could see I wasn't ever going to go back to living as a boy. I knew my truth and I've always honored my truth.

My extended family, for the most part, was not accepting of me at all. My cousins around my age saw me as inferior and the butt of jokes. I was told by my stepdad's mom that she "didn't want a 'he/she' in her family." I was told that I was going to be an ugly girl and that I would need thousands of dollars in surgery to be pretty. It was all foreign for them, and their comments made me feel further marginalized.

My parents decided that I would be better off if I moved in with my grandparents. They raised me as a Christian because my grandfather had converted from Hinduism to Southern Baptist Christian. Hearing anti-gay rhetoric at church every Sunday and Wednesday was horrible for me. I was also enrolled in the town's Christian high school, where I was constantly picked on. The kids bullied me to the point that I had to go the principal's office every week because I was accused of wearing makeup or whatever lie the kids told to get me in trouble. I was obviously not like the other boys in my freshman class of high school, and everyone knew it. They wanted me gone and they got their wish.

One day in November I was called to the principal's office, where I walked in to see my grandparents sitting with the principal. My grandmother's eyes were red from crying, and I was told I was being withdrawn from school. The principal told me, "I'd rather you leave than for parents to withdraw their kids from this school because they don't want their children going to school with a queer." I was given a cardboard box and escorted to my locker, which had "QUEER" written all over it in magic marker. I packed everything I had into that box, and I was later enrolled into a home-schooling program and put into conversion therapy.

Every Sunday I got dressed for church and sat with my "peers" for junior church, but it was the most isolating time of my life. I would sit by myself for four hours each Sunday because no one wanted to sit next to me. No one would talk to me or share their Bibles with me. The worst was that they all treated me like I had leprosy when they had to pass the offering plate my way.

It was the most terrible feeling, sitting in a place of God with people who preached Christianity but were not anything like Christ. I learned to distance myself from the religion, but I loved learning, so I studied every world religion to see if there was something better out there. I always found myself coming back to Hinduism and the teachings and stories that Grandpa had shared with me before he converted. I began to study the Bhagavad Gita and discovered that I loved Hinduism. I do have love for what I call real Christianity, too, but there is a great deal of trauma for me there. I've gone to church with my parents and enjoyed it, but Hinduism resonates much more deeply with me. I consider myself a Hindu now.

The cis women in my life during my teen and early adult years have been the best allies. During my senior year in high school, my best friend Lauren wouldn't let anyone mess with me, and my friend Christina and her boyfriend Michael always protected me. I was surprised that Michael, a cis man, went out of his way to defend me because I only knew cis men as my enemies. It was so nice to have a cis heterosexual man in my corner. These days, I have too many allies to count. I'm so blessed to be surrounded by many wonderful and loving people.

I felt out of place for most of my life until I started my medical transition. Surgeries have provided me peace of mind and have allowed for more access into cisgender heterosexual society. Being perceived by people as a woman has been a huge privilege given to me in the later part of my transition, and it was something I desperately wanted and needed in the beginning. It has allowed me to no longer second-guess myself and to live at ease.

Black trans women have the highest homicide rate in this country of any minority group. Being a trans woman of color opens you up to more discrimination and violence not just in America but also in the Caribbean and in many countries around the world. In some countries, people believe in honor killings and a family will agree to having their relative murdered because it's considered better to kill a trans person than it is for a trans person to bring dishonor to their family, society, and community. This was something I feared when I was growing up.

I'm so blessed to live in Los Angeles, which allows me to live free from constant fear. However, even though I'm perceived to be a cisgender woman, I'm still vulnerable because I'm a woman of color. I navigate both racism and transphobia and there's a big difference between a white trans woman and a BIPOC trans woman. Being a person of color shapes my experiences in a way that white trans women cannot fathom. I dream of a day where we eradicate racism and colorism.

I've had to learn how to navigate the world as a Black and brown first generation American within my trans and LGBTQ+ experience. It certainly hasn't been an easy journey, as there isn't a road map to navigating intersectionality. Marginalization comes in many forms. I'm often the only trans person in the room at big events, and often the only Black person. California has a smaller Black population, so it's understandable, but sometimes marginalization comes with being tokenized. Being perceived as a woman affords me the ability to enter spaces I normally wouldn't have access to, which is a good thing. But it's also a sad thing that trans people who are misgendered can have a much more difficult time finding acceptance in our transphobic society.

I work to overcome marginalization by calling folks out on their actions and educating them on how they can be true allies—how we can really work together to make necessary change. It's not easy, but I plan to continue the work. There are ways to be a better ally: Call out homophobia and transphobia when you hear it and see it. It's absurd that we call it a phobia when the result often is violence. In my eyes, it's a fear that stems from a lack of knowledge.

> **There is so much about me beyond my trans identity. Being a trans woman is a part of me but not all of me.**

My advice to allies is to be there for us, protect and defend us. We need you to walk next to us but even more, walk in front of us. Be our first line of defense. Open doors and opportunities and provide us seats at the table so we can make real change. Too many people call themselves an ally during Pride season but don't help us where it's needed. Don't be a rainbow sticker ally. Truly support us. Ally is a verb, not a noun!

As a Black trans woman, I see that the wider Black community could do a better job of acknowledging us and fighting for us. For every murder of a Black cis person, there are trans folks whose lives go by unnoticed. Speak up and speak out for us. Keep that same energy when our lives are taken. I especially want to see Black men uphold, honor, and protect Black women. All of us, not just the cisgender women.

I've worked as an activist in my full-time work for a nonprofit organization and in my volunteer work. I've left the nonprofit world as an employee, but I still advocate through my social media along with other volunteer efforts. I've supported pro-trans legislation in California, gone to rallies, and worked tirelessly to create access in the realms of healthcare, legal, housing, and affirming resources for my community. I am also on the Board of Directors of Parivar Bay Area, a nonprofit organization where we work to positively impact the lives of queer and trans South Asians both in the US and abroad.

I've had the honor of putting on various trans Pride events in the southern California area and each one was more special than the last. There's nothing better than seeing our community members come out and feel like they have a space that's just for them. Getting recognized for my advocacy work by two California congressmen was epic. All my hard work feels worth it when my community and my legislators recognize my efforts.

In my work life, I've been doing makeup professionally for MAC cosmetics since 2012. Makeup was always my passion and hobby but also my saving grace. It has helped me to feel confident and beautiful when I struggled with acne scars, and it has been so powerful for me to provide the same joy I've experienced to others who have sat in my makeup chair.

It's been twenty years since my original coming out and my family has progressed in their understanding by leaps and bounds. My relationships with my parents and siblings are still works in progress, but the good news is that we all get along well; there's love there. We just needed time to get to learn about each other. Truthfully, I was surprised when my mom and stepfather finally came around. The day they finally accepted me was one of the best days of my life.

My advice to youth is to continue to stand and live in your truth. Find your allies and hold them accountable for making sure you are supported. There has been so much change within the last six years, and I know greater days are ahead so that our up-and-coming youth won't suffer like I did. We all must apply pressure on those in power to make sure we all have legal protections.

My heart goes out to everyone living in states where there are anti-trans laws. They are inhumane! We are human beings like anyone else and deserve to be treated with dignity. Just as Marsha P. Johnson, a Black American gay liberation activist and a prominent figure in the Stonewall uprising, fought for gay rights back in the 60s, we need to fight now. There will always be someone to try to take you down, but you must realize deep down inside that you are divine and that you deserve to be here.

There is so much more to me than being trans. I love food, cooking, nature, fashion, plants, aesthetics, astrology, and the arts. I'm just a woman trying to live out her dreams while navigating my trans existence. I'm proud of having my poem selected for a poetry anthology. I'm proud of graduating at the top of my class. I'm proud of being a Florida State Seminole. I'm proud of singing at the 2021 Presidential Inauguration. I'm proud of performing with Demi Lovato and Noah Cyrus for YouTube Pride in 2021. I'm proud of being on CNN. I'm proud of being on my talk show, Girls Like Us. I'm proud of making it to thirty years old, and, yes, I'm proud of my journey as a trans woman.

Lana, Carlton & Patrice. Photo by Diane Bondareff

Patrice (*she/her*)

retired mental health worker, mother

I'm Lana's mom. I grew up in Brooklyn. Over the years, I worked in mental health with geriatric patients in a hospital while raising my kids. It wasn't a surprise when Lana came out to us about being a trans woman.

My husband Carlton and I were in denial, but we kind of knew it. We both were familiar with what being trans meant and we had put it under the carpet because we didn't want to admit it. My extended family kind of suspected that Lana was trans because they saw the signs. They were waiting for me to come out to them with the news, so when I did, they weren't surprised at all.

When Lana first came out, I didn't really respond to her at first. I wish I could have been more receptive but at that time in my family and in my Baptist church, being transgender was unacceptable, so I didn't want to accept it.

It took me some years to change and accept Lana being a trans woman, and at times it's still a little hard. I slip up sometimes and use he/him pronouns by mistake. It really took years for it to grow on me, but I accept her as my daughter now.

My relationship with Lana has been kind of distant because she grew up with my mom in Florida, but we are starting to get closer now. As Carlton and I have become more understanding, over the years, we've formed a much closer bond with Lana.

> **"** *I want other parents to know that you should accept your kids for who they are. Keep an open mind. Take it one day at a time.* **"**

I see that my daughter Lana has a lot of my qualities in her! Lana is very intelligent. It was a nice experience having Lana come home from California this year for Christmas as it had been several years since we had a visit. I feel that my relationship with Lana is very good now.

Carlton (he/him)
construction worker, father

I was born and raised in Kingston, Jamaica, and my work has been in construction. I wasn't accepting of Lana when she first came out, even though it wasn't really a surprise. I hoped she would move into a different direction rather than being trans. I understand now that this was not possible.

I wish I had accepted Lana sooner, but it wasn't until I started thinking less of my expectations and more about Lana's safety and comfort that I came to a better place. Accepting Lana is still a work in progress, but I would say that it keeps getting better. I think it was easier for our extended family who spoke more with Lana about her being a trans woman to accept her than it was for Patrice and me. As far as her younger cousins, we didn't really have to do much explaining to them. And we just introduced Lana to our pastor as our daughter and that was that.

As far as giving advice to other parents, we are still in transition mode and learning more ourselves. I'd want to say that full acceptance takes work. You need to get used to your child's transition. However, the most important thing is that you need to love your child unconditionally! Keep their feelings in your mind above all because their feelings are all that matter.

> **" I want other parents to know that it could be a life-or-death decision if you don't handle it right. Love your child! Carry the same love you had when they first came out of the womb, and you first saw them. "**

The bottom line is that Lana is our daughter, and we love her. Lana is ambitious, artistic, articulate, very intelligent, and humble. I like to kid around with Lana, and we laugh together a lot.

Thomas Family

Mack. Photo by Robin Rayne

Mack Thomas
(*he/him, they/them*)

college student

I was born in Massachusetts, raised in Rhode Island for the first three years of my life, and then moved to Freehome, Georgia, where our family has lived ever since in a house with my mom's parents. When I was about five, my parents adopted Montavious, who is an amazing person, just so full of life and vibrancy. Montavious came into our life at the perfect time.

From fourth grade to my sophomore year of high school, I was home-schooled by my parents. I feel lucky that I was able to stay out of the drama of public school, especially as I was in the process of figuring myself out gender-wise. I didn't feel different from other kids until I hit puberty, when stuff started going crazy for me in my own head. My self-confidence plummeted and I felt awful for so long. I didn't believe that I could accomplish anything or that I was worth anything. Nothing seemed to make any sense until I started watching YouTube videos about people who were trans and nonbinary.

I was assigned female at birth, so being anything but female was just completely unthinkable to me. Officially changing my gender identity was not even an option for me as I couldn't imagine putting my family through anything like that. It didn't matter if I thought my parents would be accepting or not. I simply thought that coming out as gay or trans would tear my family apart. Also, at the time, we had been fostering two kids for two years and we were planning to adopt them. I was terrified that if I came out, they would be taken away from us.

I was still identifying as female in high school until I came out to some people during my second semester of sophomore year. I didn't want to tell my whole school because I lived in a very rural and conservative area of Georgia, and I knew that wouldn't have been taken very well. There was only one other trans guy at my school and he wasn't treated very well. I was terrified.

To find my comfort zone, I ended up being a theater kid. When I told my friends in the theater group, they all welcomed me with open arms. Well, not all of them, but most of them. The first month after I came out to them, I was in a group chat with some friends and we were talking about *The Wizard of Oz*, the show we were putting on at my school that spring. Some guy we had never met before took one of my friend's phones and texted a bunch of mean things about how I was mentally ill and needed to go to therapy. Reading these nasty comments after I had just begun to come out solidified for me that this transition was going to be very hard. It didn't help that I had anxiety and was still very self-conscious.

On the positive side, after I transitioned and came out, I had a conversation with my theater director, Miss Valerie Bowem. She's amazing. She truly made me feel seen and gave me a platform to be myself. There was never a question of me getting a female role. It was always, "So, which male role can you fit into?" Her acceptance was instantaneous, and it was validating and felt great. I recommend to any kid who is struggling with identity or in the LGBTQ+ community to try theater, because it's truly such a welcoming environment. I became myself there.

Despite all my fears, I came out to everyone in my family in 2018. It was extremely hard! My dad had kind of figured it out because he's a pastor and I had asked him a lot of questions about what being gay or being trans meant to God. In church we had always been told that homosexuality was a sin, and the Leviticus verse that says that being gay is an abomination and that all gay people were going to go to Hell was quoted often. I was terrified of going to Hell and disappointing my entire family.

> **❝ I want to do everything that I can to make the world a better place for people like me so younger trans people don't have to go through the trauma that I went through. ❞**

One night my dad sat down next to me on the couch where I was crying. He said, "Are you crying because you're trans?" And I said, "Yeah, I am." I hadn't planned to come out to him that night, but it seemed like a pretty good time. It was terrifying. Then he said, "It's about time," and gave me a hug. Wow! I've been blessed with the best family. When I told my mom the next day, she gave me a hug and told me she loved me. She also told me she was confused, and that it was going to take her time to wrap her head around it. I said, "Okay," because it had been a tough thing for me to wrap my head around. If people are open about the fact that it's going to take them a minute, that's all that matters.

Since then, my mom and I have had a lot of conversations about being trans. When Mom asked me, "What does it mean to you to be trans? What do you feel like?" I said, "I feel like I'm the most comfortable when I view myself as a guy and when other people look at me and view me as a man. I don't feel comfortable in this female persona that I was given at birth." It took a while to get that point across to my mom, but after I started transitioning socially and telling more people in my life, including my extended family, it started to become more apparent how happy I am when I can present as the person I am.

My mom has become closely affiliated with the Mama Bears group on Facebook. We go to a Pride parade every year and my mom gives out free mom hugs at the end of the parade to kids who have been rejected by their families. So, yes, things have changed a lot in my family.

For a lot of trans people when they come out, there is a very long period when everyone is adjusting. In my family, coming through that adjustment period and the hard times of butting heads all the time has helped us become very close. Now that we've grown to understand each other, I believe that we can get through anything together.

It's not just my immediate family that is amazing. It's my whole extended family! I know how lucky I am. I want to tell everyone who finds out that some distant cousin is trans, please reach out and show your support. It meant the world to me when family members who I didn't realize cared about me gave me wholehearted support.

It took a little bit longer for my grandparents to fully wrap their heads around me being trans. In fact, I think that they're still wrapping their heads around it. I have a very special bond with my mom's parents because they helped raise me. I love them dearly and I know that they love me, a love which didn't change when I came out. It's just that we are still learning how to communicate and understand one another with my new identity. My dad's mom is amazing. I love her and she has supported me since I came out to her. I was terrified to come out to her because I didn't know how she would react, so I had my dad tell her, but she's been great from the start. And I like to think that my late grandfather would be proud of me as well.

I was attending church while I was in the process of coming out to myself. This church was very small, and we considered it one big family as my dad was a pastor there. There was a lot of support, but not for me once I started being perceived as different. One day I wore a suit with a blazer to church. I was so excited to wear it and I'd never felt more comfortable, but when I got there, I felt something shift in the way the people were looking at me. I didn't realize what it was until a couple of weeks later at my youth group's Bible study when someone was talking about how gay people are all going to hell because they're living in active sin. I left that Bible study group in the middle, and I was crying on my mom's shoulder for a while before she took me home.

My dad was the interim pastor at this church. I ran the sound board and I helped run lights during the services. It was a community that I felt part of, but it seemed like they didn't feel the same way about the lesbian and gay people who I loved. I needed to get out of the church because even though I didn't know who I was yet, I knew who my friends were. And I knew that it wasn't okay with me if my queer friends weren't welcome at my church.

After I came out, my dad decided to leave the church and become a missionary to serve the LGBTQ+ community. This work became my dad's purpose in life. Despite everything, it was hard for me to leave my church because I grew up with it as my church family. However, I'm so glad that I did leave because I was shunned there. Although I didn't fully realize that this was happening, it became obvious when I went back for a vacation Bible school theater production.

When I walked into the church that I had come to call my second home over many years, nobody in the congregation even looked at me or smiled at me. Nobody talked to me. I turned around and looked at somebody who I considered to be my good friend, and she made no eye contact with me and looked down at the floor. I knew at that point that I didn't want to worship the God they worshipped. Whatever God they claimed to serve didn't like me and didn't want me there. I feel sad for them because they miss out on loving so many great people.

Over that summer of 2019, I began taking hormones and started becoming more and more confident and comfortable in my own body. I had friends and a girlfriend. I was fully out socially, living my life as a male, and I was happier than I had ever been. I used male bathrooms without a problem at first. In fact, I made a point to mainly use the bathroom in the drama hallway because it was usually empty, and I knew everybody down there. Sometimes, however, I was in a class, and I needed to go to the bathroom, so I would use the boys' bathroom closest to my classroom.

At one point during my first semester of senior year, another student saw me in the boys' bathroom and reported me to the administration. In a total abuse of power, the principal brought me into a room and proceeded to tell me that somebody had a problem with me using the boy's restroom. He said that I needed to either use the female restrooms or use the nurse's or faculty restrooms.

I went home that day and cried with my parents. I was honestly shocked because I didn't think that anything like this would ever happen to me. My dad came into school with me the next day, and we sat down with the principal and told him it wasn't okay and that I should be allowed to use the male bathroom because I'm a male.

It was difficult to convince the principal that I should be able to use the male restroom. Finally, as we were leaving, he said, "You can use it, but try not to." Soon after, the superintendent of schools put out a notice that trans kids were allowed to use the restroom of the gender that they identify with. It was the best news I could have heard! But when he put it up on Facebook and I read the comments, it turned out that our community was outraged. Everyone was talking about how if I used the correct restroom for my gender identity, it was somehow going to cause their daughters and sons to get raped and assaulted.

The next day, the school board revoked the superintendent's decision. They said that there would be a town hall meeting later that week to have the community discuss what they thought about me using the male bathrooms at school. That week was hell for me. I still had to go to school. I still had to sit at lunch behind a table of students who talked openly about how much they disagreed with the superintendent's decision to let me use the male restroom. I heard what people thought about me. And I saw the way that my classmates looked at me and watched me to see if I went into the male restroom. I watched as classrooms got quiet when I walked in. It was hard for me to walk comfortably around my school.

The day of the town hall meeting arrived. I was at rehearsal getting ready for a show when I found out I was going to be escorted out the back of the building while the security officers watched the front. They didn't feel like it was completely safe for me to walk out through the front doors of my school because protesters were already starting to gather, and people were waiting to get into the auditorium to talk about me. It was very hurtful to think that people cared so much about preventing me from having my basic human rights respected.

I'm glad I didn't go to the town hall meeting because there was no way that I could have handled that amount of hatred in one room. There's a video up on YouTube of the whole meeting, but I still haven't watched it.

From what I've heard, it was brutal. The whole situation caused a lot of mental scarring for me because it felt like there was a witch hunt, and I was the one being attacked. That would be traumatizing for anyone.

There were many people who didn't want to hear my story before they made a judgment about me. I think I'm a very likable guy, and the only reason that people shouldn't like me is if they don't like my personality. I just want people to give me a chance, because I feel like a lot of those people who judge me simply because I'm trans would be pleasantly surprised to find out that I'm a very nice person.

Fortunately, many people came out in support of me and my LGBTQ siblings from counties all around ours. After the meeting, the principal told me I had to use the female restroom or the teachers' restrooms, most of which were locked and far away from all my classrooms. It was frustrating, and with the support of my parents we threatened to take legal action. Once we threatened to sue, the school ended up switching their position as, no doubt, they didn't want to go to court.

My situation at my high school with the bathrooms went viral. Fox News even did a whole story about it! The small county where I lived exploded. It was all everybody talked about because there's not a lot of stuff going on there. I decided to stick with my case because I didn't want any student after me to have to go through what I went through. That is still my goal.

Ultimately, I didn't pursue legal action because my lawyer advised against it for my own mental stability. I already had a lot of anxiety and PTSD, and I didn't think I had the mental stamina to go through a court battle. Ironically, the Eleventh Circuit District Court of Alabama, Florida, and Georgia was deciding on a similar case about a trans bathroom issue, so it also didn't make sense to pursue our lawsuit while that case was being heard. Amazingly, the court decided in the trans student's favor! Since that decision was handed down, trans kids are supposed to be allowed to use the bathroom of the gender that they identify with. That's terrific, but the high school that I went to still doesn't truly abide by that ruling. Even though the principal finally agreed that I could use the male bathrooms, COVID happened during my senior year, so they ended up basically getting a free pass out of the situation. The principal did support me in using my preferred name at the graduation ceremony!

I'm in college now, but I've heard from other kids at my old high school that they are experiencing the same issue as I did now that school is back to being in person. I don't know if their families are fighting back, but I'm guessing that the reason the school administrators are still getting away with flaunting the law is because nobody has brought it to their attention. Or maybe they do know that they are breaking a law, but they don't care because it's such a conservative area. My high school is in Pickens County, about an hour and a half north of Atlanta. It's 100-percent Republican. I even had a Stop Sexism bumper sticker ripped off my car.

I'm waiting to hear from my friends who are still in high school to see if they are being oppressed in this way. If so, I'm going to call the principal and discuss why it isn't legal to prevent trans students from using the bathrooms that match their gender identity. There are more out trans youth in my high school than when I was there. I was the president of the Gay Straight Alliance in my senior year when everything was going down, and I saw that a lot of the trans kids were scared to come out because they were surrounded by a bunch of people who didn't like them.

During my hardest days, when I was being attacked by the world for merely existing, I was lucky enough to have my ex-girlfriend by my side to help me through it. Her parents weren't supportive of me or our relationship and took their prejudices out on me throughout the entirety of our two and a half years together. She defended me to the best of her abilities to her parents, even as they threatened to pull her out of school and force her to quit her job. Although we are no longer together and things between us didn't end as smoothly as I imagined, I will always be thankful for the support she gave me during my difficult experiences.

I still feel scared walking into a public male bathroom because of the fear that I could get jumped. It was terrifying to know that not only was I a Black kid living in a rural white town in the south, which is already scary enough, but that I was also a trans kid in the spotlight because of the lawsuit. There sure are a lot of different things that come into play when it comes to how I interact with the world.

I got lucky. I have a great family. I have a great support system. But not every kid has that. Not every kid has a mom or a dad that they can turn to and get a hug. Not every kid has somebody who will accept them when they come out. In my view, the suicide rate among LGBTQ+ youth is so high because people are so ignorant that they inadvertently or purposefully hurt the ones that they love.

I identify as a bisexual, biracial trans man. That's a lot of intersectionality in one person! Being biracial is a struggle that I've had to deal with because it isn't fully understood or accepted where I live. Yet it's also an identity that I'm very proud of. And then I'm transgender, which is another identity that is very hard for people to wrap their heads around and accept. Trans and nonbinary people, in my opinion, are the most oppressed group. Yet I'm also a man, so I have male privilege. I'm also a very light-skinned biracial person, so I can pass as a white person and that has given me the experience of white privilege. I'm still coming to terms with my intersectionality.

I'm very outspoken when it comes to anyone but myself. That is a defense mechanism because it doesn't matter how loudly I have defended myself in the past; people still will attack me verbally. It's been amazing to have the allies that I have, because when I couldn't stand up for myself, they did, and I trust that they will always stand up for me in a heartbeat.

I'm not scared about college life. Going to college, I have the chance to present myself without being judged on first sight because folks already think they know who I am. I'm excited to be able to be myself and not be judged and potentially hurt based on how I identify. I'm excited to feel included and part of a community again, as it's been a long time since I truly felt like a part of a community outside of my LGBTQ+ community. I don't want to hide my past, but I don't want my past to define me. I want to be the person that I am now who uses the events from my past to become a better person.

Georgia State is the most liberal college in Georgia. It's in the middle of downtown Atlanta, a very multicultural, diverse, and liberal city. They have the biggest Gay Straight Alliance in the state, and I'm moving in with a roommate who is also a part of the LGBTQ+ community. I feel safe going to this college. I'm studying psychology, with a focus in younger LGBTQ+ people and neurodivergent individuals. Of course, I realize my career path is very likely to change frequently given that I'm still so young.

I'm very politically active. I have a lot of thoughts about what we need to do as a group, as a people, as a country. If I become a therapist, the community

I would focus on is one that I identify the most with, which is the LGBTQ+ community, especially young people who have dealt with trauma.

I want every trans kid to hear these words: You are completely and totally worthy of love, no matter what. You should not settle for anything less than unconditional love. Be aware that it's going to take a second to figure out who you are. But as you figure it out, you deserve to love yourself and you deserve to be loved. Your gender identity doesn't take anything away from that.

Montavious & Mack. Photo by Robin Rayne

Montavious Thomas (*they/them*)
high school student

I'm sixteen, and I learned the term nonbinary when I was thirteen. I came out to Mack as nonbinary before he came out to me as trans. I don't remember when it happened, but one day I was just telling Mack how I was nonbinary and bisexual. Then he told me that he was trans and I was surprised. Mack was always more interested in the masculine stuff and wouldn't play with dolls, but I still didn't have a clue that he was trans till that day. I liked to wear dresses when I was young, so I think my parents always knew.

At school, there were other kids coming out as nonbinary and I researched it on the internet. It means that we don't identify with either gender or any gender, and we don't have to take any specific gender roles in the way we express ourselves.

Usually, males express themselves a certain way and girls express themselves in a different way. I don't want to express myself all the time as male or as female. I just want to be in the middle. I don't want to live by the gender stereotypes. Some of it is the clothing, but I don't really care what I wear. If I want to wear a dress, I will. I've worn rainbow chokers that I've made and worn makeup out of the house.

> **"I have switched pronouns a lot. At first, I went by she/her, but it didn't feel right. And he/him didn't sound right at all. But then a little bit later, I asked to go by they/them, and that felt just right."**

I left college and joined the military for the first Gulf War, where I trained as an interrogator. I blew up my knee during training and had to resign. I went back to the Middle East as a contractor for a couple of missions,

Marshall Thomas
(he/him)

veteran, reverend, activist

but one of those missions went very badly and added to my PTSD. When I returned, I went back and graduated college. I met Stephanie and we fell in love while I was working for a small internet company in New England. When I got the call to become a minister, our family moved to Georgia where I was ordained and called to be a pastor for a Hispanic congregation.

Six months before our son Mack came out to me and Stephanie, I had a clue something was going on. He just wasn't ready at that point to tell me directly what was up, and it certainly didn't occur to me that he was trans. I just knew there was something brewing.

Mack didn't know that we were a safe family. He was worried that our relationship would change or that he'd get kicked out because I was preaching in a very conservative church, and he'd seen it happen with other people.

Eventually, I told Mack that I was sorry for anything I had said or done to him that had been hurtful. For example, I was talking to Mack about

Marshall, Mack, Stephanie, Montavious. Photo by Robin Rayne

going to a father-daughter dance together late in his transition process. It must have made him totally uncomfortable! And if you truly love your children, you want them to be comfortable in the skin that they're in. That hurts me looking back. How do you fix that? If I can't fix it, I can just try to help him to continue to go through his transition. If being comfortable in his skin meant that we found a surgeon, that's what we did. If being comfortable means that we switched pronouns, that's what we did. If being comfortable in his skin required that he be able to talk to us about anything, that's what we did! You've got to love your children unconditionally.

I didn't know a lot about trans and nonbinary terminology but when my kids came out, Stephanie and I learned right away. The internet was fantastic because there's a wealth of information. I bought Mack his first binder online.

The church that we attended was considered right-wing conservative. I wasn't the lead pastor there, but I was filling in, preaching and teaching the Wednesday night Bible study class. I'm respectful of other people's religious views, and this church believed in certain teachings that I didn't believe in.

However, since nobody ever asked me what I thought, I didn't have to address the areas of disagreement.

After Mack first came out to our family, he decided that he still wanted to go to church. One day when we were leaving, he was practically in tears. I didn't know why, and Mack didn't specify why. Later I found out that he had been effectively shunned by the Sunday school group, which was run by the pastor's wife. We left the church two weeks later and we've been doing church in our home since then. We found the Village Church, which is a progressive Christian church, and we are welcoming to all LGBTQ+ people. We've found a nice church home there.

> **"I told the superintendent of schools, 'You're on the wrong side of this battle. This is about to become the law of the land. Are you going to be with us?'"**

We moved to such a conservative white area because we wanted to get some land where the kids could go out and play. Since we were homeschooling at the time when we arrived here, racism in the school system wasn't an issue for our family. In the Black community nationwide, folks know to stay out of Forsyth County, Georgia. You get taught that. It's in the culture. But we were in Pickens County. People have been pretty good. Not that racism doesn't exist here, but they keep it quiet. I hadn't seen a lot of the racial division until the Trump administration. After his election, it became very evident which folks were ardent racists. You could recognize them as the people with those red MAGA hats on.

I'm a large Black man. People do not mess with me. When I was in college, people who hadn't met me in person thought I was either a cop or a member of the mafia. White people tend to leave me alone. Anybody who's going to have a racist moment with me would just be stupid.

LGBTQ+ issues have become a massive focus in many conservative churches and communities. Pastors use the same passages they used during the civil rights era to say that my interracial marriage was an abomination. There are Bible verses that have been used to say that Black people are not human and to justify slavery. Many pastors and conservative churchgoers are very good at using scripture to justify their cultural standpoint. At one point my sister told me that I was twisting scripture to meet my family's needs. No, I'm reading the scripture carefully and looking at society and I believe the broken part in the equation is the church.

The Bible is almost silent on most gender issues once you strip out the patriarchal structure that was in place when it was written. The kids that we've taught have read Jesus's words in the New Testament and they understood the real meaning of love. Many young people, especially LGBTQ+ youth, are leaving the church because the church doesn't support them.

When the bathroom issue with Mack began, I talked to the principal, and that didn't go well mainly because he accidentally stepped on a racial landmine. He told Mack that he could use the bathroom that was in the field house, which is far away and outside the school. His words reminded me of something that happened when I was little, when I was told that I could only use a special bathroom. It took me a couple of years to figure out that it was because I'm Black. So right away I said to the principal, "Oh, I don't think so. You can't do that to my kid or to any kid. That is, in fact, segregation. Is that what you want?" I told the principal he had to get this fixed.

At the time we had a phenomenal superintendent of schools. There was a meeting set up with the superintendent, the principal, and me. I told the superintendent, "You probably want to invite the attorney for the county because I'm going to sue you people into oblivion." The superintendent, who was a former judge, listened very carefully. I told him, "I'm seeing this play out exactly like it did in the civil rights era, using the same concepts against a trans kid as were used against Black kids. Before I had this conversation, I had already called Lambda Legal, a nonprofit organization, and had an hour-long conversation with an attorney. The superintendent agreed and said that Mack could use whatever bathroom he wanted to use. But then word got out and these racist and transphobic people in town got right on it and apparently Facebook exploded.

At the town hall, we had 700 people at that meeting who were against us. But we had around twenty people from all around the area who were there specifically to support us. We got hooked up with several hundred organizations from around the country that wanted to help us. When it comes to supporting our children, you bring every resource to bear immediately—or at least let the enemy know that these resources are available, and then it is their choice as to whether they would like to be hit by them or not. Anything short of that isn't going to work, in my way of thinking. I'm more of a Malcolm X guy than a Martin Luther King Jr. guy, although I think both of those leaders were needed to lead our civil rights movement.

The school board fired the superintendent because of his stance on this issue. They wouldn't say that was the reason, but it was 100 percent because of this bathroom issue. He was a judge. He understood the law. He saw that it was like the issue of women in the military being allowed to get into combat roles.

After the town hall gathering, I cannot say how many times I left the house thinking that I was going to come out and see something spray-painted on the side of the house or a cross burning and our car tires slashed. The school quickly realized that there was a double threat. Mack and I were Black, and Mack was also trans, so his case was going to draw national attention. The school administrators didn't have a whole heck of a lot of choice but to do what they did.

Moving out of Pickens County has been a huge relief from being under the threat of violence. I was constantly in a state of vigilance, and I already have PTSD from a combination of the military and the fire service. I can't believe the amount of stress that I was under there. Until we moved closer to Atlanta, I hadn't realized how poorly I had been sleeping for a long time. Now I sleep like a rock.

Stephanie Thomas
(she/her)
preschool teacher

When Mack came out, I was totally blindsided. I had no idea. Looking back on that day, I'm very embarrassed about the way I responded. I didn't tell Mack I didn't love him, or I didn't believe him. I just said that I'd never seen any signs of this. I did ask him, "How do you know and why do you have to put yourself in a box?" Mack had just started going to public school and I thought it was because he was hanging out with people who talked about being trans. I didn't know that he had already been exploring it. For eight months, Mack and I went back and forth, and we had so many crying fits in the car. I just didn't understand.

I grew up in a very liberal family, and we were never taught to hate anyone or that any group of people were unacceptable. Even my grandparents, when they met Marshall, said, "You're going to have some issues because people are going to view your interracial marriage as not okay, but we adore you both."

In my family of origin, being gay was never considered to be a bad thing. It was just a thing. I never knew about trans people because it wasn't something that we had any exposure to. I grew up in a very small town and there wasn't a lot of diversity, but after reading the Bible and going to church, I saw that God or Jesus never said anything against gay people. I thought, if God is love and God created everyone and God loves all His creation, well, why is this even an issue?

Ironically, when it was my child, my reaction was entirely different. I didn't think there was anything sinful about being trans, but I was terrified for him. All you hear are the stories of people being murdered and young people committing suicide after being bullied because of who they are. I was thinking, "Oh, my goodness, how am I going to protect my child? How do I parent Mack?" I had a lot of nights where I lay awake in tears. I was going downhill into a deep depression because I didn't know what to do.

As a parent, you imagine how your kids are going to grow up and what they are going to look like as an adult. You imagine them having a beautiful wedding dress and all these other things. I felt like I was on an island and that nobody had ever gone through this before—it wasn't something on my radar at all. Then I was introduced to the Mama Bears group on Facebook, and it saved me.

Mama Bears was started by a woman named Liz Dyer, who has a gay son and was looking for community. She believed that there needed to be something for these moms to latch onto, where they could talk about parenting a LGBTQ+ child, because it's not an easy road. When I joined three years ago, there were probably about 1,200 members. The last time I looked, there were over 5,000. It just grows exponentially. I might get a post that says, "I just heard about this teen who got kicked out of his house and he's in this area. Is there anybody nearby who can help him find resources?" At Pride events, we meet up and march together. Some of us moms hold signs at Pride parades saying, "Free hugs," and many of the LGBTQ+ teens are so excited to get a hug. I've heard kids say, "My mom hasn't hugged me since I came out," or, "My mom passed away." I love giving hugs to these kids. When Mack's case became public, Mama Bears from all over the country sent cards and gifts and packages with the message, "You are not alone. You are worthy of love."

Truthfully, it was such a relief for me to know that I'm not a terrible person because I cried about Mack's gender identity, and I struggled a lot with pronouns with both Mack and Montavious. I've had many people come up to me throughout the past couple of years and tell me that they are amazed at my parenting. I've said to them, "You don't see what happens at home behind my closed doors!" But I would move mountains for my kids, no matter what.

> **" We parents must love our children although we may not always understand them. They are always going to be our children, and we must learn to love them unconditionally. Helping other parents come to that realization is my mission in life. "**

Marshall and I did everything we could to give our kids a place where they could thrive and flourish and be who they are truly meant to be. I explained things to my mom when she was struggling a lot with Mack coming out as trans. She and Mack have a very special bond and always have. My mom was in tears and said, "I'm a terrible person." I said, "No, you're not. I've had the same feelings. I've had the same thoughts." Over time, I helped her to see that Mack is still Mack. He is an amazing human being. Mack has always had that specialness from the day he was born and that has not changed an iota. But the way Mack sees himself and the way he presents himself and the way that he feels in this world makes a huge difference in his joy. To see him happy again and loving who he is brings me joy.

A year into Mack's transition, he needed a checkup from our family doctor. Before the appointment, I said to the doctor privately, "I have an odd question. My oldest son is trans and I would love to have you continue to be his physician, but I need to know that you're going to be okay with that." And she said, "Oh, yes! I love the trans community and our practice has a couple of other trans patients." I was so relieved!

I work as a preschool teacher at a Head Start program. It was during naptime when I happened to look at my phone and Facebook had just exploded about Mack's situation. I had people messaging me asking if I'd seen all the comments. I just sat there with my mouth hanging open.

When I started teaching there, I told my director that I would be teaching diversity and inclusion. Often kids walk into the classroom at three years old saying, "Pink is a girl's color and blue is a boy's color," or "I'm a boy so I can't play with dolls." Day one, I stop them and say, "All colors are for everybody. Everybody can wear pink or draw with a pink crayon." I don't just tell them that; there are days when I have everybody in the class draw with pink, for example. I want to make an impression that colors have nothing inherently to do with gender. And I show them that anyone can play with dolls or trucks. My first year there, one of the kids was getting teased because he loved to play with baby dolls. I told the kids, "Hold on a second, these babies need daddies. And people have to practice being good daddies, just like girls practice being good mommies."

Now that we are moving to Cobb County, I will have a much more racially diverse Head Start classroom. I'm really looking forward to it, even though it looks like there's going to be a crackdown this year in Georgia about teaching diversity, especially about race and LGBTQ people. No matter what, I will be the teacher who will respond, "Hold on a second here. I'm going to teach my kids that no matter what color your skin is or what style of hair you have, or if you are a boy who wants to dress in a skirt, or a girl who wears traditionally masculine clothing, it's all totally okay."

The young kids today, like the youth in every generation, want things to happen right now, and they don't understand how long it takes to change society. They don't understand how long it takes to change the law, let alone the societal change that must happen along with that. Despite all the horrifying, transphobic laws being introduced all over this country, I'm still hopeful that things will change in the right direction.

Ashlee Page

DATA ANALYSIS

Ashlee. Photo by Robin Rayne

(*she/her*)

technology manager

I'm forty-nine years old and a trans woman. I was born in Seoul, South Korea, and adopted by my parents when I was three years old. I grew up in the very rural, very white Hudson River Valley area of New York state. I could have counted on one hand the Asian people in our town. In fact, I was the only one in my class for several years. I got picked on often and heard a lot of racial and ethnic slurs because people there weren't educated about diversity and tolerance back then.

For a long time, I didn't feel like I was part of my family because my father is Polish and my mother is Dutch English, and my two sisters and one brother are all white. When it came to family portrait time, I always felt like an outsider. On top of that lonely feeling, starting at the very young age of five I knew that something was a little bit different about me. For quite some time, I couldn't pinpoint what the difference was because there wasn't social media or YouTube or Google back then where I could have searched for some answers. I especially felt different during my adolescent years. I felt like I wasn't who I was expected to be, and yet even if somebody had asked me, I wouldn't have known how to describe my feelings.

Fast forward to my college years. I started to put things together and I could feel my identity as a woman emerging. However, I didn't understand my feelings as I didn't know anyone at that time who was transgender. I didn't even know anyone who was gay back then! Since I didn't know how to deal with the emotions I was feeling, I tried to suppress them.

When I got out of college, I experimented a little bit by dressing more feminine and buying women's clothing. I hid that from my family and friends, thinking that it was just something I liked doing for fun in private. I didn't grasp yet that being a woman was who I am.

While I was still living as a man, I met my future wife Holly at our workplace. We dated for a while and then got married, but I never told Holly about my urge to present as female. I thought my desire to dress in women's clothing or act in more traditionally feminine ways was something that I could tuck away in a closet and only bring out occasionally. I believed it would be my secret that I would take to my grave. For years, I attempted to live the so-called "normal" heterosexual life of being a man married to a woman, buying a house, having a stable career. Holly and I even tried having kids.

I've worked for my current employer in insurance twenty-four years, and now my office is in Georgia. Shortly after Holly and I moved here, Holly's mom got sick, and she left to be with her mom for several months. Her absence gave me time to do some reflecting about who I was. In September 2014, I attended a conference for transgender people called Southern Comfort in Atlanta so I could be around other people like me. While I was at this conference, I realized that wow, there were a lot of people living their authentic lives. I decided that I needed to come out, at least to Holly, though I still hadn't even considered transitioning full-time.

When Holly came home after her mother's death, I told her that I was a trans woman. I knew the timing wasn't right—not that there is ever a good time—but Holly had just lost her mom and here I was, her husband, telling her that I was a woman. This threw her into an emotional whirlwind, and she asked me if I was going to be a woman full time. At the time I didn't think I was going to socially transition, so I said no. It wasn't until I went to another conference for trans people that I realized I needed to be completely honest with myself and with Holly.

I decided to start hormone therapy and I quickly found a doctor and a counselor. I had a conversation with Holly about what taking estrogen would mean, and then we talked about the surgical aspect of transitioning. As soon as I made the decision to transition full-time to my life as a woman, I decided to transition surgically.

My sister Stephanie, who is a year and a half older than me, was about to have her gender-confirming surgery out in San Francisco, as she is a trans woman too. We are not blood related because I was adopted into my family, so it was especially fascinating that we were both trans women and that we came out just a few years apart from each other.

Holly and I went out to San Francisco to visit Stephanie when she went to the hospital. I presented as my authentic self the entire time I was in San Francisco, and that was the first time Holly experienced me over a long period of time as Ashlee rather than as her husband. We got along well. Holly came with me to some trans Meetup dinners, and it seemed like she was very accepting.

What made it very real for Holly is when I legally changed my name. We went to the courthouse and in front of a judge, I was sworn in and made my name change legal. From that point forward, Holly realized that her husband, as she knew him, wasn't coming back. That is when things changed for her. Holly had been very supportive of me the entire time as I transitioned, but just as I needed to be true to myself and live my life authentically, Holly needed to do that as well. A decision was made to separate and eventually to get divorced. I know it's been tough on Holly, and I want her to be happy with whoever she wants to be with, just as she wishes a good life for me. I would say that we are the best of friends, practically like sisters.

Growing up, I was raised in a Roman Catholic family and went to parochial schools. I was even an altar boy at one point, so when I was ready to come out to my parents, I didn't know how they were going to take it. When I came out to all my friends and colleagues, my mom had just begun kidney dialysis three times a week. I was planning to tell both my parents in a few months, but Mom took a huge turn for the worse. I went to visit her and realized that it was probably going to be the last weekend that I would see her alive, so I decided not to tell her. I didn't want my gender transition to be the last thing that she had to think about. She died a few days later without knowing about me. Had she been healthy I would have told her, of course, but I just felt like it was just too heavy of a thing to lay on her during her final days on the earth.

I knew that my dad was in a tough place after Mom died, so I waited a couple of months to come out to him. My dad lives in a nursing home in South Carolina, and I went there to tell him that, like my sibling Stephanie, I was also a trans woman. When you tell a parent, you wait for their reaction because you never know what it's going to be. My dad just looked at me and said, "I think you're going to look more Korean now." Of anything that he could have said, I didn't expect that response. And that was literally all he said! I felt, "Well, okay, I guess he means that as a compliment."

Since then, my dad has been very accepting of me. He does slip up occasionally with the pronouns and with my name, but it's not that often and it's not intentional either. And he's seventy-nine—getting up there in age—so I can understand that he forgets. He has never said anything hurtful or anything negative about who I am, which is a gift. When I was growing up, my dad was always very stern and not a warm and friendly person. If I had come out to him twenty or thirty years ago, I doubt that his reaction would have been so positive.

The way I explain being transgender is that gender is not just about your body parts. When we are born, people only look at our anatomy to determine our gender. My gender identity is what feels natural to me and makes me who I am.

If you were to ask somebody if they're left-handed or right-handed, they're going to come up with a response unless they are ambidextrous. As a lefty, someone might ask me, "How do you know that you are left-handed?" I'd have to answer, "It has always felt right to me that I write with my left hand. It feels more comfortable. It feels more natural." And it's the same thing about gender. Some people are cisgender. Some are nonbinary. Some are genderfluid. And some are trans.

When I was young, I wished that I could be reborn as a woman. But I never thought that I'd be alive today living fully as a woman. There were a lot of factors that came together to make that possible. I work for a very inclusive company that offers comprehensive transgender health benefits and this helped to make my dream come true. The medical plan pays for surgery for all trans employees. They not only pay for the actual surgery but also for the related costs. They cover both top and bottom surgery and if people want to do facial surgery, they'll cover major gender-affirming facial surgery. They cover laser or electrolysis for hair removal. It's wonderful to have that level of support from my organization.

Having gender-affirming surgery was a lifelong dream for me. When I had the opportunity to do it, I knew that it was going to be the right decision. It's not the decision for everyone and it doesn't have to be. I put my name on a surgical waiting list for two and a half years, during which I had the time to rethink it over and over. Every day that went by, there was no change in my thought process. Even to this day, there's no regret about it. I enjoy my female body. There's a sense of completeness for me, something that I yearned for my entire life.

When I was first coming out in 2016, I came out to my manager a few months before my planned date of my social transition at work. I did that so there was plenty of time to prepare, as obviously there were a lot of conversations that needed to take place. I made my official transition day October 11th, which is National Coming Out Day. Despite the prep work, when I went to work that day, there was a lot of awkward silence. I think people were still trying to process and understand what it meant for me to transition fully.

One woman at work asked me if it meant I was going to use the women's restrooms. And, of course, I said yes. She didn't ask me anything else nor did she question it with the Human Resources office. I think she just was trying to understand what being a transgender person entailed. However, another time I was in a meeting and after I told everyone there that I was a woman, one of the guys stood up and said, "A round of applause is in order." He started clapping and I was like, "OMG!" It was such an amazing feeling. From that day on, I didn't have any negative reactions at work, at least to my face.

> **As an Asian trans woman, I must be very mindful of what I do, where I go, and who I'm with. It's not just being trans. It's not just being a woman. It's not just being Asian. It's the intersectionality.**

There's a long adjustment period, especially when people you've worked with for years must remember to switch your name and pronouns. As far as I'm concerned, there should also be a long grace period. My coworkers would forget occasionally, but not intentionally—I can tell when using my old name is done intentionally and when it's not. We are all human beings. We slip up. When my sister came out as trans, I had to be very intentional myself as I would often forget to use her correct pronouns or her new name, and I was obviously very well educated about being trans. My experience with my sister helped me understand how hard it can be for most people to remember.

I realized that there was nobody else at my workplace who had transitioned at work. I wanted that to change, so I put myself out there in a video series for the entire organization talking about my transition. I started developing written guides for employees and leaders to help them understand what to do when a trans person comes out. After I made the video, I started getting messages from many colleagues saying, "I have a trans son/daughter/ neighbor/friend/colleague."

People started to come up to me at work and say, "I'm transgender. I don't know what to do. Can you help guide me?" It got to the point where if somebody was going to come out at work and needed some guidance, the HR department would pass along my name. I became the go-to person designated to support and facilitate the trans coming-out process. Now there's a small group at my company for trans and nonbinary people, but there are still a lot of people who are afraid to come out. For every person who comes out, there are probably ten more who are still in the closet.

I talk to the new people who want to come out at work and tell them what to expect, how to talk to their leadership, and even provide them with local and national resources. That's what all workplaces need to do to help make LGBTQ+ people feel safe. The last thing any organization wants to do is lose talented individuals because they are fearful of how they're going to be treated in the workplace. We've now added different events throughout the year to celebrate events such as Transgender Day of Visibility. I think we are making progress.

I wrote an article about being transgender that was published on the front cover of our company intranet. There I was, front and center, for 80,000 people from around the country to see. One day after the article was released, I was walking into work and a woman stopped me and said she wanted to ask me some questions. We scheduled a time to meet and the first thing she said was, "I want to let you know I'm very religious." I was like, Oh, boy, and I had no idea where this conversation was going to go.

She wanted to ask me a lot of questions about my upbringing and my identity and about surgery. At the end of the conversation, she said, "You know, Ashlee, I'm still a religious person, but you opened me up to understanding things differently now." If we can have these conversations respectfully, they can often have this type of impact.

Out in the world, it isn't always so safe. I was with a trans friend of mine at a train station here in Atlanta after a sports event, and somebody near us said something derogatory loud enough for us to hear him. I went over and called him out on it. I said, "We're not doing anything to you. We were just standing here." He didn't say a word. I don't understand why some people are so rude. I'd like to say to these people, "So what if I'm not exactly like you? How am I harming you?"

Once I was hanging out with some coworkers at a restaurant. We were just sitting around having a conversation and one of them blurted out, "You are transgender, right?" My first response was, "What difference does that make?" It was obvious to me that she wasn't asking the question in a negative way. In fact, she was trying to say it in a very positive way because she has a trans relative. But that's not what people should do. You don't call somebody out in public like that. After she asked me that question very loudly, I looked around to see if anybody was staring at me because who knows who could have heard her question? A person at the next table might not like trans people. It can be dangerous.

When I came out as a trans woman, the first thing many people questioned me about was my sexual orientation. They would say, "Now that you are a woman, does that mean you're going to date men?" When I first came out, I only dated women. But I identify as pansexual, so now I don't necessarily date based upon gender. I date based on liking someone as an individual.

Since my separation from my wife Holly, I've dated a bit, both men and women. When I meet someone who doesn't already know I'm a trans woman, I need to figure out when to tell them. I don't want to be in an unsafe situation. I especially don't want them knowing where I live.

It's hard when you hit it off with a date because you go from this emotional high of feeling a sweet connection with someone to the realization that there's probably a 99-percent chance, if not higher, that telling them that you are trans is going to end things instantly. I understand that a lot of men can't deal with dating a trans woman. There's a lot of societal pressure, especially if a guy's friends ever found out that he was dating a trans woman. They don't necessarily have an issue with me, but they don't want to deal with having those conversations with their friends and family.

I know some trans men and trans women who do not identify themselves as transgender. They identify simply as the gender that they are and only come out to other trans people. I can't do that, even though I'm almost always perceived as a cisgender woman. I would feel like I was living in fear again, like I was coming out of one closet to go into another. But at the same time, I don't want to have the fact that I'm trans tattooed on my forehead.

One of my big passions is dressing up like a 1940s-1950s inspired model, wearing that era's makeup, hairstyle, and clothing. It's a way to express myself that has nothing to do with me being trans at all. I'm a part of a pinup group called the Georgia Pinup Posse. It's a group of all women, and we get together and do photo shoots. The organization requires you to fill out an application to join and I was a little nervous putting in my application. I thought to myself, "This is a women's club. As a trans woman, do I really belong? And what do I do if they reject me for being transgender?" However, in the application they had a code of conduct that included a clause about nondiscrimination based on sexual orientation and gender identity. I was shocked. It was very progressive for a social organization down South.

We are a small group, maybe twenty of us. Last year, one of the women talked about her trans daughter and then I found out that one of the other women in the group had a trans brother. And another one has a daughter who is still trying to figure themself out! Who would have thought in a small group like ours, there would be so many people who have family members who are trans people?

The good news is that a lot of religious denominations are starting to turn around and actively embrace LGBTQ+ people and leaders. Many of the PFLAG local chapters hold their groups in churches, so that may have been a big influence in the open and affirming church movement. However, there is still far too much hatred coming from clergy who are homophobic and transphobic. At the trans march during Pride weekend in October, you always see a lot of supposedly religious folks holding signs and making negative comments. I try to ignore them. If you ignore these people, you won't give them the pleasure of being acknowledged, and often they'll just go away.

It's more common among youth today to identify as nonbinary because they want to feel free to be who they are. It can be hard for some people to grasp the concept of being nonbinary, and I've heard some older people say, "I was just starting to get a hang of this transgender thing. Now it's nonbinary. What's next?" It's not that there are more trans or nonbinary people now than there were in the previous generations. It's that people are more open to being out.

I'm a mentor to a support group out in California. It started out with only Asian American trans people, but then it branched out. One thing that I say often to the members is, "You are going to be your own worst enemy if you live in fear that stops you from being your authentic self. Sometimes you simply must take a leap of faith and know that there is going to be somebody there to catch you when you land."

Christian Zsilavetz
and Family

Christian. Photo by Robin Rayne

Christian Zsilavetz
(*he/him*)

dad, husband,
educator

I was born in New Jersey in 1970 and grew up with my older brother, who is your typical guy. I'm a trans man, but until I turned thirty-six, I believed I was female. As an eight-year-old girl, I liked it when I looked like a boy. In third grade, I had just cut my hair short for the first time and wore a white button-down boy's shirt and jeans for my school picture—the only school picture of me that I ever liked. At the same time, I got the message that if I was perceived as a boy, it was bad. It especially upset my father when we were out doing typical father-son things together and his friends would say, "Oh Frank, is this your son?" He'd say, "No, she is my daughter." I could sense his embarrassment, which he confirmed for me many years later.

When I was twenty-five years old, I married a guy I had met in high school. We moved to Seattle and two years later we got divorced. After the divorce, I began to come out to myself as a "butch dyke." Maybe the fact that the word lesbian rubbed me the wrong way was a clue to my real gender identity.

I was with a woman partner for about five years, and when that relationship ended, it was the first time in my adult life that I spent some time alone. As I looked inward, I began to realize that underneath my tough butch exterior was really a trans man. However, this concept was still so foreign to me, partially because I didn't know anyone who was trans.

As it turned out, I was wrong: a male lawyer I worked with was a very active member of the trans community. I never would have guessed that he was trans, but one night I saw him on TV talking about being at a conference for trans men. I filed that away in my memory and seven years later, we met again at Seattle's amazing conference Gender Odyssey, along with Aidan Key, Jamison Green, and several other men who would become my big brothers by choice.

When I was ready to see the real me, I took myself out to a beach and sat with my journal to write down a dialogue between me and my higher power, which I sometimes called God. That day I wrote, "Dear God, what's the good word?" My higher power wrote back, "You'll be okay no matter what skin you're in." I knew from that moment forward that I would be fine if I decided to transition, but I hadn't told another soul.

I already had a binder because I had been performing as a drag king with a group of folks, two of whom turned out to be trans guys. I went to Sears and bought a couple polo shirts that made it look like I was flat-chested when I had my binder on, a man's watch, and several pairs of boxer shorts. I was beginning my journey toward my transition.

That fateful day, I was on my way to a weekend retreat for people in recovery where I saw many dear friends. But there was also somebody there

I had never met before. When I turned to introduce myself to this person, I saw someone who looked just like my grandfather with a buzz haircut but who was wearing a tie-dyed dress. Rocky identified as Two-Spirit and sometimes used female pronouns and sometimes used male pronouns.

When Rocky first saw me from across the room, I later heard that he had asked a friend of mine, "Who is that young guy over there?" My friend told Rocky, "That's not a guy; she's thirty-six, and she's a girl." Rocky said, "Not for long." When we finally got a chance to talk alone, I told Rocky that I identified as a trans man and that I was planning to physically transition. Rocky became my mentor for many months and helped me find support groups. Seven months later, Rocky also taught me how to give myself a testosterone shot. Within a year, I was not misgendered as often and my voice was dropping. I had cut my hair much shorter, and I looked very masculine instead of looking like a butch woman. As part of my journey, I knew I wanted to have top surgery—a bilateral mastectomy with a nipple graft, which would remove my nipples and put them back in a male-patterned chest. I knew that this was my medical path.

Transition wasn't easy. I quit my teaching job and went to therapy and support groups two to three times a week. My therapist and my community helped me get used to living in the world as my authentic self. I'm so grateful for Seattle Counseling Service for Gender & Sexual Minorities and their sliding scale, as I was without health insurance. Truth be told, my therapist there saved my life. I knew that I could sit on her couch and bawl and talk about the hard things in my life, including the temporary non-acceptance of my parents, coming out to old friends and former students, and wondering if I would ever be able to teach again.

All mixed in with this part of my life was falling in love with my wife-to-be. When I first met Heather, we had both recently left long-term relationships, so neither one of us wanted to get into a committed relationship right away. We flirted around a lot and kind of danced our way into a relationship. Soon we were head over heels in love!

One day we had plans to go to a basketball game with a group of friends. I planned to tell Heather after the game that I was trans and would be transitioning physically. Of all the people I've had to come out to, Heather was the hardest and scariest one because I knew that I had to act in total faith that if we were meant to be together, it would happen. Heather had almost always identified as a lesbian and only dated guys very briefly in her past.

When we went out that night, we were shopping in the team shop and Heather said, "Let's buy a shirt we can share." She held up a scoop neck T-shirt and said, "How about this one?" I said, "Please, no! I don't want anything girly to wear ever again."

After the game, Heather drove us up to Capitol Hill in the gay neighborhood, and we went out to this cute romantic dessert place. I desperately wanted to tell her, but I'd learned that it was never a great idea to come out in the middle of a restaurant. However, I could barely stand to wait another minute. After we ordered, Heather said, "So that thing you said about the t-shirt, like never wearing anything girly again, what was that all about?" I blurted out, "I'm transitioning, and I don't know what it means for us. But this is what's going on."

> **" By being visible, I know that I'm there for students who need to know that they're not alone. When they see the rainbows on my car and my wrists and the flags in my class, they know that I'm a safe person. "**

She looked at me for a good minute and finally said, "Pack up the carrot cake, get the check, and let's get out of here." I'd broken the cardinal rule of not coming out in a restaurant, so I thought I had blown it. We went and sat in her Jeep for about four hours and then in the wee hours of the morning, we sat outside and talked for many more hours. We've never left each other from that moment on.

That night, I said to Heather, "You know, I don't know what this means for us because I don't know that relationships like ours exist. You are a lesbian. I'm a trans man. So, if I'm going to be transitioning physically, are you going to want to be with me?" She said, "Well, I guess you're going to be my special man!"

Heather saying that to me is one of the most impactful things that anybody has ever said to me in my entire life. It still brings tears to my eyes. My wife has grown in front of me and alongside me since that day in 2006. I will be forever grateful that she realized before I did that regardless of what people call our relationship, it's just our relationship.

The best word I use to describe myself is *queer* because I fully identify as a member of the LGBTQ+ community. Heather doesn't like the word queer; it just doesn't suit her. She still prefers calling herself a femme lesbian. That's okay with me as I know we are a happy rainbow family. Labels are far less important to us than unconditional love.

Shortly after I came out, Heather said, "Look, if we're going to have this relationship, I want to have a baby, and I'm not staying in Seattle. And, to top it off, I'll probably have pets for the rest of my life." (She had five stray cats and three dogs at the time.) I said, "Okay, I'm in," and we went forward into our life together.

Soon after, Heather told me, "Time is ticking on having a baby. Let's work on creating this baby now and then we can get married." What she didn't know was that I had already ordered a ring from a dear friend of ours who is a jeweler. It took us a year and a half to get pregnant using a sperm donor, and our sweet Zoe was born in December of 2008. And so here we are.

I came out to my parents four months into my transition. My parents had cut off contact with my brother over the years because of their own disagreements. When I came out to them as a trans man, I wondered if they would cut off contact with me too. My mom did not handle it well. The first time I came out, my mom said, "Don't tell Gram—it will kill her." She was so upset this time that she left the room and refused to come back. I sat and talked with my dad, and I had the most meaningful conversation I'd ever had with him. It was amazing. He asked me, "Why do you want to go to the men's bathroom?" I answered, "To pee." Then he said, "Really? Do you want to have a beard or a mustache?" I said, "Yeah, I do. I need you to know this because I'm going to start changing and I won't be able to hide that from you. My voice is going to change. My body is going to change."

My parents went back to New Jersey, and they told my brother. He called me up and said, "Are you nuts?" I hung up on him, and then he called back. Apparently, my parents had tried to convince him to change my mind. He apologized and from then on, he was cool enough with me being trans. He even wished me a happy Father's Day multiple times.

I was almost always perceived as male before my medical transition. One day during this time I went out to a restaurant with my dad and the waitress asked me, "Sir, would you like more coffee?" I said, "Dad, don't you see? I'm not even on testosterone and I'm already being seen as male, and it feels right." He was like, "I guess I can't argue with that."

But the day I called my parents to tell them Heather was pregnant, my mom called me and said, "We don't want to see you when you come home to New Jersey in a few weeks. Your dad and I need time to process your transition and I don't know when we will contact you again. We don't want to watch you as you go through this." I said, "You know, I was about to call you and tell you some great news. Heather is pregnant." Later I called my mentor and she said, "Your biggest fear has come to pass, and here you stand."

I didn't consider self-harm or suicide, but I knew that this was a crisis moment, so I called the crisis hotline, and they helped talk me through it. I was so grateful to have a community and care to help me through that time, and to have a working relationship with my therapist who walked me through all of it.

By the grace of all the amazing people I met at Gender Odyssey a few months into my transition, I was handed a lot of gifts. One of those gifts was the simple advice that dealing with your family can take time. Someone told me, "You took a long time to come out to yourself. It will take your parents time to adjust to this new reality, but don't give them the easy way out and just disappear." I was instructed to send my annual Easter card, Mother's Day card, and Father's Day card. I even sent my parents our wedding invitation, though of course I didn't expect them to come. However, when it came time to send my parents an anniversary card, I just couldn't do it. I could not honor the marriage of people who would cut off contact with their own child just because of who they were. My eighty-eight-year-old Catholic grandmother had flipped my pronouns overnight. Why couldn't my parents and brother accept me for who I am?

Almost a year after our daughter Zoe was born, Heather and I realized we wanted another child, that it felt like someone was missing from our family. We tried again with the same donor, and it didn't work. However, the clinic we were working with in Seattle had a different solution for us, and Heather became pregnant with our second daughter in late 2010. Emma was born at the end of August 2011, and we finally felt complete as a family (plus the pets, of course).

When Heather and I moved to Atlanta in 2012 for her job, I knew I could easily pretend to be a cisgender straight guy if I wanted to. But all my years in recovery taught me that if I couldn't be fully myself, I would die, and for me, that meant being openly trans. If I wasn't, it would feel like I was ashamed of being a trans man, of having lived thirty-six years in a female skin. I couldn't live that way. I also could not have my kids keeping my "secret" or being ashamed of their family.

When we got to Atlanta, one day my kids and I wandered onto the playground of a new private school that had just been in operation for a year. It turned out they were looking for a math teacher. On my application I put on all my service work, including the trans conferences I had volunteered at, but I never said a word about being trans in my interview and it would have been illegal for them to ask. I got the job!

When I needed a hysterectomy, my then six-year-old daughter ran out to the school playground and started shouting to her friends, "Hey, guess what? My dad's having—" and she was about to say, "his uterus out," when I stopped her and told her privately, "Surgery is kind of scary for some kids, so let's not talk about it right now." I turned to my fabulous teaching colleagues and said, "Zoe was trying to tell you that I'm having a hysterectomy." My colleagues were 100-percent supportive. I also learned that if I was going to continue to teach at that school and have my children go to school with me for the long haul, I needed to be out.

Yes, I'm in liberal Atlanta, but I'm still down South where there aren't any job protections for people like me. The school's wonderful principal knew that some of the parents were homophobic and transphobic, so she was scared, and rightly so. I told her, "You know what? If I'm going to be teaching here, I need to be out, so I'll let you decide if you want me to stay here." It was a private school and, as principal, it was her decision.

Two weeks later, she came to me and said, "I wouldn't want you to make a blanket coming-out statement because I think that would cross the personal/professional line." I said to her, "I have a young woman student whose lesbian mom just died. I want to tell her. I can't sit with this girl who thinks that she's got this random average straight white guy across the table from her. She doesn't realize that I'm family and that I've got her back. You are also asking me to hide from another kid here who is probably trans. He knows my classroom is a gender-affirming place, but he doesn't know that I'm trans. My dream school is where all of who I am matters, where my LGBTQ identity matters. It's imperative that I can be myself and be out and honest as an educator." The principal listened and then said, "Well, why don't you start that dream school?"

In that very moment, the idea for Pride School Atlanta was born in my mind. It took two years of hard work to get the school off the ground and the school was open for two years, in addition to the nonprofit organization we ran for four years, providing training and advocacy services for free. The school may have closed, but all the kids who went to this school are still alive!

Pride School made the front page of the *Atlanta Journal-Constitution*, and we had researchers come in from England. We were featured on dozens of news programs. Some people were critical of our school and said we were coddling the kids. We said, "Yes, we are coddling them, and we have every right to do so because why should they have to be on a battlefield when they go to school?" Some parents came to us and asked if our school could start in kindergarten, especially for their young effeminate boys and masculine girls, some of whom were starting to identify as trans or nonbinary.

When Pride School opened its doors the first year to eight students, the vision for our school was that when you drop your kid off, you will know for the first time that you can go to work and not have to worry about what phone call you're going to get from your child's school that day or if your child could use the correct restroom without getting beat up or threatened by a bully.

The kids were afraid to put a sign with the name of the school out front because they didn't want some homophobic or transphobic person shooting up the place. We were located at first inside a Unitarian Universalist church building, which closed because the city paved it and put up a parking lot. We moved to a second location, and it worked for a little while, but then, sadly, we had to close the school because we ran out of money.

Our students were very involved politically. We marched in many Pride parades and raised money for the Atlanta Pride committee. Everybody we worked with became family. I know where all our past students are and how they're doing. If they ever need anything, I'll be there.

One of the things I realized when we had to close it down was that we probably opened the school up too soon, and that's on me. Most of the kids who came were kids from the suburbs. They weren't city kids or kids whose parents had kicked them out because they were LGBTQ+. They were white suburban kids who lived far away from downtown Atlanta and whose parents had to drive an hour twice a day to make sure their kids had a safe place to go to school.

After closing the Pride School, I ended up doing training for the US State Department with people from all around the world who were at risk of being killed simply because they were LGBTQ+. Next, I worked in a public charter school in Atlanta, but before I could set my classroom up, I was told to keep the trans stuff on the down low and just let the kids get to know me slowly. Well, being trans is part of who I am, so I hung a huge rainbow flag in my classroom. I didn't talk too much about being trans to the students, but if any student Googled me, they could easily find out exactly who I am, which is what upset some parents.

I moved on from that school and taught in a public high school where 85 percent of the kids are Hispanic. It's a Title One school, which means it's a poor school. The kids were amazing, as were the other teachers. I am now working in a private Jewish high school with an even more supportive community and administration and expect to be working there for many years to come.

I believe that just because there are out teachers like me, there are kids who won't choose to attempt suicide. One student who did attempt suicide and survived told me, "I'm so glad you guys have created such a safe space for me to just be who I am."

We all need equal rights as trans, nonbinary, gender diverse, and gender nonconforming people. We teachers need to know that we're not going to lose our jobs because of how we wear our hair or if we change how our bodies look. We need to have access to excellent medical care where we can get our trans-related health care needs taken care of—especially for our youth, because if we get them puberty blockers when they need them, we will save years of therapy and many lives.

For those LGBTQ+ people who are depressed and feel hopeless, I know that having a stranger tell you that your life is worth living and that it can get better can feel like empty words. I say to them that I wish they would consider hanging around for just one more day. And another day. Know that you are worth it.

If you have suicidal thoughts, please consider calling a suicide helpline. If you are a teen, the Trevor Project online will give you information before a crisis happens and tell you who you should call in a mental health emergency. Most of all, please remember that you don't have to do this alone. If nothing else, you could be there for the next person coming behind you.

Recently, I went to visit my folks overnight and for the first time ever, my mom introduced me as her son when we ran into her best friend at the grocery store. It was one of the best moments in my life.

Heather and I are both grateful that we and our kids have the life we have. We couldn't imagine our lives any other way. We are imperfect, and we are an amazing family.

Heather Hastings
(*she/her*)

public health advisor, parent

I grew up in Chicago, the "spirited" red-headed child of a traditional middle-income family. My parents divorced when I was five and my younger brother was two. My mom headed back into the workforce, taking a job close to our apartment so that she could always be near us if needed. I grew up as a latchkey kid in an urban neighborhood with great schools and playgrounds.

In my early twenties, I earned my master's in public health while purchasing a home with my mom and my brother and working for a local community health center. I came out as lesbian, first to myself and then to them, while we were living together. I don't think my mom was surprised, but she was sad, and coming out to her was one of the hardest things I ever did. My brother was quietly horrified.

I identify as femme, preferring comfy clothes, casual hair, some jewelry, and a bit of perfume. Early on, I fell in love with a soft butch girl with a leather jacket, a Tennessee twang, and great politics. She wrote songs for me and insisted that we purchase a meat smoker for the backyard. We were together for nine years and, to my knowledge, we were the first lesbian couple to have a church "marriage" ceremony, before it became legal, in the Chicago Episcopal Diocese, though the bishop would not put it into

Heather & Christian. Photo by Robin Rayne

writing. By that time, both of our families were lovingly supportive of me and my wife.

Leslie Feinberg's book *Stone Butch Blues* was my first introduction to trans folks in the mid-nineties. We lesbians were still working on getting Ellen out of the closet, but the lesbian community has its own history around gender nonconformity. For example, at Lost & Found, a bar where we used to hang out which had no sign out front and a buzzer on the door, the older women there would talk about how they used to get arrested for not wearing a minimum amount of "feminine" clothing.

Fast forward to moving to Seattle and falling in love with Christian. He was presenting as female then and I assumed he was a lesbian like me. When he transitioned to male, the first thing many people said to me was, "But I thought you were a lesbian!" I was surprised too. I had thought I was falling in love with a nice butch girl. Except he wasn't a butch girl, though he certainly was very nice!

When Christian told me he was a trans man, I had to grieve the idea of who I thought he was so that I could focus on who he really was. I cried loudly for about forty-eight hours, and then I was ready. We both had some bottom lines. I said, "I'm going to have a baby, and I'm not living in the Northwest forever." He said that he was okay with my requirements.

The wedding was small and lovely and held outside near a beach in Michigan. Christian and I danced down the aisle together! We had so much fun and were so busy laughing that the reverend had to remind us to focus. It was a beautiful July day, and our daughter Zoe was there, five months along in my belly. I felt so loved and cared for and beautiful. Christian was so handsome and looked like the cat who ate the canary.

We had a great community in Seattle of people who knew and loved us. They were all supportive of Christian's transition and of us as a couple. My mom and my closest friends never missed a beat. And my brother shifted his pronouns regarding Christian immediately. My dear ones could all see how happy I was, and still am, with Christian, and how good he has been to me.

Since I'm perceived as being straight, I've had to give up some of my chip-on-the-shoulder sense of specialness that I had when I was in a lesbian relationship. This is good because who you love and how you identify your gender aren't synonymous with being a good person.

> **"I haven't traded in my hard-won radical-femme-feminist-lesbian-of-the-90s badge. But now I'm a fierce mom and wife of a trans man, while looking on the outside like I live in a stereotypical heterosexual marriage consisting of a mother, a father, two kids, and four pets."**

My focus is on teaching our two children to stand up for themselves and others in their schools. For me, I always have my pronouns on my signature line at work, and I come out in the various Twelve Step and parent support groups I attend. I provide materials to my friends who are therapists so they can learn more about gender diversity. Christian's classroom is a sanctuary for LGBTQ+ teens. While he hosts the queer support group at school, I get dinner ready at home.

Christian and I have been a couple for sixteen years, and I still giggle when he whispers in my ear. He talks about how I have his back and yet I also kick his butt. We laugh at the same things, and I feel understood and accepted. He balances me and allows me to be myself. Here are some great things about Christian: he juggles, plays piano, loves his students, croons, loves my mom and his mom.

Christian and I don't have the gender role struggles that many straight couples have. I have fun being a feminist lesbian married to a man who used to live as a woman. He sees through all the cultural nonsense, like when people used to tell him how great he was for staying home with the kids while I worked to earn money.

Christian and I have often said that every day is gender day. That means that walking through the world as someone who may not look or feel like they belong in the mainstream takes a lot of energy. A good ally can be a loving buffer and learning how to be a good ally isn't super complicated.

Being in our family has given me the strength to call other kids out when they say that certain clothing or toys are gendered. I also challenge my classmates on their transphobia, homophobia, and sexism. I'm glad I know that in my family I can be whoever I am.

Zoe Hastings
(*she/her*)

middle school student

My mom Heather gave birth to me thirteen years ago by using a sperm donor. The other day at school someone said I look like my dad, Christian, but since I'm not related genetically to him, I thought that was funny.

My birth story comes up in conversation a decent amount because I wasn't made the old-fashioned way. I was sort of made in the doctor's office and in a lab from a cryo tank. It's funny to imagine that I likely have many half-siblings out there who have the same sperm donor. It would be cool to meet some of them and see how much we look alike! I'm the only kid in my family with red hair, but maybe I have half-siblings who are gingers too.

The weird thing is that many people at my school like to discuss their sexuality and they view me as this normal, average, straight person, but then I describe my family. Turns out that I may look "normal" on the outside, but I have a ton of rainbows all over my room, rainbow jewelry, rainbow stickers, and rainbow socks. I don't really notice it at home, as it just feels normal-ish to me.

> **If your kid comes out to you, the most important thing you can do is to tell them that you love them and support them. If you don't, well then, DO! Figure it out or watch some videos that will help you understand what it is to be trans or nonbinary. You can even learn a lot on TikTok.**

Zoe, Christian, Emma, Heather. Photo by Robin Rayne

When I describe my family, kids say, "Oh my God, you have such an interesting family!" I'm like, "Huh?" I just don't think it's a big deal that my mother likes women, and that my father used to live as a woman but is really a man. Both my mom and my dad have had menstrual periods! How cool is that?

If homophobic and transphobic kids don't want to hang out with you, why would you want to hang out with them anyway? People are becoming more accepting these days, so hopefully soon enough it will be weird not to accept LGBTQ+ people.

I'm eleven years old. Having a trans parent is having a lot of rainbows and fun and stuff! It's nice knowing I can be he/she/they, whoever I am, no matter how I was born. And I can like boys, girls, or whoever. I love my family. They are cool.

Emma Hastings
(*she/her*)

elementary school student

Dalia and Terry Kinsey

Dalia. Photo by Robin Rayne

Dalia Kinsey
(*no pronouns*)

dietitian, public
health educator

I was born just outside the city limits of Brunswick, Georgia, to a devoutly religious couple. If
you are like most people, you have never heard of Brunswick. It's a
small coastal city that people drive through on their way to Savannah or
Jacksonville. The only impression Brunswick generally makes on people is

linked to its distinctly offensive odor akin to rotten eggs, an unfortunate blend of a decaying marsh and paper mill chemicals.

The patriarchy was strong in our home. My parents belonged to a conservative Christian church in which the head of the household was always a man, and the women were to be seen and not heard. I can't count how many times I was lectured for failing to develop a "quiet and mild spirit."

My parents, though devout, allowed all three of us kids as much freedom as possible, as long as they believed that God would approve. I always had what people would label masculine energy, and I wasn't into the idea of having to follow specific rules strictly because of the body parts I was born with. This was always an issue for me but because I was raised to be obedient to my elders, I wore dresses and ridiculous frilly pink church socks for what felt like an eternity. Despite those outfits, I was never read as femme by other people even when I tried.

I was constantly misgendered out in public. Even though I detested girly things and felt like androgyny was the bee's knees, I hated being called Sir when I was trying to follow all the rules to be seen as female. I knew I wasn't what we used to call high femme, but I wasn't male. I didn't want to be just one gender but being gender neutral or gender nonconforming was never presented as an option when I was growing up.

It's hard to narrow down why I was bullied in secondary school. Sometimes it was related to not being considered Black enough and sometimes it was standard racism against Black people. Being averse to all things feminine drew some attention, but since my hometown was incredibly small, I had known most of my high school classmates from the first day of elementary school. I don't think my gender expression stood out to them since it was consistent with how they'd always known me to be.

I frequently felt isolated and overwhelmed by a sense that I didn't belong anywhere and that I would never fit in. These feelings contributed to my anxiety and depression during my teenage years. I never attempted to harm myself but found it comforting to remind myself that at some point life would be over and I wouldn't have to deal with those heavy feelings any longer.

The most important person for me to come out to as nonbinary was myself. After I finally did that, I started coming out to friends and worked my way to my little brother. I knew they would have the largest capacity to accept me even if they didn't fully understand my experience. I was just beginning to come out to people when I met my husband, Terry. He knew who I was from the first day we met, even though I didn't have the language for my gender identity that I do now. I remember explaining to him on our first date that I felt almost like I was a teenage boy in my heart. I was just emerging!

My parents didn't accept me at all when I told them about my gender identity. While homophobia and transphobia are rampant in the South and among many Black folks, in my family of origin, religion plays the largest role in their rejection of my gender-neutral nonbinary identity. My immediate family considers me a lost soul, and they try to limit contact with me—checking in only periodically to see if I'm alright and to encourage me to come back to church. My parents literally think my sinfulness could rub off on them. My one ex-communicated sibling has kept in touch with me, but he has made it clear that his values don't mesh with mine. Losing my family was initially gut-wrenching, but I've worked through my feelings of abandonment and focused my energy on cultivating loving relationships with my chosen family.

When I started explaining to my friends about being a nonbinary person and the fact that I didn't want to use any third-person pronouns, they were supportive although they would often misgender me. My spouse still struggles with my choice not to use any pronouns, but he is making progress.

Quite a few people have asked me how I know what my gender identity is and why I tell anyone that I'm nonbinary since I can pass as "normal." I don't put much energy into explaining myself these days. I direct people to resources if they genuinely want to understand nonbinary people better. Otherwise, I explain that I consider it disrespectful not to refer to me the way I have asked them to. I don't care if they accept or approve of what they call "my lifestyle" because I don't need their approval to live my life. I require their respect to work with them or to interact with them on a regular basis. If they can't give me that, then they don't fill my minimum requirements for being in my life.

When I'm meeting new people in a space that feels safe, I just give my name and the fact that I use no pronouns because I'm nonbinary and haven't found any pronouns comfortable. Some people have misread the fact that I use no pronouns as hostile to LGBTQIA+ folks, which is exactly the opposite of who I am.

Misogynoir is intense in the Black community. According to some Black males, Black women have no value outside of the value they give to others. I find myself frequently butting heads with cisgender Black men who are hypercritical of Black femmes and feel entitled to have a say about what is "acceptable" behavior for them. I only recently learned that police violence against Black femmes is just as common as police violence against Black men.

The lives of Black women in general are not considered as valuable as the lives of Black men, and I think that is why there is so little attention given to violence against Black trans women in our culture. It's extremely disappointing, but it has led me to lean into community with other Black femme and nonbinary people more than ever.

I experienced extreme levels of stress in the early stages of the pandemic and during the second wave of the civil rights movement that was triggered by George Floyd's death. I was overwhelmed by relentless anxiety, malaise, and feelings of hopelessness. I came to a dead end when I was looking for resources that addressed treating chronic stress related to systemic oppression during acute periods of heightened stress. All the resources I found were clearly written with white people in mind and failed to address the influence that chronic stress caused by racism and homophobia and transphobia has on the health of BIPOC people.

> **" I want politicians who are making laws that harm trans and nonbinary people to know that we are everywhere, and that gender diversity isn't new. What has changed is the increased sense of safety that many trans and nonbinary people experience that allows them to show up fully. Ignoring our political interests will lead to your demise. "**

This awareness triggered me to create resources to address chronic stress by using my existing skills as a registered dietitian and a public health educator. I publish a bimonthly newsletter and produce a monthly podcast entitled Body Liberation for All. I also published a book entitled *Decolonizing Wellness* to focus on the health and well-being of QTBIPOC—queer and trans Black, Indigenous, and people of color. I also encourage people to reclaim Indigenous healing practices and to work on reversing internalized stigma.

When I started this work there were no queer BIPOC dietitians centering their work in this way. I created the very tools that I needed myself when I was younger, and my health was falling apart in response to relentless racial trauma. I'm looking forward to seeing more resources address the effect that systemic oppression and marginalization have on body image and overall health among queer and gender diverse folks with multiple marginalized identities.

I'm convinced that it will be years before we see major changes in the culture and the laws that influence the quality of life for most QTBIPOC. That's why I feel such a sense of urgency in serving marginalized folks, so that they will have access to resources that help them live their healthiest and happiest version of their lives right now. My work is dedicated to fostering holistic wellness—social, spiritual, emotional, and physical wellbeing—despite the abusive systems that we currently live with.

I want to urge younger trans and nonbinary people to remember that they can find community anywhere; it doesn't have to be in "real" life. Belonging to a supportive community online can dramatically improve your well-being. You can find people who understand your worthiness without you needing to explain your humanity to them. Don't give up on finding your people. In the meantime, prioritize your safety. If it doesn't feel safe for you to be out, you don't have to be out.

I think deep introspective work is going to be a key factor in changing systemic racism, homophobia, and transphobia. So many liberal people who don't consider themselves part of the problem refuse to see the ways that they are upholding systems of oppression. Anti-Blackness and ambivalence toward queer issues and social justice in general is a dealbreaker for me. At this point in my life, I don't develop close relationships with people who aren't concerned about actively promoting social justice.

I am hopeful that future generations will not have to struggle to find support and resources in the ways that elder millennials like myself did. But I'm not optimistic about bigotry being eliminated. It seems to be part of the human condition to crave dominating and elevating oneself over others. I don't know that that is ever going to go away completely, but I do believe that one day other people's bigotry will be less of a problem thanks to legal protections. In that world, it will not take nearly as long for gender diverse folks to love and accept themselves as natural expressions of humanity.

Terry & Dalia. Photo by Robin Rayne

I thought I'd never get married until I met Dalia. I dated a few self-identified tomboys, back when nobody used the term nonbinary.

I'm happily retired. Most of my career was in logistics. I ran a distribution center, and I met Dalia

Terry Kinsey
(*he/him*)

retired business
manager

when I was substituting as the interim manager in Dalia's hometown. We went out a few times and I liked Dalia right away. When the company decided to hire a permanent manager for the center and send me back to my home base in Atlanta, I asked Dalia to move with me. Dalia came to check out my setup in a preliminary visit and moved in the next weekend. We used to go to church events to accompany my mother, but in those settings our being an interracial couple was more of a challenge for people than anything else about us.

There is no downside to having a nonbinary partner and nothing to be worried about. We just respect each other and accept each other. It isn't complicated. There are people out there who seem to have a problem with everything they perceive as different. I don't spend my time worrying about these people I barely interact with. I focus my attention on Dalia, the person I plan to spend the rest of my life with.

> **❝ I don't explain Dalia's gender identity to my family or friends as it's nobody's business. There is no explanation needed. Dalia is Dalia. If they have questions, I answer them, but I don't need to explain Dalia to anybody. ❞**

I've always liked how quirky Dalia is. Dalia has a cheesy sense of humor that I find utterly charming. I say if Dalia was any cheesier Dalia would come with nachos. We love to travel together. Traveling with an introvert can be challenging, but these days I've figured out that it's best to get a great hotel room so Dalia can retreat whenever Dalia wants to be quiet and alone. I could talk to a wall and Dalia won't talk to anybody in a crowd of six or more. Opposites attract!

Dalia and I balance each other out. Like any other relationship, we work at it. Flexibility and communication are the keys to a happy marriage. We've grown together and we will continue to grow together for the rest of our lives.

Joy Ladin and Elizabeth Denlinger

Joy. Photo by Gigi Kaeser

Joy Ladin
(*she/her*)
writer, speaker

For as long as I can remember—since pre-school—I identified as female. I hid that from everyone in my family, fearing that I would only be loved if I presented as the boy I was believed to be. For years I thought I was the only kid like me, the only one whose sense of myself didn't fit my body. Even after I learned that wasn't true, I remained afraid that I would be shunned as unlovable if I ever lived as the woman I knew I was.

I started writing poetry as a six-year-old child in a home that was not literary at all. The problem was that as soon as I started writing poems, I considered them to be great poems even though I had no concept of literature! The good thing is that when I wrote my poems I felt connected to language—something larger than myself. When I made words rhyme, I was showing that words that seem different on the outside had an inner kinship on the inside. I wonder if that wasn't the way I felt about my female gender identification—that I could feel it rhyming with other girls, not boys.

By my mid-forties, my health was suffering from the strain of living as someone I knew I wasn't. But I was married and the father of children I had to support, so I lived as a male until earning tenure as a professor gave me some legal protection from losing my job. At that point, I went to a therapist during what I call my gender crisis—the physical and emotional breakdown I experienced after living for over forty years as a male. I told the therapist that I was ashamed of hiding my lifelong sense that I was female. The therapist asked me, "Did anyone ever teach you to be true to yourself?"

No one had, but the longing to be true to myself had led me to confide to my college sweetheart, the woman I married, that I was transgender when we were sophomores in college. She told me then that if I continued to live as a man, she would love me and stay with me. Over the next two decades, we lived by that agreement. I became what people call a successful man, professionally and as a father to our children. At the same time, I became steadily more miserable. By my early forties my body, and the male persona that I had created to go with it, had become a living hell. I couldn't eat, sleep, or feel anything but pain.

Some long-term relationships survive gender transition, but most don't. Even though we don't mean to, when we transition, we sometimes change the identities of the people who are close to us. My mother raised a son, which isn't the same as having a daughter, especially a daughter who used to be her son. My now ex-wife married a man, and she couldn't stay married to me when I started living as a woman as she wasn't a lesbian.

My gender transition ended my first marriage to the woman I had been involved with since we were first-year college students. I was terrified that transitioning would make me forever unlovable, and that the end of my first marriage meant I would have a lifetime of loneliness.

When, after several years of living alone as myself, Liz and I fell for one another, I felt truly, deeply loved. I still do. Liz and I got married five years after we met, and every day I'm grateful for our relationship and for a love that would never have been possible if I hadn't started to live as who I truly am.

Jewishness is very important to me, and I'm proud of the progress the Jewish world is making in recognizing transgender Jews. However, as I know from my own experience as a member of the Board of Keshet—a national organization working toward full inclusion of LGBTQ+ Jews—even very liberal Jewish institutions often struggle to go beyond simply adding the word "transgender" to their official welcoming statements.

When the dean at my university, a major figure in Orthodox Jewish women's education, first saw me after my transition, she said, "We personally value you very highly, but we don't think that our students or their families will accept you as a professor any longer." Then she said, "It is the policy of Yeshiva University that no man may set foot on school premises wearing women's clothing." I was put on "indefinite research leave." To the dean's surprise, and mine, a group of students protested that fall. They were outraged. The Orthodox Judaism they learned had taught them that you don't treat a person that way.

> **"None of the identities that any culture gives to us perfectly fit us as individuals or perfectly fit us for our entire lives. Being trans or nonbinary are just different ways of being fully human."**

When my attorneys sent a demand letter in the spring, I was told that I could return to teaching as myself—as a woman. Several years later, I was promoted to full professor. The fact that an openly transgender person has been able to teach at Yeshiva University offers hope to all LGBTQ people who are longing and fighting for acceptance in culturally conservative families, institutions, and communities. If it's possible at Yeshiva University, it is possible almost anywhere.

It felt awkward to get so much attention for my transition, and some of it was an awful kind of attention to receive. But I gradually realized that I was lucky. By being at that intersection of very traditional religion and open queerness, it gave me a unique opportunity. I got a front row seat to the way cultures change, and to the collision between modernity and traditional religious community. Eventually, I started to appreciate the attention.

I'm not sure if what I do in my writing and my teaching work is considered activism, but I do feel like part of my work is to help people understand what it is to be trans. For example, I pay attention to anti-trans feminists and evangelical critiques of trans identity. Not because it's fun to read that stuff, but because it's my job to understand opposing viewpoints so that I can help others understand and learn.

Elizabeth & Joy. Photo by Gigi Kaeser

Elizabeth Denlinger
(*she/her*)

rare books curator

Before I met my wife, Joy, three of my friends told me I should meet her and that we would like each other—two were queer Jewish friends, and one was a colleague of Joy's at Yeshiva University, where I had also taught. They weren't trying to set us up, but when I saw, early in 2010, that Joy was a featured guest at a queer Jewish women's retreat at the Isabella Freedman Jewish Retreat Center, I signed up and went with my ex-girlfriend.

The ex-girlfriend introduced me and Joy almost as soon as we got there at Shabbat dinner. Joy was wearing a black coat with a shawl collar, looking a bit forlorn. We started talking and were stunned at how much we had in common: we had both gone to Sarah Lawrence, we'd both taught at Yeshiva, we both volunteered at the same homeless shelter run by my synagogue in New York City, and we both put literature and Judaism at the center of our lives. None of that had to mean that we would immediately fall in love, but we did, and we've been together ever since.

We didn't get married till about five years later because I'm slow to make up my mind, but when we finally did, we did it twice. Our first wedding was on the spur of the moment, on the fifth of January 2015, with three friends of Joy's and her younger son. The officiant was the kind spouse of a friend who was free the first day our marriage license was valid. We were married on a frozen afternoon under the eaves of Emily Dickinson's deserted house in Amherst. Soon after our first wedding, we realized that we wanted more of our friends and family to celebrate with us, so we began planning our second, much larger wedding.

This ceremony was a full-on Jewish wedding that took place in Riverside Park in New York City. Our dear friend Rabbi Jill Hammer officiated. All our surviving parents were there, my siblings and their children, Joy's younger child, and our friends from work and from our synagogue. It was quite a crowd, and we went to an event room at my synagogue afterward for the reception. I had always wanted to be a bride in a traditional Jewish wedding, where you both get lifted high in the air on a chair and you hold onto a corner of a handkerchief with your beloved hanging onto the other corner. Having that experience with Joy was a wonderful moment.

Our relationship has shown me how not only is the personal political, but that politics are personal and matter in ways you might not expect. The things about Joy that have been hugely and continuously important to me

> "I don't think Joy being trans has had a particularly strong impact on our marriage. I think of it as a lesbian relationship, but as with any intimate domestic relationship, the personal aspects quickly become more important within the relationship itself. Thus, I no longer think much about the fact that Joy is trans, but I do pay attention to how she feels about that fact and how she feels about herself at any given moment."

are her capacity for, and endless pursuit of, self-knowledge, her patience, her sense of humor, her kindness, and her enormous gift for talking things through. Although chronic illness prevents her now from sharing my long walks and bike rides, she is always happy to hear what I've seen. I come home and tell her all about the hawk guarding a dead woodchuck from aggressive mockingbirds, a great blue heron flying majestically over a swamp, or a hot air balloon touching down in a field nearby.

The larger world is still mostly hateful toward trans people, especially trans women and most especially trans women of color. I see no cure to bigotry except to continue to struggle to make our world better.

Adam Miller and Family

Adam. Photo by Robin Rayne

Adam Miller
(*he/him*)

student, activist

I'm twenty-five now and I still remember the first time I ever told my mom I wanted to be a boy. I was about five years old. Being the awesome feminist that she is, Mom gave me a little talk about how "girls can do anything boys can do." It was very sweet, and totally missed the point! I have a hard time remembering my exact thoughts since I was so little, but I think the message I heard was, "It's not possible to actually be a boy, so just make do with the gender you got."

Of course, being a child of the 90s, I didn't grow up with much aware-ness of trans people or their experiences until later, and there were a great many times I felt very confused, anxious, gross, and unlovable due to my feelings around my gender. Oddly enough, even after hearing the term "trans-gender" in reference to a family friend who was a trans woman, somehow, I never worked out that trans men could also exist, and that I might be one.

All the confusion and anxiety eventually led me to becoming a die-hard perfectionist, people-pleaser, and a stereotypical golden child. I got straight A's, I had a massively competitive career as an orchestral musician, I almost never spoke my mind, and I was terrified of the mere thought of breaking a rule. Unfortunately, all the achievement just led to me stuffing my feel-ings inside even deeper.

When I finally did realize I was trans and came out as such at around eighteen, I felt more lost than ever. Through the process of hiding my LGBTQ+ identity away, I had also learned to hide all of myself in that closet along with my gender. Without having a clue who I was, what I val-ued, and where I wanted to go in life, I quickly spiraled into drug addic-tion, severe depression, and suicidal thoughts.

Coming out came in many different stages for me. I first formally came out as lesbian my senior year of high school. I'm a gay man, but while I was still living as a woman, being with other women felt more comfortable to me. I started the coming out process with the people I was most sure would affirm my identity and worked my way up to those I wasn't so sure about. My friends and brother all were affirming immediately. In fact, I believe my brother's response was somewhere along the lines of "Duh!"

My parents took a little bit more time to affirm me. Both were always loving toward me, but they were also Catholic and weren't sure how to sup-port me or how LGBTQ+ people fit in with their beliefs. That's when they first started going to PFLAG for support. Seeing them try so hard to be supportive is something that meant a great deal to me at the time, and it opened much more depth of conversation between my mother and me. PFLAG was such a beautiful gift to my family. The support and education my parents and I received at PFLAG meetings was astounding, and I feel like it freed both them and me of many burdens. Because Mom and Dad were getting such great support, I didn't feel so burdened and responsible for their struggle and their worry over me. PFLAG provides the perfect opportunity for family members to express their authentic thoughts and feelings in a way that's free from judgment and complication.

When I told my dad I was trans, his first words in response were, "I don't like that very much." Of course, I was very hurt by the statement. It took me a long time to realize he was struggling to express himself. I thought he meant he didn't like my transness, my masculinity, or maybe even didn't like me. I eventually realized that what he really meant was that he was worried about my future and about my upcoming struggles. He also worried about how it fit into his religion, and he worried he would hear people say mean things about his kid. Most of all, he worried that I would become a different person and he would lose the child he'd always known and loved.

Immediately after coming out, I still was not aware of who I was, who I wanted to be, what I valued, and where I wanted to go in life, and my uncertainties led me to constantly attempt to fit the role of what I felt a gay trans person "should" be. It was almost like stepping out of one closet and right into another. Luckily, my best friend introduced me to a Twitter hashtag called #RealLifeTransAdult, which was full of regular people posting about their lives who just happened to be trans. They posted photos of their kids, their spouses, their jobs and businesses, their families. It was, quite literally, lifesaving for me to see those pictures. At that time in my life, I felt like I could never have any of those things. While my immediate family was supportive of my transition, I still thought no one could ever love me romantically or want to marry me or have kids with me. I thought I'd never be able to find success at a job. I was sure that I would never have a happily-ever-after.

Since then, it has been a continued process of developing self-awareness, self-expression, and self-compassion. I worked very hard to get clean from drugs for what is now over five years, and I continue to work on becoming more confident, assertive, and authentic. Sometimes, taking this dive into the depths of my psyche is difficult and even terrifying work, but I have reaped so many rewards. I had never really been one to stick up for myself. Never been one to express a belief or opinion that didn't match the status quo. Through this journey, I learned to do all that, to the point where I have finally started seeing myself as a successful and joyful person. It's a path I hope to follow for as long as I live.

Inevitably, I've had some difficult experiences as a trans man. For example, I saw a man who was supposed to be an extremely reputable therapist after I had just been released from a mental hospital because I was having regular panic attacks and thoughts of suicide, and I thought a different therapist might help me. He ended up spending a good portion of the session attempting to convince me that no gay man or straight woman would ever want to date me. I remember being insulted, but even more shocked and confused at how a renowned therapist could even hold such beliefs, let alone express them to a client who was clearly already in such a vulnerable place.

> **We can face the people who scare us and walk away better for it. We don't have to feel trapped and stuck in our own lives and bodies. We can feel proud of every aspect of our life. We can choose our own destinies, and we do not have to be victims.**

I was fired from a job due to being gay. I worked at an in-patient substance abuse rehab facility. I worked in the men's wing, and I was consistently open about being gay but never shared that I was trans because a coworker, who was a wonderful ally, advised me not to make that information known. Unfortunately, since I was already out as gay, a few of the clients began to harass me and eventually complain to HR, prompting them to swiftly fire me. Even though I knew I was being fired solely due to my sexual orientation, it was still one of the most embarrassing moments of my life.

I describe myself as a gay trans man. However, in more social settings I often identify more closely with being gay than I do with being trans. I sing in a gay men's chorus, most of my friends are cisgender gay men, and I'm more involved in gay culture than I am in trans culture. I have always been a gay man at heart; gender transition was just one of the things I had to go through to get there.

An acquaintance of mine passed away recently. I didn't know him very well, but he sang with me in the Atlanta Gay Men's Chorus. Many mutual friends made posts on social media to honor him. It struck me so deeply to see the posts, because every single one, and I mean all of them, had one word in common that folks used to describe him: kind. I remember thinking,

"This is what I want more than anything—that someday, when I die, I want everyone who has known me to think of that word to describe me." My mission in life is to put more joy, hope, and kindness into the world.

The reality is that we all will inevitably cause pain. We will let people down, break hearts, say things out of anger, jealousy, etc. To tip the scales, however, we must make a conscious and continuous effort to bring joy, comfort, and laughter to others.

When I was in active addiction, I was extremely suicidal, but one of the things that stopped me from going through with it was that I could see how my addiction was already causing a lot of people very deep emotional pain. My death would have caused far more pain. If my life had ended then, I would have gone out with the scales significantly in the negative, so to speak, and I couldn't face that. This was a large motivating factor behind me getting clean, and a main reason why I have worked with both LGBTQ+ individuals and those who struggle with addiction. I want to show other queer people, through both my advocacy and my example, that we have such potential inside us. We can find love, peace, and even joy.

I had grown up wishing that someday I would be in a long-term and committed relationship. After my transition, top surgery, and a bit of weight loss, I lost sight of that goal for a while. I had felt so horrible about my body for so long that when I finally started feeling better about it, I experienced this constant need to flaunt it and receive physical attention. I would go to clubs, Pride festivals, you name it, and dance in skimpy outfits thinking I was loving the attention from all the men. All underneath that, though, was fear. What would happen if they knew I was trans? Would they still look at me? Would they still find me attractive? Would they want to date me long-term?

When I realized what I was doing, this revelation changed everything for me. I started working on becoming more courageous about asking for what I really wanted and showing the world who I really was and what really mattered to me. I stopped seeking the thrill of shallow physical validation. I downloaded dating apps that were designed for those looking for deep relationships.

After a while I started to give up hope again that I would find a committed romantic relationship because I had been told by so many that they wouldn't date me because I'm trans, or that they found me attractive but felt conflicted because of my body. While experiencing all this rejection, I started turning to some of the wonderful men who sing with me in chorus. Many of them have happy relationships, committed marriages, and some have kids. One of them even has the loveliest trans spouse. They consistently showed me by example that neither my gayness nor my transness meant it was hopeless to find what I was looking for. They gave me the hope and courage to ask for what I wanted, and to accept nothing less.

My advice to younger trans and nonbinary people who are experiencing difficult times is to realize that your life will not always be the way it is now. You can experience joy you wouldn't even dare dream of right now. And no matter what anyone has told you, and no matter what you tell yourself, you deserve for it to be that good.

Recently, it finally occurred to me that I have become the real-life trans adult I used to see in those pictures on Twitter. Nothing can quite describe the emotion I felt upon that realization. I work and go to school, I have a rich social life and a beautiful family, I'm vibrant and energetic, and I feel joy daily. I have all the things a younger me thought were impossible. So, if you're in a place where I was, feeling as depressed and suicidal as I felt, know that I see you. I feel you. I love you. Hang on because you have no idea what's to come.

Ann Miller *(she/her)*

small business owner, PFLAG regional director, LGBTQ+ activist

Parenting my son Adam was very much like parenting any other child—although I remember thinking that he was a dreamer, because he would think so deeply that it was clear he wasn't completely with us at times. I used to say that Adam lived in a parallel universe and occasionally visited ours.

Adam was very much what was called a "tomboy," loving to wear his brother's hand-me-down clothing and playing with the boys in his class. I saw an episode of Oprah when Adam was about eight or nine about transgender children and it really gave me pause. I remember thinking that I might need to watch Adam and see if that developed for him, but I never

Adam, Steve & Ann. Photo by Adam Miller

talked with Adam about it, never mentioned that some people are born transgender and what that meant. I was scared to, honestly.

I wrongly thought that talking to Adam about being transgender would put an idea in his head, and I didn't want that. I knew that I would always love my child, but being transgender sounded very difficult and I wanted to save him heartache, so I just sort of buried the whole topic. I regret doing that. I know now that there is absolutely nothing that anyone can say to make a cis child "become" trans and there is absolutely nothing that anyone can say to make a trans child "become" cis. Gender identity is innate. It is for me, and it is for Adam.

During his growing up years, Adam was driven to achieve. He was bright, musical, competitive, and accomplished. He also struggled with anxiety and was easily overwhelmed. I thought at the time that he was putting too much pressure on himself to excel and that the inner pressure was the cause of his anxiety and mood swings. Sometimes I was at a loss as to how to help, what to say, what to do; I just kept loving him and communicating the best I could about things that mattered to him, mainly his music.

I had so many emotions when Adam first told us that he was transgender. I was terrified for him, for his health, for his future. I was deeply worried about the discrimination he would no doubt face. I was scared about his mental health and the anxiety he was suffering from. I was crushed that he had suffered in silence for so many years because he was afraid to come out to me, afraid that I would stop loving him. And I was also strangely relieved when he told me he was trans. Here was something that explained so much of his life, his reactions, and his emotional swings. I never felt that I lost a daughter, although that is a common emotion for many parents. Clearly, my child was right there before me with the same blue eyes, old soul, and dark sense of humor.

No law protects LGBTQ+ individuals and their families in Georgia, and I do know families that faced job loss because they supported their transgender child. I'm extremely privileged in that I didn't have to worry about my financial security as a consequence of affirming my transgender child. I am also extremely lucky in that most of our extended family has embraced Adam. To those who do not affirm him, I completely feel like it is their loss not getting to know Adam better, because he's extremely insightful and very fun to be with. To that end, we focus on the many beautiful hearts in our extended family who love him.

After Adam initially came out, I attended my first PFLAG meeting. The group completely met me where I was emotionally, soothed some of my worst worries, and connected me to resources. It was a very small chapter, but warm and inviting. I started going every month, partly needing support but then just liking the camaraderie.

One of the leaders asked me to be a facilitator and lead groups, and I found it rewarding to help other parents. Shortly after that I joined the board of directors as the chapter president. I could see the impact we were making, and it was exciting to see the chapter grow and to feel like we were really adding value to the community.

After adding a teen support program and teen socials, we found more and more families coming to our PFLAG meetings with transgender and nonbinary loved ones. Often the parents would say that our groups provided the one place that their child felt comfortable. We began to see anxious, shy, reserved, non-communicative teens blossom, laugh, and have friendships. I know we saved countless lives.

When Adam first was navigating his gender transition, he also began college. He had suffered multiple identity crises: giving up his dream of playing classical music, a nasty break-up, and realizing that he is trans. His anxiety skyrocketed and he turned to marijuana use. As any addict will tell you, your drug of choice helps . . . until it doesn't. This seemed to be the case for Adam. He was getting great grades, transitioning socially and physically to have his outer self match his inner self, and juggling working and college life. But his dependence on marijuana was also growing.

> **Having a queer child is a gift; it really is, if you let yourself learn and be open to the joy that comes from loving unconditionally.**

Slowly as Adam's sophomore year in college wore on, Adam's personality became more and more paranoid, rage-filled, and out of touch with reality. He was spiraling and I had no knowledge of how to help him. I was petrified that he would end his life. I would text him a funny meme or just a request that he answer with one word just so I knew that he was still alive. Honestly, it's still hard to think about. I never felt like I lost a child when he came out as transgender, but marijuana addiction stole him from me during that time and almost permanently.

The rehab progress was long, twisting, and uneven, involving an inpatient stay and two outpatient rehabs. Through it all, we were right there with Adam, driving him when he was too scared to drive himself, moving him home, then back to school, then back home again, learning about addiction, listening to hard truths about our family, distracting him in the early days with soothing crafts or activities, and paying for countless therapists. Where addiction had threatened to divide us, recovery brought us closer than ever.

There's more to life than just staying clean and staying alive however, and Adam struggled greatly with finding purpose and meaning. He started and quit multiple jobs. But a vigorous life coaching program helped him became more in tune with his values and his innate worth, and slowly but surely, he began to thrive. Eventually Adam trained to be a life coach himself and launched a business coaching other LGBTQ+ individuals during times of transition.

As a mother, all I ever wanted was for my child to be safe, happy, and fulfilled. Now, as I see Adam putting himself out there in brave new ways, I realize that happiness and fulfillment will often require acts of measured risk. I can live with that. I think he knows our family home is always a safe refuge if the world becomes too intense.

To the families who have a transgender or gender expansive child or teen, I want to say that I see you. You are not alone. Seek help and support from other parents who have been where you are. Your emotions are valid but please do not burden your child with your giant emotions. Please find an outlet other than your child. Their very life may depend on that.

I hope that the world will stop seeing transgender individuals as broken. They are not. I hope that more cis people will learn to appreciate, respect, and value the lives of trans and nonbinary individuals and see the great wisdom that can be gleaned from their experiences. I hope that people will come to understand that there is nothing to fear from transgender individuals. There is nothing to fear in the bathroom, the boardroom, or the classroom. We do not need laws to protect us from transgender individuals.

My volunteer work with PFLAG became a source of greater purpose in my life, and I'm now the PFLAG regional director for the states of Alabama, Florida, Georgia, and Mississippi. Legislators in all these states have put forth copious bills restricting transgender girls from playing sports and restricting healthcare—including mental health care—for all transgender minors. Educating people about the falsehoods in the anti-trans bills has been one of my main focuses as a regional director for PFLAG. It's hard, heartbreaking work; sometimes it gets me down and I feel extremely inadequate. I do it anyway. Ally is an action word.

These bills are damaging on multiple levels: they seek to ostracize transgender youth from their peers; they seek to prevent transgender youth from accessing lifesaving mental health care and medical care. The bills all use inflammatory wording and phrases to confuse voters with no knowledge of transgender youth. Clearly the proponents of these bills do not understand the long, careful, painstaking approach that medical care providers use when treating transgender teens. The medical care ban bills are a complete government overreach of a private matter between the patient, their parents, and the medical care provider.

The main advice I have for parents when their child comes out as transgender is to let the child lead. There is no one cookie-cutter way to be trans. Some individuals will want to go slowly and just transition socially, sometimes just with the family at first. Others may want to transition socially and medically when age appropriate. Know that the medical community moves extremely carefully when working with transgender youth.

If there is any way to swing the funds, get a reputable therapist who specializes in working with trans people involved to help the process. Educate yourself on your own. Please don't rely on your child to educate you. Also please refrain from any ultimatums or hoops that you say that your child will have to jump through to access care. I've seen parents withhold life-saving medical treatment from their child by requiring them to have better grades or reach a certain age. That is very, very damaging. Please get support and get educated. I know from experience that when we affirm our transgender and nonbinary youth, we set them up to thrive.

Steve Miller
(*he/him*)

parent, financial educator, advocate for LGBTQ rights

Back in college in the mid-1970s I had a lot of exposure to the gay community, but up until the time that Adam came out as trans, I really didn't know what being transgender was all about. To me, having grown up with four sisters, most of what I saw in Adam was what I classified as being a tomboy, like all my sisters were. Since they have all become moms and wives, I assumed that was what would happen with Adam.

When Adam first came out as lesbian at seventeen, it wasn't something that I hoped to hear, knowing the struggles that being gay can present. Of course, I felt that he was and always would be our child and that Ann and I would love him no matter what. I immediately reached out to one of my dearest friends from college, who is a lesbian, and asked her for some help in understanding and supporting Adam, and that led me and Ann to PFLAG. The local group we attended really helped us understand the kind of support we needed to lend to Adam.

At some point, Ann told me that the other shoe had not dropped and not to be surprised if Adam was transgender. I didn't know that Adam was struggling with his gender identity until then and thus I began my education about what it means to be trans. I will never forget the gut-wrenching conversation when Adam told me that he wanted to be called Adam. I am crying now, remembering how much pain Adam was in because he had carried this knowledge alone for so long. I can still hear his voice and see his face contorted with anguish.

"Trans people are not scary. They are just ordinary, loving, good people living their lives without harming anyone."

Thankfully, I had written a mission statement for our family years earlier, which said, "I want my children and grandchildren to know that they can accomplish anything when surrounded by people who do not say that they cannot, and I want them to have the financial resources to support their dreams and goals." I was able to live out this mission as we responded to Adam's pain.

I am certainly the backseat driver—or maybe better described as the copilot—of Adam's support. Ann does the research and shares with me whatever she has found, and then we move forward together with what we believe to be the most appropriate steps. Has it been a struggle for me? Yes. Was there remorse? Yes. I had long held dreams for my little girl that I thought were very important! I had dreams of where my child's wedding would be and what it would be like to walk my grown daughter down the aisle. I had to let my dreams go because they were not my child's dreams. It's not that I didn't accept Adam; it was suddenly different, though—not for him but for me. He knew for a long time how he felt; I needed time to get used to it.

PFLAG became a huge part of my life after Adam came out as trans and I needed help. I needed to understand and be in empathy with others who were going through or had been through the journey. As I grew more, occasionally I would meet in person with other struggling families to help and support them. Ann and I also opened our home to be a safehouse for any trans person in danger.

As I interact in the world and with the ignorance that people have around LGBTQ+ issues, I find that most people's ignorance is not hateful. They fear the unknown and when they can connect with the real people involved, they want to learn, they soften their opinions, and often become empathetic to the issues and the challenges that trans people face. They have questions that they have never had a chance to ask. Many tell me about their own experiences with a friend or family member who is also trans, and how they still love that person too.

Amazingly, the people who do hate LGBTQ+ people typically call themselves religious. Unfortunately, "religion" is sometimes our worst enemy. I was born and raised Catholic, and I was very involved in our local parish for a long time. The final straw for me came four years ago. It was when the song "All are Welcome" was sung by the congregation. I was with my mom at our hometown church in Ohio, and I cried for the first half of the mass because I knew that my church, my faith, my community did not in fact welcome my son. I could no longer remain a hypocrite and continue to attend a church that did not support him with love and acceptance. It was a tough reckoning, and we moved on.

I remind Christians that Jesus said to love everyone. So please folks, love your children! Do your best to understand them. Be patient with your trans child. They see freedom where you see struggles. Seek out support from others who have already been through the journey.

Adam is quite an extraordinary young man. He has worked his way through challenges that I have never faced and has come out a strong individual who is positioned to help others do the same because of his own experience. Life gets better as the journey progresses. I still have my child, and he is still just as loving and loved as before, and most importantly, he is happier than ever just as he is.

My message to all people but especially to politicians is leave trans people alone! Trans people are not scary. They are just ordinary, loving, good people living their lives without harming anyone. I am sick and tired of politicians using trans people, especially young, innocent people, as their pawns to get elected. It is despicable. As legislation comes up in Georgia and all over our nation, I have personally addressed legislators about the laws they support that are harmful to the trans community, especially to the children. Because of Adam, we accept the challenge of educating others.

Marian & Adam. Photo by Robin Rayne

Marian Moore
(*she/her*)
grandmother

I wasn't surprised at all when I learned that my grandson Adam is transgender because Adam always acted like a typical boy. As a child Adam didn't want dolls and didn't like dresses or feminine clothes, so I wasn't shocked. My emotions at first were sorrow because Adam was my only granddaughter, but it was not anything that I needed to work through. I could see that; it is what it is. I just loved him. And I have of course continued to love him.

> *Even though I was in my nineties when Adam transitioned, I learned quickly to switch from using Adam's birth name and pronouns to his affirmed name and pronouns. When I made a mistake and was corrected, I could see how important it was to get it right. I tried hard because I love him.*

Transgender people have always been here, although many have lived in unhappy conformity. I believe that it's crucial to accept your grandchildren or children when they come out as transgender or nonbinary. When we get older, and I'm ninety-six now, we realize that love matters more than anything else.

Harris/McNeil Family

Brianna & Amy. Photo by Jill Meyers

Brianna Harris
(*she/her*)

mom, ski technician/
greenskeeper,
athlete

I'm a trans woman and I'm in a loving lesbian marriage with Amy, who is a trans woman too. From our previous marriages, we have three grown children, Aidan, Grace, and Liam. Amy and I live with my child Aidan in a beautiful house in Vermont, way out in the woods.

The process or journey of transition is so very complex. I knew in first grade that I wasn't the same as the other little boys in my class. I was a sensitive boy in a time when boys were expected to be anything but! Because of my more feminine ways, I didn't fit in with the boys, but I didn't fit in with the girls either as I was a boy in their eyes. This created a lot of stress in my life and a lot of bullying from many of my classmates.

In fourth grade I made the decision that since I appeared to be and was assumed to be a boy, I was going to be the best boy I could be. I decided to become an athlete, starting with wrestling and Little League baseball, and I progressed to football, ice hockey, wrestling, skiing, snowboarding, water-skiing, and rock climbing. I did as many of the so-called "macho" sports as I could and became known in school as a jock. I went into athletics to prove my masculinity and was a member of one of the "cool kids" cliques from then on.

Middle and high school went by in a blur. Average student, great athlete, lots of partying and drinking, and all the while, I was cross-dressing by wearing my mother's clothing whenever I was at home alone, just as I had been doing since I was 11 years old. I was desperately trying to hide my secret that it felt good, it felt right, whenever I dressed in women's clothing. This was in the late 1970s and I knew not to share this fact with anyone. I had escaped years of harassment as a very young child by playing the male role and putting on a façade. I knew that my life would all fall apart if it was discovered how I felt when I was dressed as a woman.

I went on living for the next twenty-four years doing what was traditionally expected of men. Over those years I had a few girlfriends, and I never questioned my sexual orientation because I was always attracted to women. In college, my girlfriend of three years discovered my stash of women's clothing and that relationship ended, further reinforcing my need to conceal what I thought was simply my enjoyment of cross-dressing.

I kept taking the next steps in the so-called normal chain of heterosexual life milestones, while hoping that my longing to feel and look like the woman I'd always been, would subside. I would often say to myself, "I'll get married and have kids, and then these feelings will go away." I hope that younger trans and nonbinary people won't have to go through this long stage of hiding who they are.

At twenty-six I married a woman, and ten years later my now ex-wife and I had a child, Aidan. Fourteen years into my marriage, we got our first computer. One night after my wife had gone to bed, I went on the internet and typed in "cross-dressing," and my world blew up. I found ten thousand-plus websites, including some dealing with what was then called transgenderism and transsexuality. The lights in my mind came on and they were blinding. Suddenly I had an explanation for what I had been feeling since I was six years old—and it scared the hell out of me!

Many late nights at the computer followed and it became clear to me that I needed to tell my wife what I had been hiding for most of my life. It was frightening because I knew that my revelation could easily destroy my life as I knew it. My wife and I had been together for twenty years, and yet she had no idea whatsoever about my cross-dressing. I pondered what to do and I just couldn't bring myself to tell her. Then one day she found a pair of women's underwear in the dryer that didn't belong to her. My wife's first thought was that I was having an affair. When I explained to her that I cross-dressed, her initial reaction was relief. She said, "Oh, is that all?"

At the time I told myself that if I could cross-dress with her support then everything would be okay. I could be happy and just go on with my life. Gradually I began going out dressed as Brianna in public and the more I was out in the world as a woman, the more I realized that I needed to transition and live fully as the female I'd always been. However, about a year after I came out to my wife, she decided that she couldn't cope with having a wife as she wasn't a lesbian. She filed for divorce, freeing me to actively pursue my gender transition. Two years after she left our marriage, I legally changed my name to Brianna. Three years after she left, in 2006, I had Gender Affirming Surgery in Montreal, Canada.

When I came out to my child Aidan after the divorce, they were only six years old. Of course, they had questions, but they took the news very well. Their first response was to say, "I'm going to miss my dad." I told them that I wasn't going anywhere and that I would always be their dad. After that conversation, Aidan took my transition in stride. They were seven the first year that they marched at Pride with me. They made a T-shirt that said, "I'm Proud of My Trans Mom!"

Aidan and I discussed how they would refer to me when we were out in public. I told them that it would be a little awkward if we were in a store and they yelled across the aisle, "Hey Dad, look at this," because I looked like the woman I was. I told them that they could call me Maddy, as a cross between Mommy and Daddy, or just my nickname, Bri, or whatever name they wanted to use. A couple of days later, Aidan settled on calling me Ma, and it's been that way ever since.

On a few occasions Aidan was bullied in school, but they always handled it well. When they were in third grade, a fifth grader made some comment about their dad wearing dresses. They just turned to the kid and said, "Well, you are just jealous that I have a dad and a mom in the same body." Aidan just turned twenty-four and they still live with me and their stepmom, Amy. We work together year-round at Mount Snow, a ski area near our Vermont home.

I had gender confirmation surgery after coming to terms with the fact that I wasn't comfortable just wearing women's clothing. For some trans people, surgery is unnecessary. For me, I needed my body to match my actual gender. But even with a woman's body, dating as a trans woman can be a dangerous proposition. Every year, trans women make up a large percentage of the victims of hate crime homicides. As a white woman I didn't face as much risk as my sisters of color do, but it still felt dangerous, so when I transitioned, I figured the romantic part of my life was over. I understood that it would be hard to meet people safely as a trans woman and I was okay with not dating. I was finally me and that felt good enough to bring me joy most of the time.

It has been sixteen years now since I began living full-time as Brianna, and the journey has had its highs and lows. At its lowest I felt so desperately alone and unhappy that suicide seemed like a reasonable alternative, but over time my life has improved so much. I've found that living authentically has been wonderful, including finding love a second time! To my absolute surprise, eleven years ago I met Amy, who is now my wife.

When Amy and I first met, she was transitioning, and her son Liam was struggling with her transition. Coincidentally, Liam was attending the same elementary school that Aidan had graduated from. The school counselor called me and asked if Aidan would be willing to talk to Liam and help him come to terms with Amy's transition. Aidan was happy to help, as they had just written an article titled "Living with a Trans Parent" that was published on the front page of their middle school newspaper.

Amy called, and we talked on the phone for over two hours the first time. Eventually Liam and Aidan met and became good friends. It also turned out that Amy's daughter, Grace, and Aidan were sitting right next to each other in their math class and had no idea that they both had trans parents. After about two months of talking on the phone, Amy and I met each other in person. The rest, as they say, is history.

> **"** *As I've learned more about being trans, I've come to believe that my purpose as a trans woman is to educate people and try to make the journey for those who come after me a little bit easier.* **"**

We began dating and Amy moved in with Aidan and me just eight months after our first phone call. We are incredibly lucky to have found each other because we deeply enjoy being together. On November 8, 2020—yup, we purposely chose election night in the battle between Trump and Biden—Amy and I got legally married. When we woke up on November 9th to the great news that Biden was likely our next President, I decided I wanted to be more out there in the world as an activist.

As I've learned more about being trans, I've come to believe that my purpose as a trans woman is to educate people and try to make the journey for those who come after me a little bit easier.

I've also found peace and a new sense of confidence through public speaking. I've spoken at colleges and universities, high schools, churches, Pride marches, and rallies in five New England states and in New York. Together, Amy and I are available to help smooth the way for others dealing with issues related to their gender identity. Not long ago, we assisted a third grader in her coming out as a trans girl at a local elementary school.

As an athlete, I've initiated the integration of trans people into local women's softball and ski racing leagues, and I've gotten back into playing ice hockey in a local mixed gender league. I hadn't played softball since before I transitioned, but around six years after my transition some local women asked me to play on their team. After I played the first game, the coach who had invited me to play came over to me and said, "Do you have an ID that says female on it?" I said, "Yeah, what's the problem?" She replied, "Somebody wrote a letter to the league's board of directors and complained about you playing on the team. The chair of the board said that if you have something that says female on it, that'll be the end of it." Sure enough, after showing the gal who was the board chair my driver's license, I never had to deal with another complaint—plus, Amy and I have both become like family with her.

When I came out at work at Mount Snow Resort, the parent company owned nine major ski resorts nationwide and yet I was the first person in the entire company to come out as trans and transition on the job. At the time I had been working at the resort for fifteen years and I was fortunate to find substantial support. I never even had difficulty with my restroom usage other than a little initial awkwardness with some coworkers. Incidentally, a few months after I came out at Mount Snow, a second trans woman came out at another of our resorts in Maine. I like to think that I may have helped, in some small way, to pave the way for her to proceed with her own transition.

All in all, I've been very fortunate to have the support of most of my family, friends, and coworkers. I've lost a few folks along the way but gained many more in the process. My life is richer for it. Living authentically is absolutely worth the struggle.

I'm a sixty-one-year-old trans woman. I was assigned male at birth in Columbus, Ohio, and moved to New Jersey when I was four. I still have distinct memories of being around four and discussing with my mother how I was certain I was

Amy McNeil
(*she/her*)

parent, electrical engineer, skier

a girl. This was in 1964 and my mother, with her typical midwestern 1960s mindset, told me: "No, you were born with a penis. You are a boy." We went back and forth, and I argued and fought hard for my belief that I was a girl, and my mom just kept repeating, "No, you're a boy. That's it. There's no changing it. End of discussion. And don't talk to your father about this." I was a child growing up in a time where there was no hint in the media of anything about being trans or nonbinary.

I was always very aware that I was different from the other boys in my school. They teased me all the time because all my friends were young girls. My town was a jock town and there was a lot of emphasis on the football and baseball teams in the school system. I didn't fit into that because I've always been a geek and I've had an interest in electronics from the time I was a little kid—my early toys were tools and things to take apart. I was lucky that both of my parents were very academically oriented, with no interest in sports or desire for me to participate in any of those types of activities.

I had a late onset puberty at fifteen, and when it really started kicking in, it kicked in hard. I remember my brain screaming, "No, this is wrong!" Puberty caused me a lot of stress and a lot of depression. The good news is that I discovered the technical side of theater in high school, and it literally saved me. Our drama club was all misfits and oddballs. Even though we were all uniquely "different" kids, we had this common bond in our love for theater. I did lighting and sound for many wonderful shows throughout my high school years and I also took four years of electronics.

My studies plus my discovery of concerts led me to my first career. I went to my first concert when I was fifteen to see the bands Chicago and the Beach Boys at Madison Square Garden in New York City. I decided then and there that I wanted to do lights for concerts for a living and that's what I did for twenty years. I also designed and built lots of special effects and custom electronics.

I've never worked harder or had more fun in my work life than I did during my time in New York. All along, however, there was always this dark cloud hovering overhead. My confusion about my gender had always been a source of deep, unsettled angst that ebbed and flowed. It was easier to bury myself in work and the long hours that were required to put on shows. I also used drugs and alcohol to self-medicate in the rock and roll world, which was an unhealthy way to take the edge off. It didn't make the pain totally go away, but it made me numb enough to be able to function.

During those rock and roll days, I only dated women and whenever I disclosed my gender issues, the relationship would end. I got to a point where I disclosed as soon as I started to date someone and on our third date, I told my now ex-wife that I liked to cross-dress. At the time, I had a relatively androgynous appearance for a man—long hair and earrings—and she said it wasn't a big deal. As our relationship grew, it became obvious to her that a lot of my clothing came from the women's aisle—my underwear was all from the women's section! I was trying hard to find a middle ground that I could exist in comfortably, but my desire to be live and be recognized as a woman was growing stronger.

I proposed to my girlfriend while I was wearing a black lace dress and high heels. I mean, it wasn't like she didn't know what she was getting into, right? But when our daughter Grace came along, suddenly my wife wanted us to be the stereotypical nuclear family. She wanted me to take on a masculine father role and she wanted to take on the caregiver mother role. It didn't sit well with me, as suddenly I was being forced to put my real self literally back in the closet. I also quickly realized that my show business career, which required me to be away for four days or even a week or two at a time, was not how I wanted to live now that we had a baby at home. I didn't want to miss those special early days and my baby's milestones.

I took my technical background and computer skills and went where the money was—Wall Street. After a while, we started looking for a place to live that was less expensive than New York City. My wife had always wanted to live in Vermont, where her mother's side of the family was from, so we visited Vermont and I fell in love with the beauty of the state. We ended up buying a house and moving up to the Brattleboro area, all while I continued working on Wall Street and drove home on the weekends.

On September 11th, my wife was nine months pregnant with our second child, Liam, and I was supposed to be in the World Trade Center that morning. I was at our data center in a building right next to the World Trade Center and I ran out right after the first plane hit. I headed straight to our main office in midtown. On the ninth floor of a building on 51st and Fifth Avenue looking south, I watched the first tower fall from the skyline.

On the ride home to Vermont that day, the poorly constructed wall that I was using to try and hold my gender issues inside crumbled. I realized that I needed to do something about my gender dysphoria, but it was a long path for me. I struggled for several years until I finally began to move forward with my transition, with a lot of resistance from my wife. Eventually we separated and a few years later got divorced. The two kids stayed with my ex most of the time as the courts awarded her sole custody. The custody decision had nothing to do with my gender identity; in those days, courts almost always ruled in favor of the mother. Fortunately, I ended up getting custody of my kids every other weekend and I made it a point to be as much of a presence in their lives as I could. I called Grace and Liam all the time.

Once my marriage ended, I made the decision that I wasn't going to hide. I lived in a small town of 3,700 in Vermont, and when I began to live visibly as the woman I am, I had no issues with any of the local townspeople. Everything continued without any sort of hiccup. Vermont is a very accepting place, and being a trans woman just wasn't a big deal up here. You couldn't ask for a better place to transition.

> **Because I chose to be very open about my transition, people could see for themselves that there was nothing to be afraid of. Being a trans woman is just who I am.**

When Brianna and I got together as a couple, I brought my two kids, Grace and Liam, and Brianna brought Aidan. When you get all five of us together, it's a fabulous family— our household is the transgender Brady Bunch! Brianna and I both accepted each other's children as our own immediately. I have always given Aidan the same level of support and occasional grief that I gave to my bio kids. I love Aidan every bit as much as I love Grace and Liam. And happily, the three kids love each other. They really acted like siblings right from the start. Now that they are all grown and Liam is at college and Grace is working and living on her own, it's wonderful when we can get everyone together and pile in the pickup truck and go somewhere as a family.

Both Grace and Aidan have come out as nonbinary. I think Liam's solidly heterosexual and cisgender, but he's not at all narrow-minded. In fact, even at a young age, Liam did not like bullies. He had been the recipient of some bullying when he was very young, so he would always rise to defend others who were being bullied. In high school, he turned out to be a strong, tall kid, so when he went up against somebody who was bullying somebody else, the bully usually turned tail and ran. Liam is studying engineering in college now—he takes after me—and he has a lovely girlfriend who is also studying engineering and is almost as tall as he is.

I play softball on a women's team and Brianna and I both bowl on a women's team, and we ski a ton. The National Collegiate Athletic Association has started laying out their guidelines for trans athletes, including requiring two years of hormone replacement therapy before they can compete. A woman who hasn't been on estrogen yet and still has high levels of testosterone might have an advantage. But after a couple of years of taking estrogen, a trans woman's testosterone level is lower than the testosterone level of a cisgender female. For example, Brianna's testosterone level is almost unmeasurable.

The Trump administration was rabidly anti-LGBTQ+, especially with their desire to turn trans people into their personal scapegoats. Their rhetoric and subsequent legislation in many states banning trans athletes from playing on teams or using the correct bathrooms have done a great deal of harm to young trans and nonbinary people. We must fight to change these laws!

A lot of homeless youth are LGBTQ+ teens who have been thrown out of their homes by their parents—which I think should be against the law. And there are still many areas of the country where the topic of gender identity itself is considered taboo. In fact, new laws are being passed right now prohibiting elementary school teachers from talking about LGBTQ+ people and banning books on these topics from school libraries. The best thing that young trans and nonbinary youth should do if they live in such places is to try their hardest to find one sympathetic adult who will at least listen to their story.

My advice to young LGBTQ+ people: Don't be afraid of exploring, but please do it safely. If you find yourself in an extremely conservative environment, work on yourself and try to find some other things that bring you some joy until you can change your situation. You can find a way to survive without self-harm until you can get out. If you are a scholarly type, work hard on your academics so you can get to a college that is in a more liberal part of the country. Colleges can be a way out and offer scholarships. If not, do your best to find a job and a place to live where there are fewer bigots and many more people who will respect you and treat you as an equal.

On the positive side, there is the fact that we trans people are now much more visible, and that corporate America, the entertainment industry, and a lot of the media have come out in support of us. By choosing to be very open about my transition, people could see for themselves that there was nothing to be afraid of. Being a trans woman is just who I am.

More and more people all over this country support us. With more education, I believe that this support will grow by leaps and bounds.

Aidan, Brianna, Grace, Amy. Photo by Jill Meyers

W hen I was around six my dad vanished from my life. Well, not really! My dad came out as a trans woman, changed her name, and became who she really was all along: Brianna Harris.

Aidan Harris
(they/them)

greenskeeper,
ski rental technician

At first, I was terrified because I felt like I was losing my dad. One night at Brianna's house, I broke down in bed and bawled my eyes out. Brianna explained, "I'm still going to be your parent; I'm just not going to pretend any longer to be a man. I'm going to be a woman because I am a woman and I always have been." I didn't really understand in a deep way what was going on, but I thought if I still had both of my parents, I could be happy. Brianna also told me that no matter how much she changed, she would always be my dad deep down inside.

Before my mom's physical transition, the best I can describe her style was very Magnum P.I., the original version of the television show starring the guy who had a thick mustache and wore Hawaiian shirts. One day, when I was around eight, I came home, and Brianna had shaved off her mustache. I just started screaming because I literally didn't know who she was. I only remember my childhood in random bursts, but I do remember that moment when my eight-year-old brain finally comprehended a bit more about what being a trans woman meant.

The year after my parents' divorce, when I was nine, Brianna and I went to the Northampton, Massachusetts, Trans Pride Parade. I covered my bike wheels with rainbow ribbons, and I got a lot of positive comments and had a great time. The next year's Pride parade was even better. I met lots of trans people, and by then I had adjusted well. I saw that Brianna and I could still do all the stuff we used to do together and more!

> **Just because folks are different than you, does that mean that they should be shunned? Trust me, if everyone on the planet were the same, we would get really bored. Being different is what makes us who we are!**

My bio mom took things a bit rougher, but she never, to her credit, tried to get between me and Brianna. I lived with my bio mom in Brattleboro until I was a junior in high school, and by then, she had remarried somebody who was extremely sexist, racist, homophobic, and transphobic. My theory is that my mom thought that her previous husband had "turned into" a woman, so she was going to find somebody who would never, ever do that again. My stepfather—now thankfully my ex-stepfather—kept telling me, "You need to be a macho man." We butted heads a lot and I had no desire to be macho!

My bio mom eventually decided it wasn't working out for me to live with her and her husband and she asked me if I wanted to live with Brianna. That sounded great to me! I moved here to Bri's house when I was sixteen and I've been living here happily ever since. My bio mom moved down to Florida to live with her parents and take care of them in their retirement, so I only see her occasionally. Since her divorce from her sexist husband, Mom and I have slowly been repairing our relationship, and to be fair, both of my bio parents have helped me become who I am—a kind and accepting person.

Since it was the early 2000s, I constantly heard anti-gay comments in school like, "That's so gay," or "You're a sissy!" I decided to write an article for my middle school newspaper about what it was like to have a trans parent. I'd already been involved with the Gay Straight Alliance at the school and some other LGBTQ+ pride groups that Bri had connected me to when she first transitioned. I felt like Brianna did her bit to educate people and now it was my turn to do my bit.

My purpose in writing the article was to show the other kids in my school that I was just a normal kid and that my normal family just had a little twist. I got a lot of positive feedback and support from my classmates and teachers after my piece was published. There wasn't any negative blow-back because Brattleboro is a small liberal town in Vermont. I was never bullied here by anyone about having a trans parent. When friends at school would find out about Bri's transition, they would just say to me, "Oh okay, what should I call your parents now?"

Today when I hear, "You're so gay," or other homophobic slurs like that, I get steamed.

Every year hundreds of LGBTQ+ people are killed. Most of the trans people killed were murdered simply because they were trans. And many suicides of LGBTQ+ kids have happened after the kids were bullied for being or being thought to be queer. I, for one, am tired of reading the news and seeing, "Fifteen-year-old trans youth commits suicide because of relentless bullying." We need to do something about this! This bullying must stop now.

I use the labels nonbinary or genderfluid to describe myself. I wear dresses some days and I wear jeans, work boots, and a cowboy hat on other days. Shortly after I graduated from high school, I was struggling to figure out my sexual orientation like a lot of kids do and now I consider myself pansexual. It's like if you are painting, you can choose whatever colors you like. Do you want purples and blues? Or do you want like orange and pinks?

Grace McNeil
(*she/her*)

lover of life and experience

When my dad came out as a trans woman, I didn't understand right away because being trans was not something that I had ever heard about before. But once it was established that Amy was still my parent, it wasn't that big of a deal to me. I thought about calling Amy, "Mom," but it just seemed weird because I already had a mom and I never really got along well with her growing up. So I still referred to Amy as my dad, but I also called her Amy and I still do.

I had a few experiences that made me feel like I needed to hide that Amy was trans, and I hid it for a long time. As the world around me has grown more accepting, I feel like I don't have to hide it anymore. No matter where you go, there are going to be some people who dislike who you are. Maybe they're going to be cruel about it, but their opinions don't matter in the long run.

> **"I consider myself agender, but I don't really label my sexual orientation at all because I find labels restrictive."**

Being queer, you need to know that you aren't doing anything wrong. There are many people who are misled and don't understand anything about gender identity or sexual orientation. They don't necessarily have any experience with it, and they are usually surrounded by people who think just like them. I don't necessarily hate transphobic and homophobic people, but I hate what they stand for and believe in.

My bio mom wasn't supportive of Amy's transition in the beginning. They had huge fights and she forced Amy to come out to me before Amy was ready. When I was growing up, my bio mom tried to keep me and my brother Liam away from Amy, and I had a lot of problems because of that. I live with my bio mom now, and she's more supportive now than she ever was before, but it's still not always easy. There have been times in the past few years that I've come to live with Amy and Brianna when I'm not getting along with my bio mom. Brianna accepts everyone and is so understanding that she makes me feel very happy. When Amy married Brianna, it made our whole family better.

I had many conversations with Brianna about my gender identity when I was first coming out. One of the things I learned about was the radical difference between my generation and Brianna's generation. When Brianna grew up, she didn't have any resources or role models, so she was forced to be in the closet. She didn't even know that there were many other people throughout the history of humankind who had felt the way she did. In contrast, I can go online and see the trans flag or the pride flag all over the place and find support groups and all kinds of resources for people who aren't cisgender or straight. For people my age, it's a completely different experience than what Amy and Brianna went through.

top: Brianna, Liam; bottom: Amy, Aidan. Photo by Brianna Harris

Liam McNeil
(*he/him*)

college student

Amy told me she was trans around when I was in first grade. She explained to me that being a woman was something she had known all her life and that it was time for her to live as her authentic self. She went on to say that no matter what happened, she was always going to love me and love my sister. She looked different than she had when she was living and presenting as a man, but she was still the same exact person. I still felt the same unconditional love.

I don't call Amy, "Mom." I just call her Amy. When I'm talking with people I've just met, I tend to just say "my dad" and use "they" pronouns because it's easier than having to go in depth for fifteen minutes about Amy being trans. Of course, all my friends know, and they are all supportive and don't care. No one I've told has ever said, "Your dad is a freak." I know I'm lucky that I haven't had to deal with transphobic people.

When I got to college, I was a little bit more reserved right off the bat because I was an athlete. When you're a college athlete, appearance is a huge thing. Not saying anything too controversial is the path most student athletes take because when you're a success-ful athlete, a lot of eyes are on you. After I had firmly established myself, I started talking more freely about my family. The response was completely positive. I'm very happy that I've never had, at least to my face, a negative reaction. I had a girlfriend this past year and the first time she came to visit over the summer I took her to meet Amy and Brianna. It went great. In fact, it went really awesome. She had no issues, no questions.

> If you have a trans or nonbinary parent, don't be afraid. It's part of who you are and it's part of your experience in life.

If you're in a safe place, don't be afraid to let people know about your family members who are trans or nonbinary. If some people judge you, you don't need to be around them anymore. Obviously, they don't appreciate you for who you are, so don't put up with any of that nonsense.

Scott Turner Schofield

Scott. Photo by Josh Stringer

(*he/him, they/them*)

actor, trans advocate

I am trans and nonbinary. I'm on a journey that I'll be on for my entire life. When I started my transition in the year 2000, I was living in Georgia, and the word *nonbinary* didn't even exist; at least I never heard it used. The expression we used back then was *genderqueer*, but that didn't feel like the right descriptor for me.

When I was six, I shaved the skin off my chin trying to shave like my dad. If he thought I was a boy, my dad would have taken the razor and let me do the whole shaving-foam-in-the-mirror thing safely. But because he believed that I was a girl, I wasn't allowed to play like that. So I tried it on my own and I hurt myself in doing it, all because my dad didn't want me to do something that was associated with being a boy. My mom was invested in me being her daughter. I'm her only child, and having an only daughter meant something to her, and I honor that. But the truth is I never was her daughter, and that created a deep misunderstanding between us that we both wish it hadn't. But gender sets up a lens that creates all these expectations, and as a result, it causes people to live in denial. I was living in denial of myself. And my parents were living in denial of my reality. We were all living a lie, and it caused so much needless pain between us.

I came out as a lesbian before I knew that I was trans. Ellen DeGeneres had come out on television and Ellen and I looked kind of similar, so I had a positive role model there. But I still had questions about my identity—I wondered if every lesbian secretly wanted to be a man, like I did. At that age, and in that part of the world, I didn't have any way to know that people like me could be transgender—it just wasn't talked about, and I never saw another person like me anywhere. At TimeOut Youth, I had met some girls who had been assigned male at birth, but I didn't know that there was a boy version of that. In fact, I didn't learn how to believe in myself and trust my intuition and my inner voice until I was twenty years old. I was in college, and I was doing a theater internship in New York City when I met another trans guy in passing. After all those years of denying who I was, I was just like, "Whoa! What?" A huge light bulb moment happened when I was able to talk to him and in the first five minutes of our conversation, he confirmed my entire life. I realized that I wasn't crazy and that there wasn't something wrong with me. The truth was undeniable.

But back when I was a queer teenager living in Charlotte, North Carolina, my first life-defining moment happened. The Pulitzer-Prize winning play by Tony Kushner, *Angels in America*, came to town. There was this massive First Amendment fight when the County Commission tried to shut the play down. They took away all the money from all arts programming, even from after-school programs for kids, the symphony, explaining they didn't want to use any government money to promote the "homosexual agenda." Teenagers think everything is about them—that's just psychological development—I was a queer kid who loved theater, and I felt like this censorship was happening to me. It was in the news all the time and politicians said horrible things like "All homosexuals should be pushed off the face of the Earth" during a televised county commission meeting. The average opinion I heard was that LGBTQ stories were not suitable for public consumption. It all made me want to kill myself—at fifteen years old. Every politician who participates in the act of speaking anti-trans, anti-gay rhetoric today has blood on their hands. As an adult, there's nothing that makes me angrier than other adults who don't realize the impact that speaking their ignorant opinions into the world will have on vulnerable kids. But this was the event that ended up setting the trajectory for the rest of my life. If those bigoted politicians thought they were going to stop anyone from being who they were—or making the world better for ourselves—they failed completely, and their legacy is one of hate and ignorance.

I went to a college with a wonderful theater program. The faculty members were very intentional about making sure that each student got to experience every kind of role, as professional development. I was getting all As and doing well in my acting classes. But the shows that they were doing did not have roles for someone who looked like me: I looked too feminine to play a man and too masculine to play a girl for roles in traditional theater.

One of my professors introduced me to Holly Hughes, the lesbian performance artist who was in the "NEA 4"—four artists who had received grants from the National Endowment for the Arts, which the US government had then taken back because of the LGBTQ content in their work. Holly was writing a book about the Wow Café, a feminist theater collective in New York City, and she let me be her intern. I met that first trans guy who turned the light bulb on for me, and was in the midst of discovering my gender at the same time I was taking the subway everywhere. I realized that the New York City transportation system was a metaphor for the way that discovering one's gender identity works in an underground way. Just like the subway, the gender path doesn't just go in a straight line—it goes in many intersecting directions, and you can get off at any point.

At the time I was exploring my transness in New York, young people were doing a lot of spoken word performance poetry. I figured that this was the way I could share my gender transition, so I created my first one-person show called *Underground Transit* for my honors thesis. And to their credit, when I got back to school, my theater professors said, "This kid has not had the same opportunities that all the other kids have had. Scott deserves a lead role." So, they gave me a full production of my own show. This was in Georgia during the early 2000s. My professors weren't activists. They were theater people who saw that an injustice was being done from an artistic, professional development point of view. And they used their professional power to see to it that I got equal treatment. Somehow, whether because of privilege or miracle or both, it was just that simple. By spring break of my senior year, I was touring my show around to other colleges. Because I was given the same opportunities to develop as a professional, I was able to build an artistic career. This is why inclusion is so important—it has profound effects.

It wasn't all roses. For five years in a row, I applied to graduate schools but got rejected from every one of them. I had a successful touring show. I had recommendations from a Pulitzer Prize winner and some of the top voices in the national theater community. I applied with a cohort of people from Emory who had taken the exact same classes, had the same recommendations from some of the same people, had the same grades, and on top of that, I was a Phi Beta Kappa, highest honors graduate. I was the only one in the group who didn't get into any graduate school. You can't say that wasn't discrimination, that my non-traditional identity and the art I made about it didn't get me excluded from traditional arts programs. I didn't get to earn an MFA, which would have put me in the running to get teaching jobs, maybe a more economically stable life than I have had. The price of exclusion is high, and long-lasting.

I spent a lot of time, after that, thinking that there was something wrong with me, that I wasn't a good enough artist. That's a very human thing to think. But instead of giving up, I wrote another one-man show called *Debutante Balls* and a third show called *Becoming a Man in 127 EASY Steps*. I got a big award from the Princess Grace Foundation and a commission from the National Performance Network—because there are progressive and inclusive arts institutions too—and I started getting taken seriously as an artist. After running a performance space for three seasons up in Alaska, I got an acting gig in France and toured a play within their National Theater system for a season. So I learned that you don't need an MFA to have a career, and I just got on with it.

I moved to Los Angeles. I signed up for an acting class, and at first, I had the thought, "Maybe I won't disclose that I'm trans." I knew I could do that because I could "pass." I don't like to use that word—because there's a connotation that if you don't "pass," you "fail"—but it's the word most people understand. I can move easily through the world as a man. In the end, I decided to disclose to my class that I was trans. Two days later, my teacher called and told me that there was a casting director from the soap opera *The Bold and the Beautiful*, who was looking for a trans actor. He gave her my name and within two weeks I had a recurring role on the second most popular soap opera in the world. They have 33 million viewers per episode, globally, and we were doing a groundbreaking trans storyline. That would never have happened if I hadn't decided to be authentically who I am.

> **"I admit that I practice my Oscar speech from time to time. I imagine that if I ever get an Academy Award, I will dedicate my Oscar to my trans community and especially to any kid who is watching who has ever been told that they are not who they know they are. I will hold up that golden statue and say, 'This is you. You are a prize.'"**

But career isn't everything. All along this decade-plus span I've just described, I negotiated relationships that meant everything to me, even more than my work.

My mom really struggled because she cares what people think. But my mom is a perfect example of a human being who struggles with things that she doesn't understand and goes on to learn more and change. It was very hard for her. But to her credit, she recognized that it was far harder for me than it was for her and that she just needed to figure it out and get over it.

There was something about me changing my name that was particularly intense for my mom. We had a big fight, and I went to my room and slammed my door shut, and I was thinking, "Oh, this is the fight that you have where nothing will ever be the same with your family." I starting to do the math about how to emancipate myself from my family. But the very next day after our fight, to her credit, my mom went to PFLAG. She did the necessary learning and bridged that gap. Now my mom helps other parents of LGBTQ+ kids because she knows what it feels like, and she knows how to talk them through.

I wouldn't have my deep and loving relationship with my mom without PFLAG and all the people who are part of it—the people who attend their support groups to the organization itself. They are teaching people a way of loving that most folks don't learn in our transphobic, homophobic society. PFLAG is helping people put back the essential building block of unconditional love and service to others. We are always going to be a minority, but every single person who loves us makes a difference. Organizations like PFLAG and Free Mom Hugs empower people to resist homophobia and transphobia. There are no words for what that means. It is wonderful and powerful, and my family is better because of it. There's a saying, "If you change one person, you change the world," so if you change one family, that is incredibly powerful.

I want to encourage all parents of trans and nonbinary children to do the work to understand that each of your kids has had an entire lifetime of knowing who they are inside. Please understand that if you disagree with your kid when they tell you from the moment they are verbal that they know who they are, your denial of their reality does so much damage to them.

For example, before I met my wife, Terra, I had been in a series of toxic relationships. I was a toxic person, and I attracted similarly toxic people. I didn't understand it then, but having done a lot of work on undoing it, I understand now that I was toxic in relationships because I didn't know how to love myself. This happens so often in our community: we didn't know what unconditional love looks like—it goes back to not being seen or loved for who we are and thus not being able to love ourselves for who we are. This is why it's so damaging not to affirm a child. Between high school and my thirtieth birthday, I attempted suicide four times, and I spent time in an inpatient psychiatric facility. That's not because I am trans: it's because of how I was treated because I was trans. I had to do so much work to know who I am and to trust that there's nothing wrong with me—I'm just trans! And I can be loved as a trans person, and the love I have to give, as a trans person, is perfect, like all love is. In a world that accepts trans people as valued humans, that wouldn't happen.

By the time I met my wife, I had recognized that I could not continue to hurt people, and I did a great deal of healing work—therapy, support groups, meditation classes. Years of work to undo all of the toxic messaging that told me I was not—could never be—good enough. Just as I had to intentionally create an authentic way of living my gender, I also had to create a code for living. I vowed I would never take out the harm that was done to me on anyone again. We can't change the past, but we can intentionally change direction, and never go back. And just because we have done harm in the past does not make us unloveable forever. And then, I was ready for the love of my life.

My wife is solid in places where I still have work to do, and I am the same for her. There are places in her life where she needed more stability and love, and I am able to provide that for her in ways that have nothing to do with gender or sexual orientation—and she does the same for me. Our very human, very deep parts really match up. Terra's family accepted me immediately. The first thing her dad said to me was that he had watched my TED talk about being transgender. He said, "It was fantastic. Thank you for making it." He and her mom approached me with love and respect and that's what a healthy family looks like. Terra and I are mutually supportive of each other, and I feel like I'm living a completely different life than before we met—a life that I couldn't have possibly imagined.

I have told this story of support and love and good fortune and privilege, but there is another story too. It's about my close family members who don't accept me, who think I'm an abomination, who won't let me be around their children. That is a part of my story, but I choose not to get into it because I don't want it to be the definition of my story. I don't want to give it that much power. Life hasn't all been roses for me and when I talk to other trans people who are suffering from rejection and discrimination, I do know what it's like. I do share that pain. I affirm that pain and the intense anger that can change who you are as a person. What I've come to, through it all, is that success is the best revenge. Success doesn't mean having a big job with lots of money, or being married, or anything anyone tells you it has to mean. Just like you, success is self-defined. It means being exactly who you are, having a life where you can still appreciate whatever brings you joy, even in the face of all the pain of the world that we can't fix or change.

Genny Beemyn

Genny. Photo by Jill Meyers

(*they/them*)

LGBTQIA+ advocate, author, speaker

I began to be harassed for not being masculine enough in middle school, when one of the bullies mocked me by saying that he could not tell at first if I was a boy or a girl. That was the start of verbal and physical violence that became so constant that I dreaded going to school, even though I loved learning and did very well academically. When my mother and grandmother found out about the extent of the bullying and saw how it was affecting me, they agreed to send me to a Catholic high school even though my family was not Catholic. While I still experienced some harassment in high school, I survived, which I cannot imagine would have been the case in public school.

When I was growing up in a working-class/lower middle-class suburb of Buffalo, I had no idea that there were options other than male and female, so I tried to fit in with other male-assigned individuals and thought my inability to relate to them simply meant that I was a different kind of guy. I was able to have some sense of belonging and gain some acceptance because I was an athlete and, at one point, was the fastest cross-country and long-distance track runner at my high school. I was not interested in drinking, but I also sought to fit in with classmates by going out to drink with them and secretly dumping out my drinks when they were not looking.

I learned about trans people in college, but it was only about individuals who were then referred to as transsexuals, who were described as being "trapped in the wrong body." While I increasingly felt that I was not male, I did not identify as female either and did not reject my body to the extent of hating or feeling disconnected from it.

My revelatory moment came through reading Leslie Feinberg's *Stone Butch Blues* when it was published in 1993. The experiences of the gender nonconforming narrator were very different from my own, even though they had grown up in Buffalo as well, but I saw enough of me in them that I was able to relate on some levels. The novel empowered me by enabling me to see that identifying outside of a gender binary was a possibility. However, I continued to feel alone, as even though *Stone Butch Blues* was based on Feinberg's experiences, the protagonist was still a fictional character, and I still did not personally know anyone else who identified as nonbinary.

Because of the lack of images of nonbinary trans individuals and the widespread ignorance about nonbinary people, even in LGBTQIA+ communities, it was a gradual process for me to claim a nonbinary identity and to come out to others. I started coming out more publicly as genderqueer after I was hired to be LGBT office coordinator at Ohio State University in 2001. I had been asked to choose a pseudonym for a study of trans people in which I was participating and decided on "Genny," after my grandmother,

Genevieve. Afterward, I realized that I liked the name for myself in every-day life. By that time my given first name, which was somewhat non-gendered when I was growing up, had become a name given only to individuals assumed to be men. But because I did not want to be seen as a trans woman, I chose to combine "Genny" with my birth name. Over time, though, I found that this part "male"/part "female" name did not work. People would still call me by my birth name only, seeing Genny as optional, or would think Genny was my last name. I eventually decided to be just Genny and let the dissonance between a "female" name and a largely "male" appearance serve to indicate my nonbinary identity, along with adopting nonbinary pronouns for myself.

I initially asked my colleagues, friends, and members of the local LGBTQIA+ community to refer to me by ze/hir pronouns. In the early 2000s, few trans people were using nonbinary pronouns for themselves and I was constantly misgendered. I quickly tired of correcting others and having to explain how to use and spell *ze* and *hir*. Even though I worked in an environment where I typically did not encounter outright discrimination as a nonbinary trans person, I regularly experienced microaggressions in the form of misgendering.

Ironically, some of the most frequent misgendering I experienced—and the most painful—came from other trans people. The trans people I knew at the time were mostly trans women who were ten to twenty years older than me. When they began to self-identify, being trans meant that you were either transsexual or a cross-dresser, so they had no lens with which to understand me as someone who felt more female than male but who was not intending to present as female and take hormones. As a result, I found myself in a surreal situation where my gender identity was more often disrespected by other trans people than by some of my cis colleagues, who had much less comprehension of trans issues but who wanted to be supportive of me. Eventually, many of the trans people I knew did see me as one of them, but only after I legally changed my name and began electrolysis (there is nothing like shared pain as a bonding experience).

In 2006, when I took my current position as the director of the Stonewall Center, the LGBTQIA+ center at UMass Amherst, I decided to switch to using they/them, hoping that I would have less difficulty in getting other people to remember and respect these pronouns, since they would not have to learn a new vocabulary. I have been misgendered less frequently since then, which is probably because of this change, as well as because I am now living in a more progressive area of the country and because cis people have become more educated about pronouns in recent years as more nonbinary trans people have come out. I think it has also helped that I legally changed my name to Genny and that I regularly speak about and advocate for trans students on campus and nationally, so that others are constantly reminded of my nonbinary identity.

In the early 2000s, as a growing number of college students started coming out as trans, I wrote some of the first articles on their experiences and needs and began to push for universities to develop trans-supportive policies. I also conducted the first national study of nonbinary trans students and edited the first anthology about trans people in higher education, and the study that Sue Rankin and I did for our book *The Lives of Transgender People* (2011) remains the largest trans-focused study in the United States conducted by individual researchers. Applying my scholarship to practice, I have helped to turn UMass Amherst into one of the most trans-inclusive colleges in the country and advocated for trans students in higher education more widely.

> **Although I tend to focus on what still needs to change to create a better world for nonbinary trans students, when I take a step back, I am amazed at how far we have come already.**

Twenty years after I began writing and speaking about trans students, I am still doing so because colleges still largely ignore or marginalize trans students, especially nonbinary trans students. No campus does enough to support trans students, particularly so that they are not misgendered and that those who knowingly misgender them are held accountable.

Colleges need to ask students how they identify their gender and the names and pronouns they go by and then respect this information in all contexts. This means eliminating a gender binary in campus housing, athletics, student organizations, and other areas of college life and treating trans students' birth names as confidential information that never appears on public documents. In addition, students' pronouns should appear on course rosters and in administrative systems, and instances of repeated misgendering by others, whether deliberate or not, should be addressed as harassment.

Some of these changes are beginning to be made. In 2021, the administrators of the Common Application, the admissions form used by more than 1,000 colleges, began giving students the ability to indicate their gender identities, chosen names, and pronouns, so that some institutions will automatically have this information about their incoming students. The University of California system implemented a gender and name policy in the 2020–21 school year that, as part of respecting students' gender identities, enables nonbinary trans students to be recognized as such on their institutional records.

A few colleges now assign all housing based on students' gender identities rather than the gender marker on their legal documents so that trans students can live anywhere on the campus and not be limited to gender-inclusive housing. And perhaps the most important change is that, as of 2021, both the executive and judicial branches of the US government consider the prohibition against sex discrimination in federal law to include discrimination based on gender identity. This means that colleges risk being investigated and charged by the Department of Education if accused of anti-trans discrimination and possibly being sanctioned if the complaint is substantiated.

Although I tend to focus on what still needs to change to create a better world for nonbinary trans students, when I take a step back, I am amazed at how far we have come already. Twenty-five years ago, I felt very alone when I came out as nonbinary while I was a graduate student at the University of Iowa and helped get the university to add "gender identity" to its nondiscrimination policy, making it the first college in the country to enact a formal trans-inclusion policy. Today, the majority of young trans people identify as nonbinary, and it can be a challenge to keep up with all the terms that they are creating to describe various nonbinary gender identities.

Moreover, even though most colleges still do not have specific policies to support their trans students, hundreds of colleges now offer trans-inclusive policies, such as including gender identity in their nondiscrimination policies, providing all-gender restrooms and housing options, covering transition-related medical care under student health insurance, and giving students the ability to have a chosen name and pronouns on campus records.

As I continue to advocate for colleges to become more welcoming to trans students, I am heartened by the many other nonbinary trans people who are now also engaged in this struggle.

Tynan Power and Family

Tynan & Randy. Photo by Shana Sureck

Tynan Power
(*he/him*)

mother, writer, faith-based organizer

My life has been shaped by many identities—white, queer, trans, Muslim, deaf, disabled, middle-class—and my roles as a writer, editor, digital media specialist, activist, organizer, and faith leader. My most central identity and role, though, has been as a mother to my two children.

That identity was born with my first child, Yahya, when I was only twenty years old. It impacted nearly everything that followed, including when I transitioned and why I chose to spend so much of my life as an activist and organizer creating space for families like mine.

My own mother was a divorced single parent, and I was her only child. She instilled in me a strong value of family and, as we moved a lot, I learned from her that home is where your family is. She also challenged traditional notions of what it meant to be a woman and made it clear to me that I could be anything I wanted to be—just not a boy.

I knew I felt like a boy as a child, but it took me a while to find the words to express that—and even longer to find the word *transgender*. When I was five, I told my mother I wanted boots so I could be a cowboy. She laughed and said I could be a cowgirl. It wasn't an unreasonable response— she probably assumed I just didn't know the right word—but I got the clear message that talking about wanting to be a boy would just lead to ridicule.

When I was a teenager and my mom and I had conflicts, I imagined running away, cutting my hair, and living as a boy. Why not run away and just be a girl somewhere else? It never even occurred to me! It was obvious that I would be a boy if I didn't have to live by anyone else's rules.

Going along with social gender expectations got me through those years, even though there were many areas of my life that were difficult. For one, I was a kid with a severe hearing loss, navigating mainstream public schools with no accommodations in the seventies and eighties. It's no wonder I didn't want to rock the boat over gender. I also didn't think there was any point. I knew trans women existed, but I'd never even heard of trans men.

It took me until my late twenties to discover that trans men existed and start to identify as trans. By that point, I had two children—Yahya and Justyn—and my second marriage, to Justyn's father, was unraveling for unrelated reasons. Transition seemed like it could only happen for people with very different lives from mine.

When I was twenty-seven, I attended the True Spirit Conference in Washington, DC, an annual conference for people who identified as FTM (female-to-male), which the organizers defined very broadly to include people who might identify as butch or genderqueer. I stayed with my uncle's family and on the spur of the moment, I decided to tell my aunt about the conference. She asked a lot of questions, listened, and told me that she and my uncle loved me and always would. Her reassurance made a world of difference at that moment and gave me the courage to tell other family members.

When I told my mother that I was transgender and felt that I was male, she said, "Well, that makes sense." Sadly, even though she said she understood, she didn't support me in transitioning. She refused to use correct pronouns for me until she was dying of cancer seven years later—by which point I had already transitioned, changed my driver's license to say "male," and grown a full beard.

Other family members learned I was trans through family gossip and had a variety of reactions, mostly of the "I don't understand, but you are family" variety. With some relatives, though, my transition added to existing strain that had started when I converted to Islam as a teenager. Some of those relationships did get better over the years, but others worsened after my mom's death.

My contact with my father was so infrequent—and so awkward—that I didn't tell him that I was transgender until years after I transitioned. How do you bring something like that up, during a once-a-year phone call with someone you haven't seen in person for years? Eventually, I sent him a letter explaining that I had transitioned because I was hoping to see him. We never talked about it, though, and he never agreed to see me again before he died a few years later.

My father never mentioned my transition to my younger half-brother, John Mark, my father's son from his second marriage. John Mark and I weren't in regular, direct contact over the years, but as adults, we found each other on Facebook and started to build a real bond. When we got in touch for the first time in years, he and his wife had just had their first baby. When I asked him if he had any questions about my gender identity, his response was, "My only question is whether you want to be Uncle Ty or Aunt Ty." That was the best response I could have hoped for because I had always wanted nieces and nephews and, being raised as an only child with my mom, I thought I would never have any.

When I first started calling myself trans, I didn't announce it to my kids, but I started presenting in a more masculine way. Justyn was only four and seemed to accept every person however they presented gender-wise, including me. Yahya was seven and had more questions. One day while I was driving, Yahya asked me, "How come there are men who feel like women and wear dresses, but there aren't women who feel like men and wear men's clothes?" I stopped the car and turned all the way around in my seat to look at Yahya. Yahya looked right back at me—dressed in khakis and a button-down shirt with my buzzed hair. I didn't have to say anything; after a few seconds, Yahya exclaimed "Oh!"

A few years later, when I started to consider transitioning, my kids knew a lot of other trans people. Justyn didn't seem to think transition was a big deal at all. To him, it was just something some people did. Yahya thought it was fine for other people to transition, but they were afraid that if I transitioned, they would lose their mom. To Yahya, losing their mom would have meant losing the nurturing parent I'd always been. I reassured Yahya that I'd always be their mom.

I've never used the term *father* for myself, though I know lots of trans men do and I support that choice. I was my kids' mother for years before I transitioned, and both my kids had biological fathers who interacted with them in more stereotypically "Dad" ways, so I felt like it made sense to stretch the definition of a mom to include me.

At the time, there were very few out trans men with kids, so there was no model to follow. Since then, models have emerged based on what trans parents want to be called and their various paths to parenthood—including the wonderful term "seahorse papa" for trans men who give birth after transition.

Transitioning completely altered how my family participated in religious life. As a devout Sunni Muslim, a lot of my faith was woven into our home life—like praying five times a day or waking my sleepy kids to have a big breakfast with me before dawn during Ramadan—and those things didn't change. Attending services at the mosque, on the other hand, became complicated. My mosque-centered Muslim community had always been warm and welcoming, but also had very strict ideas about how Islam should be practiced, ideas that did not leave room for gender transition and queerness. Like most mosques, the space itself was divided by gender, with separate doors and prayer spaces for men and women. I knew I couldn't continue to attend services in a gender-segregated space where people had known me as a woman. I would be stopped at the door if I tried to enter the men's section.

Because I no longer felt safe or comfortable going to the mosque, my kids couldn't go either. They experienced an Islam deeply rooted in our household and our family life, but not the warmth and fellowship that American Muslim community life can offer. It was especially hard after 9/11, when Yahya was the target of relentless bullying, and I didn't have a Muslim community to call on for help or moral support.

I was fortunate to find a spiritual home for my family in the Unitarian Society of Northampton and Florence (Massachusetts), a Unitarian Universalist congregation, where we were warmly welcomed as a queer and trans family. Our Muslim faith and traditions were also welcome and valued. Still, I longed to find Muslim community—I never felt it was "either/or," but rather "and."

There were some rays of hope. In 1997, I had discovered a nascent queer Muslim community forming online, in an email group called "gaymuslims." By then, I knew there were as many ways to be Muslim as there are Muslims in the world—that's roughly 2 billion—and there was no single way to be devout. I quickly learned that there had even been religious rulings that supported gender transition, although these rulings hadn't magically made things easier for trans Muslims. We were still facing transphobia at home, in our communities, and in our mosques, since even religious leaders are often unaware of these rulings or how to translate them into welcoming policies.

I also became very aware of my privilege. I could list the ways I was marginalized, but I was suddenly struck by the enormous privilege I had as a white convert, and even as a trans man who would probably never face the violence that many trans women experience. The more aware I was of the risks other LGBTQ Muslims faced, the more committed I became to being out and advocating for all of us.

That commitment to this fragile new community became the foundation of my queer and trans Muslim organizing and activism. The gaymuslims email list led to the creation of Al-Fatiha, the first national LGBTQ Muslim organization formed in the US, which was founded by my friend Faisal Alam in 1997. I joined its shura and facilitated sessions at its conferences.

After Al-Fatiha disbanded, several of us gathered to form a new organization and co-founded the Muslim Alliance for Sexual and Gender Diversity (MASGD). I served for two years as co-chair of our LGBTQ Muslim Retreat, which took place every year for seven years from 2011 to 2018. The Retreat drew Muslims from all over the country and offered a chance to be in community with others of different sexual and gender identities, varied racial and ethnic backgrounds, and a wide range of ages. For one weekend a year, we could learn, worship, and be joyfully at ease together in a thoroughly Muslim space. By then my kids were adults, but each of them participated in the Retreat at different times. Seeing them warmly welcomed there helped to heal the deep wound left by years of feeling excluded from Muslim community. The Retreat was also the first Muslim space that completely welcomed my partner Randy as a full member of the community, in the same way that Randy's Jewish community had always welcomed me.

> To me, being a mother had to do with the role I played with my children, not with my gender. Years later, a vendor at a local Pride march was selling a t-shirt that said, 'Who says men don't make great moms?' I felt so seen that I bought it and still wear it every Mother's Day.

Randy and I were married in two ceremonies in 2013 and 2014. Our second wedding was a beautiful celebration that honored both Islam and Judaism, and we were joined by friends who gave blessings from their own faiths. It may have been the only Muslim-Jewish wedding in history that included Christian ministers giving blessings in the name of Jesus. Our chuppah was a T-shirt quilt that included queer-themed T-shirts we'd each acquired over the years. The guests included queer and trans activists, local Jewish and Muslim community members, Randy's parents and extended family, his childhood friends, and their parents. Both of my parents had passed away, but I felt surrounded by family of many kinds.

In stark contrast to my previous, ostensibly straight weddings, no one from my mother's family attended. But my brother's family and his mother made the trip, and my tiny nieces were delightful as our flower girls. It was hard to celebrate a wedding after so much loss, but expanding our family to include my brother's family and Randy's was the start of a new chapter in our lives.

Together, Randy and I have built a home that honors both Muslim and Jewish traditions and prioritizes our shared spiritual values, including the values of building community and welcoming the stranger. In the time we've been together, I started the Pioneer Valley Progressive Muslims with Randy's support, and I supported Randy when he co-founded Nishmat Shoom, a queer minyan that offered Jewish high holiday services in Northampton.

Over the years, I realized that, as crucial as LGBTQ+ Muslim spaces are, trans Muslims have specific needs that weren't being addressed. When I learned that the Philadelphia Trans Wellness Conference had religious programming but didn't have Muslim Friday prayers or Muslim programming, I volunteered to create it. Allies at TransFaith gave me the support to make it happen and, later, to form the Trans and Muslim Project. Doing this work has been a deeply meaningful ministry to me. I have loved witnessing other trans Muslims find this space—a small Muslim enclave within a very queer, very trans conference—where all their intersecting identities are welcome and they can be fully seen. During the pandemic, when we couldn't gather in person and many trans Muslims were experiencing acute hardship, two of us launched the Trans Zakat Project during Ramadan 2021, creating a way for Muslims to make their annual charitable zakat payments directly to trans Muslims.

When my oldest child, Yahya, told me they identify as nonbinary, it made me realize, in a very personal way, that the trans advocacy efforts so many of us had been making were both vitally important and still sometimes fell short when nonbinary people were left out.

I didn't anticipate that Yahya would identify as nonbinary, but I also wasn't completely surprised. In the years since I'd transitioned, the trans umbrella had expanded and identity words—which are so important to feel we are understood and seen for who we are—had shifted, making more room for trans people whose identities were less about moving from Box A to Box B. Yahya as a child and then as a young adult seemed to find binary gender norms unnecessary and was happy to ignore them, so it makes sense to me that they identify as nonbinary. I am glad there is more space for them in the world today, but I also know there's still a lot more to do to ensure the safety and equality of nonbinary people.

Although I fully supported Yahya from the beginning, pronouns were still a challenge for me. Even back in the nineties, I knew some people who used nonbinary pronouns and I've always been a strong supporter of they/them pronouns. Still, changing the pronouns I used for Yahya required unlearning a speech habit I'd had for more than twenty years. Their brother Justyn and my partner Randy seemed to make the switch seamlessly, but for me it was difficult—and very frustrating. It felt like repeatedly failing a test despite knowing all the correct answers—and worse, every time I got it wrong, I knew it hurt this child I loved. It was humbling to be reminded that we can't afford to stop learning and growing, even when we think we are experts.

Building community and making space for families like ours—and, really, for anyone who is excluded—gives me hope that the world we are leaving for our children and their children will have more expansive words, more inclusive spaces, and more kindness.

I grew up in a mixed Christian and Jewish household, but I am strongly Jewish-identified today. I was a creative, imaginative kid who loved acting and singing, and I was very lucky to have parents who always supported me. When my parents divorced when I was a teenager, they tried to make it amicable, but their divorce really challenged my faith in families. Creating the family I have now has helped restore it.

Randy (he/him)
teacher

I first learned about transgender people in a job I had in high school in the 1990s. I was a peer health educator with an organization called Advocates for Youth. We included some information about trans people in our trainings, but I didn't really have a full understanding. However, I got to know many trans people when I was a student at Hampshire College.

I met Tynan when I was still in college. I thought Ty was very cool, but I didn't really get to know him until quite a few years later when I started attending religious services both at a local synagogue and at the Unitarian Society of Northampton and Florence. Ty was a member of the Unitarian Society with his kids and his partner at the time. We got to know each other, sharing experiences as people of faith and seekers of connection with the Divine. But it would still be a few years before we went on our first date.

Ty reached out to me by email, and I took over a month to get back to him because I'm terrible about my email. We went out for dinner and just talked and talked and talked. I didn't want the night to end. Our third date was when Ty invited me to see *Borat* with him and Yahya. It was terribly offensive, but we also laughed so much. That was how I really got to know Yahya too.

As we continued dating, I also spent time with Ty's son, Justyn. When I moved in, it was Yahya's last summer at home before college, but Justyn still had a few more years at home. During that period, I tried to work out how to be a good stepparent to Justyn. It was a tumultuous time, but so very rewarding. I loved hosting Justyn's friends at the house, and I got Ty and Justyn into watching the entire series of *My So-Called Life*, an important part of my adolescence.

> **"** *I've admired how steadfast Tynan is in his faith and prayer practice despite this lack of acceptance from much of the Muslim world. We've had a wonderful time together at the LGBTQ Muslim Retreats he has helped organize. There are now some spaces that weren't available when his kids were younger, but I still feel sad that Ty couldn't provide that kind of religious community for Justyn and Yahya when they were growing up.* **"**

We got legally married in August 2013 in Washington, D.C., in Dupont Circle. Our friend Daaiyee Abdullah, who is a gay Muslim imam, performed the ceremony, and Ty's kids and my parents attended. We had applied for a marriage license the year before, but we made the wedding happen in just twenty-four hours once we found out that Yahya didn't have health insurance at their new job and needed to be on my insurance. The next year, we had a big interfaith wedding, officiated by a Jewish friend and a Muslim friend. We followed the Jewish wedding format of seven blessings but included Muslim prayers as well.

My focus shifted to being more family-oriented, and I knew that my home with Ty and the kids would be my home for life. I wanted to be there for both Yahya and Justyn for whatever they needed: late-night rides home, their theater improv performances, and the occasional trip to the emergency room. All of it is part of being a full member of this family and

I treasure that so much. As the kids have grown older, my relationship with Ty has evolved and we've made our home much more just for the two of us. However, it is hard being empty-nesters and having the kids live so far away in North Carolina and New York. Ty and I miss Yahya and Justyn so much! We always keep two bedrooms available and look forward to the times when they come home to visit.

My family has always been very supportive of me being fully myself and loving who I love. They haven't always understood everything, but they've always been loving. When I started dating Ty, my parents initially felt more hesitation about the age difference and the fact that Ty had kids than because he was trans. Now we are all a close extended family.

I have an aunt who is a conservative Christian, and some people might assume that she wouldn't accept me and Ty, but she is incredibly loving to us. She has invited me and Ty and the kids over for Thanksgiving and Christmas and has always been really welcoming of all of us.

As far as religion goes, being in the progressive Jewish world, I've always been welcomed for being my full self. However, I know that Ty has not experienced the same welcome from Muslim communities. Ty's son Justyn recently commented that it felt weird that he knows the Jewish prayers so much better than he knows the Muslim prayers. I responded that Ty couldn't take Justyn and Yahya to mosques for much of their childhood and their adolescent years because most mosques were not welcoming to their family. I told him about the time Ty and I went to a mosque in the D.C. area one year for Eid prayer and the imam's sermon was all about the "evils of gay marriage."

I've learned so much about love from Tynan, seeing the way he loves his grown kids and experiencing the way he loves me. He's always there to support Yahya and Justyn and loves to have them close by so he can talk to them and hug them. As a teacher, I've worked with kids a lot, but I didn't really understand how much encouragement, support, and love kids of all ages need until I joined Ty's family.

Yahya, Randy, Tynan, Justyn. Photo by Jill Meyers

I'm Tynan's biological child. Growing up with a trans parent in a liberal college town in western Massachusetts, I knew that my assigned gender was not all that I could or had to be. I considered myself an ally and advocate for the

Yahya Alazrak
(*they/them*)

nonprofit executive director

trans and queer community, and I also felt like I was part of the community thanks to my parent, Tynan. I was confident that I was a boy until I went to college.

I went to Guilford College, a cozy Quaker liberal arts college in Greensboro, North Carolina. It was there I started to question my own gender experience. I knew that I had problems with traditional masculinity, but I also knew that I didn't identify as trans in the way I understood it then. Up until that point, most of my experience in the trans community was around people who had a more binary—or at least a more binary-presenting—journey. For the most part, I spent time with people like my parent Ty, who were raised to be women, identified as men, and were taking medical steps toward aligning their body with their own understanding of themselves.

> **Trans, as the broad umbrella term it has become, still doesn't feel 100-percent comfy for me. I prefer the terms genderqueer and nonbinary. I'm glad to be in the land of 'neither' and 'in-between.' It's roomy, there is a lot to explore, and the clothing options are endless.**

There weren't many role models back then of what nonbinary identity could look like for me. At the time, Eddie Izzard was one of the few public figures that I felt I could identify with somewhat, and even she was considered a cross-dressing man.

I remember being in my Gay and Lesbian Cinema class and talking about Judith Butler and their theory that identity is either placed on us by society or something we create in response to that; from there we perform the identity we want the world to see, like putting on make-up to be perceived more as a woman or buying a big pickup truck to appear more manly. My professor asked, "What is left when we get rid of all those layers of performativity?" Instinctively, I knew the answer was God. I had this moment of deep knowing in the class, understanding that a world where we have access to an innate sense of belonging must be a world of pure love, of holiness. But I didn't yet know what to do about it.

After college, I began to say that my pronouns were "he or they" when asked. Eventually that became reversed to "they or he." Almost three years after leaving college, I was interviewing for a job with Resource Generation, where today I'm the executive director. In the interview process, I was asked for my pronouns and shared "they or he," and for the first time ever, a group of strangers chose to use they/them pronouns when referring to me, even though I had given them the "easier" option of "he." I felt so seen.

Justyn Melrose
(*he/him, they/them*)

digital journalist

My immediate family includes my biological mom Ty, my stepfather Randy, my sibling Yahya, my biological dad David, and my former stepfather, Tim. When I was in grade school, we'd always joke that someday I'd write a memoir called "My Four Fathers," even though I still refer to Ty as my mom.

Ty's transition, the queerness of my family—these have been normal parts of my life for so long that it's honestly mundane. I was about six when my mom transitioned. For a six-year-old, everything is new. Learning that my mom was a man was no more mind-blowing than learning that my teachers existed outside of the classroom.

When I was a kid and I'd be talking about my family, I wouldn't stop to explain. I just assumed everyone was going to understand. I'd be a bit dumbfounded when someone would interrupt me and say, "Oh, you used 'he' when you were talking about your mom. You mean 'she.'" As I got a little older, I got used to the back-and-forth. I might quickly interject a footnote in there and say, "My mom's picking me up. He—my mom is trans—he should be here soon," but I usually wouldn't bother. Either way someone would get hung up on the "errant" pronoun. "Wait, your mom is trans? Are you adopted? Who is your real mom? Who is your real dad?"

It didn't bother me that people were curious, but I did find it annoying to have to stop and give a five-minute Gender Theory 101 course when I was just trying to get through a conversation or tell a story. That's still more or less how I handle the conversation. I'm not going to get into it unless I'm asked, and if someone asks, I'm happy to explain—as long as they aren't asking intimate questions about my parents' genitals.

I was Muslim when I was very young before declaring myself a "proud atheist" when I was a preteen. I was anti-religion for a long time, partly because I had seen a lot of self-described religious people being pretty ugly about LGBTQ+ issues. Anytime I thought about religion, I mainly thought about the bigoted "Adam and Eve, not Adam and Steve" brand of Christianity, which included some of the now-estranged members of my family.

That really tainted the whole religion thing for me. Also, I was a deeply curious kid and fascinated with science, and I'd say, in most grade schools around the country, science and religion don't get along well because of the "evolution" of it all.

Our family went to the Unitarian Society when I was in middle and high school, and through much of that time I identified as agnostic and wouldn't have really called myself Unitarian Universalist (UU). Around my junior year of college, I migrated back to being UU. I had started getting more comfortable with defining my religious experience through my own lens, rather than as a reaction to someone else's.

> My family is the kind of family that would make some people's heads explode. It includes a queer trans Muslim mom, a Latino dad, a Jewish stepdad, and an Arab brother.

I use he/him pronouns mostly because it's convenient, but when asked I'll often say I'm comfortable with they/them too. I'll put it this way: it's like when you're going through security at the airport and the TSA agent tells you which metal detector to go through. They've been telling me to go through the same metal detector my entire life, and I'm fine going through it, but I'd be just as happy to go through a different one—or not go through one at all. It doesn't feel like it has much bearing on who I am on a more profound level. We're all going to the same place.

I work as the executive digital producer at a TV news station in North Carolina, and I love working in news. One of the first things I learned about journalism is that you should always strive to be unbiased, that you are required to divorce your own opinions from your writing in order not to erode your credibility or manipulate your readers. When I got my first job as a reporter at a small-town newspaper in rural North Carolina, I really clung to that. I set my voter registration to "unaffiliated" and kept mum about politicians and movements. At the time, as a fledgling twenty-one-year-old writer, I was terrified that if I crossed that line, if I made the wrong comment, I'd end my career before it even started. So along with my opinions on elections and political parties, I also buried my pride in my family.

I was afraid to tell folks that I'm Latino, let alone tell folks that my mom is a transgender man. We're talking about North Carolina, home of HB2, the so-called "bathroom bill" that said that transgender folks had to use restrooms corresponding with the gender they were assigned at birth. So, I didn't put up pictures of my family at the office. I didn't talk about home at all. When folks asked me about my mom or my parents, I'd avoid using pronouns as best I could or—and I'm not proud of this—misgender my mom so I wouldn't rock the boat. I felt like a coward.

It took me a couple years before I was willing to publicly admit that my mom is a transgender man and another few years before I was willing to say I supported him in being trans. I don't think it was any kind of epiphany that changed my view. I think it was just exhaustion. I love my family. I'd say we're closer than many others out there. And I was trying to keep all of that hidden away. I felt so isolated, like I was living a half-life, like I had lost my family. I still spoke with them regularly; it wasn't a tangible kind of loss, but I felt like I was betraying my family every day. I don't think there's a good comparison for that ache you feel when you lie about someone you love, especially when it's out of a perceived self-preservation.

It was only in the last few years that I decided that I'm not going to let anyone tell me that my family is "too political" for me to talk about. I still value and respect the journalistic tenet of unbiased reporting, and I stand by it, but I've decided that it doesn't have to be mutually exclusive with valuing and respecting and loving my family. Every journalist I know with a nuclear family has a picture of their wife or husband, their kids, whomever, in their office. It took a bit to convince myself that I deserved that too—and my mom deserves a son who is proud of him. It should never be controversial to say I love my mom or my dad or my sibling.

Last year, I was moved into a bigger cubicle at the television station, and I framed a few photos of my family and put them up in the most prominent spot I've got on a shelf above my computer. It's my shrine to my goofy, loving, very-non-nuclear family. I love them and I support them. Always have. Always will.

Blake Alford

Blake. Photo by Robin Rayne

(*he/him*)

retired truck driver, activist, public speaker

I was born in Atlanta, Georgia, in 1948, which makes me seventy-three. I came up in the era where there wasn't very much information about being a transgender person. Back then I was the object of bullying at school because I was considered "different" than the other girls, and the negative term at that time for being different was "queer." Being called a queer in school was one of the worst things you could possibly be back then, especially in the South.

My parents, God love them, they tried, but they didn't understand me at all. They kept saying to me, "What did we do wrong?" Well, they did nothing wrong! They did everything that they possibly could have done based on what they knew to do. They tried sending me to a doctor, of course, and the doctor told them, "Here's the deal. You have a child who is what we call a homosexual, and you're going to have to deal with this child because this is what you have."

Despite this advice, nobody in my family understood where I was coming from. This made things very hard for my mother because she was brought up Southern Baptist with strict anti-homosexual views. My dad tried to adjust, but you could tell he was struggling very hard with it.

My mom kept trying to turn me into the girly girl she wanted me to be. My grandmother on my dad's side would say, "She's a tomboy—just let it go." And my mother's mother didn't really care because she ran mules on a farm and worked in the fields, so she wasn't into dressing like a typical woman anyway.

Personally, I've never looked feminine a day in my life. If my mom put me in something girly, it was coming off before I could get out the door. From the age of about six, I knew that I was a boy in a girl's body, and the only thing I could do to feel like myself was to dress in anything boyish that I could find.

At school I was bullied all the time. My books were thrown down the stairs when I'd go from class to class. When I'd try to pick them up, the bullies would push and shove me. I'd go to my locker to grab my stuff, and somebody would cram my head into the locker and slam the door right on me. Or if I'd go into the girl's bathroom and a football player had seen me go in while his cheerleader girlfriend was in there, he waited till she came out. She'd tell him, "There ain't nobody else in there," and then the football player would come in and stick my head in the toilet. There was really no way to get help or support. Nobody really gave a damn about me, to be honest. Many days I'd end up in the counselor's office with the principal and they would both say, "Well, if you would dress normal like a girl and act more like a girl, this wouldn't happen." I kept saying, "I'm dressing as best as I can as who I am!" That never got me anywhere.

When I tried to play girls' sports at school, which I was very good at, nobody wanted me on their teams because they didn't want me in the locker room or the shower room with the other girls. Luckily, I had a gym teacher who was a lesbian. Nobody knew she was a lesbian, of course, but she allowed me to shower in her private shower room so I could play basketball on the girls' team. She also allowed me to sit with her on the bus trips to play games so I wouldn't be bullied. Having her support was the only way I was able to play sports.

In church I sang tenor, so I had to sit with the boys. The girls were pissed because I got to sit with the guys, and I was pissed because I couldn't sit with the girls. The truth is that the leaders at church didn't really want me there at all because they thought I was a homosexual. The church members got to a point where they didn't want me involved in anything and they were making it unbearable for me to be there. The pastor's sermons were frequently about those sinning homosexual people, and whenever there was a church function people hovered around me, making sure I wasn't going into the bathroom when the other girls went in. I was constantly being supervised. If they had a roller-skating party, they would always have somebody watching every move I made.

Eventually, I was run out of the church. The mother of a girl who was at a skating party with me came to my mom's front door and angrily told her, "Keep your damn daughter away from my daughter." That was the straw that broke the camel's back. My mother was so upset and angry with me. She told me, "I don't know what it is that you're doing, but you've got to stop. You got people coming to my door now, telling me to keep you away from their daughters." I said, "I wasn't doing anything except roller skating." After that, I packed up my bag with as much as I could carry, and I hitchhiked to Atlanta at age sixteen.

I went into Mama Mia's Italian Restaurant and Bar on 14th Street in downtown Atlanta and sat down at a booth with my sack of clothes and belongings. This little Italian lady came over and looked at my raggedy sack and said, "Are you going somewhere?" I said, "I don't know," and she said, "Do you need a job?" I said, "Yes, ma'am." Then she said, "How old are you?" I said, "Seventeen." She said, "You can sweep my floors and clean up around here for me and I'll give you a place to stay because I don't think you have one, do you?" I said, "No, ma'am." She said, "Tonight when we close, you'll go home when I go home, and I'll show you where you are going to stay."

That kind woman helped me for quite some time until I met two drag queens who took me in and taught me how to take care of myself. They taught me the commonsense ways to stay alive. I stayed with them until I was nineteen, before they went their way and I went mine. They kept me alive and for that I'm forever thankful.

I stayed downtown and worked in the bars, doing drag shows or anything I could do to make a dime and working at Mama Mia's restaurant on the side. I remember cleaning off a table for her one night and this guy grabbed me, turned me around, and slammed me up against the wall. He said, "We are raiding this place and you are under arrest." I looked at him and said, "For what? I'm cleaning off the table," and he said, "I saw you move that beer can from in front of that person right there and that person is underage," I said, "I just work here clearing tables. I don't check IDs." He said, "I don't believe a damn thing you're saying. You're under arrest for interference with the law and moving a beer can in front of a minor. You're going to jail," and he threw me in the back of the paddy wagon and took me to jail.

I was left in that stinky jail where the matron came up to me and asked me if I had anyone who could bail me out. She told me that cops bring "folks like you" to jail because they think it's funny. Then, to my surprise, she said, "It's not funny. The cops do this to the drag queens too. I just work here at the jail and there's nothing I can do about it except that I'm going to let you make a phone call."

Oh, my dear God, I had to call my dad! He came and got me out and brought me home and sat me down and said, "You need to figure out what you want to do. I don't want you to become a drunk and be out on the damn street without a way to make a living. You need to figure out what to do with your life before you ruin it totally. I can't bail you out every time you get in trouble." I decided right then that I needed a job that I could get away with doing as a guy. I asked my dad to put me in truck driving school, and he did. There were twenty-one guys in my truck driving school class and me, and I graduated third in my class.

When I went to apply for my first job, my waist was twenty-nine inches. I was barely 5'4" and probably didn't weigh much more than 120 pounds soaking wet. I went into the interview and handed the guy my papers from school, and he looked at me funny and said, "I don't know about hiring a woman to drive my truck." I looked at him and I said, "Well, I can drive." He said, "I'll give you a road test." He had me drive a truck with him to Chattanooga and as I was coming back up this steep hill—which nobody else had ever been able to get up without having to try two or three times—I changed gears three times. I didn't even slow down. When we got back, I whipped the truck into the yard, backed it up, and put it in the spot he wanted me to put it in. He just got out and shook his head and turned around and said, "You got a job right now."

> **I grew up being called queer, dyke, butch, lesbian, and now I'm called a trans man. Personally, I don't like labels. I'm not a can of beans. I am Blake. In my eyes, I'm simply a man. All my life it's been about trying to find the right label. Please don't label me. Meet me, get to know me, and then let's talk about it.**

As far back as I can remember, I always had this dream of being a guy and having a wife and a family. I wanted to have a typical guy's job and I wanted to be able to go to work and wear a suit and tie. Well, at least I was doing a typical guy's job. I became a long-haul truck driver for many years.

The first trans guy I ever met who had transitioned was visiting Georgia from New York City. He told me that he had to go back to New York because he couldn't get his medications down South. He explained that he would "turn back into looking like a woman" if he didn't get his testosterone and that without the hormones, he couldn't continue to be seen as the man he really was. I turned around and said, "What?" He looked at me and said, "I'm a transgender man." I'm like, "Get out of here." He says, "No, seriously. I really am a transgender man. The South is not ready for this. People who transition from female to male like I did have a problem getting our meds down South."

My mother and father were both still alive at that time, and in the back of my mind I was thinking maybe I needed to move up North. Not long after I met this trans man, my dad passed away with cancer and then my mother got sick, so I stayed to take care of her. After she died, I decided it was about time for me to go up North.

I was sitting with a bunch of my friends at a bar a few weeks after my mother's death. I got up to go to the bathroom and when I came back to the table my face was beet red. I sat down at the table, took my fist, and slammed it down hard in the middle of the table and said, "That's it. I'm done. I'm through!" One of my friends said, "What is all this commotion about?" I said, "That smartass woman at that table over there came into the women's restroom and told me I didn't belong there." I'd always tried to avoid public bathrooms because every time I'd go in one somebody always said something catty like, "Are you sure you're in the right bathroom?" Sometimes I'd even go out, open the door, look at the door, and go, "Yeah, I'm in the right one. Are you?" They'd go running to the door to see if they were in the wrong bathroom.

My friends all started laughing and said, "That happens to you all the time, so what's the big deal?" I said, "This time, I told the woman that she was right and that this was the last time that this guy is going to be in a restroom for women." Then I announced to my friends that I was going to transition and publicly be the man I always have been. I explained, "My mother's gone, my daddy's gone, and I don't owe anybody anything. It's finally my time to be me. I'm tired of being a chameleon! First thing tomorrow morning, I'm going to tell my therapist that I want to get my transition started. I'm no longer going to have anybody else tell me I don't belong somewhere. I'm done!"

One of my best friends is named James. When I finally found out I could transition, James was my hero. I said to him, "I'm too old to do this," and he said, "You're never too old to be who you are." Years later, I crossed paths with a trans woman who was starting her transition at seventy-eight years old. I realized that James was right. I'm not too old to be who I was born to be.

The next day I made that phone call, and within a week I took my first dose of testosterone and got started on the path to living as the man I really was. I've never been so glad I've done something in all my life. I really wish I would have known about being trans when I was younger—it could have changed my whole life if I had transitioned earlier. I didn't transition until I was fifty-six years old because I waited until both of my parents had died.

Getting testosterone, or T, in the South was trial and error at first. I had to get my doctors to work with the insurance companies and send them letters saying that T was a necessity for me to stay alive. The insurance company didn't want to give me the drug and the doctors had to explain that I would need to have this shot every five days for the rest of my life. It took some fighting to get the insurance company to approve my drugs, but they finally did. Thank God I've got some good doctors, that's all I can say. They've been extremely helpful to me. Taking T has made me very calm! It was truly amazing the difference it makes in how I handle things. I used to be a very angry person when I was hiding my true self. Now I think before I act.

After I transitioned, my brother said, "What do you hope to accomplish by doing such a thing to yourself?" I sat down face to face with him and said, "I don't expect you to understand this, but I've never been respected as myself in fifty-six years. Now I can walk into a store, and nobody says, 'I don't want to wait on the queer.' And when I go into the bathroom, nobody goes flying out. I walk with my head held high every day." My brother said, "But I never got to mourn the death of a sister. I just suddenly woke up and had a brother. How am I supposed to deal with that?" I said, "I'm not dead. Believe me, I'm still here."

My brother finally came to terms with me two years ago when I got stung eighty times by yellow jackets and damn near died. It's gotten to where he speaks to me almost like he knows I'm a human, and we're getting along much better. I live in my parents' old home now, so I still bump into some old neighbors who say, "Hey girl," when they see me at the mailbox. I don't care. Just treat me like I'm a human being.

I tell people that I simply existed for fifty-six years, but that I have lived my life ever since my transition. Sadly, I lost most of my life, and I don't want to sit back and watch another child go through what I went through before they get to be who they are. I try to help these kids as best I can.

Many old friends tell me that when they talk to me now, I look them straight in their eyes instead of looking down at the floor. I can stand at a podium and talk to a huge room full of people and make them understand where I'm coming from. I've even been asked to help train police officers about how to treat trans people. I watched how the police department cadets were reacting to the way our scenarios were going, and I thought that we have a problem not only with the police but with society itself.

At the trans conferences I speak at, I tell the younger ones, "Don't wait like I did. Don't lose your life because you can't get it back." If I had known that I could have been this self-confident and made something this good out of myself by transitioning, I would have done this when my parents were alive, because I think they really would have liked Blake better than Rebecca.

I carry both my driver's licenses, my old one and my new one, because a lot of people say they don't believe I'm trans. I'll hand them my two licenses and they'll just flip out. I'll out myself in a heartbeat if it's for the good. It's mind-blowing to watch the expression on some people's faces when I do.

A few years ago, I had a terrible accident when someone hit my truck and had to retire. I've had four back surgeries, and the last one just about broke my spirit. I guess it's my age because I'm not bouncing back like I did from the rest of them. When we get a little bit older, we don't bounce back so easily. I've been living with tremendous pain, and I pray that I recover some of my energy and mobility. I'm single now because I can't get out there in the world and meet anybody who wants to have anything to do with somebody my age who has a severe disability. I can't support myself right now because I don't make enough with the government aid I get.

Cisgender people are not going to accept trans people until they realize that we are decent, normal human beings. We are here to work and live among them. I wish all people could see the trans community for who we really are. We just want to be treated as equal with respect and dignity.

Louis Mitchell and Family

Louis. Photo by Krysia Villón

Louis Mitchell
(*he/him*)

minister

I was probably only four years old the first time I recognized that I was different from most little girls. My dad had come home on leave from Okinawa, and I put on all his military gear. I can still remember how I felt really at home in it. Although I had no idea what that meant, it was my first memory of not fitting into the gender box that my family had put me in from the time of my birth.

I was raised up in the church and I believed in miracles. Every night I would pray to God that I'd wake up as a boy. When puberty hit, I was furious that my prayers hadn't been answered. I was like, "Okay God, what are you doing? What on earth could be more important than my prayer that you're supposed to be answering?"

As I became a teenager, I found out that people who were embodied like I was, who were attracted to girls the way I was, were called lesbians. Being a lesbian was fine and dandy with me, but in my mind, I always felt that being a lesbian wasn't quite it. I just didn't know there were any other options out there because back then, I had never even heard of transgender people. So I went along merrily, being a lesbian. It was a great time in my life!

When I first came out as a lesbian, my mom, who is very religious, had a hard time. My dad was a little crunchy about it as well. What I said to them, in not so many words, was, "I'm not asking your permission. I'm just telling you what my life is like, and you can do with it what you wish. If you want me around, you'll treat me respectfully."

I wasn't bullied in my school at all. In fact, my best friend in high school got mad at me because there were all these rumors floating around that I was a lesbian, and she was angry that I hadn't told her right away. She said, "Why didn't you trust me with that?" I said, "I was scared." We are still friends after all these years.

I grew up in the Baptist tradition where I often heard anti-gay preaching, but I tried to disregard it. In my view, there was a fair amount of sexism, misogyny, and homophobia all wrapped up in their interpretation of Biblical text, and yet behind the scenes there was a fair amount of queer activity going on among the congregation. I couldn't figure out how they reconciled their Monday through Saturday life with their Sunday life.

At that time, I didn't have the self-esteem or the imagination to envision the kind of life I have now. I was a raging alcoholic and addict between the ages of sixteen and twenty-three and made several suicide attempts. I just didn't want to be here on earth, but I wasn't sure why. Maybe it was the gender stuff. Maybe it was the notion my mother's church had taught me that I couldn't be loved by God if I were a lesbian. I don't know. It was probably a combination of the two. All I can say is that I am so grateful that I survived and got sober when I was twenty-three years old.

I couldn't have dreamed where it would lead when I started working the Twelve Steps. There's the Third Step where you turn your will and your life over to the care of God as you understand God. When I said yes to that step, I don't think I read the fine print! I didn't have a clue yet that God or the Divine Essences had always been in me urging me toward ministry.

I was a young adult at the beginning of the AIDS epidemic. I was often invited to pray with people who had AIDS because I was the only person they knew who prayed. Together, the combination of trusting in a power greater than myself and my willingness to be of service led me to ministry.

My gender transition came first. When I was around thirty-five, I met my first trans man. "Okay," I thought to myself, "this is possible!" I realized that I had some hard decisions to make because I was already entrenched in a lesbian community that I loved and respected. I knew I was going to lose friends and safety and comfort and possibly my mom. I was very nervous about the idea of coming out as a trans man, far more anxious than I'd been when I came out as a lesbian.

My dad had already died, and I realized on some level I was waiting for my mom to die so I could live authentically as a man. Since I didn't want my mom to die even in my subconscious, I decided to risk losing her while she was still alive and come out. I wrote my mom a letter instead of calling because I was afraid. I didn't want to shock her by visiting her in person. I had already started taking testosterone and my voice was changing and I just couldn't pretend I had a cold all the time. She wrote me back and said, "I may never accept your choices or understand them, but you are an adult and I love you." That was literally all I needed to move forward—to know I was still going to be loved by my mother!

I transitioned while living with my former wife, Krysia, in San Francisco—liberal, crunchy, San Francisco—and I was pulled over literally 300 percent more often in my first six months after becoming a Black man than I had been in the previous twenty-three years of driving while being a Black butch lesbian. When I say, "pulled over," that's a euphemism because twice I was just sitting in my parked car when the police came over to interrogate me. Once I was parked right outside of my apartment on a one-way street, and this officer went down the street and then made a U-turn and came the wrong way up the one-way street just to ask me why I was sitting in my car. He said, "Do you live here?" I said, "Yes, and obviously you don't live here, or you would already know that." He went on to ask me what I was doing, and I answered, "I'm sitting in my car reading. What about me sitting in my car seems threatening to you?" Obviously, being a Black man had radically changed the way I could move in the world.

I've seen both ends of the spectrum with the police. While living in San Francisco, I had just gotten a puppy. I was driving with her one day and I made an illegal lane change because I didn't want the puppy to pee in my car. I was trying to get to the park. I got pulled over and the officer looked at my driver's license and said, "Are you going through a gender transition?" I was surprised and had some trepidation about what would come next, but I said, "Well, yes." He then said, "The reason I raised this is because your ID no longer matches you and you need to take care of that right away." His kindness and respect for me was a surprise, as I was in the same town where I had been interrogated for simply sitting in my car.

One of my first jobs during my transition was with a San Francisco cab company where most of the drivers were male. When I went for my interview, the boss looked at me and my identification, which still read female, for a long time and I said, "Yeah, I'm a trans guy." He said, "I don't care, just drive safely and make me some money." At the cab stand none of the bathroom stalls had doors and I thought, "This is going to be problematic." I had to figure out where in the city I could go to the bathroom while I was out on my route, something none of the cisgender male cabbies had to contemplate!

I had already transitioned and was fully out when Krysia and I moved to New England in 2001. It made the most sense for me to tell people right away so they couldn't use my trans identity against me later if it got revealed. A lot of trans people who blend with cisgender society choose not to disclose their gender histories. I feel that everyone should make a choice about disclosure that makes the most sense for them.

When we settled in western Massachusetts, we found a wonderful church, Old First Church in Springfield. Unfortunately, the once vibrant congregation had begun to dwindle and they closed. From there I went to South Congregational Church just down the road and I became very involved.

After some time, one of their interim pastors hired me as an assistant pastor and eventually I became the bridge pastor.

This congregation was progressive, but progressive means a lot of things to a lot of people. They were a mostly older, white, straight, and cisgender congregation. I invited all their questions, and they accepted me fully and unconditionally as their pastor.

I went to seminary in the Boston area at the well-regarded Andover Newton Theological School. I didn't finish because I have a learning disability, which I didn't know back then. I just thought I was stupid and lazy. I told my association, the ordaining body of my denomination, "Listen, I can't afford any more student loans. I can't pay the ones I already have. So, I'll take one class a year if that's what it takes, but I'm just going to keep going." And they said, "We are going to ordain you anyway." I said, "Can you do that?" And they said, "Yes, we can," and so they did. I became a minister in the United Church of Christ, a very progressive Christian denomination. I was able to be fully out and open about my gender history, which was wonderful.

One of my very traditionally religious parishioners told me that someone had transitioned at his workplace and that person had been afraid to tell him because he was known as "Mr. Bible Thumper." But when the trans man finally told my parishioner, he said, "No, no, I completely get it. I support you. My pastor is a trans man too!" That is the kind of gift that results from being completely open about who I am.

At my church on Tuesday mornings, we had a knitting club. I called them by the nickname a friend had given them, the Itty Bitty Knitty Committee. One of the women there confided in me that she was nervous when a big Black guy had walked into the parking lot where she parked her car that morning. I said, "What was he doing?" She said, "He was just walking through the parking lot." I asked, "Why were you nervous?" She hesitated and I said, "You know that in every parking lot in the country, I'm that big Black guy. Do I make you nervous?" And she said, "No, of course not, but I didn't know him." I said, "Do you understand that the assumptions you're making based on race and size and gender could do me harm?" She said, "No, I never really thought about it." I responded, "I think about it every single day of my life." She said, "I get it," and I said, "Okay, you've scratched the surface of it. I'm not telling you not to be aware of your surroundings, and as an older woman, I want you to be safe and vigilant. But I want you to stop assuming criminality whenever a big Black guy walks near you."

I am still shocked and appalled by the assumption that all Black men are criminals. I was so naïve. If you look at the world and think there are all these scary, dangerous Black men that need to be contained, jailed, or killed, you've been indoctrinated by white supremacy. There are scary, dangerous people of all races. Black men are not especially devious or dangerous, regardless of how the media portrays us.

The most recent time I had an incident was when I was leaving the church to deliver something to a parishioner. I was four blocks away from church and there was an arrow on the road indicating that the lane I was in could only turn left. There was a car on top of the arrow, so I didn't see it till the last minute and I drove straight. Immediately an officer pulled me over. As he was approaching my car, he put his hand on his gun and said, "Put your hands on the window." And I said, "Wow, just for a traffic violation! Do you do that for everybody?" And he said, "I don't know you." I was afraid and I was also mortified. I mean my car looked like an advertisement for the United Church of Christ. I had all these bumper stickers and stuff all over it! I thought, "Really? Really? You feel like you need your gun to tell me I went straight when I should have turned left?" That happened only a few years ago.

I recently moved back to the West Coast at the request of my mom. I'm currently serving as the bridge pastor at a United Church of Christ congregation in West Seattle, Washington. Apparently, my calling is to work with liberal white people. I enjoy these folks, and they have the desire right now to re-envision the church into a multi-faith community center. I've only been at this church for a couple of months, but we're moving forward; we're doing the work.

If you are a young trans, nonbinary, and/or gender nonconforming person reading this book, then you already have some access to support. Your support may not be in the town where you live, but it's out there. Seek and find it! It's essential to know that you're not alone. You've never been alone; all of history sustains you being just who you are.

"Throughout history, those of us who are in the gender kaleidoscope have always been created to be the ones who move around all the crossroads of life to apply clarity, correction, and healing. Genderfluid or gender non-conforming people have always been the people at the intersections of so many cultures around the world."

Whatever the preachers have told you about LGBTQ+ people, God loves you. Bad theology can't erase you. You don't need to harm yourself, no matter what others might say. If you need to get out of an unsafe environment, find help to get out. I made decisions that were not very smart when I believed that God didn't love me. I'm grateful that I lived to tell the story.

It's a totally different world for trans and non-binary youth compared to when I was coming up. The language is out there, the information is out there, the ability for people to name themselves accurately is out there.

I'm my mom's only child, her only little baby girl and I'm not a girl anymore. I know that a lot of my life decisions have been challenging for her, but she's been amazing, and she has changed over all these decades. Here we are many years later; I'm sixty years old and my mom is eighty and I'm visiting my mama's house! She still loves me, and I'm her son. I've taken on the primary male role in her life—the role that traditionally passes from the husband to the eldest son.

> **"Throughout history, those of us who are in the gender kaleidoscope have always been created to be the ones who move around all the crossroads of life to apply clarity, correction, and healing. Genderfluid and gender nonconforming people have always been the people at the intersections of so many cultures around the world."**

Our relationship is better than I ever dreamt it could be. Sure, my mother's confusion about my gender transition led to some rocky times at first. However, what was always true was that with or without her full acceptance, with or without her understanding, my mother consistently loved me. When people misgender me or address me improperly, she corrects them, and that's it. We just keep it moving.

I have more gratitude for my life. My mom loves me, I have a kid who loves me, and I'm out to my kid. I have a nine-year-old daughter named

Kahlo. Her mom Krysia and I were together for many years. In fact, I transitioned medically during our marriage. Krysia gave me my first shot of testosterone, and it was special to share such a life-changing moment with her.

Taking T was easy. The hard part was the discomfort of all the itchy, scratchy hair growing all over my body. And who knew I would start losing the hair on my head? Then I had top surgery, which freed me and made me feel so much safer. I told my mom when I was going into surgery. In fact, she kind of joked about it. She said, "I wish you could give your big breasts to me." I said, "I wish you had said something sooner!"

After Krysia and I separated, we've remained the closest of friends. When Krysia found out she was pregnant, we were already separated. I asked her if she wanted me to be an uncle or godfather to her baby and Krysia said, "I've only been able to envision a family with you as the father." I instantly said, "I'm in." My name is on the birth certificate and Kahlo is my daughter. Kahlo has met her bio dad a few times in Peru where he lives, but he's called "Uncle" and I'm the only dad she's ever known. Krysia and I are still legally married until we take care of paperwork, but we are family for life. Kahlo is an amazing kid, with a kind and tender heart. She's never mean to anyone who is different.

Since I stopped living with Krysia, I haven't been in a lot of relationships. I've dated some, but I'm not an off-the-rack guy. I'm trans and I'm queer and I'm a clergyman who is clean and sober. I'm an old, fat, bald guy—clearly not everybody's cup of tea. I'm pretty much a recluse, but my outgoing personality fools a lot of people into thinking that I'm a fun guy. Truth is I'm just as dull as paint drying!

Trans Faith is an organization that was started by my friend Chris Page, although they claim me as a cofounder. It's an organization by and for trans folk of every identity, and it is there to support the vitality of every kind of faith and spiritual practice. We work with existing denominations and churches to increase their trans awareness. We also offer some liturgies for clergy who are trying to find more trans and nonbinary inclusive language.

When people ask me to do something to support the trans and nonbinary community, I try to say yes whenever I can. It doesn't really feel like activism to me; it feels like holding family and community by the hand.

My form of activism now is supporting other activists in their self-care and well-being, mostly behind the scenes. There are many Black trans men, women, and gender nonconforming people around the country doing incredible work, and I feel like my role is to be an elder and a support person for them. I don't need to be out in front. It's time to hear new names and new voices and new visions!

The best way to be an ally is to spend some time getting to know trans and/or genderqueer people. Ask the questions that you have and do not make assumptions. Also do not assume that everybody you meet is a cisgender man or woman. When I lead trainings for allies, I ask them, "You say you've never met a trans person, but how do you know you haven't?"

Honestly, I'm just so stoked about my life. I feel like I've won the million-dollar lottery of life—and I did everything I could to leave this planet. Wow, I think about all that I would have missed if I had killed myself.

I've suffered incredible loss from violence aimed at Black people in general and particularly at POC trans women. It's hard for me when we read their names on Transgender Day of Remembrance. Often there are people on the list that I've known and held in my arms and broken bread with. So no, I'm not living in some pink cloud of joy and happiness. Life is full of suffering and grief. But I'm so glad and grateful that I didn't miss all the joy and love that was also coming my way!

If you are new to transition at any age, I beg of you to just stay in your body and keep praying. You have no idea how good your life can get. And I'm happy to help if I can. I'm easy to find.

Krysia Villón
(she/her)

mother, chef, business owner

I'm a mixed-race Latina, of Peruvian-Quechua and Polish descent. I was born in Boston and grew up in a middle-class suburban neighborhood where I didn't really know anyone else like me. I mean that in so many ways. I was raised Catholic, yet always carved my own path spiritually and left the Catholic church behind at the age of thirteen. While I never knew anyone else who was queer-identified in my

Krysia, Kahlo & Louis. Photo by Priscilla Harmel

family, I always seemed able to pick up on others who were like me and felt drawn to them. My sexuality was a mystery to me until I met my first butch girlfriend in college and fell madly in love. It was then that I understood myself a little better. I was, and still am, attracted to masculine energy.

When I started dating Louis, we were both lesbians—classic butch and femme. Louis let me know shortly after we started dating that he was planning to transition. Honestly, it did not surprise me, as his energy felt distinctly male, but I was nervous about what this would mean for me and for us. He shared that he had already started collecting information on the process and had spoken to his doctor about it. The only thing holding him back, he said, was his fear of telling his mother. So, I knew right from the start that Louis would likely transition while we were romantically linked.

I was enjoying the rollercoaster ride of falling in love again when, what felt like only moments later, Louis finally got his prescription filled for testosterone. It was about three months after we started dating. He had chosen his thirty-ninth birthday to take his first dose of T. I gave my dear Louis his first shot and many, many more shots after that as well. It was fun to see his body change, to hear his voice altering, to see hair sprouting in various places.

When Louis first started transitioning, one of my fears was that the more he looked like a man, the less I would be attracted to him, as I had never in my life been attracted to cisgender men. I was afraid I was going to have to shift my lesbian identity! Looking back, what I feared happening did in a sense come to fruition, but it was a positive experience. I had to wrestle with this label I had claimed for myself and that by holding on to my lesbian identity, I was in fact being dismissive of the identity of the man I loved. Did I still see Louis as a man who was once a woman, or did I simply see Louis as the man he always was? I realized that my lesbian label, no matter how important it had been for me, did not leave room for the love I had for this man I had married. I loved a man. I loved Louis. It did change me and shift my lesbian identity and the way I saw myself. The way I see myself.

> **" Gender and, in my case, sexual orientation can be fluid or static. None of it needs to be understood. It all just is. "**

Whether being trans or nonbinary or queer is genetic or biological or if it's environmental or any of these things, we just don't know the answer. I look at all these things the way I look at the concept of God. God, to me, is so big that there's no way that I could ever possibly understand what it means or what God looks like and doesn't look like. Gender and, in my case, sexual orientation can be fluid or static. None of it needs to be understood. It all just is.

One afternoon Louis and I went to a shopping area south of San Francisco, where not many people knew us, to visit a men's shop called Big and Tall. I was so used to being guarded with my lesbian partners, never showing too much affection in public. Even in San Francisco, a gay mecca, I was always very careful. When Louis began being affectionate with me in the store, I felt myself clam up until I realized that people were smiling at us. I was like, "Oh, we're being seen as a straight couple!" It was one of those "aha" moments that brought a mixture of feelings. It was exciting that somehow we had gone undetected, and then there was this sadness that I wasn't being seen as a lesbian anymore. This moment, and subsequent moments over the next few years, was filled with these kinds of mixed emotions.

When Louis and I moved to Massachusetts, it was about two years into our relationship. At that point my language was beginning to change. I no longer saw Louis's transition and his being accepted as a man in society as "passing." Instead, I realized that Louis had become the man he always believed himself to be. He wasn't passing as a man. He was simply being who he is.

Louis is not one to stay in the closet, and we developed beautiful friendships and connections to the trans and queer communities as a couple and individually. While we are no longer together as a couple, our relationship continues to have a profound impact in the way I view gender and gender expression and the way that sexual orientation intersects with gender.

When Louis and I became parents to Kahlo, I wondered what kind of adults and teachers we might be. I have to say, I'm amazed at how, no matter the complex natures of who we are individually, we continue to be so patient and transparent as coparents. I'm forever grateful for our loving, decades-long relationship and this road of happy destiny we've traveled and sometimes trudged together. We've created something quite beautiful.

Louis is my offspring, and I will always love the child God blessed me with. Louis had always been a strong-willed person, but

Mrs. Joyce L. Irving (*she/her*)

mother, retiree

when he first told me he was transgender I did not think he would go this far. I understood what it meant, but I cannot remember what I said to him that day.

> **" I will always love the child God blessed me with. "**

I believe my relationship with my son is solid. I do sometimes wish I had a daughter to talk with woman-to-woman. That was my lifetime desire for us before Louis transitioned from female to male.

I had no problem explaining Louis's transition to most of my family or to my friends. I just told it like I understood it. I also received complete support from my fellow Christian friends, though some of the older family and friends had a difficult time understanding and accepting the change.

Joyce & Louis, photo by Krysia Villón

As a Christian widow, I felt like someone had stuck a dagger in my chest when Louis told me he was transgender, but my biggest problem now, many years after Louis came out, is my use of pronouns and remembering when I see Louis not to say, "Hey girl," or "Here she comes." I love everything about the fact that I have a grown child who I can communicate with candidly. Louis makes me laugh all the time, especially when he uses, as my family and I call them, his "ten-dollar words!"

Heatherland/Park/ Heatherly/Landis Family

Noël. Photo by Robin Rayne

Noël Heatherland
(*they/them*)

social work intern,
domestic abuse survivor,
equality activist

I was born in Georgia in 1983 and grew up near the Florida/Georgia state line. I was the oldest child in a household with two parents and a younger sister. When I was in college my parents had another child, my little brother. My mom and dad attended an Independent Baptist Church, which is fundamentalist in nature, meaning that everything written in the Bible is taken literally. The preachers I grew up with would spew sermons about hellfire and brimstone and occasionally mention homosexuals as sinners. One time when I was a child my dad took a business trip out to San Francisco and when he came home, he laughed about the "fruits and nuts," describing his reaction to a gay man who supposedly hit on him.

My family homeschooled me from second grade until I graduated from high school. They used the same curriculum used by the Duggars, a reality TV family on the show *19 Kids and Counting*. Many people, including myself, are now in survivor support groups to heal from the wounds of church teachings that controlled everything in our lives, including gender roles within the home and in our community, what music we could listen to, and what we could wear. For example, people assigned female could only wear long "modest" dresses and skirts.

It has taken years of therapy, self-healing work, and spiritual effort to rewire my brain and learn that love isn't based on how well I adhere to a certain set of standards. Although my parents are out of the cult now, they have retained a lot of the thought patterns and it has made having a relationship with them virtually impossible.

My sister and I tried to maintain a relationship for a while, but ultimately both of my siblings decided to side with my parents. My brother was born after our parents left the cult, so he had a very different upbringing than my sister and me. Additionally, he is still reliant on their financial support. So for multiple reasons, it's easier for my siblings to stay aligned with our parents. I wish with all my being that it didn't have to be this way, but I also understand. Most days I've gotten to a place where I can be okay with our estrangement, but there are some moments when it hits me like a ton of bricks.

I remember knowing I was different as a child, but I didn't have the words to explain why. Even if I'd had the words, it wouldn't have been safe for me to be open about it with anyone given that we only associated with other people who attended our church or used our home-schooling curriculum. The sense of difference little Noël had developed was from a combination of being neurodivergent, bisexual, and nonbinary, but at the time I didn't know about any of these labels.

It's challenging to have a deep inner knowing that your true self is vastly different from those around you and to know that the way you truly are inside cannot be visible. It makes for a very traumatic childhood. My childhood had positive moments, but I spent most of my time masking and covering up key aspects of my identity out of fear, lack of exposure to diversity, and wanting to please my parents.

One time when I was about sixteen, my family went out to eat. I was wearing a hat and corduroy pants and the server referred to me as a boy. I remember being slightly pleased, but based on my parents' reactions, I also learned that this was not acceptable and that I shouldn't continue to dress in a way that could cause this mistake.

After I graduated from high school, I got my undergraduate degree at the University of Georgia. While I was at college I got involved with the AIDS Coalition of Northeast Georgia, which was my first exposure to queer people. I was nineteen, and I knew immediately that I felt at home for the first time. I didn't understand why yet, but I somehow knew that I belonged with these people. It was a major turning point in my life.

I came out to my parents as bisexual a few years later. As you can imagine, it didn't go well, and could have ended in my suicide without the support of my chosen family and friends. My parents used the Bible to tell me that I was causing God to grieve because of my "choice," and they said they would never be willing to meet a same-sex partner.

About a year later, I started dating a person who identified at the time as a woman. I fell in love, and within a year got engaged during Atlanta PRIDE. Soon after our engagement, my fiancée told me that he was a trans man and would be transitioning to male. While I had quite a few trans friends, it threw me for a loop. I was shocked, but I loved this person and I wanted to be supportive. We proceeded to get married and were cheered on by wonderful friends. My mother and an aunt even decided to attend the ceremony.

I was seeing a queer therapist to give me space to process my feelings around my partner transitioning genders. I tried my best to keep any challenges I was experiencing in the therapist's office while maintaining positivity outside until I reached the point where I wasn't struggling at all. I finally came to a place where I felt fully supportive of my partner's transition.

In 2019, I had what I consider to be a small mental breakdown of sorts. I think my nonbinary identity, suppressed for so long, was trying to come to the surface and had a lot of walls to break through. Once I realized why I was having such intense feelings, I told my spouse at the time that I was nonbinary and that I wanted to explore what that looked like. I felt so relieved and thought how wonderful it was that we were both trans.

Unfortunately, my spouse's response was to say, "I'm so tired of you and all your changes. I just wish we could have a calm, stable life." That broke my heart. Thankfully I had other people who were supportive, but it's hard to not be supported at home. In 2020 I started micro-dosing testosterone. I am still taking T, and I do feel better when I'm on a low dose. I sometimes wear a binder, and sometimes do not. Some days you may see me in a dress and makeup and other days a hoodie with no makeup. What I wear depends on how I am feeling that day. I'm comfortable with long or short hair. Regardless of how I am presenting, my pronouns are always they/them/theirs.

> **"** Having LGBTQIA+ friendships and chosen family is why I'm still here today. Sometimes parents are worried that if kids know a trans or a gay person, it will 'turn them queer.' Honestly, having LGBTQ+ relationships as a child would probably have saved me from a lot of psychological torment and self-hatred. **"**

Not long after coming out as nonbinary, I had some trouble at the coffee shop where I was working. At a store-wide team meeting, I decided to come out to everyone, so when I introduced myself, I said, "My name is Noël, and my pronouns are they/them." The store manager was a cisgender man in his fifties. I assumed he would be a safe person since the store chain was known for having inclusive company values. I was wrong! His response was sarcastic and rude, asking, "What is *they/them*?" I was so embarrassed, and then angry. Instead of filing a complaint or leaving, I chose to send him some educational articles. That didn't work. Despite multiple conversations, he never respected my pronouns and after I requested an investigation of his behavior, he was let go.

I chose my new name in 2021 after leaving my spouse due to domestic violence. *Noël* means rebirth and represents coming out in December. *Ly* means reason or lion and has a similar meaning to my original first name. Heatherland combines my chosen family members' last names, Heatherly and Landis. Using parts of both of their last names to create my new last name is a daily reminder that I have people caring about me and thinking of me even if we may not see each other every day. Even if I get married again one day, I plan to keep the last name I've made from theirs because it means so much to me. Sam, Jarrett, and I have a lot in common from our backgrounds, which has made it easy to have conversations about deep topics. Sam and I also share our struggles as nonbinary people, and they came out as nonbinary and switched to they/them pronouns not too long after I did.

I've known my dear friends Sam and Jarrett for around six years. I met Sam through mutual friends at a New Year's Eve party and I met Jarrett at a LGBTQ+ church that we both attended at the time. We all quickly hit it off with our passion for social justice. Soon after we met, we attended a protest together to fight the ban on transgender troops. During the protest, a car almost ran me over, and Sam was right there to pull me out of the way. They have saved my life on more than one occasion!

Several times during my marriage, when I was overwhelmed by my ex's alcoholism and bad temper, I called Jarrett. Jarrett was a listening ear when I didn't know what to do. I had to stay at friends' houses a couple of times to stay safe. Once things started to get to the point where I knew I couldn't handle it on my own, Jarrett, Sam, and I worked together to come up with options.

When my ex escalated his behavior, Jarrett and Sam were right there. Who else would have been there? My parents hadn't talked to me in about two years. My sister lives several states away and I'm not a priority in her life. In the middle of one night, Sam sent someone to pick me up to get me to safety. Jarrett took my dog and got him delivered to the domestic violence pet safety program. Both Sam and Jarrett came with me to the courthouse to help me safely retrieve my personal belongings. Jarrett, Sam, and a couple of other friends were there when my ex tried to push my door open to get to me. They held me while I sobbed on the floor. They listened and comforted me.

Jarrett and Sam both knew, as queer people themselves, how hard it is to lose my family of origin and to lose the small family system I had created with my husband. Jarrett and Sam assisted with filling out paperwork when I was too much of an emotional mess to write out my own name. They both sat with me during court proceedings and Sam held me while I sobbed during the hearing for the restraining order. They got me food when I didn't want to eat. They checked on me regularly and made sure that I survived. They made sure I knew I wasn't alone and that I still had family.

This is the power of queer chosen family! Sam and Jarrett both did way more for me than anyone should ever be asked to do. I truly don't know what I would have done without them as I needed them in every possible way. They gave me the support I needed to leave my spouse and get free.

Sometimes I've wished being trans or nonbinary was a choice. When I've been depressed, I've thought, "If I wasn't nonbinary, maybe my marriage would have stayed intact," or "maybe I would still have a relationship with my parents." After all, who would *choose* to lose their parents and their partner? Who would *choose* to have to deal with severe conflict at home? If it were a choice, I could go back to living as my assigned gender at birth.

Today it made me sad for a second, and then I thought "Thank goodness I don't have to try and associate with relatives anymore who think negatively of me because of things that are just parts of what makes me me." Parents and siblings shouldn't be like this to their queer or neurodivergent family members. Yet the positive aspect of losing your family of origin is having more time to invest in people who are empathetic and accepting.

I wish I had met trans and nonbinary people or read a book about them when I was younger. I am sure it would have saved me from some of the pain I've experienced. I'm a two-time suicide survivor and have dealt with bouts of major depression starting in my teens. Not feeling comfortable in my body and holding back parts of myself led me to use drugs to be able to survive and function. I've also been diagnosed with post-traumatic stress disorder from chronic traumatic events throughout my entire life. The good news is that I've been sober for almost two years! I'm healing!

Healing from religious trauma is still an ongoing process, but I'm thankful for learning what works for me and embracing my own spirituality. Because I've had a mixed experience with Christianity, I combine my Christian practices with other healing arts and sacred texts, rituals like using rosaries, Buddhist meditation, tarot cards, aromatherapy, movement, and positive affirmations. This variety works well for me. Religion should be a safe place where people are protected, but for so many LGBTQIA+ people, religion contributes to more depression, self-hatred, and suicide. There is nothing God-like about transphobia!

I wish someone would have explained to little Noël, "Your sexuality is queer, your gender is queer, your neurotype is queer, and that is all okay. I know you feel like you are having to suffocate so much of yourself. Keep taking it day by day, and one day you will have way more family than you can imagine. The name you are going by right now isn't even your name; you'll pick your real name later. There are changes ahead, and it will be a wild ride, but you are going to be so happy you stayed alive to go on the journey. Know that you are not alone! Other nonbinary and trans people are out here waiting for you when the right time comes for you to join us."

I want to help increase family acceptance for queer children and contribute to queerness being celebrated rather than being seen as a flaw or a character defect. I'm currently getting my Master's in social work so I can do more work with LGBTQIA+ young people and their families. I'm on the Board of Georgia Equality, and we work hard to increase inclusivity and acceptance of queer people in the state of Georgia, to ensure queer and trans people are elected to office, and that legislation that is friendly to us is passed and legislation unfriendly to us is not passed.

I'm dating Mallory, a transgender bisexual woman who lives near me. Some people may say that being trans or genderqueer makes you impossible to love, but I have my chosen family of Sam and Jarrett who love me as family, and Mallory who loves me as her romantic partner.

Every dating situation is unique and if you find that someone isn't accepting you but only tolerating you, move on. I promise you it can get better. Being nonbinary or trans does not make you worth any less than anyone else. In my experience, the specialness and uniqueness and beauty and strength that nonbinary and trans people bring to their daily lives, including to their relationships, makes them more fascinating and enjoyable. Being nonbinary myself and loving trans people has made my life richer and made my heart expand to previously unknown capacities.

If you are being raised in a religious environment where you know it's not safe for you to come out, please don't rush. I want to tell trans and nonbinary youth that I'm proud of you for surviving and making it to this moment. One day, you will be able to come out and live authentically when you are able to do so safely. Hang in there.

My psychiatrist showed up to our last appointment with his fingernails all glittery gold and an outfit that looked like it came off a *Queer Eye* episode. It was the first time I've ever seen him outside of his white lab coat attire and it made my day! Sometimes it means a lot to see your own identity and traits mirrored in people who are taking care of you and whom you respect. It increases my comfort level to share honestly. Thank you to all professionals who choose to be visible and represent trans identities in their fields. It means a great deal to many of us.

All humans can love beyond a box, beyond a binary, and beyond society's limits. We know it's possible to love bigger, for love to change and expand, and to learn new ways of loving. As hard as it has been at times, I wouldn't change the experience of being outside of the binary even if I could.

I'm proud of myself and grateful for my life. I wouldn't have made it here without the help of other people, especially Sam and Jarrett. I have a roof over my head in a nice place, all three of my pets are caught up on their veterinarian visits, I have groceries, my medical care is current, I'm working on building my business back up, I'm restarting school, and I have a beautiful woman as my partner.

I'm doing so much better than I was a year ago. I'm so glad I chose to stay alive. If you are in a dangerous or unhealthy situation, look for helpers and down the road you will get a chance to be a helper to other people. Accept help. You deserve to live and be happy, and my co-worker and his fiancé invited me to move in with them. It's been wonderful living with these friends. When they decided to move back home to Georgia last year, they invited me to come with them. I always wanted to live outside of Arizona, and this was the perfect opportunity. While I miss my home, I've never been happier.

Moving to Georgia has been a blessing in more ways than one. I met someone who very quickly became a very big part of my world. I was first introduced to Noël through an online Facebook group that we both belong to. We both are polyamorous, and I had joined the group hoping to make new friends after my move.

My chosen family members also adore Noël. In fact, sometimes I joke that they like Noël more than they like me! I've found a love with Noël unlike anything I've ever experienced before. The best parts of my days are spent with them, and I could not be happier.

Mallory & Noël. Photo by Robin Rayne

Mallory Park
(*she/her*)

mortgage pricing
analyst

I'm a forty-two-year-old transgender woman from Mesa, Arizona. I grew up the only child of a single disabled parent. My parents divorced when I was only six months old, and they shared custody of me. At ten years old, I had no interest in spending time with my father. I never really formed any type of attachment to him, so not seeing him was easy. My mother worked full-time, and I spent a great deal of my childhood with my grandparents. My mother would drop me off in the mornings and I'd go to and from school from there. My mom would pick me up in the evenings and take me back home. It all seemed to work well for me.

I first became aware of being transgender around the age of seven. I began raiding my mom's closet for clothes to try on when she wasn't home. I always liked the way I felt in women's clothes as it seemed more natural, and I felt at peace when I wasn't dressed as a boy. Of course, I had no way of understanding why I felt this way. Terms like transgender were not in use and people labeled transexuals were used as props for laughs during daytime television.

As I grew older, I kept my feelings hidden from everyone. I don't think I necessarily felt in danger, rather that it would be completely unacceptable to ask to be recognized as a girl. Instead, I assumed the "man of the house" role early on and stuck to it as best as possible.

The secret of my hidden self, like any big secret, wore on me as I aged. I would continue hiding until I turned thirty-eight. I was suicidal and had just left an abusive relationship. Fortunately, I decided I didn't want to die without even trying to be my real self. Without telling anyone, I started seeing a therapist, began hormone replacement therapy, and eliminated anything that would stand in the way of realizing my goal to transition. I spent a total of eighteen months on hormones before even coming out to my close friends. It's funny that the people I was worried about losing turned out be the most supportive people in my life. Conversely, some of the people I was least worried about had the most hurtful reactions.

> **The best evidence against the idea that being trans is a phase is the happiness of people who live as their true selves. The male person I was before coming out as a trans woman, well, he was just a phase that unfortunately lasted for far too long.**

I was almost forty before I officially came out in a public way. All my friends, save one, were accepting and supportive, far more than I could have ever imagined. Living my truth has strengthened these relationships in many ways.

My mother was a different story. Instead of showing acceptance or any desire to learn about me, she chose skepticism. She couldn't accept the fact that she had a daughter, not a son. To this day she misgenders me, and still introduces me as her son to other people. It just makes her look like a fool in all honesty.

Although I spent a great deal of time growing up as an altar boy for our church, I never felt a strong attachment to religion. I've always been much more interested in learning about the world and the experiences of the people who live in it. I've found that a belief in a single religion has a way of tarnishing a person's views of those who believe something different.

Religious beliefs can also create a lot of hate for the transgender community. I have been fortunate to have experienced very little compared to others. I've only encountered one time out in public when someone felt the need to make a scene. I was walking out of a store and heard someone yelling behind me. I wasn't really paying attention, but the yelling followed me as I approached my car. I turned to see a middle-aged, cis white guy following me, screaming about how much of a disgrace I was to mankind. I simply got in my car and left. I didn't want to create an altercation for simply living my life authentically. Besides, he was just making himself look bad in front of hundreds of people.

I don't believe being transgender is something anyone who isn't trans can ever fully understand. Those in the community know the pain of hiding ourselves away, sometimes even from ourselves, out of fear of rejection. I would love for people to learn tolerance and realize that not everyone is going to believe the same things, and that it is okay. We need to be more trusting and supportive. We need to make decisions based on science and facts rather than fear.

It's very important that trans and nonbinary youth feel safe expressing themselves as they see fit. There is a reason that trans suicide rates are so high, and it's not because we are trans; it's because the world tells us being trans is wrong. Nothing could be further from the truth!

Since transitioning, I've been able to find joy in my life. I was fortunate to work for a company that affirms and supports their employees during the first few years. I've been able to mentor and provide guidance to others in the trans community, and to several seeking to be more active allies. Every time there is a panel discussion or celebration in the workplace, I am first to volunteer.

I've also been fortunate enough to find my chosen family. I was living with my mother, which wasn't the best situation for me, and my co-worker and his fiancé invited me to move in with them. It's been wonderful living with these friends. When they decided to move back home to Georgia last year, they invited me to come with them. I always wanted to live outside of Arizona, and this was the perfect opportunity. While I miss my home, I've never been happier.

Moving to Georgia has been a blessing in more ways than one. I met someone who very quickly became a very big part of my world. I was first introduced to Noël through an online Facebook group that we both belong to. We both are polyamorous, and I had joined the group hoping to make new friends after my move.

My chosen family members also adore Noël. In fact, sometimes I joke that they like Noël more than they like me! I've found a love with Noël unlike anything I've ever experienced before. The best parts of my days are spent with them, and I could not be happier.

Jarrett Heatherly
(he/him)

actor, loan officer, photographer

I identify as queer. In the past I have said gay, bisexual, and even straight when I tried to go through therapy to "pray the gay away." My sexual orientation is fluid, but I would say *queer* is the word that resonates the best.

Noël and I met at church when the pastor suggested we meet since we were both attending a queer Christian fellowship conference. We connected at the conference and began to spend time together outside of church. Our bond was immediate, and we chatted about dates and sexuality, and deconstructing and reconstructing faith, and got deep real fast.

We have recently started spending portions of holidays together as both of us have some estrangement from our bio families, who have chosen their theology over affirming their children.

66 Only true love can repair what has been lost in our relationships. 99

My bio family has always been kind, albeit traditional cishet Southern Baptist in their way of approaching me and other queer folk. I was never chased away with shotguns—although it was something I feared would happen. They are mostly quiet and do not like to let me know how they really feel unless I speak up—which I do often in hopes of getting the affirmation that they love the openly queer and proud Jarrett as much as the closeted one. It's sad not to be embraced when you have the courage to live authentically. I pray that they will one day have a spiritual awakening and see how big God really is—and that They are a God who transcends gender and sexuality and political beliefs.

Learning that Noël wanted to create a new last name using mine and Sam's felt endearing. As they explained the loss of a core family unit and choosing me to be someone who fills that gap, it made complete sense. My initial reaction was that I wasn't proud of my last name and how my family was responding to me as a queer individual, but when Noël explained that Heatherland was a combination of my last name and Sam's, it felt right—especially with our shared experiences as queer, neurodivergent, and survivors of domestic violence.

Noël and Sam have become part of my journey, and I love and care for them both. They give me companionship and challenge. Having them walk with me patiently through their process of coming out as nonbinary has been enlightening and has helped me hold others to the fire when I've heard anti-trans sentiments in my day-to-day life. I love that they both challenge my perception of gender, and I've learned to expand my thinking. They are my chosen family!

I'm twenty-six, and I'm nonbinary and queer identified. I was born in Mobile, Alabama, and grew up in Birmingham, the oldest of four. My siblings and I were all home-schooled after elementary school. Our family was a very Christian family, very involved in church. My dad's family was Mennonite, and we went to a variety of mostly conservative evangelical Christian denominations. We were living in a small bubble where everyone I knew thought very much alike.

Sam Landis
(they/them)

advocate, designer

I knew from a young age on that I was different from most kids. In fact, I was always drawn to other kids who were outsiders. All throughout public elementary school, I was friends with the few Black kids in my mostly white, conservative, straight world.

As a child, I loved playing dress-up in all kinds of costumes. I especially loved my grandmother's box of skirts and dresses that I would try on and I would also make dresses out of blankets and walk around in my grandmother's high heels. In a beautiful way, my family allowed me to do that if it was in a private secure setting.

I remember wanting a Barbie and my parents didn't give me a Barbie, but they did get me a Ken doll. I received subliminal messages that acting in feminine ways was wrong. One example that stands out in my mind happened at my birthday party in kindergarten. Pink was my favorite color, so I wanted a pastel pink birthday cake. My mom told me, "Sam, maybe let's do a red cake instead. Red is very close to pink!" I think that she did that to protect me, but it was a message that stood out to me. Around that time, I lost some of that sense of freedom to explore my feminine expression, and I started trying to conform a little bit more. I had crushes on a couple of boys in elementary school, but I didn't understand why or what they meant. Even before I really knew what it was that made me different, my parents took me out of the public schools to homeschool me with my siblings.

It wasn't until early adolescence when I began to search the internet that I sort of figured out my sexual orientation. My parents discovered some of my searches on the computer and got concerned. They wanted me to talk to the youth pastor at our church, and I told him that I thought I was gay. He suggested that I immediately see an ex-gay therapist. I went to her for a little while, but I had panic attacks each time I had an appointment to see her. It was really confusing for me because the therapy was all about rewiring a part of myself that I never felt like I had chosen in the first place. Her explanation for why people were gay was that they had bad parents or they were sexually abused. Clearly, neither was the case for me. My parents tried to do the best they could, and I always had a close relationship with them. Her explanations never made sense to me, and I became increasingly confused.

At around fifteen, I was going to a homeschool co-op where home-schoolers take classes together and I met a couple of students who were gay. This was the first time I began to open to other perspectives, and I began to question whether being gay was wrong. My parents discovered that I was posting on a gay dating website and told me that they had gotten tickets for me and my dad to go to an international conference. It was run by Exodus, the largest "ex-gay" organization that existed back then. By the end of the conference, I thought that maybe it wasn't wrong to be gay, but that it was probably not what was best for me.

I agreed to go back to the counselor again, and I read all the books that she and my youth pastor recommended. I tried doing all the things they suggested such as not being friends with girls because I was supposed to see girls romantically. That never worked for me because I preferred being friends with girls as I didn't have anything in common with the guys.

Throughout my high school years, I felt isolated because of my inner struggle with my sexual orientation. Some of the people I told that I might be gay ended up not being safe. For example, I told my best friend during our freshman year, and she seemed okay with it, but during the summer before our senior year, she told me she couldn't be friends with me anymore and outed me to the other students. I became increasingly isolated and felt ostracized by many of my peers.

Around that same summer, Exodus announced that they were closing because the Founder/President, Alan Chambers, declared that his organization was doing more harm than good and that 99.9 percent of people who had tried to become straight had not experienced any change. It made sense because I had been doing everything that this group had told me to do for three years, and I hadn't experienced any change in my sexuality whatsoever.

When I graduated from high school, I went to the prestigious Savannah College of Art and Design (SCAD). What a shock it was that whenever I told a fellow student that I was gay, no one had a problem with it at all. I no longer had to have three-hour conversations about the state of my soul or questions about whether I was saved or not whenever I told someone I was gay. My fellow students at SCAD would just say, "Okay, cool, whatever." My personal world began to broaden, and I also realized that the world was way bigger than Birmingham, Alabama, and the people that I was raised with in my hometown.

In my freshman year, I started getting involved with the LGBTQ+ group on campus. At the end of that year, the president of the group was graduating and there really wasn't anybody else that could step up and so he asked me if I would take over his position. I was barely out myself so I didn't know if I could do this. I thought about how it had been such an important space for me coming from Birmingham where I didn't know any queer people. Just being surrounded with like-minded people, I no longer wanted to die. So I did step up and became president of the queer student group. Being the leader of this group was one of the most extraordinary experiences at college because I met so many different people. I learned so much about myself from all of them.

It was around this time that I began to contemplate gender in a deeper way because being transgender was something that I still couldn't wrap my head around. My first step was when I began to hang out with some trans people.

There have always been parts of me that are very feminine, and it made sense to me that I didn't want to box myself into identifying as one gender or another. I still don't feel the need to change my physical body. As my understanding of the meaning of being nonbinary grew, it made more sense to me. I began to understand that gender and sexuality were two different things and it helped me understand and accept all those different parts of myself.

When I went back home for the summer after my freshman year of college, I felt like I had to go back in the closet. But in June, I went to a Pride Parade in Birmingham and after it was over, I decided that I wouldn't go back in the closet to make other people happy. I came out on Facebook because up until that point I felt like my parents controlled so much of my story and who I was allowed to tell and who I wasn't. I felt like I needed to take back my own story, which caused a lot of conflict in my extended family.

My parents took my coming out so publicly very personally and were worried about how it might impact them in their social circles. The truth is that my parents were ostracized in their community, which broke my heart. It's painful for me to go back to that time because the trauma blurs some of my personal history. It's still hard for me to talk about it.

As terrible as that summer was, it was a catalyst that led our family to the place we are at now. Thankfully, I have a much better relationship with my parents as they've become very affirming of me and my gender identity. My mom even went with me to Noël's wedding and has become a kind of surrogate mom for Noël. I think it's proof that people who choose love can grow and open their minds to change.

One thing that really helped my mom change was when she joined some of the online Facebook groups that support parents of LGBTQ+ offspring and help them find community. I also think that my grandparents helped my parents accept me. My grandmother had a gay brother who died of AIDS, so she had dealt with gay issues sooner than most people in her part of the world. She was one of the positive voices in my parents' ears. I also had a wonderful aunt, my mother's sister, who supported me from the moment I came out when I was a teenager. I believe that the reason I survived middle and high school was the love I received from my grandparents and my aunt. I don't know where I would be now if I hadn't had them at my side.

I'm probably more liberal than my aunt now, but at the time she was the most liberal person in my family. She is a nurse practitioner and a very open-minded person. She gave me and my mom tickets to a Reformation Conference, which was a place where LGBTQ Christians could meet. This conference was a starting point for my mom as it was the first time she met some gay Christians and figured out that people can be gay and Christian and live good lives. I am proud of my parents, especially my mom, for accepting the invitation to grow and become more open.

> *People spend way too much time trying to figure out why trans people are trans. So many people feel like they need to understand everything before they can offer acceptance and love. If you start first with love and acceptance, your understanding will grow from there.*

My dad is still more on the conservative spectrum of politics, but he shows me his love and recently has tried to become more intentional about using my correct pronouns. I think it's been extremely helpful on their journey that when they come to visit me and meet my friends, they see the good life that I've made for myself. My siblings and I were all close when we were young children, and as we grew up there have been some rifts and divisions, but I have a lot of hope that we will also continue to grow closer as we get older.

When I went to college in the fall for my sophomore year, a bunch of people from our student LGBTQ+ group wanted to do drag for the first time and I figured if I was ever going to try drag, that was the time to do it. And so *Christian Mingle,* my drag persona, made her first appearance onstage. I have to say that it was a liberating experience for me to get dressed up, put on the makeup and the wig and the dress and heels, and perform for an audience who loved our show.

This experience opened something inside of me that I had buried down for so long and had not let myself look at with clarity. I discovered that I wanted to do small courageous things to show myself that I could be brave. I would think, "If I want to wear floral prints, I'm going to wear florals." And those were the kinds of small, but meaningful things I could do for myself. Over the past few years, it's been such a gift to explore parts of myself that I didn't know existed. It felt a bit like peeling an onion as I

Sam, Noël & Jarrett. Photo by Robin Rayne

revealed more and more parts of myself to the world and to myself. It has been a truly liberating experience for me.

During the period when things were not so great with my birth family—like many LGBTQ+ people—I began to create my own chosen family and Noël is a major part of that family for me. I recently joined the Georgia Equality Board with Noël because I love that our friendship is very rooted in activism. We don't get to see each other every week or even every month, but whenever we do, it is always special, and we always show up for each other in the important moments. Noël was one of the first people that I reached out to when I was first figuring out how to get sober because I knew that they were sober. That is a testament to the importance of chosen family—the people who show up for you no matter what else they have going on.

When Noël decided to change their last name to include my last name, I was honored that they would choose to take on part of my name. It was a big step, and I think Noël was trying to show their commitment to me and to our other chosen family member, Jarrett. Jarrett has been one of those people who has shown up in the moments that are very important for me. I don't have any bio family here in Atlanta, so it's very special to have both Noël and Jarrett, my chosen family, living right nearby.

An important reason to be out in the public eye is that I'm surrounded by people who had claimed not to know any trans or nonbinary people. It's been a cool gift to get them to open their minds to who we trans and nonbinary people are. There have been countless people who have reached out and told me that I've helped change their perspective about gender diversity.

Selected Resources

"Love—the beauty of it, the joy of it and even the pain of it—
is the most incredible gift to give and receive as a human being."
—Elliot Page

As this book celebrating trans and nonbinary people and their families ends, the journey of self-discovery continues for the participants and for you, the readers. Whether you are trans and/or nonbinary, questioning your identity, have trans and nonbinary loved ones, or perhaps all of the above, please remember always that you are not alone. In every moment of your lives there are opportunities to strengthen your pride and acceptance of all people, including yourselves.

Dear readers, I am wishing strength and loving kindness to all of you. Please take good care of each other and your beautiful authentic selves. Here below are some resources for support, deeper learning, and advocacy.

—Peggy Gillespie

Resources for Exploring Identity

Gender Identity Workbook for Teens: Practical Exercises to Navigate Your Exploration, Support Your Journey, and Celebrate Who You Are by Andrew Maxwell Triska (2021)

The Queer and Transgender Resilience Workbook: Skills for Navigating Sexual Orientation and Gender Expression by Anneliese A. Singh (2018)

Seeing Gender: An Illustrated Guide to Identity and Expression by Iris Gottlieb (2019)

You and Your Gender Identity: A Guide to Discovery by Dara Hoffman-Fox (2017)

Resources for Family Members and Allies

The Gender Creative Child: Pathways for Nurturing and Supporting Children Who Live Outside Gender Boxes by Diane Ehrensaft (2016)

The Reflective Workbook for Partners of Transgender People: Your Transition as Your Partner Transitions by D. M. Maynard (2019)

Trans Allyship Workbook: Building Skills to Support Trans People in our Lives by Davey Schlasko (2017)

The Transgender Child: A Handbook for Parents and Professionals Supporting Transgender and Nonbinary Children (2022, rev. and updated ed.) by Stephanie Brill and Rachel Pepper

The Transgender Teen: A Handbook for Parents and Professionals Supporting Transgender and Non-Binary Teens (2016) by Stephanie Brill and Lisa Kenney

Organizations to Follow, Support, and Learn From

There are many worthy organizations, from large national networks to small regional ones, that are doing vital work to support transgender and nonbinary people and their families. The following selection represents just a few good sources for up-to-date information, resources, and advocacy opportunities. Be sure to look into advocacy groups, support networks, and trans-led organizations in your local area to access resources tailored to your region.

Equality Federation (equalityfederation.org): an organization that does grassroots state-based organizing across the United States to advance pro-LGBTQ policies and defeat anti-LGBTQ legislation, including anti-trans bills

Family Equality (familyequality.org): an organization that works to resource and advocate for families with LGBTQ parents and/or children through community-building, media projects, and legal advocacy

GenderCool (gendercool.org): an organization that shares positive stories of trans and nonbinary young people and works to dispel myths about trans and nonbinary youth through speaking engagements and inclusivity consultation

Gender Spectrum (genderspectrum.org): one of the leading US organizations offering training and support for educators and other professionals, with the goal of creating gender-sensitive and inclusive environments for all children and teens

Genders & Sexualities Alliance Network (gsanetwork.org): a national US network of GSAs that supports youth-led LGBTQ groups and trains queer, trans, and allied youth leaders to advocate for safer schools and communities

Global Action for Trans Equality (gate.ngo): an international advocacy organization working toward justice and equality for trans, gender diverse, and intersex communities

GLSEN (glsen.org): the longest-running US network of students, families, and educators working to create affirming school environments for LGBTQ students through resources, research, and policy work

PFLAG (pflag.org): the first and largest US organization dedicated to supporting, educating, and advocating for LGBTQ+ families, particularly parents and other family members of LGBTQ+ people, with hundreds of local chapters across the country

Transgender Law Center (transgenderlawcenter.org): the largest trans-led organization in the United States, working toward trans liberation through advocacy, litigation, organizing, and movement-building, rooted in racial justice

Transgender Legal Defense & Education Fund (transgenderlegal.org): an organization working to end discrimination and achieve equality for trans people in the US through public education, test-case litigation, direct legal services, and public policy efforts

Trans Lifeline (translifeline.org): a trans-led organization that connects trans people to the community, support, and resources they need to survive and thrive, including microgrants and a peer support hotline

Trans Youth Equality Foundation (transyouthequality.org): an organization that supports trans, nonbinary, and gender nonconforming young people through support groups, retreats, and other resources

The Trevor Project (thetrevorproject.org): the world's largest suicide prevention and mental health organization for young LGBTQ+ people, offering youth crisis support, legal advocacy, research, and educator training

Acknowledgments

Above all, my utmost gratitude, respect, and admiration go to each of the truly remarkable and courageous trans and nonbinary individuals and their family members in this book who took the time to be interviewed and to do photo shoots. I have laughed and cried with each of them and feel privileged and honored to know them all. They are rock stars! I am proud to have gotten to know their authentic selves.

In the process of creating this book I interviewed and had photographed more trans and nonbinary people and their families than we had room to include. In addition to those in this book, I want to thank Jamil-Jack Abreu, RJ Appleberry, Lupa Brandt, Istredd Cheng, D'Lo, Izzy Heitai, Glen Michael, Elijah Nicholas, Penelope Rothschild, Rev. Dr. Erin Swenson, Asher Thye, Reverend David Weekley, and all their family members. They will all be in the traveling photo-text exhibit distributed by Family Diversity Projects, and I want to thank them for sharing their incredible and moving stories with me.

I want to praise and thank PFLAG National and its many branches around the USA. Many of the trans and nonbinary participants in this book spontaneously told me that PFLAG had literally saved their lives by supporting their family members. PFLAG has done groundbreaking work for fifty years and I appreciate all that they continue to do to support LGBTQ+ people. Special thanks to PFLAG's Director of Communications, Liz Owen, for spearheading our collaboration. I'm appreciative of Stephen Baruch at ID Talent, who helped me and PFLAG National reach out to people in the performing arts world. And my deepest gratitude goes to Executive Director Brian Bond for his heartfelt preface for this book. His dedication and wisdom make him one of the heroes in the LGBTQ+ world.

I am eternally grateful to Jeanette and Jazz Jennings for contributing their wonderful foreword to this book and for their activism and visibility in the wider world. I'm an unabashed fan of this wise, talented, and inspiring mother/daughter duo.

I want to thank Khadijah Silver, former Communications Director at the Transgender Legal and Defense Fund and their current CEO, Andy Marra. I'm grateful for the legal help they provide to so many trans people, including the case they recently won for Anna Lange, who is featured in this book.

Special kudos to the remarkable photographer from Atlanta Robin Rayne, who found so many of the families and photographed them with such artistry and sensitivity. I couldn't have done this book and exhibit without Robin's amazing non-stop help. My thanks also to all the other photographers who contributed their beautiful images and treated their subjects with great kindness and care. I also want to thank four participants: Feroza Syed, Ann Miller, Myles Markham, and Jozeppi Morelli, who introduced me to many of the people included in this book.

Thanks, of course, go to Jack Pierson, my long-ago Smith College intern at Family Diversity Projects. Jack proposed and then created the original exhibit under our auspices. I also want to thank fabulous photographer Gigi Kaeser, who took two of the photos in this book but photographed many people for the original exhibit. She has been my work partner, collaborator, and friend for thirty years as Co-Director and photographer of Family Diversity Project's many traveling exhibits and books.

Our financial donors at Family Diversity Projects are too many to list, but I am appreciative of each one of them. A few deserve special mention for their astonishing generosity and support. My gratefulness, above all, goes out to our organization's angel Nancy Poor, who gives year after year from her heart to support our mission to fight prejudice and bullying. I thank the wonderful E. Rhodes and Leona B. Carpenter Foundation for their unwavering support for our nonprofit and their commitment to projects that challenge homophobia and transphobia in all faith traditions. Thanks also to the renowned multicultural educators and authors Dr. Sonia Nieto and Dr. Patty Bode, who have contributed support to the work of Family Diversity Projects in every possible way. In addition, a deep bow to friends and major donors over the years: Mary Applegate, Marge Dimond, Robert Jonas and Margaret Bullitt-Jonas, Karen Clay and Mary Heney, Ellen Grobman, David and Linda Maraniss, Micky McKinley, and Amy Kahn and Jeff McQueen for their ongoing commitment to make this world a safer place for all people.

A special thanks to the members of my beloved Christopher Heights Assisted Living writing group (ages 74–96), where I lead a weekly workshop. I have appreciated their curiosity and probing, open-hearted questions about trans and nonbinary people: Margaret Allen, Linda Schein Greenebaum, Monica Hamkins, Alan Kimmel, Joyce Mazur, Elizabeth Peters, Irene Whitman, and Peggy Wilson. They inspire me to do my best writing work always.

Thanks to authors Lesléa Newman and A. J. Verdelle, who both deserve loud shoutouts for their enthusiastic support for this book and their contributions to literature.

I'm so grateful to writer/educator Emily Merriman, educator Krysten Lobisch, and graduate student Lauren Arienzale. They helped transcribe the interviews and their wonderful editorial questions and suggestions helped me edit the final narratives. Thank you to educator/artist Alisa Greenbacher for creating an original curriculum to help schools use this book and exhibit to reduce bullying and bias.

How can I begin to thank the best editor ever, Mary Benard, Publishing Director at Skinner House Books? The best I can do is offer my profound gratitude for choosing to publish *Authentic Selves* and for gently but firmly nudging me to the finish line like a spirited midwife. She cares deeply for social justice and her keen editorial eye guaranteed that the book is true to the mission at Skinner House Books.

My heartfelt appreciation goes to editor and consultant Alex Kapitan, who has given more than just time, but heart, to working on the narratives to make them read as clearly as possible and help make sure the language in the book affirms everyone. Also, my thanks to Larisa Hohenboken at Skinner House, who has also contributed their vision and expertise to editing the narratives. Big thanks to warm-hearted and wise publicist Pierce Alquist from Skinner House, who has been working tirelessly on promotion for this book. I am deeply appreciative of the talent, flexibility, and time Jeff Miller, the book's designer, devoted to making it beautiful and getting it to press on deadline.

I am enormously grateful to beloved powerhouse publicist Cathy Renna, Communications Director at the National Gay and Lesbian Task Force. Cathy has worked nonstop to make sure this book gets out into the world in as wide a way as possible. I also greatly appreciate the ardent activist and director of Parity, Rev. Marian Edmonds Allen, who made it possible to work with Cathy Renna and has done so much herself to make the world a safer place for all.

I appreciate the kindness of all my closest gang of friends who are my chosen family forever. You kept me going and provided nourishment throughout the process of creating this book: Deb Abrams, Adi Bemak, Steve Berman, Carla Brennan, Steve Eipper, Amy Kahn, Jeff McQueen, Hardy Merriman, Lyssia Merriman, Nan Niederlander, Rob Okun, Lenny Schoenfeld, Gail Shufrin, Adin Thayer, Vivian Weiss, and Shari Weldon. Your excitement and your questions about this book encouraged and challenged me. Thanks also to my longtime Bristlecones group for the balm of your support: Carla Brennan, Rebecca Bradshaw, Linda Harris, Rebecca Reid, Susan Theberge, and Kate O'Kane. I also want to thank my younger queer friends and allies over many years: Vanessa Anspaugh, Lani Bemak, Amber Bemak, Ava Berkofsky, Morgan Cain, Grace Merriman, Lewis Merriman, Lizzie Moulton, Casey Oparowski, and Ailey Verdelle. I'm glad that the world is now in your creative and capable hands. Thanks also go to my newer friends and wonderful neighbors, Linda Eichengreen, Doug Beattie, Beth Grams Haxby, and Wendy Bleiman, for generously loaning me their homes and offices to work on this book.

My acknowledgments couldn't be complete without expressing my endless gratitude to performance artist Taylor Mac and choreographer/ dancer Bill T. Jones, two brilliant MacArthur Foundation "Genius" Fellows. They are both my inspirational guiding stars and heroes. They challenge gender and sexual stereotypes in their work and in their lives, and it is their inspiration that continues to open wide my heart and mind. Bravo to their bravery and artistry!